Library
New Hampshire Vocational - Technical College
Manchester

D1417222

HOW MANAGERS MOTIVATE: THE IMPERATIVES OF SUPERVISION

HOW MANAGERS MOTIVATE: THE IMPERATIVES OF SUPERVISION

William F. Dowling, Jr.

Leonard R. Sayles

COLUMBIA UNIVERSITY
GRADUATE SCHOOL OF BUSINESS

McGRAW-HILL BOOK COMPANY

*New York, St. Louis, San Francisco, Düsseldorf,
Johannesburg, Kuala Lumpur, London,
Mexico, Montreal, New Delhi, Panama, Rio de Janeiro,
Singapore, Sydney, Toronto*

Library
New Hampshire Vocational · Technical College
Manchester

For George Strauss

How managers motivate:
the imperatives of
supervision

Copyright © 1971 by McGraw-Hill, Inc.
All rights reserved.
Printed in the United States of America.
No part of this publication
may be reproduced, stored in
a retrieval system, or transmitted,
in any form or by any means,
electronic, mechanical, photocopying,
recording, or otherwise,
without the prior written
permission of the publisher.
Library of Congress Catalog Card Number 70-143447
07-017654-X

4 5 6 7 8 9 0 K P K P 7 9 8 7 6 5 4

Photo Credits: page 2, Al Lieberman; page 44, Raymond Juschkus;
page 76, Arthur Swoger; page 124, ILGWU; page 166, Eva
Shaderowfsky; page 198, Anna Kaufman Moon; page 236, Hiag
Akmakjian; page 268, Hiag Akmakjian; page 308, W. Eugene Smith;
page 338, W. Eugene Smith; page 366, Al Lieberman; page 398,
Mary Ann Akmakjian.

Contents

6. The communications problem: dimensions and solutions   198

7. A balance theory of supervision: using interaction to solidify leadership   236

Preface

For decades managers and business educators alike have agreed that the first-line supervisor is the most critical member of the management team. Here is where the action is; where operating work gets performed. While there is no disagreement on the importance of face-to-face supervision, the subject has not attracted many major textbook efforts. There are probably thousands of courses within companies and colleges that seek to train young men and women to become effective supervisors. Most of these consist of more or less adequate collections of speeches, readings, articles, and notes. Given the quantity of first-class behavioral research that has been done in this area and the need for its application both in the classroom and in organizations, we sought to write a new type of text on face-to-face supervision.

Our objectives in developing this text are threefold: first, to include a broad range of research findings from the leadership and organizational behavior field; second, to express these in ways that would appeal to the reader because the text would contain lively first-hand examples of supervisors on the "firing line"; and third, to emphasize the actual behavior and analytical thinking required of supervisors, not abstract "principles" and traditional "theories."

We have sought to give equal emphasis to behavior and systems. The new or prospective manager doesn't get much help from being told what attitudes he should adopt and what his feelings *ought* to be. Sentiments are a result of what happens to you, not the cause. Therefore we have consistently dealt with styles and patterns of behavior—how the supervisor handles himself with subordinates, colleagues, his boss, the union—in a wide variety of situations. The particular situation determines what particular strategy will prove successful, rather than a memorized formula good for all seasons.

As many of the newer studies have shown, it is just as reasonable to expect that high-performance work groups *cause* employee oriented supervision, as the reverse. There is no one "best" style. Technology and the kinds of jobs being supervised will have a profound impact on what the supervisor can and should do. The supervisor's job is not neatly compartmentalized into planning and doing, controlling and directing, and the other traditional categories. Instead almost every action the supervisor takes has elements of all these embodied in it, and he is most likely to cue a subordinate as to what he wants when he least expects to do so!

We recognize in each chapter that the supervisor and his department are always part of a total system that includes the operations closely related in some work flow, often a variety of staff departments (that both service and control him), perhaps a union, his boss, and the larger organization. For any supervisor to play the "management game" successfully, the heart of the matter is to understand the importance of these interrelationships and dependencies. He must weigh carefully the impact of his actions and decisions on each one, as well as the role played by individuals he supervises and the group norms which have evolved. More often than not he must compromise and negotiate, accepting half a loaf, so to speak, rather than any ideal solution, if he hopes to minimize conflict and provide a realistic accommodation between the goals he seeks and the constraints that surround him.

Because our primary audience is managers-in-training, we have not sought to footnote any significant number of references. Footnotes, while useful and relevant to advanced work in the field, often discourage the new student or supervisor. We chose what we believe is a better road to impress the reader with the origins of the field. We have included brief selections from twelve scholars who have contributed greatly to modern management. By choosing men with broadly disparate backgrounds, we have sought to illustrate the breadth of knowledge and experience relevant to the job of the manager: psychology, sociology, anthropology, economics, engineering, to name the more important.

We are indebted to some great teachers, most of them friends and colleagues. While mentioning a few may do some injustice to the remainder, parsimony has been a guide in the preparation of the total work. Miss Patricia Haskell, Professor George Strauss, Dr. Eliot Chapple, and the late Professors Robert McCloskey and Douglas McGregor have been among our instructors, although grades were given sparingly.

A book is the product of many hands. Miss Cynthia Newby, our editor, provided us with a great deal of professional assistance, personal encouragement, and consistent good advice. Miss Penny Nathans skillfully clothed our "plot" and concepts in the continuing case which follows each chapter. The Misses Sue Cohen, Rosalind Gold, Fanny Williams, and Mrs. Ann Goodwin typed our many drafts conscientiously and with good cheer.

William Dowling
Leonard Sayles

HOW MANAGERS MOTIVATE: THE IMPERATIVES OF SUPERVISION

1. Motivating people: How to match human needs to job demands

You just set the work before the men and have them do it.
Henry Ford

When he was a teenager, Henry Ford's hobby was taking watches apart and then reassembling them. Legend has it that no watch he reassembled ever failed to tell the correct time. And, as everyone knows, he went on to perfect the assembly line and make a billion dollars. Henry Ford knew everything about machines—that's one side of the coin. The other side is suggested by the quotation above. He knew very little about what moves human beings. And it was his fantastically simplified view of human nature that more than anything else brought his company to the brink of bankruptcy in the latter days of his management. He really believed that all that was involved in the human side of management was to "set the work before the men and have them do it."
If only it were that simple!

MAINSPRINGS OF WORK

Why do men work? Ask yourself the question. If there were a dozen men answering it, we would guess that each one would list at least eight to ten reasons. And if each man were listing his reasons in order of their importance, no two lists would read exactly alike. Men differ in the expectations they bring to their jobs and the satisfactions they derive from them. That's as you would anticipate.

The problem is that many jobs in both plants and offices are poor motivators as measured against any man's list of expectations and satisfactions. They offer a man a week's pay in return for his services and very little more, for the nonmaterial rewards and satisfactions are slender.

This gap between the needs men bring to their jobs and the ability of their jobs to meet them is one of the central topics of this chapter. We will describe the principal needs that the majority of men bring to their jobs and the problems faced by higher management and supervision in trying to fulfill them.

WHY IS MOTIVATION IMPORTANT?

The problems of job expectation and satisfaction are important to even the most hard-boiled managers because, in the last analysis, management pays a heavy price for dissatisfying work—friction on the job, substandard output and quality, high turnover, absenteeism, and tardiness, to give only a partial list. The positive side of the motivation coin is of equal significance. The motivated worker is also the most productive worker, the worker who sometimes equals or excels any standards his bosses set or would contemplate setting for him.

Several years ago, Professor Argyris of Yale wrote a book entitled *Personality and Organization,* in which he outlined the basic conflict between the demands of the healthy human personality and the requirements of the formal organization. It might better have been titled *Personality versus Organization* since, except for a few scientists and top decision makers, it was clearly in the nature of the organization to stunt the personality of those it employed and frustrate their desires for self-expression and self-fulfillment.

In this chapter, we're not going to be as grim as Professor Argyris was in his book. We can see that there is a substantial gap between what most men want from their jobs and what they're currently receiving, but we think that Professor Argyris has substantially exaggerated the size of the gap. And we also believe, drawing on recent research in behavioral science, that it's possible to show how much of that gap can be bridged and the organization made at once more satisfying to the worker, more effective, and more profitable.

Simple Men—Complex Methods

Many management thinkers have tackled the needs side of the job equation and come up with different, sometimes seemingly contradictory, answers to the question: Why do men work? Forty years ago, *scientific management,* the then dominant mode of business thinking, concentrated on the method, not the man. The aim was simple: Divide each job into a large number of small, easy-to-learn tasks and devise the one best way for achieving each one of these tasks.

As for the worker, to quote Frederick Winslow Taylor, the founder of scientific management, "Each man must learn how to give up his own particular way of doing things, adapt his methods to the many new standards, and grow accustomed to receiving and obeying directions, covering details large and small, which in the past have been left to his individual judgment."

Taylor's thinking was eminently pragmatic. He based his conclusions on a series of experiments he had conducted at the Midvale Steel Company, a predecessor of Bethlehem Steel, where his approach had resulted in dramatic increases in productivity. The classic example involved an ironworker named Schmidt who, following Taylor's instructions, quadrupled the amount of pig iron he shoveled during an hour. What was in it for Schmidt? A 61 percent increase in wages and the satisfaction, to quote Taylor again, of being a "high-priced man." In other words, scientific management saw the worker, at least the hourly employee, as essentially a passive economic man with strong muscles and a weak mind only capable of absorbing the simple routines of mass-production technology—and incidentally, a man willing to accept a 61 percent increase in wages for a 362 percent increase in productivity.

Mass-production technology, for which scientific management provided a rationale, was enormously efficient. Few businessmen questioned the theory when the practice worked so well. Scientific management probably reached its peak when Henry Ford outraged his partners by using some of the profits generated by the assembly line to give his workers—the year was 1914—the unprecedented wage of $5 a day. This historic move probably had its unselfish side, but primarily Ford was interested in getting the most work out of the best workers and he was appealing to them in the only terms that he thought had any meaning—economic ones. He had accepted completely the assumption that, in the specialization of industrial labor, a few people will do all the thinking while the rest will do the work. But let him be his own witness—his candor makes him a natural. "The average worker, I am sorry to say, wants a job in which he does not have to put forth much physical energy—above all, he wants a job at which he does not have to think."

The Power of Recognition

If it took Saint George to slay the dragon, it probably takes a psychiatrist to slay an engineer. At any rate, the human relations school of employee motivation, which pretty much has vanquished scientific management, got most of its impetus from the studies conducted at the Hawthorne works of the Western Electric Company under the guidance of Elton Mayo, an Australian psychiatrist turned Harvard Business School professor and practicing sociologist. The studies, conducted roughly over the five-year period 1927–1932, attempted to determine what made employees productive—Hawthorne management being convinced that its workers were far from realizing their potential. At the core of the Hawthorne research was the now classic study of the relay assembly girls. As Fritz Roethlisberger, an associate of Mayo, explained it,

---

The idea was very simple: A group of five girls were placed in a room where their condition of work (assembly of a telephone relay) could be carefully controlled, where their output could be measured, and where they could be closely observed. It was decided to produce at specified intervals different changes in working conditions, and to see what effect these innovations had on output. Also, records were kept such as the temperature and humidity of the room, the number of hours each girl slept at night, the kind and amount of food she ate for breakfast, lunch, and dinner.[1]

Over a five-year period, Mayo and his associates collected and analyzed "literally tons of material."

What did the material prove? What were the correlations? At the level of physical environment, there were no correlations at all. But with the introduction of each variable, production kept increasing. The answer to the puzzle lay in the changing social environment. From an ordinary group of workers performing routine jobs with little or no recognition from management, they had been transformed into important people. "Their physical health and well-being became matters of great concern. Their opinions, hopes and fears were eagerly sought," observed Roethlisberger. Nor was this all. They were questioned sympathetically and at length about their reactions to working conditions by investigators—frequently in the superintendent's office. They could chat as they wished on the job and they set their own production quotas.

The chief direct impact of the Hawthorne research at the Western Electric Company was an elaborate listening program—critics called it practicing "cow sociology." Employees were urged to discuss their problems with trained counselors in the apparent hope that the simple act of "blowing off steam" would relieve many of their tensions and dissatisfactions. However, this was only one ripple emanating from Hawthorne. The impact on motivation theory and management

---

[1] F. J. Roethlisberger, *Management and Morale*, Harvard University Press, Cambridge, Mass., 1949, pp. 11–12.

practice continues to this day. The emphasis on human relations in management stems from Hawthorne, including the major themes in most of the supervisory training classes attended by the past generation and a half of supervisors. Interpretations of Hawthorne varied with the interpreters. But one message everyone got: It was difficult, after Hawthorne, to view the rank-and-file employee as a pure economic being, to maintain that optimum output was a function of an appropriate wage scale with a minor assist from good physical working conditions.

In Search of Complexity

Not long after Hawthorne, Chester Barnard, the president of the New Jersey Bell Telephone Company, wrote a book, *The Functions of the Executive,* which still makes rewarding if difficult reading. In it Barnard argued that any organization secures the services of its employees by the incentives it offers them. Material inducements—salaries, bonuses, fringe benefits, and similar advantages—headed the list, not because he thought they were the most important but because they had been the incentives that had received the greatest emphasis—"relative to other incentives it is the material things which have been progressively easier to produce and therefore to offer. Hence there has been a forced cultivation of the love of material things among those above the level of subsistence."

The other incentives to which Barnard gave at least equal billing were the following:

Personal, nonmaterial opportunities for distinction

Desirable physical conditions

Ideal benefactions—what we more commonly think of as pride of craftsmanship or aesthetic satisfaction derived from work

Social compatibility or associational attractiveness, particularly with the members of a particular work group, including its boss

Conformity to habitual practices and attitudes

Feeling of enlarged participation

Condition of communion, which Barnard understood to mean the opportunity for comradeship and mutual reinforcement of personal attitudes

Barnard himself, perhaps influenced by the Hawthorne research but more likely reflecting his own experiences as a successful manager, emphasized the role of social compatibility. "Men often will not work at all and will rarely work well under other incentives if the social situation from their point of view is unsatisfactory." Money thus becomes a secondary incentive, one that only gets a chance to function once the employee views the social situation as satisfactory. We've traveled a long way from scientific management.

HIERARCHY OF NEEDS

The deemphasis on money and material things generally as a motivator has reached its apparent peak in the hypothesis of the needs hierarchies developed by two noted social psychologists, A. H. Maslow and Frederick Herzberg. The two hierarchies are separate but similar. In Maslow's, physical needs occupy the lowest rung, followed in ascending order by *safety* needs to be free from fear of deprivation, danger, and threat on the job and off; *social* needs to associate, to belong, to accept, to be accepted, to like, and to be liked; *egotistic* needs to obtain respect, recognition, and status; and finally, at the top, the need for *self-actualization* which Maslow defines as "the desire to become everything that one is capable of becoming."

Herzberg divides his needs into five job dissatisfiers and five job satisfiers. As dissatisfiers, he lists company policy and administration, supervision, salary, interpersonal relations, and working conditions, which correspond roughly to Maslow's physical and safety needs. His job satisfiers are achievement, recognition for achievement, work itself, responsibility, and advancement, which correspond to Maslow's social and egotistical needs and the need for self-actualization.

Herzberg, impressed by the analogy to preventive medicine, labeled his five dissatisfiers "hygienic factors." In his opinion, "A good hygienic environment can prevent job dissatisfaction but cannot create true job satisfaction or happiness."

What lends particular interest to Herzberg's theories and what accounts in large measure for the recognition they have achieved is the amount of empirical research that verifies and supports them. They began as the conclusion of a study conducted by Herzberg about fifteen years ago among 200 engineers and accountants in the Pittsburgh area. Since then, he has repeated the study over fifty times in a wide variety of occupations from the sciences to housework—and the theory has checked out every time. Like "the Colonel's Lady an' Judy O'Grady," the scientist and the blue-collar worker are brothers under the skin—they have the same basic job needs and so does the white-collar worker.

Let us assume—for the moment at least—that Herzberg is correct: Those who work with their heads have the same job needs as those who work with their hands. And let us further assume that Herzberg has correctly analyzed and ranked these needs. What are the practical implications of his theories for the supervisor who is charged with seeing that those reporting to him contribute as much as they are capable of to the effectiveness and profitability of the organization? In other words, having read Herzberg and been converted, where does the supervisor go from there?

The Supervisor's Dilemma

"Nowhere very fast" is an accurate although partial and not very satisfactory answer. One problem is exemplified by Maslow's observation that "the U.S. citizen is 85 percent satisfied in his physiological needs, 70 percent in his safety needs, 50 percent in his social needs, 40 percent in his ego needs, and only 10 percent in his self-actualizing needs." If to be satisfied is to be satiated, then the supervisor is going to get very little mileage from his effort to make the employee's job safer and relatively little from efforts to improve his pay. The big payoff in terms of effort and performance will come from making it possible for the employee to realize more of his potential on the job.

SATISFACTION AND THE STATUS QUO

In theory, this sounds fine. Applying it presents several obstacles. First, the supervisor must make sure that any favorable factors in the work environment stay that way. True, he can't use the status quo as a motivator with employees, but let current conditions deteriorate from the employees' point of view and he will be in serious trouble. We well remember a discussion we had several years ago about Eastman Kodak's bonus plan with the then vice president of industrial relations. The plan dates from the days of George Eastman (he died in 1932) and provides an annual employee bonus based on the combination of salary, seniority, and the size of Eastman Kodak's dividends. It was the industrial relations director's contention that the company didn't get an extra ounce of effort from any employee on account of the bonus—everyone had long since taken it for granted. Water down the bonus? Scrap it altogether on the grounds that it provided no incentives to improve performance? Impossible. The negative consequences of tampering with it were difficult to predict, but no one in the company dared to risk them. Eastman Kodak was stuck with the bonus.

Similarly, the supervisor is stuck with the task of trying to maintain the positive elements in the status quo of his own little organization—whatever they happen to be. Maintaining them won't make his employees a bit more effective, but failing to maintain them may motivate them to become less effective or even quit. In short, the supervisor must work hard at maintaining whatever elements are present of Herzberg's "good hygienic environment."

SATISFACTION AND EMPLOYEE PERCEPTION

Another problem arises from the fact that any job, as viewed by an employee, can be and usually is both satisfying and dissatisfying at the same time—a phenomenon freely conceded by Herzberg. One reaction does not cancel out, preclude, or produce the other. The supervisor starts with limited resources—of time, energy, and money—as well as limited authority. If he wants to improve performance, where should he focus his attention? The answer, according to Herzberg, would seem to be on improving the job satisfiers rather than on removing the job dissatisfiers, with the qualification already made that the job dissatisfiers shouldn't increase while the supervisor's gaze is fixed in another direction.

Once again, behind the obvious answer lies a sticky wicket. At one level, the problem is one of definition, with Herzberg the villain or at least the source of ambiguity. He talks about motivation as lying at the root of any man's desire to excel in his work and he criticizes monetary incentives for their alleged failure to motivate. The distinction, however, seems more semantic than real, for Herzberg describes the failure in these terms: "The promise of money can move a man to work, but it cannot motivate him. Motivation means an inner desire to make an effort." To the hard-pressed supervisor with a limited supply of the true motivators and an even more limited control over their disposition, the distinction between moving a man to work and motivating him to work probably would appear academic. Results are what concern him, and apparently it's possible to obtain the same results from decreasing the sources of job dissatisfaction as it is from increasing the sources of job satisfaction. The difference lies not so much in the way the employee performs as in the way he feels about his performance—what he gives freely and cheerfully in the latter case, he concedes as part of the work bargain in the former.

How Much Can the Supervisor Do?

A much deeper problem is the ability of the supervisor to dispense the several sources of job satisfaction defined by Herzberg: achievement, recognition for achievement, work itself, responsibility, and advancement. Boss and employee alike confront the same barrier—the job. Whether or not the supervisor is able to provide the five motivators depends more than anything else on the intrinsic nature of the job. No exercise is more futile than for the supervisor to concern himself with motivators that he is largely or totally unable to provide. On the classic assembly line where the moving machine determines the pace, not the man, where the operation performed is simple, repetitious, and monotonous, where whatever knack that is needed to run the machine is acquired in days or weeks, not months or years, where promotions are few and far between—under circumstances such as these, it's ludicrous to harangue the supervisor about the necessity of developing a sense of achievement, of building pride in the work itself, of increasing the employee's responsibility on the job, or of motivating him to strive harder for advancement. The potential satisfactions just aren't there, and the gap between what the employee needs from the job, and what the job itself permits is large and unbridgeable. It's a great pity because men without satisfying jobs rarely have fully satisfying lives.

Of course, we chose the example of the assembly-line worker with due deliberate care. And we make no apologies. Hyperbole is a legitimate way of making your point as long as you don't pretend that it's anything else. In other words, few jobs are as barren of motivators as that of the production worker on a typical assembly line. In some factory operations, you have, at the other extreme, skilled craftsmen such as the tool and die maker, where a high degree of responsibility, achievement, and pride of workmanship are inherent in the job. Providing the tool and die maker is the skilled craftsman he's assumed to be, the supervisor can take his job satisfactions and motivations for granted—they're built into the job.

The potential of many other jobs for providing satisfiers

or motivators is greater than would appear on the surface. Take, for example, a half-dozen men in a chair factory, whose job it was to bend several pieces of steel and attach them so that the end result would be a bridge chair. A "nothing" job with few if any possibilities for developing pride in the work itself? That's not the way these men felt about their job at all. As the best of ten or twelve teams engaged in the same work—theirs was the fastest and the most coordinated—each member of the team developed enormous pride in the superiority of his work group and its acknowledged position in the plant.

Two points are clear. First, the capacity of work to provide motivators and satisfiers, as defined by Herzberg, depends largely on the intrinsic nature of the job—the supervisor can do something to affect the picture but not much. Second, in factory work only a small number of jobs offer significant motivators and satisfiers, at least as defined by Herzberg.

As a partial confirmation, consider a study by Dubin of "the central life interest" of industrial workers. On the basis of a forty-item questionnaire, he found that only 24 percent of the rank-and-file employees regarded work as a central life interest. For the satisfactions that made life meaningful or even bearable, the worker had to look outside his job. Contrast this with a second study that found that 79 percent of the professional nurses queried regarded work as a central life interest, and with a third study of 331 supervisors—first through third levels—in six Michigan companies, in which 54 percent of the supervisors considered their jobs as a central life interest.

The figures, although gloomy, are not surprising. The nurse, after all, is a member of a profession with a deep sense of calling. The work itself continually feeds her sense of achievement. Patients keep on getting better, at least partially, as a consequence of her efforts. In short, the job offers psychic satisfactions that are frequent, immediate, tangible, and significant. Under these circumstances, the surprising thing is that one nurse out of five did not regard her job as a central life interest. The figure is a measure, perhaps, of the degree to which some doctors make nurses feel that they are second-class citizens of the healing community.

Another surprise in the Dubin study was the finding that almost half the supervisors didn't regard their jobs as a central life interest. Again, we can hypothesize that this figure is an index of the degree to which authority, power, and initiative are centralized in the typical industrial organization and, as a corollary, it is an index of the degree to which lower levels of supervision lack authority and are unable to exercise initiative in meaningful ways. They are courtiers, not managers.

WHAT'S WRONG WITH A "HIERARCHY OF NEEDS"?

Let us relieve the gloom by pointing out what we consider the central flaw in the motivational theories advanced by Herzberg, Maslow, and company—their monolithic quality. They assume that all men have a universal set of needs in common—more than this, that these needs are shared to the same degree. In other words, men have the same needs hierarchy. They maintain that the relative standing of one need versus another reflects, not a basic difference in human nature but, instead, the extent to which a man's needs are currently being satisfied and his ability to concentrate on his higher needs, once his lower requirements are satisfied.

By contrast, we believe in the happy diversity of needs. Few men want the same things, at least to the same degree. And we reject as irrelevant the intellectual arrogance embedded in the notion of a needs hierarchy. "Better Socrates dissatisfied than a pig satisfied," thundered John Stuart Mill. The supervisor, however, is not dealing with a race of heroic men like Socrates, but with real men and real needs. His problem is how to meet these needs within his always circumscribed abilities.

Furthermore, we feel there is a tendency for men with a certain set of job needs to seek a job where these needs are congruent with the demands of the position. The big question, and one we don't pretend to answer, is the extent to which the process of matching job needs to job demands is a conscious one and the extent to which men learn subconsciously and over time to adjust their needs systems to the opportunities afforded by their jobs.

We suspect, however, that with most people, both factors play a part in the matching process. Men initially seek out a job that satisfies their needs as they understand them. As time passes, they readjust their personal needs system to inflate the needs that the job can satisfy and downgrade those which the job simply isn't equipped to fulfill. Not that we've come full circle from gloom to euphoria. The matching of job needs to job demands is neither automatic nor uniformly successful. Each organization has its quota of round pegs in square holes, and as Aldous Huxley warned, "Round pegs in square holes tend to have dangerous thoughts about the social system and to infect others with their discontent."

WATER SEEKS ITS OWN LEVELS

In attempting to demonstrate our thesis that most people seek jobs with a capacity to satisfy their particular set of needs, we have to rely pretty much on anecdotal evidence (of which there is a sufficiency), personal observation, and common sense. If we could marshal large bodies of statistics to serve as heavy artillery for our thesis, we would. Lacking such support, we take what comfort we can in the absence of any impressive statistics that would tend to refute our thesis.

Let's begin with simple needs and simple demands—those of the happy morons at the Utica knitting mill cited by Argyris. They performed their jobs with such a high degree of efficiency that management expressed surprise that they were considered subnormal. In addition, their attendance was good and their general behavior compared favorably with that of any other group of employees.

Are we saying that some jobs are fit only for morons? And are we implying that only morons could find satisfaction in holding down such jobs?

Not quite. Taylor might well have answered yes to both questions; at least, that's a reasonable inference from his comment that "one of the very first requirements for a man who is fit to handle pig iron as a regular occupation is that he should be so stupid and so phlegmatic that he more resembles an ox than any other type." All it required of a worker to perform one of the minute tasks made possible by the subdivision of labor into the smallest discrete elements, was enough ability to "execute punctiliously the orders given, down to their minutest details."

What Makes a Job Beautiful?

We will not go as far as Taylor would probably go—but for somewhat different reasons. We agree that there are many positions, including the overwhelming majority of assembly-line jobs, where the work itself could provide a challenge and offer positive satisfactions to few men above the level of morons. Our point is, instead, that many of the men occupying these jobs, although far from morons, are not unhappy on their jobs, are not living lives of quiet desperation, and are not round pegs in square holes. Since the work itself provides few satisfactions, employees seek their satisfactions elsewhere on the job. Take, for example, the analysis of workers in a public utility made by Dr. Harry Levinson, then of the Menninger Clinic. He found a clear correlation between the kind of work a man did and the expectations he brought to his job: The bulk of employees in routine, unchallenging positions valued job security, the noncompetitive character of operations, the informality of work activities, and the opportunity to develop close personal relationships—exactly the benefits afforded by the jobs they were in. The only workers who emphasized expectations having to do with their specific work were the relatively few with highly individualized work responsibilities: the chemist in the power plant or the clerk who worked alone in the company office in a small community with few opportunities for interpersonal contact.

In other words, we reject the idea that the man with a routine job is, of necessity, unhappy, frustrated, and bored. Many are, of course—but many more are not. We tend to study the components of such a job, then shake our heads in dismay and say, "No one should be doing that." What we have done is to universalize our own feelings and needs—we have confused ourselves with everyman. What we haven't done is to remember that the beauty of the job is in the eye of the beholder.

We agree with Professor Sexton of Notre Dame, who sampled the reactions of 200 electronics workers performing routine, semiskilled functions and found that routine work actually promotes freedom on the job. What's the explanation of that apparent paradox? The task is not monotonous unless the individual is forced to concentrate on it, Sexton emphasizes. A routine job rather quickly becomes a task performed automatically—or at least without conscious thought—such as dressing, eating, or walking. Because the sense of monotony presumes thought, the routine job loses its monotonous character early in the game. The worker is free to daydream or talk with his fellow employees, and usually neither his gossip nor his fantasy life interferes with his doing an acceptable day's work.

More than one organization has experienced unwelcome, as well as unexpected, difficulties in transferring its clerical employees to more responsible jobs because of the advent of the computer. Management's thinking made surface sense:

The computer did take over many routine clerical duties. The people who formerly performed these duties were retrained and then moved to new jobs which were, in almost every instance, more challenging and responsible—and in most instances, somewhat better paid. In the majority of cases, the upgrading process succeeded, but with a significant minority, it failed. The upgraded employees actually seemed to miss their dull, monotonous old jobs. They resented the continuous attention that they had to give to their new duties and felt that the extra pay fell short of compensation for their extra effort.

We challenge the behavioral scientists to say that the employees were wrong. Most behavioral scientists, of course, would be repulsed by the prospect of performing a clerical job. But most such scientists have different aptitudes, different temperaments, and most important, different value systems.

Choosing the Right Company

At one level, a man betrays his value system or his need system (the two are practically interchangeable) in his initial selection of X company over Y company as a place to work. Of course, we're presuming the freedom to choose between alternatives, a freedom which exists except for the rare case of the man with limited abilities living in a community with limited opportunities—a community dominated by one industry or one company—and even he has mobility. Freedom is the price of a bus ticket.

One side of this largely unconscious process of selection is that safe people—people preoccupied with safety needs—gravitate toward safe companies. They want the company that, in comparison with other employers, offers stability, job security, and the status of being affiliated with an organization that has real clout in the community. Leading banks, the electric light company, the local telephone company, and any large and long-established manufacturer are typical institutions to which they are drawn. Among the factors which do not attract them to an employer are an unstructured job situation in which duties and responsibilities are loosely defined, the chance to move ahead fast but at considerable risk to both job security and peace of mind, and the chance to grow with a fledgling enterprise if, as, and when it grows.

Contrast the typical employee of a firm such as Polaroid, that operates on the perimeters of scientific knowledge, with the typical employee of AT&T. We're not denying Polaroid its share of safe types or Ma Bell its quota of hard drivers and risk takers, but we're talking about the average, not the exception. We still maintain that there is a major difference between the two, a difference of organizational climate that, in turn, determines the organizational image and reputation of the two enterprises. The man who is attracted to one would probably not be drawn to the other, and if he unwittingly made the wrong choice, it is likely to turn out to be an instance of the round peg in the square hole.

When Levinson argues about how important it is for the supervisor to accept and gratify the legitimate dependency needs of his subordinates, he's talking about an organizational setting that is apt to attract people with strong dependency needs in the first place and to foster their further development—a public utility.

The question of why people are attracted to some types of organizations rather than to others also illustrates the impact of culture on a worker's system of needs. Among lower and lower-middle class men of Irish descent in the northeastern United States, for example, there existed for two generations a tradition of regarding three institutions as the logical route to status and recognition (we're omitting the Catholic church as a special case): the police force, the power and light company, and the telephone company.

The source of the mystique is unclear. Certainly it had little or nothing to do with pay. We suspect it was a survival of the class system and the acceptance of class distinctions as part of an obscure but unchanging and unchallengeable natural order. The jobs themselves may not have been much, but the occupants felt a glory that gave them some of the prestige they felt was occupied in the community by the institutions they served—and sometimes loved. When they talked about the company, you could hear the capital letters.

At times, the cultural impact may lighten the task of the organization and the supervisor. A long-time Sears executive and a man of great sophistication in personnel matters, for instance, praised and explained southern employees in these terms: "A great many of these young people have had religious upbringings which, together with parental admonitions, emphasized the rightness of hard work and the moral obligation of the employee to give his employer a full day's work for a full day's pay." Lest we start a new wave of industrial migration south of the Mason-Dixon line, let's hastily add that this is an accurate description of a South that is rapidly disappearing, not the South as it is becoming.

PREFACE TO THE SELECTED READINGS

In about the middle of each chapter, we're including a few pages written by a classic management thinker on an aspect of the topic you are studying. Which raises the question—who is a classic management thinker? But first a comment that is not a criterion. Compared to philosophy, political science, psychology, and history, to use some examples, few first-rate minds have concerned themselves with management. Maybe it reflects the citation given each year to all graduating MBA's at the Harvard Business School that refers to management "as the youngest of the professions." Of course, no work of permanent literary or intellectual worth has emerged from the oldest of the professions either. Anyway it makes the anthologist's chores lighter.

Not to beg the question: A classic management thinker is a man, first, whose work is intrinsically first-class. He originated, not regurgitated, and what he had to say was a contribution then—and now. Second, he has achieved wide recognition among his peers and among the book-reading wing of management. Third, there is pleasure in reading him, whether it's for his preciseness, the breadth and depth of his thought, the elegance of his simplicity, or in some cases, such as Taylor, Mayo, and McGregor, his eloquence. Passion is not the monopoly of priests, poets, and politicians.

For each reading, in the brief space allocated, we will attempt to say a few words as to what makes him a significant thinker. Our purpose, beyond introducing the men and their ideas, is to stir some of you to read further in these men who thought deeply at what they were about.

Whitehead said "the justification of a university was to serve as a connection between knowledge and the zest of life." We are addressing ourselves primarily to the same public about whom Whitehad was speaking. We hope that these excerpts and the book as a whole have a like justification and fulfill a similar purpose.

FREDERICK WINSLOW TAYLOR (1856–1915)

Poor Taylor. He has had a terrible press for the past generation and, as the tone of his testimony in the selection would indicate, he was very much on the defensive back in 1912. He was the prototype of all efficiency experts, the father of time-and-motion study, the man who dehumanized factory work by breaking each job down into the smallest possible components, thereby robbing it of the slightest interest or challenge for any sentient man.

Not at all, Taylor would have responded—and did on many occasions. The division of labor permitted the laborer to devote all his energies to performing the work at hand; thinking was practically excluded. Furthermore, because the worker was on incentive, the more he produced, the more he got paid. Of course, management got higher profits because of the increased productivity. In Taylor's system there were no losers: Time-and-motion study ensured that things were done "the one best way" at the "one best speed"; the worker was spared the burden of thinking about what he was doing and made more money to boot; management had the satisfaction derived from efficient planning—and larger profits.

Taylor's ideas had tremendous appeal and wide application: the lesson of the famous Schmidt, who weighed in at 130 pounds, but nonetheless, using Taylor's methods consistently loaded 47 tons of pig iron per day versus the prevalent 12.5 tons, was not lost on a generation of employers. Scientific management became the religion of efficiency, with Taylor as high priest, and Henry Ford as lord high practitioner.

What went wrong? Why did the movement run out of steam? To what extent were its deficiencies inherent in Taylor's ideas? A few suggestions. Taylor's view of the working man—and for that matter the executive too—as a purely economic animal was always a partial view. His belief that the increased wages made possible by the division of labor would more than offset any loss caused by a shrinkage of the intrinsic interest of the job was never as generally palatable as Taylor assumed and became progressively less acceptable to the better-educated blue-collar worker with higher expectations in the two generations after him. In short, there were never as many Schmidts as Taylor had assumed and they became in increasingly short supply.

Beyond that, Taylor's ideas were appropriated by many so-called efficiency experts who in the name of scientific management did institute speed-ups and exploit working-men—by almost anyone's standards. Scientific management, and Taylor, got an undeserved bad name in the process.

Most important, technology passed Taylor by. The times had been ripe for Taylor in the 1890s. One hundred years

before, Eli Whitney of cotton-gin fame had put forth
pretty much the same ideas, but he was decidedly pre-
mature. Today it's only in assembly-line operations, which
now account for a small fraction of total factory production, that the minute division of labor still makes economic
sense. In other words, the same logic of efficiency that
once carried the day for Taylorism has dethroned it.

Taylor belongs more to the past than any other of our
classic thinkers. However, his is an important voice of a
past that is still with us. On this ground alone he is
worth reading. The task is easy; all his key works have
been assembled in *Scientific Management,* Harper and
Bros., New York, 1947.

What Is Scientific Management*

Scientific management is not any efficiency device, not a
device of any kind for securing efficiency; nor is it any
bunch or group of efficiency devices. It is not a new system
of figuring costs; it is not a new scheme of paying men;
it is not a piecework system; it is not a bonus system; it is
not a premium system; it is no scheme for paying men; it is
not holding a stop watch on a man and writing things
down about him; it is not time study; it is not motion
study nor an analysis of the movements of men; it is not the
printing and ruling and unloading of a ton or two of blanks
on a set of men and saying, "Here's your system, go use
it." It is not divided foremanship or functional foremanship; it is not any of the devices which the average man
calls to mind when scientific management is spoken of. The
average man thinks of one or more of these things when
he hears the words "scientific management" mentioned,
but scientific management is not any of these devices.
I am not sneering at cost-keeping systems, at time study, at
functional foremanship, nor at any new and improved
scheme of paying men, nor at any efficiency devices, if
they are really devices that make for efficiency. I believe
in them; but what I am emphasizing is that these devices
in whole or in part are not scientific management; they are

---

* Reprinted by permission of the publishers from Frederick W.
Taylor, *Scientific Management,* Harper and Bros., New York, 1947,
pp. 77–80.

Excerpt from testimony of Frederick W. Taylor at hearings before
the Special Committee of the House of Representatives to Investigate
the Taylor and Other Systems of Shop Management, January 25, 1912,
pages 1387–1389.

useful adjuncts to scientific management, so are they also useful adjuncts of other systems of management.

Now, in its essence, scientific management involves a complete mental revolution on the part of the workingman engaged in any particular establishment or industry—a complete mental revolution on the part of these men as to their duties toward their work, toward their fellow men, and toward their employees. And it involves the equally complete mental revolution on the part of those on the management's side—the foreman, the superintendent, the owner of the business, the board of directors—a complete mental revolution on their part as to their duties toward their fellow workers in the management, toward their workmen, and toward all of their daily problems. And without this complete mental revolution on both sides scientific management does not exist.

That is the essence of scientific management, this great mental revolution. Now, later on, I want to show you more clearly what I mean by this great mental revolution. I know that it perhaps sounds to you like nothing but bluff—like buncombe—but I am going to try and make clear to you just what this great mental revolution involves, for it does involve an immense change in the minds and attitude of both sides, and the greater part of what I shall say today has relation to the bringing about of this great mental revolution. So that whether the details may be interesting or uninteresting, what I hope you will see is that this great change in attitude and viewpoint must produce results which are magnificient for both sides, just as fine for one as for the other. Now, perhaps I can make clear to you at once one of the very great changes in outlook which come to the workmen, on the one hand, and to those in the management on the other hand.

I think it is safe to say that in the past a great part of the thought and interest both of the men, on the side of the management, and of those on the side of the workmen in manufacturing establishments has been centered upon what may be called the proper division of the surplus resulting from their joint efforts, between the management on the one hand, and the workmen on the other hand. The management have been looking for as large a profit as possible for themselves, and the workmen have been look-ing for as large wages as possible for themselves, and that is what I mean by the division of the surplus. Now, this question of the division of the surplus is a very plain and simple one (for I am announcing no great fact in political economy or anything of that sort). Each article produced in the establishment has its definite selling price. Into the manufacture of this article have gone certain expenses, namely, the cost of materials, the expenses connected with selling it, and certain indirect expenses, such as the rent of the building, taxes, insurance, light and power, maintenance of machinery, interest on the plant, etc. Now, if we deduct these several expenses from the selling price, what is left over may be called the surplus. And out of this surplus comes the profit to the manufacturer on the one hand, and the wages of the workmen on the other hand. And it is largely upon the division of this surplus that the attention of the workmen and of the management has been centered in the past. Each side has had its eye upon this surplus, the working man wanting as large a share in the form of wages as he could get, and the management wanting as large a share in the form of profits as it could get; I think I am safe in saying that in the past it has been in the division of this surplus that the great labor troubles have come between employers and employees.

Frequently, when the management have found the selling price going down they have turned toward a cut in the wages—toward reducing the workman's share of the surplus—as their way of getting out whole, of preserving their profits intact. While the workman (and you can hardly blame him) rarely feels willing to relinquish a dollar of his wages, even in dull times, he wants to keep all that he has had in the past, and when busy times come again very naturally he wants to get more. Thus it is over this division of the surplus that most of the troubles have arisen; in the extreme cases this has been the cause of serious disagreements and strikes. Gradually the two sides have come to look upon one another as antagonists, and at times even as enemies—pulling apart and matching the strength of the one against the strength of the other.

The great revolution that takes place in the mental attitude of the two parties under scientific management is that both sides take their eyes off of the division of the surplus as the all-important matter, and together turn their attention toward increasing the size of the surplus until this surplus becomes so large that it is unnecessary to quarrel over how it shall be divided. They come to see that when they stop pulling against one another, and instead both turn and push shoulder to shoulder in the same direction, the size of the surplus created by their joint efforts is truly astounding. They both realize that when they substitute friendly cooperation and mutual helpfulness for antagonism and strife they are together able to make this surplus so enormously greater than it was in the past that there is ample room for a large increase in wages for the workmen and an equally great increase in profits for the manufacturer. This, gentlemen, is the beginning of the great mental revolution which constitutes the first step toward scientific management. It is along this line of complete change in the mental attitude of both sides; of the substitution of peace for war; the substitution of hearty brotherly cooperation for contention and strife; of both pulling hard in the same direction instead of pulling apart; of replacing suspicious watchfulness with mutual confidence; of becoming friends instead of enemies; it is along this line, I say, that scientific management must be developed.

The substitution of this new outlook—this new viewpoint—is of the very essence of scientific management, and scientific management exists nowhere until after this has become the central idea of both sides; until this new idea of cooperation and peace has been substituted for the old idea of discord and war.

This change in the mental attitude of both sides toward the "surplus" is only a part of the great mental revolution which occurs under scientific management. I will later point out other elements of this mental revolution. There is, however, one more change in viewpoint which is absolutely essential to the existence of scientific management. Both sides must recognize as essential the substitution of exact scientific investigation and knowledge for the old individual judgment or opinion, either of the workman or the boss, in all matters relating to the work done in the establishment. And this applies both as to the methods to be employed in doing the work and the time in which each job should be done.

Scientific management cannot be said to exist, then, in any establishment until after this change has taken place in the mental attitude of both the management and the men, both as to their duty to cooperate in producing the largest possible surplus and as to the necessity for substituting exact scientific knowledge for opinions or the old rule of thumb or individual knowledge.

These are the two absolutely essential elements of scientific management.

WHAT'S THE MATTER WITH MONEY?

So far, we've talked a lot about the plurality of human needs and the different ways in which they are satisfied on the job. And we have stressed that many people seek jobs and that many more accommodate themselves to jobs which afford few of the satisfactions delineated by Herzberg and Maslow, yet they remain reasonably content and reasonably productive for years or even decades. These satisfactions run the spectrum from job security to the freedom to daydream, the opportunity to develop meaningful interpersonal relations, the pleasure of working for a superior who is both boss and father figure, and the reflected glory of association with a powerful and prestigious organization. Most workers, of course, bring to their jobs a complex of needs and expectations which, in turn, they find satisfied to a greater or less degree. Happily, in our society—at least, until he's well into middle age—a man who finds few of his major needs satisfied in his current job is in the position to leave it, fortified by the knowledge that he can find another and hopefully more satisfying position.

Up to this point, we have omitted any evaluation of the motivator that previous generations regarded as the mainspring of performance and that this generation, among academics at least, has banished to the sidelines—money. Have we been intimidated by the current vogue among behavioral scientists to downgrade or dismiss money as a motivator? Possibly, although we don't think so. We've been deterred much more by the difficulty and complexity of the subject and by the problems involved in distinguishing between illusion and reality and of separating the two.

Does Money Motivate?

A few instances stand out where it is difficult to deny that the worker puts a very high value on money, indeed.

The classic ratebuster on an incentive job drives himself from start to finish, has no time for sociability, usually incurs the active hostility of his coworkers and the passive antagonism of his supervisor (by implying that higher management may get the idea that he should make the other employees do as much work), and ends the day with little energy to spare. All this is evidence that the size of his paycheck means a lot to him. In fact, the only other likely motivator is whatever satisfaction the ratebuster derives from being the winner of a race which, typically, no one else cares to enter—cold comfort, we should think.

In one sense, we would agree that money has ceased to be an effective motivator—the ratebuster being the exception, not the rule. The reasons were neatly summed up by Lawrence Appley, chairman of the board of the American Management Association: "A person who is born into a world of legislated and sizable security benefits must have a different point of view from one who is not. An individual who starts work in a world of great organized union strength must have a different point of view from one who does not. That individual who expects, receives, and is accustomed to high pay unrelated to quantity or quality of work done must think different from one who does not." Mr. Appley exaggerates when he talks about high pay unrelated to the quantity or quality of work—but not by much. In other words, to a degree undreamed-of by any previous generation, the basic financial needs of most workers are satisfied from their very first day on the job.

An obvious objection arises: Aren't unions forever demanding more and more money for their constituents, who already have all the money they need? Are we claiming, then, that the unions are misrepresenting the needs of their members? Not really. The process at work, a pretty complex one, has been encapsulated best by Argyris. Many elements of the work situation frustrate the employee, and he responds by asking for more money—"wages for dissatisfaction," Argyris calls them. The union presses his demands and management reinforces the importance of the dollar drive by the publicity campaign that inevitably follows any wage increase. In turn, the worker feels more strongly than ever that the answer to any job dissatisfaction is more and more money.

Several factors are at work here. One is cultural lag. When Samuel Gompers, the founder of the American Federation of Labor, summed up the goal of the organization in behalf of its members as "more," he was talking primarily about money in an era when the value of wage increases was real rather than largely symbolic. Unions and managements both are conditioned to argue about money—the union usually has a pretty good idea as to what the company can afford, and the company usually has a pretty good idea as to what the union will settle for. Bargaining about recognition, restructuring of jobs, and making work more meaningful are complex, nebulous, and unfamiliar activities. By contrast, money talks in terms that everyone understands. Yes, but money, at least as it is seen in nine-tenths of the wage increases granted to the rank and file or exacted in their behalf, doesn't talk loudly enough. Increases that weren't sufficient by and large to make any real differences in the recipient's standard of living, increases that were granted to everyone irrespective of merit, increases that were sought in the spirit of exacting revenge and granted in the spirit of offering a bribe—all these work against the raise providing any real satisfaction for the employee and any real incentive for him to do a better job. We have never heard of a case where a blanket increase led to better performance. At best, it maintained the status quo.

The paradox is that no one really knows whether money could function as an incentive for the rank-and-file worker because no one up to the present time has really tried it. The use of money in meaningful amounts as an incentive has been restricted to the upper executive echelons where the weight of the evidence suggests that it can be a highly effective motivator. To cite just one outstanding example, consider Ernest Breech and the "whiz kids" Bugas, Harder, McNamara, Miller, and the others whom Henry Ford II recruited— largely from General Motors—at the end of World War II to turn around a company that was losing 10 million dollars a month. They accomplished the turnaround and not the least of the reasons were stock options guaranteed to make all of them multimillionaires if they succeeded.

We're realists. We know that there is nothing about the potential contribution of the average worker to justify making him a millionaire. However, we think that management collectively is missing the boat by its failure to view money as an incentive with the rank-and-file workers because of its preoccupation with a wage policy whose principal purpose is to achieve equitability and minimize frictions. We agree with Gellerman that "money may well turn out to be the costliest motivator of them all, but money may also prove to be the most potent motivator of all, at least in certain circumstances, and when used on a sufficient scale."

We are suggesting that management try using money on jobs where the worker's efforts have a large and direct impact on productivity, on jobs where most workers are realizing only a portion of their potential, and on jobs that offer few other satisfactions. We are also proposing that management be willing to utilize the lion's share of any productivity gain as an incentive bonus—45 percent more productivity might, for example, yield a 40 percent bonus. Most so-called incentive systems now in effect don't work because (1) the standards are so tight that it takes extraordinary effort to effect any substantial increase and get a meaningful bonus, (2) the worker is afraid the system will be revamped to his financial disadvantage if he consistently makes a large bonus, or (3) he fears social ostracism by the work group if he produces too much. The approach we have in mind would take care of the first two objections. The potential for earning large bonuses would be built into the system—we wouldn't advise this use of money as an incentive where workers were already producing 80 percent of their capacity or more. There should also be built-in guarantees that the incentive system would remain the same as long as the production process was unchanged. And with the first two objections erased, the work group probably wouldn't object to rapid raises in output. But we don't think the expectation of a 5, 10, or even a 15 percent pay increase will motivate a man. Our guesstimate is that money as a motivator begins with the 20 percent increase.

JOB DEMANDS DEFINE INCENTIVES

Now that we've finished discussing the principal incentives, we can see their importance to our central thesis: the interrelationship between the needs the employee brings to the job and the demands the job makes on him. The nature of the job sets limits to the possible satisfactions a man can derive while holding it. Many men derive satisfaction from their work by the subtle and largely subconscious adjustment of their needs structure to accommodate those satisfactions permitted by the job, while others buck the job and derive satisfaction from beating the system—seeing how little they can do for a week's pay. Still others quit in disgust and get another job.

In any case, the job itself defines the satisfactions anyone can derive from it and sets limits on the incentives even the wisest and most socially conscious managements can provide. Returning once more to our favorite horrible example, let's consider the moving assembly line. Listen to one assembly-line worker: "The job gets so sickening, day in and day out plugging in ignition wires. I get through with one motor, turn around, and there's another staring me in the face. It's sickening." Excessive specialization of the kind we've just described deprives the employee of almost any chance to be independent, to do quality work, or to feel that he is accomplishing anything worthwhile. Work that has been so subdivided and simplified that it takes almost no time to learn and requires no attention provides little or no interest.

There's also little opportunity for advancement in the typical assembly-line job. Most such positions require similar levels of skill and reward the worker with similar pay. Many workers hold on to their dreams of advancement or a business of their own for a while, but by age 40, they've said goodbye to Horatio Alger.

Even on the social side, the assembly line, at least in an automobile plant, affords few satisfactions. Workers are restricted to a very small area and can only talk with those directly on either side, or occasionally across the line. Moreover, since most workers dislike the job or feel, at best, indifferent to it, they're not particularly interested in making friendships which carry over after their shift is over. Most of them want to get away from every aspect of the job at quitting time.

What makes the jobs endurable?

The pay is considerably higher than it is in most semiskilled jobs that are more interesting. The jobs make limited physical and minimal mental demands on the occupant, leaving him comparatively fresh for his real life once he's finished putting in his time on the assembly line. And there's always the freedom to fantasize, since assembly-line jobs make few demands on the employee's attention span.

Of course, not all mass-production workers wear blue collars. In many clerical operations, the eye can take in literally hundreds of desks and work tables. The jobs are minutely described, broken down into mechanized short-cycle tasks requiring such tools as card-punchers or typewriters, and they are time-studied just as their counterparts on the factory floor. Also, there's the same continuous pressure to make the standard.

Small wonder that many clerical employees derive few satisfactions from the job itself. For example, here's part of a self-description provided by an office worker in a large insurance company: "As an operator, I had to complete 720 units in four hours with no more than eleven errors. This quota was often very difficult to meet, especially on nights when the packs were of more than average difficulty. The job was extremely boring." Whatever satisfactions the woman derived were social and associational. Furthermore, for the vast majority, the jobs are temporary positions which they expect to leave as soon as marriage and motherhood make it feasible.

CONTINUOUS-PROCESS AUTOMATION AN EXCEPTION

Continuous-process automation affords significant exceptions to the lack of built-in satisfactions in fragmented blue- and white-collar jobs.

Continuous-process automation occurs in industries, such as chemicals and petroleum, in which the product flows continuously from entering raw material to finished product through a number of interlinked stages. In these plants, the employee spends much of his time monitoring gauges and control instruments. Aside from monitoring, he handles breakdowns, start-ups, and changeovers. The skills required are not necessarily greater, but as Walker commented in his study of an automatic rolling mill, they are different in kind: "of the head rather than of the hand; of logician rather than craftsman; of nerve rather than muscle; of pilot rather than manual worker; of maintenance man, not operator." The work cycles are long, and the employee retains some control over the work rhythms. In breakdowns, it frequently takes a great deal of skill to remedy the stoppage, and in between, employees derive satisfaction from being responsible for keeping some very complex and expensive machinery in good working and running order. Employees also see themselves progressing on career ladders that naturally evolve as they gain experience and express a willingness to accept responsibility. The top crew-chief positions involve enormous responsibility and challenge.

Let's consider the case of the worker's soup described by Blauner as an illustration of the difference between the auto assembly line and continuous-process technology. A chemical operator mentioned that he often warmed up a can of soup on a hot plate in the automated control room—*a procedure requiring perhaps ten minutes*. What if the soup is ready when the operator is about to make his round of instrument readings—something that takes 30 minutes? "You can eat the soup first and do the work later, or you can take the readings earlier than scheduled, in order to have the soup when it's hot" was the operator's reply. The auto assembly line worker, by contrast, who wanted a bowl of soup would have to wait for his allotted relief time, purchase his soup from a vending machine, and probably gulp it down on the run on his way back from the lavatory—relief times being both fixed and brief.

In summary, continuous-process automation is the opposite of Taylorism and the specialization of labor. The latter tries to make the job something that anyone can do by breaking it down to its smallest common denominators and, ideally, assigning one element to one man. Continuous-process automation, on the other hand, looks at the work process as a whole and utilizes the actual abilities of the rank-and-file worker to integrate jobs, not fractionate them.

Unmeasurable Performance and Incentives

What about workers on jobs that don't lend themselves to precise, quantifiable measurements and direct production bonuses? How much should they be rewarded? And how frequently?

We repeat our contention that money spent on modest merit increases is money thrown away if the purpose of the merit increase is to motivate the man to do even better work in the future. In fact, a 5 or 10 percent increase may leave him with a feeling of being cheated and may demotivate him— motivate him to contribute less, not more. Instead, save your merit increases for your top performers and give them 20-25-30 percent annual increases if you want to motivate them.

As for frequency of increases, management would do well to heed the latest behavioral theories, which demonstrate that the best way of getting desired behavior is to reward that behavior immediately after it takes place. We know of one successful manager who tries to incorporate, or at any rate approximate, this approach in giving out merit increases. First he determines how big each employee's total annual increase should be. Then he divides it into several segments and awards one of them to an employee after an incident of performance that is way above average, even though the man's last raise may be only a couple of months old. Of course, this also gives the manager the option of withholding the segmented raises if the man's performance should unexpectedly deteriorate. (More on rewards in Chapter 5.)

MAKING THE JOB MORE MEANINGFUL

So far, we have talked about the limits imposed by technology on the satisfaction of employee needs as if they were immutably fixed and could not be changed. The truth is much different. Many organizations have redesigned jobs within the framework of the existing technology in order to make them more meaningful to their employees, or have made other changes in the circumstances of work intended to make the job more interesting or to give the employee more initiative or control.

Why have they taken the trouble? Social consciousness or philanthropic instincts have played little or no part in most managements' decisions. We know of only one major company—Polaroid—that has made making work meaningful to its employees a central and explicit goal of the organization. With an annual growth in earnings of 18.56 percent in the decade 1959–69, Polaroid can afford the luxury of a social conscience. In the other organizations, management decided to make the jobs more meaningful because it was convinced the time, effort, and expense would pay off on the bottom line.

The other satisfactions and incentives present in any job situation—including money as it's presently used (we would argue, misused)—are real enough. But at best they are motivators to stay on the job, to show up for work most days, to contribute what the employee defines and what the company pretty much has to put up with as a fair day's work. On the other hand, if you make the job itself more interesting and more challenging, if you give the worker more control over the job and more responsibility for performing it, you might actually hope to motivate him to do more work, better work—or both.

Of course, there are limitations to management's ability to make the job more meaningful. In some cases, reversing the process of the division of labor is technologically unsound. No dividend gained from motivating workers can offset the savings lost. To advocate the introduction of job enlargement, for example, on the automobile assembly line, would be to deserve the retort Theodore Roosevelt made to union leaders who objected to using steam shovels instead of men with shovels in building the Panama Canal: "Should we dig it with teaspoons?"

Companies, such as IBM and Texas Instruments, that have been in the forefront of job enlargement have discovered in their operations a number of "stupid" jobs where job enlargement doesn't pay. In consequence, IBM uses job enlargement or job enrichment, as one IBM spokesman put it, "whenever we can"—in other words, wherever management is convinced it will pay dividends.

Job Enlargement

What changes in work methods and procedures do we have in mind? Nothing we're talking about is very new. Many companies have tried one or all of them with a considerable measure of success.

Let's begin with job enlargement and a story about the late Thomas Watson of IBM. He approached a middle-aged woman on the assembly line in Endicott, New York, in the early 1940s and asked her an unusual question: "What don't you like about your job?" "Doing the same thing over and over again," was her frank response—Mr. Watson had apparently caught her off guard. It led IBM to pioneer job enlargement and make most IBM operators responsible for both setup and inspection on their jobs. The result: generally improved operator efficiency, fewer errors, and fewer inspections.

In other instances, IBM enlarged the scope of the actual production job. For example, it decided it would get better results at its Lexington, Kentucky, typewriter plant by having one person put together an entire tab mechanism for the machines rather than the six who had done the job previously.

WHY DOES IT WORK?

The explanation for the improvement you won't find surprising. Since specialization uses only a small portion of most workers' abilities, most employees respond to job enlargement because it makes their tasks more interesting and intellectually more challenging. If you make the workers responsible for quality, as IBM has done, you also give them autonomy and develop their sense of responsibility.

A few more instances of job enlargement, together with some payoffs: Maytag, the appliance maker, over a seven-year-long period undertook twenty-five job-enlargement projects for its blue-collar workers. Previously, for example, the company used a group of five or six operators on a small production line to assemble a twenty-six-part water pump for automatic washing machines. Now each worker puts together the complete pump and tests it as well. The result: Direct labor costs have been cut 16 percent for simple time-and-motion reasons. The various parts of the pump can be arranged more efficiently within the employee's work area than along an assembly line. Moreover, there's been a significant increase in the quality of pumps—the average reject rate has dropped to less than 0.5 percent from 5 percent.

Texas Instruments in its "Meaningful Work Program" has gone several steps beyond IBM and Maytag with job enlargement. In addition to doing their own testing and inspecting, many TI workers daily set their own quality and quantity goals—with results that management finds very satisfactory. In some instances, TI has experimented with giving workers almost complete control over jobs, delegating to them responsibilities for planning, organizing, and controlling their work that are usually monopolized by management. In short, TI has practiced vertical job enlargement and, at times, has achieved spectacular results.

One such success occurred with a group of women assembling a complex instrument. At the beginning of the experiment, it took an average of 138 hours to assemble a single unit. In a problem-solving meeting, the women came up with many ideas for improving work methods, including a rearrangement of the assembly procedures. All of them were adopted. Subsequently, they set their own production standard for the unit—86 hours. Unknown to them, industrial engineering had determined on a standard of 100 hours. They made it in 76 hours. After a second problem-solving session and the introduction of still more employee suggestions, the goal was reset at 65 hours—this time, they did the assembling in 59. Later, they got the assembly time down to 32 hours. Some improvement from 138 hours! Nor was this the only benefit. Absenteeism, turnover, learning time, employee complaints, and trips to the health center all fell off.

SOME RESERVATIONS

Not all attempts at job enlargement have worked out nearly so well—at Texas Instruments or anywhere else. At times, most of the problem lay with some of the employees whose jobs were being enriched. They liked their old routines and disliked their new responsibilities. The duller-witted among them probably found the old job as much of a challenge as they could handle, and the rest were lazy, indifferent, or had been conditioned too long to adjust successfully to the change. When Non-Linear Systems, a manufacturer of electronic measuring instruments, for example, abandoned its assembly line and made the women responsible for a much larger proportion of the total task, reactions ranged from those of women who wanted larger segments to those of women who wanted nothing larger than what they had been accustomed to. Eventually, Non-linear had the women themselves decide the size of the segment they would assemble.

In one survey of assembly-line operators conducted by Professor Kilbridge, of the Harvard Business School, he found that over half the sample preferred smaller assembly tasks, 37 percent were indifferent to the size of the task, and only 12 percent preferred larger tasks. Mechanical pacing was not distasteful to the majority of workers with whom he talked. What we can't know, of course, is to what extent their reactions were based on anxiety about the unknown and how different their reactions might have been had their jobs been enriched. Another study of assembly-line workers at a pharmaceutical plant found that they liked their jobs on the assembly line, but two years after the change to a whole job approach wherein each employee secured his materials, performed nine operations, and did the final inspection, employees indicated their reluctance to return to the old method.

Finally, as Professors Turner and Lawrence have warned, managements shouldn't introduce job enlargement and simultaneously diminish other job satisfactions. They cite an instance where fifteen workers on a rotary conveyor were given work stations surrounded by high banks of parts, and each was assigned to assemble the total product according to a carefully predetermined method and sequence. This particular form of job enlargement emphasized variety at the expense of autonomy and the opportunity to interact with coworkers— and it failed, for obvious reasons.

Sometimes the problem with job enlargement, particularly with vertical job enlargement, lay in an overall climate that didn't support the enrichment of the job. Foulkes quotes an official at Texas Instruments on the reason why the Meaningful Work Program sometimes succeeded but sometimes failed: "Many times the behavior of top and middle management ran counter to the value of the Meaningful Work Program and thus TI was not getting the necessary mileage out of the program." The point he made could be generalized to include any effort at job enlargement, whether vertical or horizontal. The program must be consistent with the overall plant or office system, of which it, after all, forms only a part. If the employees, for example, are given more so-called responsibility but their supervisor insists on inspecting every piece of work, they will see the program for the empty gesture that the supervisor has made out of it, and the consequences for motivation and performance are more likely to be negative than positive.

Job Rotation

Some companies are seeking to reduce boredom and provide challenge not by changing jobs but by moving employees from one job to another, a process that almost always involves some jobs that are more demanding and more rewarding than others. Herzberg has warned that you can't provide meaningful work by adding meaningless duties to a paltry position. Similarly, job rotation accomplishes nothing if you move an employee from one inconsequential job to another that is of no greater consequence. Job rotation also provides variety, permits the employee to see more of the total operation, and requires him to learn new skills.

Polaroid has done as much with job rotation as any other company, in part because of its general concern with making the job life of its employees more worthwhile and in part because of a survey of production employees that isolated the eight opportunities they felt were the keys to an interesting job. These were the opportunities: (1) to learn something new, (2) to move about, (3) to show initiative, (4) to be in contact with others, (5) to visualize end results, (6) to make job-related decisions, (7) to vary one's regular duties, and (8) to be fully competent at what one does. Job rotation began with the "Pathfinder Program" and the rotation of personnel at intervals that varied with the job—some weekly and others monthly—between their regular position and one that was more interesting and provided more of a challenge. The program proved to be a mixed success and Polaroid abandoned it after three years. What went wrong? After a brief period of adjustment and a longer period of enjoyment—typically three months to a year—most employees became frustrated with the routine part of the job. They wanted to keep rotating only if they could hope for permanent, full-time assignment to a better job. As a lesser problem, supervisors objected to the burdens of adding a dual supervisory job to their other responsibilities.

Other organizations haven't experienced Polaroid's problems with its Pathfinder Program, probably because their rotation, although it involved some jobs that were more challenging than others, was restricted to a single production process, and occurred during a single day. That way, workers couldn't develop the same sense of identification with the better job and the same sense of frustration over having to return to the lesser job. There were too many tasks to perform and too little time spent on the individual task, each one of which contributed to the same end result.

In place of Pathfinder, Polaroid substituted a "Job Exposure Program" under which an employee interested in a better job would be loaned to another department free of charge for a limited period—say three to six months. At the end of the period, he could either apply for a full-time opening in the department if one existed or return, without prejudice, to his old job in his old department. Up to the present time, hundreds of employees have taken advantage of the Job Exposure Program and a large number of them have made the transition successfully.

Job rotation, as a technique for making the job more interesting and employees more valuable, is not restricted to blue-collar workers. The Boston Safe Deposit and Trust

Company, for example, uses it with many clerical employees.
Moreover, many companies practice it in their management-
training program for recent college graduates.

AN UNUSUAL CASE

Some applications of job rotation seem far out—but they
work. Take the case of the Steelcraft Manufacturing Co.,
which sent draftsmen to Toronto for a week to call on
architects and try to sell them on specifying its products—
metal doors and frames. How did these draftsmen make out
as salesmen? They batted .500—in half the cases they were
able to convince the architects to specify Steelcraft's products.

There was also a substantial bonus. The men returned to
their drafting boards with a better understanding of what
the firm's salesmen were talking about when they described
customers' needs, likes, and dislikes. They're no longer drawing doorways in a vacuum.

Job rotation, then, is another important technique for increasing job satisfaction and efficiency—under the proper
conditions. Once again, it's necessary to hedge. Job rotation
won't be appreciated and won't work with many employees if
they are deeply rooted in their job and regard it almost
as a piece of personal property, or if they work on jobs that
demand no attention so that they can daydream to their
hearts' content. Polaroid, where participation in the job-
rotation program was optional, found that many workers—
in fact, more than a majority—elected not to participate.

The truth is, there are people who would keep digging
holes and filling them up again if they enjoyed the company
of their fellow diggers.

The Right-Sized Job

Most people get a feeling of accomplishment from completing
a whole job. But if the work unit takes too long to complete,
the goal is too far away to be much of a motivator. And if
the natural unit is too small (such as, say, tightening a bolt),
the units are too trivial to be meaningful and completing one
of them doesn't give anyone a sense of accomplishment.

The question inevitably arises—how large is an optimal
unit? One study suggests that it should last from an hour
to an hour and a half, depending on the situation. Think of
your own household chores. You may have maintained a minimal level of interest in mowing the lawn, for example, by

the device of dividing it into small sections as you went along.
Many companies have applied a similar technique called
"Short Interval Scheduling" (SIS) to jobs where the work is
repetitive and the time required for the task is relatively
short and fairly constant. SIS is a technique that replaces the
usually weekly or daily job assignment with a series of
smaller, short-term performance goals. The length of the interval varies according to the type of work assigned. For
example, a typist might finish eleven letters and envelopes
per hour, a maintenance electrician might take four hours to
modernize a load center, or a draftsman might need three
hours to complete two detailed drawings of specific units.
But within any category, the interval will be the same for all
employees.

Employees get a sense of achievement every time they
complete an assignment in less than the scheduled time, which
usually happens several times a day. Some managements let
the worker who finishes ahead of time sit back and take it
easy, with leisure as his reward. Others offer some form
of bonus pay for extra production.

CONCLUSION

Why do men work? What needs do they have that are
gratified on the job? To secure the means of subsistence, to
enjoy the company and support of their coworkers, to be
identified with an organization far more powerful than themselves, to make a meaningful contribution to a product they
think of as important, to test their abilities on a challenging
task—these are a partial catalog of the needs men hope to
satisfy by work.

The potential for satisfying this galaxy of needs varies
greatly from job to job. We think it's useful to distinguish
between needs satisfied *on the job* and needs satisfied by *the
job itself.* In a Michigan survey of 401 men, 80 percent said
they would continue to work even if they inherited enough
money to live comfortably, and one-third identified the
socializing aspects of work as what they would miss most if
they did not work. On many jobs where the work itself is
trivial and monotonous, there are continuous opportunities for
socializing. In other words, the absence of satisfactions from
the job itself are offset, to a greater or less extent depending
on the individual employee, by the satisfactions he finds on
the job. Also, it's difficult to generalize about the satisfactions

employees derive from the job itself. Men with dull wits may find a job challenging that a more intelligent man would deem intolerable. It does indeed take all kinds to do the world's work.

Of recent years, many managements, for economic reasons, have become more and more concerned over the large number of situations in which the job itself offers minimal satisfactions. The problem, oversimplified, is that on-the-job satisfactions almost never motivate a worker to make more than an acceptable contribution—many companies have resigned themselves to a 60 percent day. Only when the employee derives positive satisfactions from the job will he exert himself and come close to realizing his full job potential. Hence, many organizations have redesigned the jobs—made them more varied or more complex, or have given the worker more control over the job and more responsibility. In fewer instances, the jobs have remained the same but the employees have been rotated from job to job.

How have these efforts worked out? Have they accomplished their goal of motivating the worker to more and better performance? There are no overall figures and what figures there are suggest a mixed picture. Successes are frequent— they probably outnumber failures—but in some instances the employee himself doesn't respond to the new challenges; more often the employee responds but his boss and his boss's boss do not and by their actions they negate the planned benefit of the job change.

As for the big picture, it's changing—and most people would agree that it's changing for the better. The assembly line hasn't vanished, but it's in full decline.

Blauner estimates that assembly-line workers in all industries make up no more than 5 percent of the total work force. In fact, there are probably more white-collar workers in clerical assembly jobs than there are assembly-line workers in factories. The crucial trend is away from low-skilled manual occupations of every kind, which offer few from the job satisfactions, and more toward the jobs, made possible by continuous process automation which substitute different kinds of skills and build responsibility—and the satisfaction that flows from it—into almost every job.

One final word about an almost forgotten man—the rank-and-file employee's boss. We've pretty much neglected him, in large part, because we're going to have so much to say about him in the pages that follow. We've stressed the importance of the demands inherent in the job in defining and limiting the satisfactions possible from the job—and we're not about to retract our emphasis. The supervisor works within the same framework as his subordinates, but within that framework, there is much he can do to increase or diminish whatever satisfactions his employees derive from the job. His actions, in fact, add a dimension to the motivational picture. All other things being equal, loyalty, affection, and respect for the supervisor can motivate employees to turn in a better performance. Reverse the picture and the supervisor's actions will act as a demotivator.

Take Elton Mayo's classic study of workers in a Southern California aircraft factory. Absenteeism was generally high throughout the plant and production generally low. A few departments in which the opposite was true stood out. When Mayo investigated, he found the explanation to be the way the supervisors in the successful departments managed: They spent most of their time facilitating the work of their men, acting as buffers between them and higher management, listening sympathetically to whatever complaints they had. In short, the supervisor always has an impact on motivation and performance. Sometimes it's decisive.

SELECTED REFERENCES

Argyris, C., *Integrating the Individual and the Organization,* Wiley, New York, 1964.

Blauner, R., *Alienation and Freedom: The Factory Worker and His Industry,* Chicago University Press, Chicago, 1964.

Foulkes, F. K., *Creating More Meaningful Work,* American Management Association, New York, 1969.

Gellerman, S., *The Management of Human Relations,* Holt, New York, 1966.

Herzberg, F., Mausner, B., and Synderman, B., *The Motivation to Work,* Wiley, New York, 1959.

Kuriloff, A. H., *Reality in Management,* McGraw-Hill, New York, 1966.

Mayo, E., *The Social Problems of an Industrial Civilization,* Harvard Graduate School of Business Administration, Boston, 1945.

McGregor, D., *The Human Side of Enterprise,* McGraw-Hill, New York, 1960.

Roethlisberger, F., and Dickson, W., *Management and the Worker,* Harvard University Press, Cambridge, 1939.

Taylor, F. W., *Scientific Management,* Harper, New York. 1947.

THE ARROW PLASTICS COMPANY:
A CASE STUDY

DIALOGUE BY PENNY NATHANS

The Arrow Plastics Company, located in Traverse City, Michigan, is a small (200 employees), family-owned business with a record of forty years of profitable operation. Using injection-molding equipment, it manufactures both high-volume and custom-order small plastic parts for use by equipment and computer manufacturers. The company recently hired a new supervisor, Greg Horning, who is in his mid-twenties and a graduate of a technical institute with course work in industrial engineering. This is Greg's first management position, and the case which follows each of the book's chapters describes his first six months on the job as supervisor of the custom-molding group.

Greg's work group, injection molding, is a part of the production department headed by Steve Phillips. Work flows from mixing (mixers, pelletizers, extruders; headed by Joe Barber) to molding to shipping. His group includes a day crew and a night-shift crew, but Greg spends most of his time with employees who work on days. Among the key employees are:

Molders:
Alfred Cameron
Henry Creegmore (who had expected to be named supervisor and who is very influential among the work group)
Phil Martello (union steward)
Ted Kilpatrick (the most senior employee)
Rick Cohn (the youngest employee)
Inspectors:
Jeannette Greely
Helen Kowalski

The other parts of the organization with which Greg must work, the staff departments, are the following:

Industrial engineering: Frank Granto, manager
Personnel: Albert Sykes, manager
Maintenance and materials handling: Ed Brisco, manager

THE EDUCATION OF GREG HORNING:
JANUARY 15

Greg Horning thought he knew what he was up against when he had been hired to supervise the injection-molding department at Arrow Plastics. Steve Phillips, the production manager, was not an overly communicative man, but Greg had gotten the picture. Phillips had decided to go outside the department—in fact, outside the plant altogether—to replace the old foreman when he had retired. The crew had been spoiled under him, and Phillips wanted fresh young blood to turn it around.

"The shop puts out 85 percent of standard now," Phillips told Greg. "Without busting a gut, they should be making 110 percent. That's what I'm counting on you for—to get that extra 25 percent."

It was a challenge, but Greg would be able to use all the knowledge he had been cramming into his head in technical school for the past two years—he felt he could handle it.

Things had gotten off to a bad start. When Phillips had brought him into the shop on the first day, Greg had realized immediately that there was no love lost between the production manager and the men in injection molding. Phillips had introduced Greg curtly and left. The crew had listened, sullen and silent, then turned their blank, unfriendly faces toward the new supervisor.

Greg hadn't expected that hostility to be directed toward him. It made him feel defensive and extremely young. He said something about having a lot to learn and counting on their help and the importance of teamwork.

"If we all play on the team," he finished lamely, "we can make this the smoothest running operation at Arrow Plastics." The crew faced him with the same unenthusiastic expressions. He hadn't blamed them—he hadn't believed what he'd said himself. Trying to smile, and muttering something about learning how the records were kept, he escaped into his office.

And that's where he stayed during much of the week that followed. He was going to be sure of his ground before he made any moves. Reading through the records and reports that were available and watching the workers through the glass partition that separated his office from the floor, he observed the places where procedures were not being followed and where bottlenecks in the operation occurred.

There were plenty. He decided that he would start off with an obvious one—the location of the two girls in the group. Jeannette Greely and Helen Kowalski, who checked the pieces that the men produced, were working close to each other rather than to the machines they inspected. By moving the girls closer to the machines, he would cut down on movements and waste motion by as much, perhaps, as 25 percent. He would also cut out their steady stream of conversation. They talked constantly—Greg couldn't measure what that did to their efficiency, of course, but he was sure it didn't help.

There was no hesitation from either woman in rejecting Greg's plan for their new job stations.

"It'll never work, Mr. Horning," Jeannette declared flatly.

"Now, look," Greg said, "and by the way, call me Greg—it makes much more sense than the way it is now. You see, you'll both be much nearer to your machines. The operators will be only a couple of yards away instead of 70 feet—in case you have to ask them anything."

"But you don't understand," Helen said, with a determined look. "Jeannette and I—we have to check back and forth with each other a lot. When I'm not sure if I should reject a piece, I ask what she thinks. And she asks me."

"Two heads are better than one, as they say," Jeannette added in support.

"No, no. There's no need for that." Greg's voice rose and took on an edge—he was no longer trying to be persuasive. "The standards are clearly spelled out and you girls are both experienced. Of course, there will be borderline cases, but you should bring those to me, anyway. That's one of the reasons I'm here."

Greg paused, looking from Jeannette to Helen. Neither of them said anything. They had been given an order and their tight, glaring looks were sufficient to tell Greg what they thought of it. Well, he hadn't expected them to be very enthusiastic over the idea—they'd have to fit all their gossiping in at lunch—but they'd just have to get used to it.

"So we'll try it my way for a while," he said more heartily. "Once you get used to it, I'm sure you'll see how sensible it is." Starting back toward his office, Greg added, "And don't forget, my door is always open if you have any problems."

Feeling more confident now that he had taken this first step, Greg decided to go right on to the next. He stopped at Henry Creegmore's machine and asked him into his office.

"Please sit down, Henry," Greg said. Then, picking up a single-spaced mimeographed page from his desk, he handed it to Creegmore. "Does this read the same as your copy, Henry?" Greg had received job descriptions for the whole crew from the industrial-engineering department three days ago; this was a description of Creegmore's job. Glancing at the paper and then looking fixedly at the wall behind Greg, Creegmore answered.

"I guess it's the same."

"Well, I just wanted to make sure of that, Henry, because

I have the impression that you don't always follow the job description.

"And?" Now Creegmore focused directly on Greg's face. Greg shifted in his chair.

"Well, Henry," he answered, "I think you should. I want you—and the others too—to stick to the descriptions from now on. After all, industrial engineering has put a lot of work and study into figuring out what's the best way to do the job. When people do things their own way instead of sticking to what the description says, production falls off."

"You've watched me and you see I'm doing things that aren't in the rules, you say. Well, how do you know my way isn't better?" Creegmore was studying the wall again.

"I don't know that, Henry. But if you feel what you're doing is an improvement, why don't you describe the changes to me in detail? I'll be happy to talk it over with industrial engineering."

"Yeah. That's nice. Very nice." Creegmore stood up and leaned over just slightly toward Greg. "Tell me. Just what makes you so certain that the industrial engineers have the right answer to everything? You accept everything they say as gospel, just like that?"

"That's their job," Greg snapped. "So, I'll take their word, at least until someone proves they're wrong. And my crew will take their word too, and follow their instructions until I tell them differently. Have I made myself clear?" Greg had raised himself up out of his chair and was leaning over the desk. Creegmore looked at him for an instant, then stepped back.

"Quite clear," he answered, his voice quiet and hard. "You're the boss. Do you have anything else you want to say to me?"

"No Henry," Greg said, "I guess not." But, as Creegmore started toward the door, he went on. "Henry, I hope you see that I'm just trying to get this shop running more efficiently."

Without answering or looking back, Creegmore opened the door and went out.

QUESTIONS

1. If you had been in Greg's shoes, how would you have handled the opening remarks to the crew?

2. How impressive do you find Helen's and Jeannette's objections to Greg? Were their reasons only rationalizations?

3. Do you feel that Greg could have handled Creegmore in a way that would have made him happy to accept his criticism? How?

4. On balance, do you feel that Greg did anything right in his encounters with the crew?

2. *Adapting to job requirements*

What is a job and how is it supervised? On the surface these look like simple questions. You expect to hear answers like this: A job consists of a series of duties which the employee is supposed to perform in a prescribed fashion—and the supervisor makes sure he does them! But this really isn't an answer.

WORK FLOW AND THE SYSTEMS APPROACH

Modern management recognizes that the supervisor's major emphasis should be not on individual jobs but rather on the *interrelationship* of jobs. After all, the purpose of work is not so much to complete a task or an assignment as to complete goods or services. A file clerk may work incredibly hard, but if no one else can retrieve the material she has filed, her work has not been useful. Even an engineer or a technician who energetically and conscientiously solves a problem in equipment failure may not be working effectively from the point of view of the total organization if his solution creates problems for others, for example, for those who must repair or use the equipment in the future.

Experienced supervisors concentrate on the interrelationship of jobs, on how employees work as a team. Good teamwork means that each person does his job in such a way as to complement or fit into the work of other employees. Evidence of poor teamwork—everyone is out for himself, completing his own task but not caring about how it affects his fellow workers. For example, you might hear this:

Hey, Joe, you're dropping metal filings all over the place and they're getting on my tools and gauges!

Look, Barney, don't bother me. I'm behind on my sched-ule for the day. It would take me half an hour to readjust this machine to stop spraying those filings.

Another way of saying this is to note that emphasis has shifted to the *flow of work*, the movement of material or papers or communications from work station to work station. The ideal that every supervisor seeks is to keep this move-ment *continuous* and *regular*. Such continuity, the absence of breakdowns between work stations, is the primary source of efficiency—not speed or sweat. This is one of the major conclusions and implications from the substantial emphasis on automation in recent years. Automation provides this continuity and regularity. It is the manager's job to keep things going, which really means to be concerned with the interrelationships between and among jobs more than with the individual job. To put this in another way, the supervisor ought to concentrate primarily on the *system,* on how jobs feed into one another and impact one another.

How the supervisor achieves and strengthens these interrelationships will be the focus of this chapter. Let's look first at jobs that can be individually programmed, that is, the method of doing the job can be precisely specified in advance. Then we will try to cope with the more difficult task of the supervisor's relationship to less programmed work.

PROGRAMMED INDIVIDUAL WORK

The coordination among jobs such as those found in a good deal of manufacturing can be accomplished by explicitly defining in advance what each worker must do. The typical assembly line "works" because some engineer has carefully thought through the tools, motions, and placement of each employee. Each worker's job is designed in advance so that if everyone does precisely what he has been told, the work will progress smoothly from job station to station through to completion (as shown in Figure 2-1). This is what we mean by the word "programming."

Of course, we have described this in Chapter 1 as the source of monotony and dissatisfaction: the requirement that a job be performed as some supervisor or industrial engineer has prescribed. The supervisor's job, then, is to make sure that the employee is adequately trained and is capable of doing the work. He sees that the job is actually being performed as planned.

Completed product

Each job is designed so that it is separate from
every other job, and yet nothing is left out:
everything that needs to be done is assigned to
someone. Thus there are no overlaps or gaps between jobs.

Figure 2-1   Programmed work

Training for Programmed Work

The supervisor (sometimes with the assistance of specialized training personnel) makes sure that the employee understands the "what," "how," and "why" of the job and is given adequate practice (under supervision) to guarantee his proficiency. A good capsule account of a typical training procedure follows:

1. A job description is worked out that breaks the job down into a series of motion sequences that can be described. The trainer identifies the special techniques required, the special precautions that need to be taken, the criteria that indicate whether the job is being performed correctly, the quality and safety levels necessary, and so forth. These are *key points* of the job.
2. At the beginning of the training session, the equipment and supplies are arranged in the way in which the worker is expected to keep them.
3. The trainer puts the learner at ease, finds out what he already knows, explains the relationship of his job to other jobs in the organization, and shows him the correct working position.
4. The trainer describes the job completely, stresses the key points, and then performs the job, describing "what" and "why" at each step. The learner is encouraged to ask questions.
5. The learner then tells the trainer how the job is to be done and the trainer follows his instructions.
6. The learner does the job, explaining to the trainer at each step "what" he is doing and "why."
7. The trainer follows up with periodic checks and tells the trainee where he can go for help if he runs into difficulty.[1]

Of course, the supervisor needs to remember that training is not a one-way street. The employee must ask questions and get feedback on his performance. What will be easy for one will be difficult for another and what seems like a clear instruction may be misunderstood by some. (Problems of communications are discussed in Chapter 6.)

Also, this carefully planned training of the employees must reflect the usual pattern of learning, which is often called a learning curve. At first, new material is absorbed slowly, then

---

[1] Leonard R. Sayles and George Strauss, *Personnel,* 2d ed., Prentice-Hall, Englewood Cliffs, N.J., 1967, p. 526.

there is a rapid phase in which the new ideas and motions suddenly begin fitting together. This is followed by another slower growth period, often involving a sense of frustration for both pupil and teacher, in which additional progress seems painfully difficult. Then there is usually another breakthrough as the employee attains reasonably full competence. The supervisor and the employee must learn to be patient during both the early, clumsy stage and the later, slower periods. Otherwise this can lead to either quitting ("I just can't learn this new job") or long-lived enmity between supervisor and trainee ("He's unfair and pushy—I'll never get used to working with him").

How Much Programming for the Employee?

Jobs differ, of course, in how much programming they require for their effective performance. Some jobs can be learned in a few minutes, others require weeks, still others, years of training. Often what seems like a simple job may require many weeks of practice to perfect. Thus even a simple assembly-line job may not be done with adequate speed and accuracy for a number of weeks because all the muscle movements, the hand-eye coordinations, take time to integrate into smooth, semiautomatic actions. The same is true of any athletic ability. You can learn to swim in a few hours, but becoming a good swimmer may take months or even years of practicing the same few motions.

Organizations sometimes have a choice of how much employee programming is required. In what we call mass-production industry, jobs have been meticulously subdivided (providing the morale problems we have already discussed) and the employee can learn these in quite rapid order. On the other hand, many craftsman's jobs (in construction, maintenance, and printing, for example) have not been so finely subdivided, so much more training is required either before the employee is hired (in schools or apprentice programs) or after hiring. In either case, these will be more expensive, valuable employees because of the complexity of their programming.

And then you find professionals like chemists and lawyers whose internal programming is the most complex of all. They have learned great varieties of problem-solving and diagnostic techniques which tell them how to handle a wide range of problems. Similarly, social workers, nurses, and managers themselves have this type of programming. These jobs usually are found in services and areas where technology has not progressed to the point that jobs can be minutely subdivided and aided by machines.

THE SUPERVISOR'S ROLE WHERE JOBS ARE PROGRAMMED

Where jobs can be well defined and are reasonably independent, the supervisor functions in the following ways:

1. He may help to define the jobs: the specialization that will divide up larger tasks into small, programmed units. As we have said, it may be difficult and expensive to find and hire fully trained craftsmen or professionals. However, if you supervise a medical laboratory, for example, you may be able to define the activities necessary to do a particular blood test so that a willing new employee with no knowledge of biology or chemistry can do this specific test.

2. Then the supervisor helps train the individual employees to do the job, using patience and understanding and encourages them to practice, to ask questions, to learn to cope with all the problems that may occur, and to understand a few of the underlying principles, since this "theory" will help them to know what to do when.

3. After the employee has demonstrated his or her competence, the supervisor makes periodic checks to be sure the job is being done as prescribed and with adequate quickness and concern for quality. How can this best be done?

SAMPLING

Although we shall look more intensively at this whole subject of controls in Chapter 5, it is worth noting here that most supervisors learn how to *sample* the behavior of the employee. The objectives are to:

1. Avoid the implicit pressure and even distrust communicated by continuous watching, as well as the cost in supervisory time.

2. Avoid having the employee "show off" when the supervisor is watching.

3. Distribute observations sufficiently broadly so the boss gets to see all the various parts of the job, but at different times of the day.

In practice, this means a supervisor may walk by an employee when he is finishing some work and thus have a chance to observe the last stages. Later in the day, he manages to come by at a time when a new job is just being started, and at some other time he looks at the middle portions. Of course, all the observations need not take place within one day, and the better trained and more able the employee appears, the more widely spaced the checks. Where an employee seems to be having troubles, shows some incompetencies, has quality problems, and such, more frequent observations are made. (As for what the supervisor does when he observes that the employee is not doing the job as prescribed, see Chapter 4.)

Delegation and Technology

Even when the employee is well trained, highly motivated, and working on a job with a reasonable amount of programming, there will be subjects or problems on which the supervisor wants to be consulted. He doesn't want the subordinate handling these things by himself. How much leeway the subordinate has versus how much the supervisor wants to be involved is often called the *amount of delegation*. Let us see if we can discover what determines how much or how little delegation the superior gives his subordinates.

How much the supervisor intervenes is a function of the technology and the amount of training the subordinate has, but the relationship is a somewhat complicated one.

AMOUNT OF TRAINING

In some industries, as we have noted, it pays management to hire a well-trained employee who is, in fact, already "programmed." Both advanced education and experience can prepare an employee to handle a wide variety of problems without calling on the supervisor. Thus you can hire a lawyer or an engineer or even a well-trained bookkeeper, give him a broad assignment, and have some confidence that he will know what to do in a broad range of cases and with a wide assortment of problems on the job, most of which you couldn't predict anyhow. In a sense, the company is trading a higher salary for lower costs of supervision (and also of equipment). For the most part (although the relationship is never a perfect one), the better trained and/or more experienced the employee, the less supervision he requires.

COMPLEXITY OF THE JOB

On many jobs, if the supervisor is to intervene effectively, it will be necessary for the subordinate to spend a great deal of time informing his boss what he himself has already learned, what has been going on, and what the unique circumstances of the case are. Thus, an engineer faced with a technical problem may not be able to get help from his superior without spending hours telling him all the things he has already tried, the special properties of the immediate situation, and exactly what he is trying to accomplish. "Bringing the boss on board" is costly in terms of both managerial and employee time.

AVAILABILITY OF LIMITS OF DISCRETION

Some technologies allow the supervisor to say, in effect, "You handle all the easier problems and bring me the more difficult ones." This assumes that "easy" can be defined in meaningful terms. For example, an insurance claims adjuster may be told he may handle all cases up to claims of $500. Or a salesman may be permitted to extend credit to a customer so long as the amount is not over $100. A machinist may use his discretion about waiting for material or repairs as long as the time involved is under fifteen minutes, and a secretary may be encouraged to handle all telephone requests for information that come from certain specific departments in the organization.

PATTERNS OF DELEGATION

When the job goes outside these explicitly defined limits, the employee has the responsibility of calling in the supervisor. However, we are really oversimplifying the use of "limits of discretion" in defining the amount of leeway delegated to subordinates. The supervisor actually has a broad array of choices open in defining when the subordinate should act on his own, in terms of his own internal programming, and when he, the supervisor, should be called in. Here are most of the possibilities. (See if you can think of a realistic situation to fit each category.)

1. Within these limits, you take action based on your best judgment. Don't contact me.
2. You take action, but keep me informed as to what you did (after the fact, in other words).
3. In these kinds of situations I want you to look into the

problem and inform me what you intend to do. You can go ahead as long as I don't say not to.

4. (Same as point 3) but delay any action until I have given positive approval.

5. In these situations, I want you to assess the situation and the problems and let me know what are the possible actions that should be taken. Tell me the relative pros and cons and recommend what action I (the supervisor) should take.

6. (Same as point 5) but just give me all the facts. I'll make the decision on my own.[2]

Obviously, the lower-numbered alternatives are most suited to jobs being handled by employees with more internal programming. But note that all depend upon the ability of the supervisor to pre-define, to specify in advance, the limits within which the subordinate acts *alone* as compared to where the boss must be involved. On jobs where it is difficult to be somewhat precise, the supervisor must rely on his own observation of how well the subordinate is doing or on measures of his performance (which are called "controls").

Ambiguous Jobs

The supervisor needs to distinguish between those jobs for which explicit guides for performance are available and those which are inherently ambiguous. For example, a typist's job is reasonably objective. You can assign a specific quantity, observing the speed and the quality performance. But ask an employee to clean up his work area and you can anticipate that there will be very substantial differences in interpretation. How clean is clean? Do the corners have to be scrubbed? Should furniture be moved or just cleaned around?

Two extremes are dangerous. Start telling an employee in too much detail how and what he should do, and there can be serious resentment built up very quickly.

My boss told me to go to our upstate branch tomorrow and do some sales-planning work with the branch manager. He said it would be a good idea to leave on the 5:55 plane this afternoon, stay at the Corgan Hotel, rent a car at the airport to get to the hotel and to the office, and ask for the 10 percent company discount.

---

[2] For this list we are indebted to Harvey Sherman, *It All Depends*, University of Alabama Press, University, Ala., 1966, pp. 83–84.

I've done this dozens of times in the past. What does he take me for? Can't I be trusted to use my own judgment as to how to get there? I was so angry when he finished I asked him if he wanted to buy my ticket too!

On the other hand, no specifications for the job can be disastrous unless the employee is very experienced. In any case, the more ambiguous the job, the more the supervisor must rely on previous training, knowledge, and motivation. The last is the most important because such jobs will always have aspects which are difficult to judge, where the employee works alone and must use his own discretion as to how much work to do and how carefully to do it.

Imagine the problem of hiring a gardener to maintain the land around a house. How free of weeds should the flower beds be maintained? How straight should the borders be cut, and how often? How often should the grass be cut and fertilizer be used, and what amount of trimming and what shaping are satisfactory for trees and shrubs? When should the lawn be rolled? Should the sidewalks be edged? There is really no end to such questions, which is what makes such relationships difficult, to say the least.

Except for the most rigidly controlled assembly-line type of job, it is hard to find jobs which do not have some significant discretionary component. It is much too easy to ignore this—to accept the commonplace assumption that most people work best when they do precisely what they are told and that consequently there is little room for discretion in modern organization. The facts are really just the opposite: Most jobs have a substantial, unprogrammed content, and the supervisor must be concerned with how well this is performed. Look at the kinds of decisions a file clerk may well have to make on her own:

How to rate concurrent demands for filing service coming from several sources at the same time, that is, how to decide which should be met first.

Whether to go to his supervisor and ask for assistance to meet a temporary flood of work, or to allow himself to get temporarily into arrears.

When to open new files for correspondence which was previously filed under a bulging "miscellaneous" category.

Whether particular documents are or are not intended for filing in his center.

How to develop original work methods in order to get through more quickly.

Immediate availability of back correspondence is very important to managers, but even the most thoroughly prescribed routine will not ensure this, because much depends on the wise use of discretion by filing clerks.[3]

In appraising the effectiveness of the employee, the manager may well want to concentrate on these unprogrammable elements. While obviously the file clerk has to be able to do the programmed parts (if she can't or won't she may have to be discharged), the difference between an average and an excellent file clerk will be found in how the discretionary elements are performed.

UNPROGRAMMED WORK

Many managers tend to overestimate the degree to which jobs under their jurisdiction are programmable. Many jobs which seem very simple and precise on closer examination turn out to be much more variable. The variability usually results from the fact that the jobs are not as separable as the supervisor thought. Let us take an example.

Two employees perform simple computational tasks on weekly sales reports. In order to do their work, they must periodically go to some central files to take accounting records which they then work with at their desks. Obviously, there will be times when one of them wants to keep a specific record out and use it for a while. Similarly, they will face the problem of who handles what files, and there will also be many times when one of them has some information or some skill that the other can use, for example, when a mistake is discovered.

We have seen many cases in which the supervisor's efforts to develop rigidly programmed job descriptions and rules of

---

[3] Interestingly, a recent study of new managers identifies one of the most successful as a young engineer who was assigned the job of maintaining a file of reports for a vice-president. His initiative in converting this routine, uninteresting "dog-work" type of job into a challenge—by developing original indexes and techniques for updating the file—made a superb impression on his boss. It was an important step in his rapid promotion in the company. Cf. W. R. Dill, T. L. Hilton, and W. R. Reitman, *The New Managers*, Prentice-Hall, Inc., Englewood Cliffs, N.J., 1962, pp. 39 ff.

Leonard R. Sayles, *Individualism and Big Business*, McGraw-Hill, New York, 1963, p. 156.

procedure are self-defeating. By attempting to preprogram the job, he may well decrease productivity as well as motivation. For example, the supervisor may insist that

1. Each employee does his own work and cannot ask for help.
2. Each employee must do exactly one-half of each day's files.
3. No accounting record can be kept for more than fifteen minutes and an employee can have only one record out at a time.

The result: Some files will be easier than others, so it's likely that one employee will be idle while the other works. Useful information cannot be exchanged. Many times they will need to make several extra trips to the files because of the time limits and because they cannot pass things back and forth.

This is a very simple work situation and purposefully so. In practice, most jobs have a much wider variety of "motions" associated with them. Employees have to learn to do these motions in such a way as to complement and not interfere with the way their fellow workers are doing their jobs. Thus, clerks in a store must learn to allocate customers, help each other find merchandise, and handle certain complex sales-slip problems. Even an assembly-line worker may discover ways of doing his job that make it easier for the employee next in line to do his job.

It is always amazing to the outside observer to note how frequently the formal rules of procedure for any job have to be modified in the light of special circumstances. While Bill and Joe are not supposed to help each other, now that Joe occasionally has to work on very large pieces, Bill's help in getting the parts into the machine can save ten or twenty minutes or prevent the need to call for a special laborer. Similarly, many times employees are told not to repair their machines—that is the job of maintenance men. An alert employee, however, can spot certain things and make minor adjustments that will save a good deal of maintenance time. Even when this isn't practical, by watching carefully when the equipment appears to malfunction and reporting this to the mechanic who comes to fix it, the worker saves the mechanic a good deal of diagnostic time. Again, this isn't in his formal job description!

In all these cases, the supervisor's attention is drawn to the *interface* of the job. He wants to see how jobs intermesh, which workers help each other, and which make work difficult for one another. Unlike programmed work, the supervisor recognizes that these jobs do overlap and that employees must decide on the spot how to handle the overlap (for instance, the need to share files or a common work space). And there are always aspects of the work that are left out of any job description, but alert, efficient employees will do certain things even though they are not formally part of their jobs (like tipping off the maintenance man when the machine begins malfunctioning). The aspects of interfacing jobs are sketched in Figure 2-2.

Semiautonomous Groups

There are times when the supervisor makes little or no effort to divide work among a group of interrelated workers. In effect, he says to the whole group, "Your job is to complete this task, and in doing so, you are going to have to develop your own division of labor, deciding who should do what and when." This approach is particularly useful where supervision is difficult, the employees are facing unpredictable and changing circumstances, and they have somewhat similar status.

The situation that fits this description is found in certain kinds of heavy construction or mining work. The group is held responsible for total performance, but there may still be some rudimentary division of labor within the group. A famous study of small mining crews in England found that the men had separate tasks to do, but that a number of unpredictable and unprogrammable factors (water leakage, rock slides, and more difficult terrain) required them to help each other a

Some jobs have a certain amount of
overlap; there are tasks
that cannot easily be assigned to
any specific job in advance of
the actual work situation.

Figure 2-2   Unprogrammed work

great deal. Similarly, during the war it was noted that radar crews plotting the approach of enemy planes were more effective when they learned to supplement each other's efforts—to fill in the blanks, you might say.

Now the supervisor is acting much like the coach of a good athletic team. Each man has his position to play, but the important thing is how they play together. This can't be predetermined by any abstract formulas. A good second baseman is good because he coordinates with the shortstop and the third baseman, and each one's strengths and weaknesses are taken into account in what the others do. And what each player does depends on where the ball is hit; there isn't a fixed pattern. They learn by practicing as a team, not as individuals.

The more critical that teamwork is, the more a supervisor must consider how disruptive replacing any one member by another will be and what impact his actions might have on individuals. Obviously, he cannot influence any part without influencing the whole.

Job Design to Facilitate the Flow of Work

Once we see that the primary objective for the supervisor is to manage the jobs under him in such a way that they feed smoothly into one another, we can establish some critical criteria for job design.

One common problem is that a job requires a lower-status employee to get a higher-status employee to do something. For example, one of the duties assigned to the mail room clerk was to go to the bookkeeper's office to request that certain statistical information be prepared quickly for the use of the personnel office. Whenever the mail boy would ask one of the bookkeepers to stop what he was doing and get this information for personnel, he would be greeted by a crescendo of complaints about how busy everyone was and how he was interfering and to come back later, etc., etc.

THE PROBLEM OF STATUS

Most people are not used to having their actions impacted by people they believe are doing less important work. (The same reluctance can be observed in the community. Apartment dwellers resent being told by the building superintendent, whom they often call the janitor, how to handle their rubbish or when to use the laundry room.) Whenever a job requires that a lower-status person push or initiate or make demands on a higher-status employee, you can expect problems. Good job design tries to eliminate this by having workers of relatively equal status make demands of each other or having the initiator be of higher status (as suggested in Figure 2-3).

HANDLING PRESSURE

Another criterion, similar to the one above, is that the supervisor should try to avoid creating jobs which require too much responding to others.

Bob Allen's job was to pass out certain tools and jigs in a small shop in which every worker was on a piecework incentive. The company was short of some of this equipment, and he could not keep the workers supplied. But many employees believed the toolroom personnel just used favoritism. In any case, there were constant pressures from the employees to move more quickly, to find parts, to give them something so they wouldn't be delayed. The pressure was so bad that Bob quit after a few weeks and so did the next three men who filled his job.

Particularly where such pressures are unpredictable and erratic and the jobholder can't reverse them, the supervisor can expect that he will have difficulty getting someone to hold the position or to hold it without constantly losing his temper or becoming morose. Obviously, some personalities are better than others in taking pressure from other workers, just as some waiters or waitresses are very good at "fielding" customer demands. This is a good technique that a supervisor can teach some of his employees—turning around the pressure so they are initiating to their would-be tormentors. Here is how a first-class waitress does it as the number of

Job A   Job B

A should be of higher status when the
flow of initiations is from A to B.

Figure 2-3   Status and flow

customers she must serve increases and the kitchen is getting delayed:

Waitress to table 1, even before the customers can ask for service: Let me at least give you some water while you're waiting; it will take a while because the kitchen is so busy. But don't worry—I won't forget you. (And she walks off.)
Waitress to table 2, whose occupants have already said they are in a hurry: Why don't you order the prime ribs? They're ready to serve and there's no delay. And if you'll give me the vegetable orders all together, that will save some time, too.

There's a girl who knows how to take the initiative and turn around a job in which the other person usually does most of the initiating! The toolroom man could be taught some of these devices to equalize the interaction pattern, too.

In fact, a good rule of thumb is that the supervisor should try to have most of his jobs designed so that an employee can initiate to others roughly as much as he is initiated to. Look closely at how many people, how frequently, come to him in getting their jobs done. Then see if the supervisor can build into the employee's job the need and the opportunity to go to others with requests of about the same quantity. Of course, this is much harder to do for service positions, where the major component of the job is to be responsive to others.

Studies in hospitals have shown that maids, for example, quit more frequently when they work by themselves because everybody, including nurses, aides, doctors, patients, has requests to make of them. Equally menial tasks performed by laundry personnel in the same hospitals don't create this problem because the laundryworkers interact with people of their own status and there are not many requests made directly to them—except by their supervisor and by a fellow employee when there is a work-flow relationship.

WILLIAM F. WHYTE (1914–   )

Perhaps the best-known field worker and writer in the
organizational behavior field has been William F. Whyte,
who is a professor at the New York State School of Industrial Relations at Cornell. Following on the anthropological
field-work success of the bank wiring-room part of the
Western Electric studies (in which researchers sat back and
watched and became part of the furniture), Whyte instituted studies in such diverse locales as Chicago restaurants, Oklahoma oil refineries, a midwest steel container
plant, and a fine glass blowing plant in New York State.
His detailed and vivid descriptions of work groups and
worker-supervisor relations have been captured in his
books: *Human Relations in the Restaurant Industry, Money
and Motivation, Men at Work, Pattern for Industrial Peace*.
Both Sayles and Strauss worked with him in some of his
research studies at Cornell and all three with Chapple share
this emphasis on observation rather than questionnaires.
Chris Argyris of Yale, whose work in human relations has
also become very famous, was a student of Whyte's.

Thus Whyte and his students have emphasized the
importance of field work as distinct from abstract theorizing. Whyte's work shows that managerial activities differ
substantially depending upon the nature of the technology.
Oil refineries do not pose the same challenge as restaurants, and the manager better comprehend the pattern
of relationships among employees, among managers, as
between staff and line managers, necessary to maintain
coordination. His work emphasizes the actual give and take
required among people to fulfill the requirements of the
underlying technology.

In recent years, Whyte has returned to his earlier
anthropological interests and has been studying the problems of a developing country: Peru. His work there illustrates the significant applicability of management theory to
a wide variety of social and political problems, not just
business. Whyte's broad interests make it difficult to
categorize his work; it includes both sociology and anthropology, business and public administration.

From Kitchen to Customer*

The girls themselves blamed the downstairs countermen

* Reprinted from William F. Whyte, *Human Relations in the
Restaurant Industry*, McGraw-Hill Book Co., New York, 1948, pp. 72–75.

for much of their difficulty. Their explanation was simply that the downstairs countermen had difficult personalities, whereas Sam, the chief upstairs counterman, was very easy to get along with.

There are several things wrong with such an explanation. In the first place, all the downstairs countermen had been with Jessup's for years, and were very highly regarded by the management. This would not prove that they had "pleasant personalities," but it does show that we are not talking about the unstable short duration employees upon whom so many of management's problems were blamed. Furthermore, the men were known to get along well with each other. Then, comparing them with the upstairs men, we can say that while Sam equalled them in experience, his various coworkers were inexperienced and—according to the waitresses—difficult to get along with.

When we hear that an individual has a good personality, we should ask, good to whom? We must recognize that the same individual may be easy to get along with in one relationship and very difficult in another. This discredits the personality explanation.

The layout of the counter was very important. While men, being on the average taller than the girls, could look down at them across the counter, the girls had to stand on tiptoe to talk effectively with the men. Even then a counterman could step back or bend over and drop out of sight. This enabled the men to ignore the waitresses or else to drop verbal bombshells across the counter when they were least expected.

When everything was running smoothly, there was no need for countermen and waitresses to talk with each other. Hours or even days could go by in which there was virtually no contact between them. This meant that the countermen were not accustomed to responding to the waitresses. And since the height of the counter was a bar to informal conversation, nearly all the talk that went across the counter was in the nature of gripes, demands, protests, and indignant denunciations. While the total amount of interaction was small, such frictions were not balanced by any informal adjustment, and the waitresses found the situation very hard on their nerves.

Upstairs the situation was quite different. Sam had his formula to take the pressure off himself, and, through his informal ties with the girls, established outside of working hours, he built up relationships through which it was possible to adjust many of the conflicts arising out of the nervous tension. Even when there was trouble with one of his coworkers, Sam was there to smooth things out. The girls were able to tell him of their troubles, and he told them of the problems he was facing, so that they were not left in the dark as were the girls downstairs.

This does not mean that the low service counter is superior from a human-relations point of view. Sam's adjustment with the girls was something that had simply grown up between them. It was not determined by the layout of the counter or by the policies of management. If, for example, Lew had been substituted for Sam, then surely there would have been trouble at that counter. We can only say that a waist-high counter makes possible an informal adjustment—or a pitched battle.

When we ask whether a high or a low counter is better, we must also ask, better for whom? The men behind the high counter found it an ideal arrangement and would have been very much upset if the barrier had been lowered. The waitresses took the barrier for granted and complained only of the personalities of the men behind it.

What can management do in this situation? Any move by supervisors that results in better coordination of production with service will automatically lead to more harmonious relationships. Since restaurants differ so much from each other, we cannot undertake to work out any detailed plan in this general study. We can only point to this as one of the key problems of the industry and suggest that it needs the most thoughtful attention of restaurant people.

The point of contact between waitresses and pantry people also deserves special supervisory attention. In Jessup's restaurant, when supplies did not come up, the waitresses felt frustrated not only because they were delayed but also because they could not understand what was going on. When they demanded the attention of the countermen, this only created friction. If the pantry supervisor had been able to step in between the two groups, explain the situation to the waitresses, and let them blow off steam to her, it seems likely that the flood of tears could have been avoided. It may be worth while to experiment in developing a go-between role for the pantry supervisor.

Before we leave the service pantry, we should look at the social role of the insignificant-looking spindle. It serves to fend off from pantry people a good deal (but not all) of the pressure exerted by waitresses. Where we have men (unaccustomed to taking orders from women) behind the counter, it seems likely that the spindle makes the difference between a workable system and one that would blow up.

There are still other ways of handling spindles in the counterman-waitress relationship. We observed one restaurant in which the waitresses handed all their written order slips to a pantry supervisor (male), who in turn placed them on the proper spindles where they were picked up and acted upon by fry cooks and countermen. Completed orders were placed in warming compartments where they were picked up by the waitresses. If the girls had any complaint about the service they were getting, they did not speak directly to the men behind the counter but turned instead to the supervisor, who explained the situation or took other appropriate action. Under this system, the men behind the counter had to respond to only one man, the supervisor, and contact between waitresses and pantry workers was completely eliminated.

The spindle is also of great importance where we have middle-aged counterwomen and young waitresses. Where the counter is waist high, there is a temptation for waitresses to call in their orders instead of taking the time to write them out. The dessert-pantry woman in one restaurant frequently allowed waitresses to dispense with the slips, but she stood on her rights when she was dealing with a waitress who was less than half her age and seemed to enjoy ordering her around. "If you want desserts," she said once, "you'll have to learn to write them out. I positively will not serve you any more unless you do." Later the pantry woman said, "I can't stand that kid. She's too fresh for me—snippy little thing."

To sum it up, wherever the people on the receiving end of the orders are related to the order givers as males vs. females, or older vs. younger, then it is important for the pantry people to have some impersonal barrier to block the pressure from themselves. Even when such differences are eliminated, the use of spindles makes the job easier for the pantry people.

ACTIVE COORDINATION—INTERDEPENDENT JOBS

Job design, training, and delegation are passive methods of supervision since they are really "before the fact." The supervisor must also be actively engaged in making sure that employees properly coordinate their work where jobs are interdependent.

Of course, there are some systems which make it easier for him to do this. An assembly line is really acting as a supervisor's impersonal coordinator. It tells an employee *when* to do something—as the work passes in front of him—and as long as he reacts to the timing of the line, his work will be coordinated with that of other employees who are responding similarly. Some studies have suggested that an impersonal supervisor—such as an assembly line—creates less worker resistance to its "orders" than do the *personal* requests of a boss. This is really the purpose of an assembly line—to tie together the efforts of a large number of employees who are part of a single work-flow system. The line is timed so that each job can be completed and moved to the next station in time for that worker to do his task. Naturally, each task has to be thought through so that the worker has adequate time to do his job.

Other jobs can be coordinated by the clock: "Every hour, take a sample from the 302 vat up to the laboratory." There are also built-in coordinating points within the job: "Whenever you process an order from the Middle Atlantic states, telephone Don Jenkins in sales and give him the order number and the total."

Groups of employees can develop their own coordinating mechanisms and may be required to do so when their jobs are interdependent. (For the supervisor's role in developing a group spirit and group identification, see Chapter 7.) Singing and chanting provide a beat by which a group can be responsive to the same stimulus. Like a conductor's baton or a metronome, the tempo of the song helps to keep people doing things in unison and mutually responsive. Watch a football team coming out of a huddle chanting or calling out numbers and you will see the adept responsiveness of a well-coordinated group, each of whose members moves in response to this common source of timing. The same techniques apply at work. Crews doing heavy work or work that requires each to move in response to the other will often say, "Now all together, when we say one, two, three . . . PULL! O.K., one, two, three . . . *Again!*"

Obviously, being able to see each other is a help or maybe

an absolute requirement of coordinating two jobs. For example, in a plant assembling washing machines, the body was built on a line located on a balcony, and the men at the end of that line were supposed to slide the body down an incline to the first floor. At that point, the group that was building the frame was to attach the body to the frame. The bodymen were told to slide their unit down as soon as the frame men had attached the previous unit and passed it along their main-floor line. Unfortunately, the two groups could not easily see each other and the balcony group frequently slid its work down the slide before the next group was ready or held back too long and interrupted the pace of the frame assemblers. There was constant squabbling between the two groups, each claiming the other went out of its way to be difficult or to interfere with their own work pace. In fact, it was simply that these jobs were designed in such a way that the employees ought to be able to see each other and time themselves accordingly: dynamic coordination.

Barriers to Easy Give-and-Take Relationships

We have seen that most jobs require employees to collaborate even though their actions, at first glance, appear to be quite independent of one another. Why doesn't this cooperation always appear spontaneously among people who must work together over an extended period?

One obvious reason: New employees haven't had time to learn personal idiosyncracies and how they can best do the job so as to facilitate the work of the other workers. Therefore the supervisor can expect, when one or more employees are temporary or new, that there will be a substantial quantity of inept coordination. One hears comments like:

Hey, Joe, I can't handle these cartons if you are going to keep sliding them every which way.

Nearly all those computer mistakes are your fault because you keep writing the serial number in the middle of the form instead of in the upper right-hand corner where the punch-card operator looks for it.

I'm getting tired of doing your work for you. From now on, you just get your own fixtures from the toolroom.

Whenever you get a customer who starts to dawdle, you drop her and then try to beat me to the next one who looks like a real buyer, and that's not taking your turn!

You'll have to clean that grease off the floor yourself. My job is just to do mechanical maintenance work, and I can't help it if some of the grease we put on drips down.

These are workers who are physically or psychologically colliding with one another, each defining his or her job in such a way that it clashes with the jobs of the others. Usually, informal groups serve to rub away these rough edges that each person may have around his own conception of the job. Through subtle and not so subtle pressures, the group encourages its members to help one another, to extend themselves a little, and to refrain from doing their job in such a way that satisfies only themselves, but this takes time.

Of course, where groups can't form easily, this type of mutual aid isn't likely to be forthcoming. If a supervisor has a man working in an out-of-the-way location or in a spot where he identifies with another group, he can expect coordination difficulties.

COLLIDING INTERESTS

Often two supervisors will have to spend a great deal of time untangling coordination problems when each supervises a part of what is essentially an integrated operation. In a clerical department we observed, one supervisor handled clerks who processed salesmen's orders when they first came from the mail room. Two other supervisors were responsible for clerks who checked the correspondence for mathematical errors, the warehouse instructions from which the merchandise was to be shipped, and the credit status of the customer. All three supervisors were constantly fighting over whose fault it was that a customer's order could not get through these various stages in a single day (as the company required).

The problem was that each group did things for its own welfare and the flow of work was impeded. Group 1 would often wait until they had a large batch of orders before delivering them to group 2, which introduced one kind of delay. If someone was absent in group 2, the other employees might or might not pitch in and help out, depending on whether groups 1 and 3 had recently done them a favor or had insulted them.

The chances are good that people who are separated from each other by physical or group boundaries will blame one another for whatever work problems they have rather than try to seek ways of overcoming them. In the large office just described, it is likely that the 2s began to say that the 1s were just unfriendly, not to be trusted, and always tried to do things in the least convenient way. This is another example of the general tendency to have the stranger become a scapegoat for your own difficulties.

Under these circumstances, one often sees *self-confirming* prophecies at work. I forecast that Mr. B is not going to be very helpful when I have to go over to his department to get some help. Believing he will not be cordial, I speak to him rather sharply or with some hostility in my voice. Detecting this feeling or this pressure, B is likely to be discourteous or reluctant to extend himself to help me, which confirms my initial prophecy: B is no good!

Gradually, a kind of cold-war iron curtain is built between two such employees or two such groups, and then the supervisor really has a difficult time getting work done because, whenever they must collaborate, there will be trouble. It is therefore the supervisor's job to try to detect the sources of these problems.

Where the supervisor has everyone who must engage in close coordination under his jurisdiction, he can help build the group into a social unity in which these aggressive feelings cannot flourish. Where communication is difficult, such feelings tend to fester until workers are either not talking at all to one another or are actually and purposefully sabotaging one another's work.

CHECKING THE INTERSECTIONS

The supervisor himself will be wise to watch the point at which two jobs intersect when checking to see how the work is progressing. This is the most crucial point in the work flow, the point at which the most difficulties are likely to occur, personal as well as technical. To do this, he keeps in mind the primary rule of *work-flow* supervision: Is employee A doing his job in such a way that it complements and assists employee B and vice versa? Put another way, he is observing whether work is moving smoothly between work stations, since this is the major determinant of productivity.

He will be able to observe such problems as these:

1. B never appears ready when A brings him the work.
2. B has to undo some of the things A gives him because they make it difficult for him to proceed with his steps.
3. B is frequently rushing A to finish so that he can begin his work.

4. B complains to A that the quality of A's work is such that it makes it more difficult for him to do his.

Of course, the supervisor is just as likely to see any of these reversed so that A is the one with the problem. In either case, such observations suggest that the supervisor must intervene and seek to identify the work-flow problem. Investigation may disclose:

1. A personality problem: A and B rub each other the wrong way and can't seem to learn to be mutually responsive.
2. A job-design problem: A's or B's job has not been designed to fit well into the other's. Or one or the other has inadequate or too much time.
3. A training problem: A or B needs more training as to the method of doing the job so that the work is mutually complementary.

The Supervisor Ensures Coordination

Thus the supervisor's task is to make sure that both the men and the machinery under his jurisdiction operate at their maximum capability. Specifically, his responsibilities are to:

1. Make sure that jobs are designed in such a way as to feed into one another, so that if worker A does his job in the prescribed fashion, it will facilitate the efforts of worker B. (Here is a good example of the opposite: Shelfmen in a grocery warehouse were told to do the job of putting new stock on the shelves as rapidly as possible, which meant that they pushed the older merchandise to the back of the shelves when placing new cans in stock. The pickers, who took food from the warehouse to the store shelves, on the other hand were told always to bring the older merchandise first. This meant that they had to first remove the new cans, then reach way in back for the older cans, and then replace the newer merchandise. The two sets of jobs were designed in such a way as to frustrate the real objectives of the work-flow system.)
2. Ensure adequate training, given the amount of delegation that will be provided. Where employees are going to be delegated a rather substantial amount of autonomy, meaning fewer supervisory checkups, more on-the-job or previous training and experience will be required.
3. Observe the "intersections" between jobs and detect breakdowns in the flow of work.

OVERVIEW

It is easier to supervise jobs which can be made very independent and those which can be programmed. On these,
the job of the supervisor is to make explicit through *training*
the task or tasks required, and then to make sure by periodic
sampling that the subordinate is doing the job as prescribed.

A complication is added when a job contains some elements in which the supervisor himself wants to participate or
get involved. Then the *delegation* decision arises and the
supervisor must establish clear criteria which enable the subordinate to know when he can handle a matter by himself
and on what he must consult the supervisor. Obviously, a
number of employees doing the same job may differ in the
amount of discretion and tasks which they are delegated. The
better-trained, more experienced, and more able employees
are encouraged by the supervisor to take on more tasks. This
saves supervisory time and can give employees greater job
satisfaction in assuming more responsibility. Less delegation is
given to those who are less well prepared or able.

It is a time-saver for the supervisor to give as broad
responsibilities as possible to employees and to check the
quality of work performed *after* completion. This way he can
use sampling and check performance at times when it does
not interfere with his other supervisory duties. However, to
require an employee to check with him *before* beginning a
task or while doing the task is much more time-consuming—
for both employee and manager. This is another compelling
reason encouraging fuller delegation, giving employees more
autonomy in doing their work. Whenever the supervisor must
get involved during the job cycle, scarce supervisory time is
going to be expended.

On jobs which are *not* independent of one another, where
employees' work is interdependent, the supervisor's job
changes. Many supervisors are misled into concentrating on
individual job performance, but work efficiency depends
upon completed activities—something "going out the door,"
so to speak. Even though a given employee may work
diligently and almost to the point of exhaustion, if his work
does not fit in with the work being done by others, much of
his effort is probably wasted.

Thus, where jobs are interdependent, the focus of supervisory action shifts from the individual job to the flow of work,
the interrelationships among jobs, the work *system*. The
supervisor is concerned with the smoothness with which work
progresses from one employee to another and with identifying

and correcting whatever serves to block or inhibit that smooth flow of work.

It will sometimes be matters of personality, although supervisors often are misled into thinking two or more employees can't work together effectively when job-design factors are responsible. Usually the pressures of the work group serve to iron out personal idiosyncrasies that get in the way of cooperative efforts. The alert supervisor can spot job-design barriers to teamwork. These may include communications problems. If workers have to collaborate, they must engage in a good deal of give-and-take, usually much more than the supervisor recognizes.

Harry and I do the final design drafting. Each of us knows what we are supposed to do and our jobs are pretty well separated, at least in the boss's eyes, since I handle the electrical and he does the mechanical. But, boy, heaven help us if we can't keep going back and forth to each other's board. There are countless things the engineers left out or aren't clear on that one or the other of us has more information about. Also, each will be doing things that the other ought to know about if the final plans are going to be clear. We used to work in separate rooms and I would save up problems to check with him, but then I would forget some and on others I just couldn't wait because I wanted to get on with the drawing. As a result, a lot of stuff had to be done over. Now we just yell across to each other and have developed a real helping spirit. He not only answers my questions but also gives me a hand on some of the tougher interpretations.

Many managers are guilty of underestimating the amount of effort that must be placed on the *interface* or boundary between jobs. This give and take cannot be programmed because its quantity and quality depend on personality factors as well as on a hundred little things that affect how a job is performed. Thus a supervisor's efforts must be concentrated on looking at the total process of cooperation and coordination, not on individual, separated jobs. And the supervisor must also seek to identify the environmental or structural factors (like physical proximity providing ease of communication) that facilitate or inhibit group efforts.

Four Types of Jobs: Four Types of Supervision

We have talked about four types of jobs and their distinctive supervisory requirements. The categories (as illustrated in Figure 2-4) are these:

1. Programmable individual jobs: Here the supervisor (S) concentrates on the "inside" of the job: Is the employee doing

Figure 2-4 Four supervisory approaches

the various elements correctly, sequentially, with adequate speed, and without interfering with others?

2. Programmable interdependent jobs: Here the supervisor, while having some concern with correct job performance, watches the boundary between the jobs to make sure that there is adequate mutual assistance, complementarity, and a smooth flow of work.

3. Nonprogrammable interdependent jobs in which the employees cannot easily communicate or are parts of separate work groups: The supervisor should anticipate spending a disproportionate amount of time resolving conflicts and disagreements between these employees. They are not close enough to evolve an easy give and take and mutual assistance. The supervisor sometimes will also have to act as a link or coordinator between them.

4. Nonprogrammable group tasks: Here the supervisor concentrates almost entirely on the total task and only slightly on the interrelationship between jobs and the "inside" of jobs. "The group's the thing." His job is to develop the group's capacity and willingness to work as a team.

A FINAL NOTE

It is worthwhile to obtain some historical perspective on the types of jobs that the supervisor in the United States will be managing. In 1900, the chances were one out of three that a supervisor would be handling farm laborers, probably as the owner himself. It took a third of our labor force to grow the products we needed for food and clothing.

By 1968, agricultural workers made up no more than 5 percent of the labor force, however. We had 50 percent of our work force in factories—the blue-collar workers—in the 1920s, but today these employees (who are more likely to be handling programmed jobs) are down to one-third of the work force. At the same time, the numbers and proportions of white-collar workers have been steadily increasing to where, today, they comprise 50 percent of the work force. To be sure, many of them perform routine, programmed jobs, but a large porportion, including some professionals, are highly trained. They are both able to and demand the autonomy to determine for themselves the best way of doing their jobs. In fact, there are now 10½ million professionals, perhaps 15 percent of the work force, and this segment is increasing each year.

At the same time, more and more of the work is being

done outside of factories: in schools and government bureaus and hospitals and laboratories. This is the age of the white-collar worker and the professional because our technology has shifted from orientation toward extractive and production industries to focus on service and consumption.

SELECTED REFERENCES

Burling, T., Lentz, E., Wilson, R., *The Give and Take in Hospitals,* Putnam, New York, 1956, part IV.

Sayles, L., and Strauss, G., *Human Behavior in Organizations,* Prentice-Hall, Englewood Cliffs, N.J., 1966, chap. 16.

Whyte, W., *Human Relations in the Restaurant Industry,* McGraw-Hill, New York, 1948.

THE EDUCATION OF GREG HORNING: JANUARY 17

Greg looked up in surprise to see Alfred Cameron standing outside his office. He had already pegged Cameron as a follower—Creegmore's usually—he rarely acted on his own initiative.

"Come on in, Alfred," Greg called out. "I hope you haven't been out there long. It slows us down, you know, taking time out to talk. Why didn't you call me? I'd be glad to come out to see you at your machine if you need me for something."

"Well, it's not exactly that I need you," Alfred said. Greg had not asked him to sit down and he stood beside Greg's desk, shifting his weight from one foot to the other. "You see, it's this new mold brace. I wanted to ask you about it. See, I found out I can lock it in with an extra clamp. It improves the tolerances that way. And then I don't get Helen coming around all the time, all exicted, bringing me back pieces. So I was wondering if . . ."

"That's fine, Alfred," Greg interrupted. "If it works, that's just fine. But, look. What about right now? Your machine is turned off and we're wasting time. You know we need every piece we can get out to fill our orders and get them delivered on time."

"Oh, that's all right, Greg, my machine is going and Henry is watching out for it. See, we spell each other all the time so we don't waste time if one of us has to step away for a minute." Alfred smiled now, feeling more confident. "Now as I was saying, you know, about that extra clamp . . ."

But Greg cut him off again. "I've spoken to some of the

others about this, Alfred, and as long as you're in here, I might as well make it clear to you too. I don't want any of you doing anyone else's job. The description that you have from industrial engineering tells you exactly what you should be doing. They've worked out a fair work load for each man. It's very carefully set up. How can Henry do what he's supposed to do when he . . . Now, you see what's happened, Alfred? What's going on out there, anyway?"

Greg had gone over to the window that opened onto the floor as he was talking. "Would you just look at that? You see, Alfred, it proves what I was telling you. Henry isn't watching your machine at all. He isn't even paying attention to his own—damnit. He's way over on the other side of the room shaking his fists at one of the materials handlers."

"Oh, I know what that's about, all right," Alfred began explaining eagerly as he looked out. "See, they've been putting our supplies in the wrong place. And Henry keeps telling them and telling them, but it doesn't do any good. Those guys! You ask them to do something and they've always got an excuse. 'The night men won't like it,' they say. Or it's not their job and it's too much trouble and they can't be bothered or . . ."

"All right, Alfred, don't worry about it—it's not your problem or Henry's either. Go back to work and don't leave your machine alone again. If you need me, call me over or wait until there's a break or a changeover when the set-up man is there."

"Okay, Greg," Alfred muttered. "I guess we can talk about that clamp idea some other time, maybe?" But Greg, looking out at the floor again, didn't seem to hear. Alfred fumbled with the door handle for a moment, then left.

Creegmore was back at his machine by the time Alfred came out. They exchanged a few words and looked over at Greg, then both men returned to their work.

But Greg was disturbed. Creegmore had no business fighting with the materials handlers; that was something he should have brought to his supervisor's attention. But too much time had been wasted already for one day and Greg decided not to make an issue of it.

Another thing was bothering Greg—what Alfred had said about Helen returning unsatisfactory pieces to him. That just didn't sound right to Greg. Going out on the floor, he went over to Helen and asked, "What do you do, Helen, when you feel the work you're getting from a machine is defective?"

She was in her new location, breaking the flashes off a batch of completed gears. This was another aspect of the job the girls did; before sorting and packing the orders for shipping, they cleaned the extra bits of plastic from the edges of the pieces. Helen finished up the gear she was working on and put it in the box beside her before she answered.

"Well, I go right over to whichever operator it is and tell him he'd better keep his eyes open and stop doing wrong the thing he's doing wrong."

"But, Helen, how do you know what he's doing wrong? You're not a methods person or a set-up man. That's not your job and you're not trained to do it."

"But we've always done it this way, Greg. Jeannette and I know bad work when we see it and the men know we do. Now take Rick—you know he likes to race and sometimes . . ."

"No, Helen," Greg interrupted. "That's not the point. Of course, you can spot bad work. But what I'm talking about is you wouldn't know *why* it was bad. You see, that's my responsibility. I'm the one who has to maintain the quality in this department, so I should be called in on these things. From now on, Helen, when you or Jeannette spot a bad piece, I want you to call me over. That way, I'll be able to see what's going wrong and figure out how to fix it."

Helen had gone back to the gears she was working on. "All right, Greg," she said without looking up. "If that's what you want, that's what you'll get."

Greg got it. Coming back from lunch a few days later, he found a box of several hundred tape drives on his desk. There was a note beside the box! "I thought you would want to see these pieces. They're no good. Helen."

A hell of a help that was. She hadn't said what was wrong with them and he couldn't tell. Greg started out to the shop, then realized that the girls were still out to lunch.

"Of all the . . ." Greg muttered out loud in frustration. "When are they going to realize I'm doing all this for their own good? He took a piece out of the box and slammed it down on the desk.

QUESTIONS

1. Comment on Greg's handling of Alfred's suggestion.
2. Under what circumstances should Greg allow Alfred and Henry to help each other and when not?
3. How do you evaluate the desirability of having Henry talk with materials handlers and Helen "correct" the molders?
4. How can Helen make Greg's job almost impossible?
5. What is the delegation problem here?

3. Informal groups and
the invisible organization

At first glance, the title of this chapter resembles a paradox wrapped within an enigma. If the groups we're talking about are informal, that is, unrecognized by the formal organization and have no legal status, how can we link them to the development of an organization, and an invisible organization at that—one that lacks the formal authority both to make rules and to enforce them? These are two indispensable attributes of any organization. If the invisible group lacks both of them, why bother spending time studying it?

INVISIBLE STANDARDS

To start unwrapping the enigma, let's take the case of Hank Brewster. At home in his basement workshop, Hank is a whiz with a lathe—very fast and very accurate. But on the job, it's a different story. He's still accurate—he hasn't changed in that way. But speed is a different story: Hank works at about half the pace he consistently makes in his home workshop.

How come? After his first few days in the department, a couple of the men took him aside and "wised him up." "There's no sense in killing yourself, kid. A fair day's work around here, for your job, is twenty to twenty-five borings an hour." That was the essence of their message. And because Hank was eager to be accepted by his coworkers, he not only got the message—he also took it very much to heart. Over the past two years, Hank's production has deviated very little in either direction from the norm set by the informal—what we call the invisible—organization.

In another instance, the worker who always makes sure the safety guard is in its proper position on the power saw in his home workshop will leave the safety goggles in his locker. Why is he cautious at home and careless on the job? The same reason as in the case of Hank Brewster: At home he is conforming to his personal values, and at the plant, he is adjusting to the standards of the informal organization.

A couple of things may strike you about these hypothetical but true-to-life illustrations. First, in both cases the employee, in conforming to the standards of the informal organization, is in conflict with his own value system. Second, his behavior also conflicts with the norms of the formal organization— obviously, management wants higher production and wouldn't have issued safety goggles unless it wants them worn on the job. Evidently, the informal organization within the informal group sets up norms that can motivate employees, on occasion, to behave in ways that contradict both their own value system and that of the formal organization. All of which suggests that the reasons why employees form informal groups must be many and powerful.

Let's take time for a definition and a qualification. In the case of the informal group and the informal organization, it's easy to tell which is the chicken and which is the egg: The informal group always comes first, but not all informal groups achieve organizational status, a state in which the group develops explicit standards along with explicit sanctions to make these standards stick. The qualification is that even in the most cohesive group, not all the members live up to all the standards all the time. However, a pretty high batting average on conformity is the price of membership, at least in any group deserving of the designation "informal organization."

WHY EMPLOYEES JOIN INFORMAL GROUPS

The propensity of employees to become members of an informal organization, at first glance, looks surprising when you consider that they are already members of a formal organization with a specified role and specific duties, explicit channels of communication, and a definite line of command. What more could they need?

A good deal more—obviously. Looked at one way, and a quite legitimate way it is, employees develop informal groups to meet needs that are left unsatisfied by the formal organization. To what needs are we referring?

Friendship

First, not in order of importance but because it's the simplest need and the one that comes most readily to mind, is friendship, companionship—call it by whatever name you will. Man is a social being who spends about half his waking hours at work. He needs and enjoys the social contacts with his fellow workers—joking, sharing experiences, getting his opinions off his chest, obtaining a sympathetic hearing to his troubles when necessary.

Take the case of the supervisor of a typing pool who learned the importance of sociability—what sociologists prefer to call interaction—the hard way. The lady felt that the girls in the pool did entirely too much gabbing, but none of her verbal admonitions took. Finally, she decided on a drastic step and, with the office manager's permission, had plywood partitions installed between the workplaces. What happened? By Monday noon all work had ceased and a delegation of the girls informed the supervisor that they would not return to work unless the partitions were removed. She had no choice but to yield to the ultimatum. Yes, sociability does count.

And in the group context, it counts even more. The adage is wrong—familiarity *doesn't* breed contempt. Quite the reverse. Usually, the more people interact with one another, the friendlier their feelings toward each other become. To say it another way, in the informal group, which is characterized by a high frequency of interaction between the members, companionship becomes an increasingly attractive reason for membership as progressively friendlier feelings develop between the members.

Identification

Linked to it but separate from friendship as a motive for joining an informal group is what we call *identification* or sense of belonging—and what Barnard rather grandly called "the condition of communion." We all need to belong, to associate with others in purposes and goals that may encompass and also transcend our individual self-interest. Of course, the formal organization has its goals and purposes. The problem is, at least in an organization of any size, that these purposes appear abstract, remote, and meaningless to the average employee. What rank-and-file worker can identify himself with a chairman of the board and his purposes?

However, he can and does identify with his immediate work group, which is one of the reasons he becomes affiliated in the first place. Let's take one example from the military to illustrate our point. Studies conducted during World War II showed that bravery and the willingness to make sacrifices have little to do with a person's grasp of the overall objectives of the conflict, a commitment to them, or a devotion to the triple abstraction "honor, duty, country." On the contrary, they have almost everything to do with the individual soldier's loyalty to his immediate group—his desire not to let his buddies down. And so we suspect it's been since Thermopylae—and even before. George Homans, in his classic study of the human group, summed it up thus: "That both self-interests and something else are satisfied by group life is a truth that is the hardest for the hard-boiled—and half-

baked—person to see. As Mayo says, 'if a number of individuals work together to achieve a common purpose, a
harmony of interests will develop among them to which individual self interest will be subordinated. This is a very different doctrine from the claim that individual self-interest
is the primary human motive.' "

Thus, one reason why Hank Brewster went along with the
production quota laid down by the informal organization was
that, in general, he had, as an employee, subordinated his
personal goals to those of the group. He had, as it were,
exchanged the satisfactions of independence for those of
association and, typically, he felt better for it.

Protection

Another motive for Brewster's going along with the group in
setting production quotas suggests another reason why employees form groups: to attain protection for the membership,
especially protection from what the members feel are
impositions and encroachments by management. This time
the adage works—in unity *does* lie strength. Although it's
true that employees may occasionally band together to defend
themselves from another work group, nine-tenths of the time
the enemy is management and the protection the workers
seek is from management's demands for additional output,
longer work hours, higher quality, restriction of customary
privileges, and other constraints. Many organizations, for
example, introduce changes in work methods at a faster pace
than the individual employee can comfortably adjust to. On
his own, he can accomplish little. Conform or quit are his
alternatives. However, when the group as a whole objects and
the supervisor faces the prospect of slowdowns, discreet
sabotage, or a concerted campaign to put him in a bad light
with his superiors, he is likely to do whatever he can to make
the introduction of the work methods compatible with the
group's ability or, to speak more precisely, its willingness to
accept them.

Getting back to Hank Brewster: An individual employee may
have his personal concept of what constitutes a fair day's
work. As long as it remains his personal concept, it will
avail him little if it's contrary to management's definition.
Over the comparatively short run, the employee has to bend
or be bounced. Once again, the group is in a different position. With a concerted opposition to its standards of what
constitutes a fair day's work, management faces an altogether

unpleasant alternative: Fire the whole group or live with its production quotas. Just as long as the standards set by the group permit what management feels is a reasonable output and a reasonable rate of return, and when the group is relatively difficult to replace, most managements elect to put up with its standards. We've come a long way from the joys of undiluted ownership and unregulated enterprise as exemplified by Colonel Borden of Fall River, Massachusetts, a lord of the loom, who, when his workers demanded a ten-hour day, replied, "I saw that mill built stone by stone; I saw the pickers, the carding engines, the spinning mules and looms put into it, one after the other, and I would see every machine and stone crumble and fall to the floor again before I would accede to your wishes." Against such an attitude and such a man, any group would be helpless. However, we repeat— we've come a long way.

Exploitation

We've been talking about protection against management as one reason why employees join groups. Less frequently, they join in order to exploit the strategic advantages inherent in their work position. Whereas the posture of most informal groups toward management is defensive, theirs is offensive. By presenting a united front to management, they seek to gain—and are frequently successful in gaining—advantages not enjoyed by the rest of the work force, such as looser standards, more discretion over work methods, more overtime, and other concessions. To cite a flagrant example, in one plant the automatic screw-machine operators were the only hourly employees to enjoy a paid lunch hour—a case of discrimination which surely rankled the less favorably placed and hence less favored members of the work force. Such groups, generally small in number but positioned so they can disrupt overall operations at will, usually aren't hostile to management. They're often high-producing groups, composed of clear-eyed opportunists bent on using their strategic advantage as a lever to extract whatever benefits they can from management.

Assistance

Nor are these the only reasons why employees join groups. When the employee has a problem, it's natural to ask for help from a member of the group instead of from the boss.

The assistance given is usually just as valuable, and the employee has spared himself the tension and embarrassment frequently involved in admitting failure to the supervisor. In the bank wiring room of Western Electric, members of the group frequently helped each other even though the rules forbid it. The fact that helping and being helped made them feel better was the simple but adequate explanation the men gave as to why they violated the rule.

Groups also help to facilitate the use of creativity and initiative even when the job requirements are rigid and the jobs themselves simple and undemanding. This exercise of initiative is sometimes desirable from management's viewpoint. Exchanging jobs in the bank wiring room, for example, even though contrary to the rules, probably made a positive contribution to morale and efficiency. On other occasions, such as when a group puts its heads together in order to beat a complicated incentive formula, it exercises its creativity at management's expense. The key point is that on jobs which provide little intrinsic opportunity for the use of intiative or creativity, employees manage, under the umbrella of group sanction, to exercise both. The individual employee on his own wouldn't risk it, most such expressions being clearly contrary to the rules or outside them. However, with group approval and support, the risk is less and the satisfaction greater.

HOW GROUPS BECOME ORGANIZATIONS

In our discussion, we're restricting ourselves to work groups whose members share common job interests. We've neglected friendship cliques because they are of secondary importance to the supervisor and to the organizational process in general. Given the parameters of our concern, it's fair to state that all informal groups have the potential to become informal organizations and that all aspire to this goal. Not all of them make it. As we indicated previously, a work group that has achieved organizational status is one that has norms or standards accepted by the group, plus an effective procedure for punishing members who violate them. In short, a norm is more than an ideal. Conformity to the norm almost invariably results in rewards, and nonconformity almost invariably ends up in punishments.

What type of norms are we referring to? Do all groups have the same norms? A double-barreled reply would be that the things groups care about—that become embodied in their norms—show striking similarities among groups, but that the content of the norms themselves show equally striking diversities. The informal organization usually develops norms that cover chiseling, squealing to management about a coworker, standards of behavior between group members, and quality and quantity of work. This list is by no means exhaustive, but it does include the areas most frequently subject to norms. Within the areas, the norms vary widely. In an informal organization composed largely of skilled craftsmen, quality norms typically will be very high. Among semiskilled workmen, they will be much lower. What passes for officious behavior in an informal organization of electronics workers might be totally acceptable among a group of coal miners. Between plants and sometimes even within the same plant, there will be significant differences between output norms: One informal organization may progressively restrict productivity while another may sanction increasingly higher output. Instances of both practices abound.

Output control deserves special mention because it's the one type of norm found in every informal organization. And for good reason. As one of the authors of this book wrote in an earlier study of industrial work groups—and the thesis is also valid for white-collar work groups: "Output control is a basic objective of group action as well as an essential element in maintaining group stability. Not only the relation of the members to one another but the durability of the worker's relation to his job depends on the efficiency of the process." He cited instances of "runaway" output where group controls were feeble, and young and low-status employees exceeded the production and earnings records of their "betters." "The results were calamitous for the internal status hierarchy of the department and ultimately for the effectiveness of the formal organization."

Norms

Because output control is the prototype of all norms, we should get a viable insight into the overall process of the formation of norms once we understand—*really* understand— in even one instance how the norm of output control has been determined. Back to the bank wiring room! (We make no apologies for this backtrack. After nearly forty years, the Hawthorne studies, and the bank wiring room study in particular, are still the most systematic, exhaustive, and illuminating investigations of informal work groups.) In the bank wiring room, the wiremen decided that 6,000 or 6,600 completed connections a day, depending on the type of equipment being wired, were a proper day's work—a figure well below what management considered a desirable norm. That the norm represented what many of the wiremen had been used to reaching, that it reflected a depression atmosphere in which the fear was very real that too much output might result in one or more members of the group losing their jobs (some workers in the plant had been laid off prior to the development of the norms), that it indicated a measure of thankfulness at not being unemployed when so many were together with a sense of resentment at the supervisor for pressuring them for more output—all these elements illuminate but don't fully explain the quota. We know that the operators frequently stopped wiring when they had finished their quotas even though it was not official stopping time. And we also know that the concept of a day's work was related to a variety of fears—that the rate might be cut, that it might be raised, that the "bogey" might be raised, that someone might be laid off, or that the supervisor might bawl out the slower men. All these fears somehow contributed to the formulation of a specific production quota.

We say somehow. The process is mysterious and will remain so largely, as Homans states, because the process was subconscious. "The behavior of the employees could be described as an effort to protect themselves against such changes in routines and human associations: to give management the least possible opportunity of interfering with them. When they said that if they increased their output 'something' was likely to happen, a process of this sort was going on in their minds. But the process was not a conscious one. It is important to point out that the protective function of informal organizations was not a product of deliberate planning. It was more in the nature of an automatic response." In other words, the group decides what the finish line should be after it starts to run the race—norms emerge from activities with a previous track record, but the decision is reached via a subconscious consensus.

Sanctions

With sanctions, we're on more solid ground. The process by which the punishment is matched to the crime may be just as elusive as the process by which the norm that occasioned the sanction evolved, but the sanctions themselves are usually visible. One worker summed up the informal organization's ability to control its members as follows: "You have your choice between standing in with the group and standing in with the boss. And if you don't go along with the group, the gang can make it mighty unpleasant." That it can. The informal organization's most potent disciplinary weapon is rejection or ostracism. The employee who doesn't conform will find himself on the outside looking in. Initially, discipline may be mild—a warning that he'd better fall into line. If this doesn't bring him back into the fold, he can expect to be cut off from the group's social activities—lunching together, bowling after work, exchanging small talk at coffee breaks. If the group considers the recalcitrant employee a real threat to its stability, it may take more extreme measures, such as spreading malicious rumors about him or sabotaging his tools. Ultimately, it may try to get him fired or make his life so miserable that he quits.

Because output control is the sacred totem among norms, you would expect an exceptionally severe handling of deviance, and you'd be correct. The typist who persists in averaging eighty words a minute when the group feels that sixty words is a fair pace stands an excellent chance of being ejected from the group. Her equipment may be "adjusted" while she is away, or her coworkers may withhold information or be slow in delivering supplies. In a plant, if the group thinks it unwise to produce more than 500 units a day, steps will be taken to control the worker who consistently produces 600. Such steps can be drastic up to and including "binging"—pounding a ratebuster's arm until it's so sore that he can't possibly maintain his deviant output. In the bank wiring room, on one occasion, a worker identified as W. 8 told W. 6, one of the two men who consistently exceeded the group standard, "If you don't quit, I'll binge you." When W. 6 persisted, W. 8 struck him and then chased him around the room. W. 6, momentarily chastened by this experience, quit his own wiring, saying, "I've got enough done." Then he went over and helped another wireman.

GOAL CONFLICTS

In our discussion of the norms evolved by the informal organization, two facts stand out: Some of the norms developed by the informal organization may be in conflict with

either the employee's personal norms or the norms of the
formal organization—sometimes with both. And yet, time after
time, the norms of the informal organization take precedence.
The employee forsakes his personal preferences and risks
retaliation—whatever steps his boss may take to bring him
into line—from the representatives of the formal organization.

Conflict between Groups

Let's add another dimension to the problem. There are also
conflicts *between* groups and they frequently coalesce around
the differences between the group norms. Conflicts between
work groups that share the responsibility for the same product
are inevitable—mistakes will happen and buck-passing is a
universal phenomenon. The extra measure of exacerbation is
provided by the fact that cohesive groups (groups that have
achieved informal organization) are peculiarly suspicious of
outside groups. We're talking about something that you may
have observed yourself as a member of a group—or will if
you think about it. The more friends like each other when
they're in a group, the more they tend to dislike outsiders. As
stated in the hypothesis formulated by Homans: "The greater
the inward solidarity, the greater the outward hostility." The
bank wiremen, our tried and tested examples, found themselves, after they had developed cohesiveness, antagonistic to
the men who hadn't taken part in the study and who had
remained in the department. The study group claimed that the
stay-behinds were discriminating against them in various small
matters.

What we have is the potential for a circular and vicious
pattern: The members of a cohesive group start off with a
chip on their collective shoulder vis-à-vis other groups; the
first possibility for a conflict with the other group is joyously
embraced and blown up out of reasonable proportion; the
other group retaliates in kind; both groups treat the other as
an enemy—and the group that started it all basks in the
dubious satisfaction of a self-fulfilled prophecy.

To take a hypothetical example, a work group on the night
shift of a nail factory finds that the bins contain a lot of
defective material. To the man, they leap to the conclusion
that the day shift is trying to make them look bad. Actually,
the handlers had delivered a batch of material too late for
anyone on the day shift to inspect it. So, in retaliation, the
night group works only on the good material and leaves the

defective material in the bins for the day shift. The day shift, in turn, takes one look at the bins and swears to get even "with those miserable idiots on the night shift." So it goes.

The problem would be compounded if the day shift, for example, has the responsibility of inspecting work done by the night shift—as sometimes happens—and evaluating the quality of the work performed. If the quality norms of the two groups are different, as they will almost certainly be, it would be difficult to exaggerate the resentment and retaliation that might ensue.

Conflict between Informal and Formal Organizations

As we've indicated, an even more serious kind of outsider-insider conflict occurs between the informal organization with its goals and the formal organization with its goals—what the sociologists like to call the problems of suboptimization. We've said enough about them already to indicate the gravity and frequency of the problem. Let's just give one simple illustration by way of example.

The shelf-fillers in a supermarket had developed their own procedures for doing the work, one of which was tackling the aisles in rotation, with the entire store being worked on within each six-day period. Logical and neat? Perhaps. However, the system contained two aspects that delayed customers and even prevented the filling of orders: An unexpected run on an item might denude the shelves even though refills were no further away than the store basement. More serious, each Saturday, hordes of shoppers found at least one aisle jammed with crates and cartons a good part of the day. In short, the two prime norms of the formal organization, sales and service, were under attack by the work procedures developed by the shelf-fillers.

Whether or not the store manager could successfully buck the norms and keep his aisles cleared and his shelves filled would depend on a number of factors—the unity of the group, how much these norms meant to its members, their attitudes toward him, his skill in dealing with the group and its leaders, his ability to replace some or all the shelf-fillers if necessary—and we've sketched only the most obvious factors. Very possibly the manager would conclude that he must put up with the crowded aisles and give the customers such specious apologies as "Sorry, we're temporarily out of stock."

THE MAINSPRINGS OF COHESION

We've just stated that the store manager's getting his way with the shelf-fillers would depend in part on how united they were, on whether they had formed a cohesive group. The statement is true as far as it goes, but we haven't said very much. We've also seen that groups differ greatly in the degree of cohesiveness they achieve, a fact of prime importance for the plant or office supervisor and his relationship with the informal groups. But why are some groups cohesive and others disunited? Why do some groups develop norms and a capacity to attain them despite resistance from within and pressure from without, while other groups have few if any norms and lack the stamina to defend those they do possess? As with most questions involving the human behavior in an organization, there is not one answer but several, all of them interrelated.

STATUS

Status plays a part. The member of a high-status group is keenly conscious of being part of an elite, with privileges, pay, and deference that set it off from the rest of the community. He naturally identifies himself with the rest of the group. This was so with the mandarin class in Imperial China and it is so today with the diemakers and pattern-makers, the mandarins of the industrial work force.

CLOSE CONTACT

Smallness of group size helps. We've already seen how constant, face-to-face contact develops strong feelings of loyalty and friendship. In short, the small work group tends to be cohesive. Another obvious by-product of the constant interaction in the small work group is ease of communication. And exchanging views, developing a consensus, and making strategic moves to defend or extend their norms all require frequent interaction among members of the group.

COMMUNICATION

The key determinant of ease of communications, however, is not geographical proximity. In the typical assembly line, workers are physically close to each other, but the structure of the line limits each employee's interactions while working pretty much to the men immediately preceding and immediately following him on the line. In some steel mills and foundries, the noise level makes verbal interactions almost impossible, so the employees are reduced to communicating simple messages by banging a hammer against a steel plate. On the other hand, widely scattered workers, such as maintenance men and materials handlers, communicate with ease and frequency because the nature of their jobs requires frequent interaction. We even know of one highly cohesive group of electric utilities substation operators who never saw one another but whose work required them to communicate constantly by telephone.

SIMILAR WORK

Performing the same or similar work creates a sense of common economic self-interest among group members. This, in turn, leads to frequent interaction and the development of feelings of friendship and identification which transcend the bonds of self-interest and lay the basis for an informal organization. Similar jobs, of course, don't always contribute to cohesion—witness the sometimes frantic competition of store clerks for scarce customers. Our hypothesis is that similarity of jobs among members of a work group is a cohesive factor unless the higher earnings of one member of necessity result in lower earnings for another—except where, although the members are pitted in direct competition with one another, even the minimum earnings appear sufficient to motivate the group. We recall, for example, a chat with one of the bartenders at the King Cole Room at the Saint Regis Hotel in New York. He confided that they each made at least twenty "purple fish" ($20,000) a year. And those were 1946 dollars. Presumably, competition for tips among such affluent employees wouldn't inhibit the development of group cohesiveness.

In exploring the mainsprings of cohesiveness, we have thus far done most of our digging within the group itself. If only cohesiveness were that simple!

COMMON BACKGROUND

We have overlooked secondary but influential factors such as the behavior of the supervisor. He can discourage cohesiveness by fostering competition between group members, encourage it by nurturing and rewarding cooperation between members (as discussed in Chapter 2). Then there are influences of age, sex, marital status, and ethnic, cultural, and religious orientation. No one of the last six is very influential by itself. But if you combine several—for example, if you have a work group composed predominantly of middle-aged, married, female, Irish-Catholic high school graduates such as you would find among many groups of light assembly workers in electronics plants along Route 128 in Massachusetts—you have a combination of factors that would contribute to the development of cohesion.

Power—the Mystique of Success

Contribute to the development of cohesion is right, but such a group would probably not become cohesive because it would lack the most important requisites for the development of group cohesiveness—power and the mystique of success. In an earlier study, one of the authors of this book determined, after extensive research, that the most cohesive groups studied were those who possessed the heaviest clout—the greatest power—within the organization and therefore presented the strongest threat to the formal organization. Their members' skills were indispensable and next to impossible to replace. Their position in the technology of the organization was such that if they decided on a work stoppage though they were usually few in number—they would paralyze the entire operation and nullify the efforts of ten, a hundred, or even a thousand times as many workers. The patternmakers and diemakers are two such groups. So are the automatic screw-machine operators, the cutters in the clothing industry, and the ding men who make the final repairs on the metal body of an automobile assembly line. Slightly less powerful and even more aggressive and cohesive are such groups as metal polishers, in-plant truckers, and welders. Apparently, they have more need to throw their weight around.

The relationship that exists between power and cohesiveness is a complex one. The groups, high in status and power but recognizably not at the top, are like Avis—they have to try harder. As for the groups at the top with few demands left to satisfy—objectively speaking, management has more gripes against them than they have against management (witness the paid lunch hour for the screw-machine operators cited earlier); they tend to become complacent and somewhat lax in chastising deviations from their norms. They develop a measure of toleration for eccentric behavior, one of the hallmarks of a well-established group or class.

The success mystique is almost self-explanatory: The more powerful the group, the more successful it will be. Power contributes to cohesiveness and also to success, which in turn reinforces the sense of cohesiveness. With many such groups, it would take nothing less than a revolution in the technology of the production process to weaken their power position or undermine their cohesiveness.

To reformulate our definition of cohesiveness: All other things being equal, the smaller the group, the more similar the work performed, the greater the ease of communications between members, and the higher its status, the more cohesive the group will be. Some things being more equal than others, however, we add the codicil that a highly cohesive group depends on its being in a position, by virtue of the state of technology, to exert continuous and effective pressure on management in pursuit of its goals. In short, in a power struggle it has management at an overall disadvantage. Most of the time, giving in to its requests will appear less costly to management than the risks involved in refusal.

Let's also make a qualification: A measure of cohesion sometimes develops where you would least expect it, such as among workers in an automobile assembly line where the majority of jobs are semiskilled, the opportunities for interaction (as we've seen) are severely restricted, and the turnover among the group is typically very high. The reason for the development of group sentiment in such infertile soil is probably that, without a group to identify with, workers in situations such as the automobile assembly line have a feeling of anonymity and powerlessness which many people abhor and for which they seek compensations. Group cohesiveness, under these conditions, represents the triumph of strong feelings over an unfavorable environment.

GROUP LEADERS—AND HOW THEY ACHIEVE LEADERSHIP

Most groups, certainly all cohesive groups, develop leaders— and leaders come in many sizes. Selection of informal leaders is a complex and varying process. In some instances, the informal leader is the functional head of the work group, a man with quasi-supervisory duties who is frequently known as the crew chief or "straw boss." Of course, the crew chief doesn't have to be accepted as the informal leader, but because management and the union (where there is one) turn to him in dealing with the group, it's hard for the members to reject him. Any attempt to do so would result in a real donnybrook, tear the group apart, and cause no end of trouble for the manager.

In other cases, informal leaders—and we stress the plural because a work group seldom has a single leader—evolve as the result of natural selection. But different leaders perform different functions. In a group concerned with adjusting the small parts that go into telephone equipment, for example, one leader dealt with any outsiders while another handled the enforcement of standards of output and behavior. One was, in effect, foreign secretary, and one was home secretary. In other groups, leadership is even more specialized. One man may deal with management, another with the union, and a third with maintaining internal unity. In part, this division of responsibility reflects a recognition of the strengths and weaknesses of the men involved, but it also reveals the fact that opinion in the group is rarely unanimous on all matters. Some of the leaders' actions in negotiating with management may be unpopular with a strong minority of the group. Diffusion of leadership may be necessary to maintain group cohesion.

COHESIVE GROUP—CONFORMING LEADER

What kind of men are the informal leaders of the work group? In a really cohesive group, they are its most representative members. They may also be more articulate, more personable, or more gregarious, but these qualities count as nothing if they do not also conform—and conform more completely than most—to the norms of the informal organization. In the bank wiring room, for example, the leader (in this case there was one clearly identifiable leader) conformed to the norms more rigidly than any other member of the group. As Homans wrote of Taylor, the group leader, "He is not the most, but the least free person within it." Leadership was thrust upon him, and this was the only route to power the group would tolerate.

UNCOHESIVE GROUP—THE BEST LINE WINS

Other groups, with less cohesion, are suckers for the charismatic leader, the strong personality with an overpowering ego who imposes his purposes upon the group. Some loosely cohesive and erratic groups align themselves for no rational reason under the banner of a particularly aggressive individual with a promising line. The same group for no more rational reason may transfer its allegiance overnight to a slightly more aggressive individual with a presumably even more promising line. And some groups are so weak and so disorganized that they have no recognizable goal and no identifiable leader.

When you look at the situation closely, there are only two legitimate roles for any leader of a group. They were identified almost two hundred years ago by Edmund Burke in his letter to the Electors of Bristol: A leader either reflects the views of those he represents as closely as possible—the mirror theory of representation—or else he feels that it is his duty to mold them, educate them, and represent their potential and presumably better sentiments, not necessarily their current beliefs. (The latter point of view was espoused by Burke himself.) We're not in the business of picking sides, although we might call attention to the fact that Burke's position cost him his constituency and he had to seek refuge in a tiny district whose allegiance traditionally had been up for purchase. The analogy, on the other hand, is clear: When the group is intelligent and united, the leader must either bow to its will or persuade it to change its mind through an appeal to reason. When it's disorganized, with its power weak and its position unclear, the leader can manipulate the members and leadership belongs to the most skillful demagogue among them.

DEALING WITH THE LEADERSHIP

Most groups have leaders. How does the supervisor deal with leaders? Again, there is no single, simple answer. Let's first take a look at two minicases. You could label them "right way" and "wrong way," but if you did, you would be more wrong than right.

The Shipping Room Gets Its Comeuppance

Bert Fogarty, the supervisor of shipping, was hopping mad—the superintendent had just bawled him out about the productivity of his crew.

"Those characters must just sit around on their butts all day," he had said. "They handled 20 percent less work last week and earned 10 percent more overtime. What are you doing, Fogarty, anyway—telling them to conserve their energy until three o'clock so they can earn more overtime?"

A properly chastened Fogarty cornered his crew and told them: "All this business of coming in ten to fifteen minutes late in the morning and coming back ten to fifteen minutes late from lunch stops here and now. Anyone who's late—one minute late—gets no overtime. Understand?"

Three weeks later, Bert looked over the production sheets and permitted himself a slight smile—he wasn't an expressive man. Production up 10 percent, overtime down 10 percent. "Well, it worked and I should have done it before," he mused to himself.

The Drafting Room Delivers a Message

Tom Hilson, the supervisor of the drafting room at Pioneer Astrodynamics, looked at the summary work sheets for the week. Just as he thought, output was down. Sure, there was an unusually large number of new men—four out of twenty in the past four months. But to Hilson, that wasn't the whole story. "These characters drift in one at a time—it's not nine but nine-thirty with many of them, and the real goof-offs have the guts to come in at ten. Not that I don't appreciate that the bums get a phony round of applause from the rest of the guys. They don't like it much better than I do."

Hilson slept on it, then acted. He called the drafting room together: "We're way under budget and we've got to make it up. One way is to make sure that everyone starts to work on time. From now on, there's no such a thing as being 'a little bit late.' " That was the essence of Hilson's message.

Three weeks later, Hilson looked at the records and moaned softly. Tardiness had declined all right—by 30 percent. But look at the other figures—absenteeism up 20 percent, completed work down by 15 percent—plus his feeling that interest in the projects at hand wasn't what it should be or even what it had been. Just yesterday, Jeff Welsh, the best-liked man in the drafting room, had approached him and, after a couple of petty questions (probably a pretext for their conversation), dropped the remark that "The guys really resent your getting on their backs to be on time. We'd all be a lot happier if you would relax a little." Jeff's inflection rose a bit on "relax a little." He was a pretty subtle guy.

"So I should relax a little." Hilson looked at the sheet again and pursed his lips.

Why did Bert Fogarty succeed and Tom Hilson fail? After all, their problems were similar and their approaches to solving it were much alike, too. Fogarty *acted* tough while Hilson merely *talked* tough—an important distinction, but not, we think, the reason why one man was successful and the other was not. The real explanation lies in the different nature of the two work groups.

Fogarty faced a group of shipping-room employees, men at the bottom of the plant's power and status totem pole—

with easily acquired skills, low pay, and undesirable jobs. Such a group, which an author of this book has previously dubbed "apathetic," is characterized by passivity, lack of cohesion, and little or no recognizable informal leadership. Here, getting tough works: Fogarty, with threats, was able to cow the group into submission.

Not so with Hilson. Merely talking tough resulted in a surface compliance with his request, together with a tacit resistance that was far more damaging to the efficiency and productivity of the drafting room than the tardiness problem which had caused him to act in the first place. The shipping room folded under pressure, whereas the drafting room stiffened its resistance under pressure and fought back—it was that kind of group. The members had a sense of themselves as professional employees with distinct skills that were much in demand. They combined pride of technique with the knowledge of being valued as a group and difficult to replace. They had also, apparently, developed an informal leader—Jeff Welsh—a factor which Hilson was either unaware of or preferred to ignore.

Hilson made two mistakes, one major and one minor. His minor mistake was in failing to recognize and use Welsh as a medium of communication to the group instead of trying to "bull his way through." His major error was in failing to appreciate that you can't bully or intimidate this kind of group. After all, the group with its mock applause was already applying a type of censure to the ten o'clock stragglers who were violating an apparent group norm—showing up before nine-thirty was O.K., but later than that was taboo. We suspect that wisdom, for Hilson, would be to swallow a bit of pride, take Welsh's advice, and see what the records looked like in two or three weeks' time. There are worse things that can happen to a supervisor than having people a little bit late.

Respect the Group Leaders' Position

We said that Hilson made an error in not recognizing Welsh as the informal leader of the drafting room and using him as a means of communicating his views to the group. In general, how should the supervisor treat the informal leadership of a cohesive group? "Respectfully" is a good one-word answer. "Share his leadership with the informal leaders of the group" is a more precise and accurate answer, but one calculated to enrage many supervisors or at least arouse their opposition. They resent sharing their leadership. Some even overreact and end up repressing and destroying their capabilities for leadership. Either they become laissez-faire managers incapable of giving guidance, or they turn into "bureaupaths" who guide only by citing directives or statements from higher authority.

The psychological threat of sharing authority with the informal leadership is a real one for many managers. But consider the alternatives. Take the story of two supervisors (not in industry), one who worked with the group through its leadership and one who did not—in this case, through ignorance, not choice. They were social workers in charge of recreational centers in a slum area, and they faced a similar problem. The younger boys were supposed to leave the centers at 9 p.m. to make way for an older crowd who hung around outside and generally made a nuisance of themselves. One social worker pleaded with them again and again, in the interests of fair play, to go away and leave the center alone— but always to no avail. The other man faced the problem just once and solved it promptly. How? He went outside and said to the ringleader, "Listen, Joe. The time's up. Be a good fellow and take your gang out of here." This is a simple but dramatic illustration of the advantages of working through the informal leader. Of course, this wasn't the first contact between the successful social worker and Joe. He had made a regular practice of working through him at the recreation center.

It's true that in a nonunion situation, it's possible for the supervisor to pick off the informal leaders of a group one by one by getting them transferred or fired. However, in the end, you have at best a resentful but cowed mass of individuals who docilely follow orders. At the same time, they usually show a lack of initiative or teamwork, and their performance is likely to be substandard in most respects. Enough said.

Identify the Group Leaders

Assuming that it's desirable to work through the informal leaders, how does the supervisor, particularly the new supervisor, identify the leaders of the informal group? How does he make sure that he isn't being taken in by appearances—by the guy who talks all the time or the one whose clowning and kidding make him the center of attention? The answer— there's no substitute for close observation. The supervisor should look for the men the other employees go to when they have something on their minds—these men are usually the same people who make the most sense when the supervisor is talking to them himself. One supervisor, somewhat uncertain of who the group leaders were—"the heavies," he called them because they carried the most weight with his crew—went around and asked each employee whom he wanted to work with on a special job. The two men who got the most votes were, he figured, the two whom everyone listened to the most—and that's the way it turned out. The key determinant, proved by continuing observation, is who has influence over the group, who sets the pace. Most cohesive groups contain a few men of whom it can be said, "if they say go, it's usually go."

Work through Informal Leaders

How does the supervisor work with the informal leaders? Let's assume that he has thought up a rearrangement of work stations that would reduce motion and save time. He should try it out on the informal leadership before announcing it to the group. They may have objections he hasn't anticipated and can't answer. In any event, he will need their assistance in selling the change to the group.

Equally important: Before the formal announcement of any change, the supervisor should let the informal leaders know in advance. Their feedback may reveal information he may want to pass on to higher management, and he's more likely to have their help in getting the change accepted if he has taken them into his confidence.

He might extend recognition to an informal leader by asking his help in breaking in a new employee, confident that he'll clue in the new man to the group's norms as well as to the formal rules and regulations. If the supervisor has a disciplinary problem with an employee, he should try airing it with an informal leader. Because the leader has the confidence of that employee, he may give the supervisor a new insight into the problem. If he agrees with the boss's diagnosis of what's wrong, he may see that the group itself brings the man into line.

One thing the supervisor shouldn't do is to show favoritism toward the informal leaders, do special favors for them, or give them easier or higher paid assignments. Nothing can undermine their leadership position more quickly. The supervisor should extend recognition to the leaders and reinforce their status with the group by consulting with them—nothing less but also nothing more.

GEORGE ELTON MAYO (1880–1949)

Mayo is a hard man to write about—a difficult nut to crack. His strength was diagnosis; he was the overall director of the Hawthorne Studies, and he brought to the study of the industrial work setting the perspectives of the trained clinician. He recognized that in studying the employee in the work setting, just as in studying the patient in the sick bed, you had to concentrate on the uniqueness of what you saw, not on what previous experience and previous theorizing had indicated you should see under the circumstances.

He more than any other man was responsible for discovering the importance of the small work group. He saw that where it existed many workers ceased to think or behave like the classic economic man, that the social well-being they derived as associates in closely-knit groups ranked first with them. He tended to view the formation of such work groups as spontaneous and instinctual, although the selection we have chosen emphasizes a case in which action, more or less planned by the supervisor, had a lot to do with the formation of work groups under conditions that admittedly were not very promising.

So far, so good. Anyway, up to this point few would dispute the validity and importance of Mayo's core insight. But Mayo couldn't stop there—he was a born generalizer. His instincts were in conflict with his training as a psychiatrist. In 1300 he would have been a theologian; in 1750 a *philosophe*. In any age he was a holist, one of those who is never satisfied—intellectually or emotionally—until he has wrung a general theory out of the frequently recalcitrant facts.

What Mayo did was to generalize from some of the evidence uncovered about the formation and functioning of work groups at Hawthorne and a handful of other experiments and conclude that what was true for them was true for all work groups. He theorized that groups exist because "the industrial worker wants ... first a method of living in social relationship with other people" and "happiness and such sense of personal security as may be found in subordination of an individual to a common purpose."

Mayo saw a society in which the customary ties of of family, race, and community had largely been dissolved; in which the worker obtained a measure of meaning to his life through his membership in the plant society. It was this romantic and conservative vision of Mayo's—we say conservative because if we take it at its face value, all industrial conflict is social disease and all cooperation social health—that touched off a veritable civil war among sociologists over the writings of the Mayo school. We call Mayo's vision romantic because it depends on a selective reading of the facts: To cite a simple instance, the weight of the evidence in the bank wiring room shows that group feelings developed there primarily as a means of resisting change, more specifically of resisting changes that the workers felt might be instituted by the management, changes that would work to their disadvantage.

A personal note: One of the authors confesses to a long-standing bias against Mayo's ideas. As a young man, he called Mayo—to his face—a "psycho-administrative fascist." He wasn't sure then or now exactly what the accusation meant, beyond the fact that Mayo was conservative, no Democrat with a small 'd'; he was sure that Mayo would use manipulation whenever it promoted stability and cooperation, and that he was omniscient. Mayo the man, we might add, was different. The accusation resulted in an invitation to dinner—and a fascinating evening from which this author emerged charmed but unconvinced.

We suggest that there is no substitute for reading Mayo and making up your own mind. After three decades, it's still a heady experience.

The Human Problems of an Industrial Civilization, New York, MacMillan Co., 1933.

The Social Problems of an Industrial Civilization, Boston, Harvard Graduate School of Business Administration, 1945.

The Political Problems of an Industrial Civilization, Boston, Harvard Graduate School of Business Administration, 1947. (The last is little more than a pamphlet.)

Teamwork and Management*

No palliatives external to the work situation can remedy a fundamental defect of organization. In respect of the

---

* Elton Mayo and George F. Lombard, *Teamwork and Labor Turnover in the Aircraft Industry of So. California,* Harvard University (B.R. Studies No. 32), Oct. 1944, p. 25–30.

human organization of these plants, much remains to be done. Personnel counselors and exit interviewers can do much to clear a worker's personal preoccupations. But counselors at present are rarely sufficiently trained to be thus effective. Consequently, once again the findings of research point back to administration of working groups as the critical factor in determining the extent to which teams will come into existence in an organization.

COMPARISON WITH OTHER STUDIES

This study points to the importance for management of teamwork and the direct relation of administrative method to the formation of teams. This finding is supported by earlier studies that we have made as well as by the experiences of others. We shall refer briefly to some of these.

a. *East Coast absenteeism study.* In the east coast industrial locality that we studied,[1] one of three casting shops proved superior to the other two. We append three charts, Charts 22, 23, and 24, that compare the casting shop situations of the three metalworking companies during the first six months of 1943. The absence record for Company C is better than those of the other two companies. The diagrams apply only to the "veterans" of the departments, those who were continuously employed from January 1, 1942, to June 30, 1943, but the superiority extended to the whole casting shop. The casting shop of Company C had an absence rate below 2% for every month but one in the 18-month period, Company B's rate rose to an approximate 5% or 6%, and Company A's rose above 10% and thereafter fell to about 5%.[2]

Company C had effective methods of securing teamwork. The first part of this method was an insistence that foremen should "listen" to individual workers, should be patient, and should avoid "emotional upsets"; and arrangements were made to give foremen time to listen.[3] The second part of the method was to constitute each line of furnaces a unit led by linesmen (technical experts); the three shifts in every line were paid in accordance with the 24-hour output of the line. The third part of the method was to have the foreman and individuals of a shift arrange which day "off" (one day in seven) each individual should

---

[1] *Absenteeism: Management's Problem.*
[2] Ibid., Chart 16, p. 20.
[3] Ibid., p. 19.

have. If one worker absented himself unlawfully, the arrangement for the others was upset; the consequence of this system was a pressure exercised by the group on the individual to hold him to the arrangement he had made, a pressure that "management would never dare to exercise."[4] The management of Company C thus took definite steps to assure itself that the individual was content with his work and also that there was mutual responsibility and teamwork. The consequence is clearly portrayed in the diagram; workers are concentrated at the regular attendance end of the scale.

b. *Hawthorne Plant, Western Electric Company.* The well-known "test room" experiment at the Hawthorne, Illinois, plant of the Western Electric Company[5] began with a degree of labor turnover. When, however, the new worker at No. 2 bench assumed informal leadership of the group and identified the team wholeheartedly with the company experiment, all labor turnover stopped and casual absences sank to a fraction of their former dimension and to a fraction of the rate in the department outside the test room.[6] "A change in morale had also been observed. No longer were the girls isolated individuals, working together only in the sense of an actual physical proximity. They had become participating members of a working group with all the psychological and social implications peculiar to such a group."[7] The effect of the mutual responsibility thus created was remarkable: the "layout" girl, for instance, had been absent, before the teamwork began, 85 times in 32 months; after it began, she had not ever been absent during 16 months.[8]

c. *Philadelphia textile mill.* More than twenty years ago, we were asked to study the mule-spinning department of a textile mill near Philadelphia.[9] The turnover rate, 250%, was very high by comparison with other departments in the mill; 100 men were taken on every year to maintain a working force of 40. We introduced several innovations,

[4] Ibid., p. 19.
[5] F. J. Roethlisberger and William J. Dickson, *Management and the Worker* (Cambridge, Harvard University Press, 1939); Thomas North Whitehead, *The Industrial Worker* (Cambridge, Harvard University Press, 1938).
[6] F. J. Roethlisberger and William J. Dickson, op. cit., p. 84.
[7] Ibid., p. 86.
[8] Ibid., p. 83.
[9] Elton Mayo, "Revery and Industrial Fatigue," *Personnel Journal,* Vol. III, No. 8, December, 1924, pp. 273–281.

such as rest pauses, and we were also permitted to put a qualified nurse in charge of a small clinic in the mill. Serious cases or medical questions she reported to a Philadelphia hospital; minor cases, a splinter or cut, she handled herself. Her chief duty was to encourage spinners to talk over any personal preoccupations. In addition to the provision of this personal outlet, the workers had been told by management to take control themselves of the new rest-pause system, and to make arrangements with one another as to alternation and time. This responsibility had the effect of inducing consultation, discussion, and teamwork. Turnover sank almost immediately to an approximate 5% and remained at that figure until the mules were taken out, about five years later.

d. *Experiences of others.* We have gathered from various sources a number of reports of experiences that show the importance of teams. Many companies have been able to achieve astonishing production records during the war because their managements have built up team relations among the workers.[10] Few of these industrial reports specifically lift out the importance of teams in the situations that they describe. Indeed they often seem to be unaware of the real conditions that lie behind the effective work in their situation. Some of them place the credit for what they have achieved on the payment system which they use, often in these cases some form of group incentive plan, without seeing that the payment plan is effective because teams of workers actually exist to give it reality. In other words, it is not so much the payment plan as the administration of the payment plan that is important. A report on combat fatigue, however, written by Lieutenant Commander George N. Raines and Lieutenant Lawrence C. Kolb of the United States Navy Medical Corps,[11] clearly

---

[10] See, for examples, the following references: R. Coughlan, "Jack and Heintz; Cleveland War Plant Is Paradise of Bonuses, Sunbaths, Wolf Calls and Free Florida Vacations," *Life*, Vol. 14, March 22, 1943 p. 74; "Incentive Pay: Lincoln Electric Company's Bonus System," *Time*, Vol. 39, June 8, 1942, p. 82; J. Campbell Bruce, "The Iron Men of Hendy," *The Reader's Digest*, Vol. 44, No. 266, June, 1944, p. 76.

[11] George N. Raines and Lawrence C. Kolb, "Combat Fatigue and War Neurosis," *United States Naval Medical Bulletin*, Vol. XLI, No. 4, July, 1943, p. 923, and No. 5, September, 1943, p. 1299.

In this connection, reports on the group known as "Carlson's Raiders" of the United States Marine Corps are also of interest. See for instance: Don Burke, "Carlson of the Raiders," *Life*, Vol. 15, September 20, 1943, p. 53; "The Psychiatric Toll of Warfare," *Fortune*, Vol. 28, December, 1943, p. 140.

points to the importance of team relationships among the crews of Navy ships as one of four main preventives of breakdowns resulting from combat fatigue.

CONCLUSIONS

In all these instances, attention by management to the organization of the human needs of their workers was followed by an apparently spontaneous development of teams and of mutual responsibility, diminished turnover and absenteeism, and improvement in the quality and quantity of work. The teams took over, as it were, and participated with management in securing the accomplishment of some of the tasks that had previously been performed by management alone, such as, for instance the disciplining of members of the teams as to production and attendance. Once the teams had taken over these functions successfully, their performance became a source of satisfaction to the workers. No longer were they united by a sense of failure to accomplish the impossible. Indeed, both the mule-spinners, above cited, and the girls in the test room were intensely surprised by the ease with which they accomplished a level of production and quality they had previously thought beyond their powers. And once these teams had realized their success, the pressure that the group brought to bear on those individuals whose behavior deviated from the standard was infinitely more effective than anything management could do.

Department IV and Work Center 3 of Department I, second shift, above specified, do not differ from these instances; in California with its background of seething population movement, which to superficial observation seems so unfavorable to steadiness, these departments show records of self-discipline that compare well with any records anywhere. Of 55 persons in Department IV, 50 had a regular attendance record; 37 had a rate of under 2 absences yearly; 13 had a slightly higher rate because of the inevitable interference of external circumstance—illness, family troubles, transportation difficulties, and the like. In Work Center 3 of Department I, second shift, of 30 persons, 24 had a regular attendance record, 20 being perfect or almost so, and of the latter 17 were newcomers.

Indeed, when we look through the many scores of attendance records that we have of East and West alike, we are struck by the invariable persistence of the human desire for active association in teamwork with others, and our conclusions from the various experiences cited may be simply stated:

First, the desire of individuals for association in work with others is deep-seated in humanity, and is sure to find some form of expression.

Second, there is thus no question for industry as to whether there shall, or shall not, be working groups. The important question for management is whether, in a particular situation, the attitude of these groups is:

a. *Hostile.* This attitude is fortunately rare and usually evanescent.

b. *Wary of wholehearted cooperation.* This, unfortunately, is the usual attitude. Our own and other inquiries[12] show that workers often are on guard against the engineer or newcomer. The behavior of the members of such groups is often as though they sought to maintain themselves in the *status quo,* rather than to contribute their efforts wholeheartedly to the changes which the promotion of the purpose of the larger organization of which they are a part may require. As such groups develop their self-identity rather than their identity with the rest of the organization, they become what are sometimes called "cliques," and in extreme cases may tend to the openly "hostile" attitude named above.

c. *Cooperative and friendly.* This attitude finds illustration both in the experimental test room at the Hawthorne plant of the Western Electric Company and in the Work Center B of Department IV described in this report. In both instances, management, or supervision, has worked for the result and has got it.

Third, it is clearly unwise to leave the method and form of group formation wholly to circumstance or chance. In such a situation, which is unfortunately usual, the team formation is fortuitous and may exclude, capriciously, many workers who should "belong." A consequence of this exclusion is that such workers constitute a ragged edge or fringe who become discontented and provide a population for absentee or turnover statistics. The neglect of the problem by management seemingly does not greatly matter in small organizations or in peacetime; but this is only

---

[12] See, for example, Stanley B. Mathewson, *Restriction of Output among Unorganized Workers* (New York, The Viking Press, 1931).

seeming. Company C^{13} enjoyed an enormous advantage over Companies A and B in respect to the problems of absenteeism, labor turnover, and labor shortage; the management had worked for and earned this advantage. Leadman Z in Department IV also had worked for what he had achieved in his work center.

Fourth, and for this report perhaps the most important of our conclusions. It is possible in a situation characterized by constant and almost chaotic change that the natural processes of group association may be almost wholly defeated. Something of this has been true of the scene in Southern California. Management under the pressure of dire necessity has moved individuals and groups by so-called loans and transfers to such an extent that, as we pointed out earlier, the labor turnover within a plant was greater than that at the factory gate. In this situation it was probably impossible for management to act otherwise. Our only comment would be that management does not seem to have been aware of the probable consequences of such action.

This fourth statement is entirely in accord with the first above. In other words, the desire for association in work is deep-seated and sure to find expression. This expression, if the deep-seated desire is defeated, will take the form of exaggerated absenteeism and labor turnover, so that management by its inattention to the organization of teamwork in the factory is in a significant way responsible for the conditions for which it blames workers.

IMPLICATIONS FOR MANAGEMENT

This report, based as it is on one short study, cannot attempt to answer all the questions about the formations of teams which it raises. It has already pointed out the method of administration used by one man who successfully made of his workers an organized team. The study, *Absenteeism: Management's Problem*, describes in an entirely different situation the strikingly similar methods of human administration taught by another man and adopted by his company. Wide understanding and practice of these methods, essential as they are to a society in chaos, will

---

13 *Absenteeism: Management's Problem.*

not be easily achieved. Research and training in the methods are the only answers.

Short of the attainment of these objectives, what can be done more immediately to promote, or at least not hinder, the formation of "natural" groups? The answer to this question must be approached with caution. An adequate fund of intelligently criticized experience is lacking. The present study nevertheless seems to point clearly to a few questions of practical importance which illustrate the kind of action that can be effective.

1. Where large numbers of people must work geographically together, what can be done in the organization of their work to stimulate the formation among them of small, effective groups? Although the question of the size of a work group has often been studied from the point of view of technical and operating efficiency, we do not know that it has been done from the point of view of a situation as a whole, its technical, operating, and human needs together. Such studies as have been made from the human point of view relate chiefly to what methods can be used outside the work situation by way of recreation, entertainment, and so forth.[14] As we have observed, no such remedies external to the work situation can compensate for a defect of organization in it.

2. To what extent can similarities of past experience and of life outside the factory, as, for instance, with the Oklahomans already mentioned, be used as a basis for the self-creation of teams? In particular, to what extent in emergency should people who know one another and apply for work together be placed together irrespective of whatever untrained manipulative skills they may possess? To what extent would the enthusiasm resulting from the social satisfactions thus maintained lead to a more willing interest in acquiring the new skills necessary to getting out production? There is a minor danger in this: if a team forms around such a core and if the reason for the team's existence continues to be not the work itself but its members' mutually shared experience in the past, there is danger that the group will fail to identify itself wholeheartedly with the purpose of the enterprise of which it is a part. Indeed, it might conceivably become openly hostile to it. Again,

---

[14] On this point see especially Mass-Observation, *People in Production,* (London, John Murray, 1942).

the task of administration is to guide the group from this course.

3. To what extent is it possible, when the organization of operations requires loans and transfers of workers, to transfer in groups those who on their regular assignments work together, and thus encourage human association in spite of a disorganization of operations?

4. To what extent can mangements select, as the persons through whom they make their communications to workers, the leaders of teams instead of, as so often happens, the highest producer, who frequently is not a member of the team at all? Would selection of such leaders increase the likelihood that communications from management would be, in the first instance, acceptable to workers as coming from their recognized leader instead of from someone "outside" the team? This selection can adequately be made only if all levels of supervision give close attention to those aspects of organization that we call human. From close attention a supervisor will know with certainty those persons in his group who are ready for the responsibilities of leadership, that is, those in the work group to whom, even before they have received formal recognition from management, others turn for help and counsel on personal as well as technical matters. Such men, when given even brief training designed to crystallize in their own minds the experiences which they have already had in helping others and to make explicit to them the skills which they have been using, will be fully capable of establishing the kind of communication between managements and workers of which we have been speaking.

5. To these a fifth question resulting from our earlier study and the experiences of others, but needing emphasis in this report, can be added. To what extent can group incentive payment plans be administered to promote the formation of teams? Clearly a group payment system applied to a number of workers, who because of the arrangement of their work cannot be a team, can have no effect. Nevertheless, such a plan can be effective when considered in the light of the actual relations of persons at work, as was Company C's plan discussed above.[15] When not so considered, a payment plan may, as individual piecework plans sometimes do, tend to force individuals into isolated

---

[15] See p. 25 and *Absenteeism: Management's Problem*, p. 16.

competition, when the reality of the work and their own latent desires call for them to act as a social group. The evidence[16] seems to show, however, that the more usual result of a payment plan not so considered is to encourage in the workers an attitude wary of whole hearted cooperation with management, the second type of attitude mentioned on page 28 above.

Our study raises these points as important in determining the kind of a situation, the "climate," in which teams can grow. The study did not continue long enough to allow us to demonstrate by means of experiments the effectiveness or ineffectiveness of this or that method in the promotion of team formation. Such confirmation can only come from researches set up as were those at Hawthorne and Philadelphia, mentioned earlier in this report. Here the effect on production of changed employee attitudes could actually be verified from carefully kept records of the attendance and production attained by the group before and after the change had occurred. The achievement of such a change, necessitating as it does a measure of control over operations by a research group, cannot be had without full understanding and participation of top management and line supervision.

Labor turnover and absenteeism, though exaggerated in an emergency period, are not merely phenomena of such a time. These problems existed before the war began and will continue when it is over. Except for the researches already reported, we had not made extensive studies of them earlier, and we do not know of others who have used the approach of this report. We believe that it is correct to say, however, that the patterns of turnover and absenteeism reported in this study and in *Absenteeism: Management's Problem* hold true in stable as well as emergency situations. Although we show that the proportion of "irregulars" to the total group varies, we believe that in a sufficiently ordered situation there are usually some workers who cause most of the irregular attendance and some workers for whom regularity of attendance is high. We believe also that the policies and actions of management taken together constitute an important determinant of the incidence and proportion of turnover and absenteeism in every particular situation, peacetime as well as war.

---

[16] Cf. Mathewson, op. cit.

During the war, this country can no doubt afford to pay the high cost of absences and labor turnover. But after the war and during the period of contract terminations, neglect to consider existent teams in the selection of workers for discharge can, as surely as Selective Service, strip our industrial organizations of whatever patterns of human collaboration have been achieved. This result will inevitably occur if through inadvertence existing teams and, more important, those informal leaders who have the capacity to secure teamwork in others are discharged first. Under competitive conditions of manufacture, neglect of the problem of the organization of teamwork may increase costs to the point of forcing many plants out of business. The plant that does not know how to organize teamwork, that shrugs it off as mere humanitarianism, will be little equipped to meet the critical postwar problems of securing cooperation from persons of such diverse experience as civilian war workers and returning veterans.

THE SUPERVISOR VERSUS THE INFORMAL ORGANIZATION

We've described in some detail how the supervisor of a closely knit group should work through its informal leaders and share his authority with them. But what if he faces an informal organization with several norms, including one on output, that are opposed to the norms of the formal organization? What should the supervisor do then? How should he treat the leaders of such a cohesive group?

Emphasize the Positive

First of all, he needs to put the group into perspective. True, all cohesion in a group means is that the members will adhere closely to the group's standards, whatever they are. However, from the manager's viewpoint, cohesive groups have many positive characteristics. Morale is higher in a cohesive group, and turnover and absenteeism are usually lower. Members tend to work smoothly together, so the manager escapes the bickering, bad feelings, and poor workmanship frequently found in a disorganized group. Supervision is easier, too. The manager doesn't have to transmit orders and information to every member individually or consume time with formal meetings. He can depend on the informal leadership to act as the unofficial but effective channel of communication. Under many circumstances, then, the manager will want to encourage cohesiveness within the group, not try to suppress it. As for the informal leader, if he doesn't exist already, it will be necessary for the supervisor to invent him, or at any rate to develop whatever leadership potential is on hand within the group.

This holds true with groups that develop only a slight degree of cohesion on their own. Walker, Guest, and Turner found, in their study of workers on an automobile assembly line, for example, that the most effective managers were those who fostered group cohesiveness by delegating informal responsibility to the leaders of the group or by allowing the group—with guidance, to be sure—to establish informal systems of job rotation. Comparing many work groups, an author of this book found that those with the highest degree of cohesion ranked substantially above the apathetic groups in overall plant performance and cooperation.

All well and good—but cold comfort to the supervisor

with a cohesive group that has enshrined low output as its number one norm. A little more perspective on the problem is needed before we talk about solutions. What about the output of the isolated employee who has to rely on pressures from his boss, the urge to make more money (provided he is on incentive pay), and the dictates of his conscience in determining how much work to turn out? Most employees who fall into this category have undistinguished output records (the minority of ratebusters who somehow manage to exist even in cohesive groups being the spectacular exception). Deprived of the pleasures of group association and saddled with jobs that are for the most part intrinsically of little interest, these employees settle for making a minimal contribution to the organization.

Cohesive groups show a different output pattern. Seashore found that highly cohesive work groups were likely to have output records that diverged in either direction from the plant averages. A similar study of output among groups of clerical workers emerged with the same conclusion. High productivity among cohesive groups is something you would expect. After all, restriction of output is born, in part, of fear, and the cohesive group with the ability to protect and advance its interests and to win justifiable grievances can afford to be productive. If management should take advantage of high output to raise standards, for example, the group could fight back and probably win. Most managements, with a healthy recognition of the group's power position, probably wouldn't even try.

A norm of low output is more difficult to understand. In some cases, the norm may be vestigial, a hangover from the days when the group forged its original cohesion largely in the successful effort to resist what it thought were unreasonable encroachments by management. Attitudes, once formed and institutionalized in low output norms, are difficult to change, even though the facts which prompted and justified them may have disappeared. Another factor which may partly or totally account for the low output norm in a cohesive group is the supervisor's attitude. He may have what one team of researchers called a "frozen group." They referred to a group made up of men who had decided (1) that management's plans for them were based on the conviction that they, like the machines they operated, would do no more nor less than they were told to do, and (2) that like machines, they were not expected to know more when they

retired than when they were hired. Under such circumstances, decided the researchers, the group leaders had
instinctively decided that their only chance to feel human was
to stick together and give the company as little work as
possible.

The Employee-centered Approach

To the extent that management's attitudes as symbolized and
interpreted by the supervisor are the reasons for the low
output norms of a work group, what should the supervisor do
to turn things around? Sometimes the group's restriction on
output is simply one way in which it expresses its frustration
and discontent. The restriction gives the employees the chance
to revenge themselves for what they see as deprivations.
The implication is that the manager who recognizes his
employees' needs and tries to meet them is less likely to have
a department of restricters. Take the study of absenteeism and
productivity made during World War II by Elton Mayo in an
aircraft plant in Southern California (referred to in Chapter 1).
Mayo found that absenteeism was high and productivity low.
But there were some departments where absenteeism was
phenomenally low and productivity was phenomenally high.
What was the explanation for the difference? These were
departments in which the development of team spirit was the
central objective of the managers in charge. They devoted
themselves to facilitating the work of their men and to
listening to whatever complaints or suggestions the men might
have. As a result, the employees felt that they were important
rather than taken for granted, and as a group they exerted
pressure to raise output, not to restrict it.

Consider another study made several years later by Rensis
Likert and Daniel Katz of the University of Michigan. They
examined the relationship between productivity and supervision in twenty-four departments of a large insurance company, twelve of which were low-producing and twelve, high-
producing. As all the employees did similar work and had
similar backgrounds, the researchers looked to the environment for the explanation of the disparity in production. The
key difference, they found, was the supervisor's approach to
managing his department. The supervisors seemed to fall
into one of two categories: There was the employee-centered
supervisor who considered managing people rather than
expediting production to be his main job. And there was the

production-centered supervisor who considered his main job to be getting the work done and viewed his workers as merely the tools for accomplishing that objective. He supervised with strict controls, while the employee-centered supervisor gave his subordinates more leeway and responsibility in handling their jobs. Significantly, the researchers found that the employee-centered supervisor was likely to be in charge of a high-producing group, while the production-centered supervisor's department was usually a low producer.

We're talking about the fact that, under the right conditions, the supervisor can accomplish wonders simply by practicing what two generations of experts have identified as good human relations. In a leaderless, disorganized group, the supervisor who cares about his people, who presents their grievances to higher management, who listens sympathetically to their complaints, will be able to build cooperation and teamwork where little or none has existed before. And he will be the leader of the group in fact as well as in name.

The cohesive group asks much more of its supervisor, however. Tea and sympathy are not enough. Its members have already developed cooperation and a sense of teamwork among themselves. The group doesn't need to be made to *feel* important—it already *is* important, with the fruits of its victories over management and the supervisor to prove it. In other words, the successful supervisor must tailor his approach to the type of group he is in charge of and to the amount of functional power the group wields in the organization. Politics has been defined as the art of the possible, and management should be subject to the same definition. The manager who perceives the power situation realistically and makes the necessary concessions to circumstances is living out the spirit of that definition. One caveat: There is no sure formula for turning low-producing groups into high-producing ones, even though a generation of theorists and practitioners has been systematically overturning stones in its search for one.

Share the Decision-making Power

Caveat aside, there are things the supervisor can do to help get the cohesive group on his side. One set we have already discussed at length. In addition, he should share his real power with the leadership of the group—recognize, consult with, and be influenced by its leaders on just about any question of consequence. By so doing, he saves time and energy, expedites workable solutions to pressing problems, and permits the realistic adjustment of potential conflict situations. And under certain conditions, the manager should go even further and share his power with the entire group. Because the group and its leadership are as one, he can resort to group decision making without undermining the position of its leaders—or even seeming to try.

You may be surprised at the scope of decisions made with employee participation that have turned out to the advantage of all concerned. For example, take the touchy area of sales goals. The chemical department of McKesson & Robbins at one point enabled each salesman to play a major part in setting his sales goals for the forthcoming year. It gave this approach most of the credit for a substantial increase in sales volume per man after the system was first introduced. The salesmen have consistently set high goals for themselves, in some cases higher than the goals their managers have thought reasonable and attainable.

Again, take performance appraisal—a real hot potato because it's linked, whether people admit it or not, to salary increases and promotions. Yet, in the personnel department of a large chemical company, each professional man on the staff rates each member's performance including his own, and the results of the ratings are open to discussion among the group. The personnel director is not bound by the group consensus, but on several occasions the group's final rating has persuaded him to change his initial evaluation.

The same department has made the annual budget subject to group participation and one year reduced expenditures by 30 percent in the process. The biggest cost variable in the department, next to salary, was travel. So the department head asked each member of the group to answer these questions for himself: Where do I need to go? Where do I want to stay? For how long? How much do I need to spend? Then, the group as a whole set travel and training allowances on a per man, per year basis. The man with above-average training or travel needs is offset by the man whose budget need is below average. The group tackles each major budget item in a similar fashion.

Not that the successful application of group decision making is restricted to cohesive groups. We're arguing only that the approach is especially suited to such groups because the possibilities of achieving a consensus are the greatest. Thus

the supervisor can frequently achieve results that he couldn't
get in any other way, since the groups have a built-in tendency
to resent pressure and reject outside influence even—or
maybe even more—when the sources of pressure are
their own bosses.

Take the case of the industrial engineers in a metal-plating
plant who were repeatedly frustrated in their efforts to
figure out an equitable way of dividing up the girls' work.
Every time they made a suggestion, the girls were quick to
prove that it was unfair to someone. Finally the girls asked,
"Why not let us decide?" In a short while they had worked
out job allocations that even the engineers agreed were
superior to their own recommendations. In the solution there
were no losers. The girls had the satisfactions of exercising
greater control over their jobs and of accomplishing something
on their own. Management got a better decision and one
that was more likely to be followed—employees are more apt
to obey rules they set down themselves.

Guidelines for Group Participation

Participation by the group is no panacea, however. Let's
consider some of the ground rules for successful group decision making and also some of the problems. Let's assume,
for a moment, that you're a manager with little or no experience in holding group meetings of the problem-solving
variety. Your experience has been limited chiefly to informa-
tion-giving meetings in which you have offered people a
chance to ask questions or even raise objections. But that's
as far as you've ever gone. Now you're thinking of holding
a problem-solving meeting with your subordinates and you're
looking for some guidelines. We offer four that have helped
many managers in setting up and running such a meeting.

1. Select a problem where the acceptance of the solution by
the group is at least as important as the quality of the decision. Management, for example, doesn't care how vacations
are scheduled, so long as jobs are covered and the time
allotments are not exceeded. No vacation schedule will fail
to alienate some people, so the manager who passes this responsibility on to the group saves himself a headache. And,
because the group has made the decision, it's more likely to
be implemented by all the members.
2. Set clear limits to the area of discussion. You will obviously

want to keep the group from encroaching on areas of decision making that higher management has decided are not its concern. Suppose management is interested in refurbishing the ladies' lounge. You, as the supervisor, might say, "We have $500 allowed us. How should we spend it?" This is obviously vastly preferable to asking the question, "How much should we spend?" The chances of management's figures and the group's figures being the same or even coming close are small.

3. Make it crystal-clear whether you're asking the group for suggestions on how to solve the problem or delegating the solution to the group. Both approaches are valuable. But the group that thinks it's making the decision will be frustrated and embittered if you end up the meeting by vetoing its solution, which you have never thought of as more than a suggestion.

4. Don't confuse the cause of the problem with its solution, at least not at a problem-solving meeting. You might, for example, begin a meeting by saying that the question is: "How do we get production back to acceptable levels?" After much talk, the group may zero in on tardiness as the cause of the problem. Fine, but you're only halfway home. At this point you might want to ask a loaded question such as, "Well, boys, what do you think we should do about tardiness?" or "What do you think is a reasonable time to come to work?" You know what the solution is, but you want them to name it because, if they make the decision, it's more likely to stick.

But what if they decide that starting work fifteen minutes late consistently is O.K.? Then you will have learned a valuable lesson and the dangers of letting the group decide. You misjudged the temper of the group, not realizing that it was unable to come up with a solution that management would be willing to accept. Your bosses will feel you have made a mistake in holding that sort of meeting, and you will lose face with the group because you won't be able to go along with its decision. In other words, always know how much rope you have before you give it to the group, or you may be hung with it.

One note of caution: Successful group participation, whether formal or informal, depends in large part on the climate of the organization and the attitudes of the supervisors. Several years ago, Professor Mason Haire of the University of California and his associates surveyed 3,000 managers in fourteen countries, including the United States. Most managers in these countries viewed the ordinary individual as preferring to be directed, wishing to avoid responsibility, and having little talent for leadership. If the organizational climate is hostile to group participation, the supervisor shouldn't try for it. His efforts will probably fail and he will end up frustrated and in worse favor with the group than before he began. Group decision making is a delicate organism—you don't grow Jeffersonian practices in a Hamiltonian climate.

If the supervisor adopts group participation as a gimmick but really doesn't believe in it, castastrophe is on its way. "It is better to be feared than loved," said Machiavelli's prince. Maybe so. But the manipulation game is a dangerous as well as a shoddy one. Experience shows that employees sooner or later see through the pretense and, in the resulting atmosphere of resentment, the manager's position becomes almost intolerable. He's more despised than feared, more resisted than obeyed.

CONCLUSION

We've seen why groups develop and the important role they play in the on-the-job existence of most employees. We have explored some of the internal workings of groups— how their leaders emerge and how their norms develop. We have noted also that the mysterious, spontaneous, and seemingly inevitable development of informal organizations is simultaneously a boon, a spur, and a thorn to those responsible for running the organization. Without cohesive groups the organization would be hard-pressed to retain or motivate many of its most valued employees, but once it has them, it faces competition from the groups for their allegiance to their coworkers or to management.

How to reconcile the two allegiances? That's the challenge and the problem. The supervisor who shares power with the informal leadership and who involves the group directly in consulting and in making decisions will plaster over many differences between the organization and the group. The drives for status, recognition, power, initiative, and protection against pressure, which led many members to affiliate with groups in the first place, will be satisfied by the joint action of management and the group. In other words, group decision making is a mechanism for channeling energies into working with management that might otherwise be used in combatting it.

Observers have long recognized the swing position of the first-line supervisor: Caught in the middle, he represents management to the worker, and the worker to management. We would argue that the supervisor of a cohesive group, proud of its skills and independence and conscious of its position and power, will best serve management's interests by devoting most of his energies to representing the group to management, an activity which he alone is equipped by function and knowledge to do. In other words, he must somehow presuade management that the price of performance is to let the group have its way most of the time—that management should forget about its prerogatives and concentrate on results.

We don't want to sound like a Pollyanna. Given the proper encouragement, most of the time cohesive groups and management can reach an agreement. However, there will be other times when agreement between superiors and subordinates, between the groups and management, may be impossible—and output controls might be one of the issues involved. There are times when every manager must go contrary to the wishes of the group which he supervises. Call it what you will—the demands of a higher loyalty, bowing to the dictates of authority, or simply the price of survival.

SELECTED REFERENCES

Homans, G., *The Human Group,* Harcourt, New York, 1950, chaps. 3–6.

Maier, N., *Psychology in Industry,* Houghton Mifflin, Boston, 1965.

Roethlisberger, F., *Management and Morale,* Harvard University Press, Cambridge, Mass., 1941.

Sayles, L., *Behavior of Industrial Work Groups,* Wiley, New York, 1958.

Seashore, S., and Bowers. D., *Changing the Structure and Functioning of an Organization,* University of Michigan Press, Ann Arbor, 1963.

Whyte, W., *Street Corner Society: The Social Structure of an Italian Slum,* University of Chicago Press, Chicago (rev. ed.), 1955.

THE EDUCATION OF GREG HORNING:
FEBRUARY 15

Greg had sent out for lunch so that he could stay in his office and think this thing out. The turkey sandwich he had ordered tasted as if it had been made with yesterday's bread and he threw it, half-eaten, into the wastebasket. The session with Phillips that morning had pretty much killed his appetite, anyway.

Not that Phillips had told him anything he didn't already know. Instead of production increasing to anywhere near the projected goal of 110 percent during Greg's first month, it had fallen 5 percent and was now down to 80 percent of standard.

Greg took a sip of his coffee and began to pace back and forth in front of his desk. That only made his office seem smaller and more closed in. That was it. He felt so boxed in. The way Phillips had talked down to him that morning had made him feel like he was a kid in school again and hadn't prepared his lesson. But he *had* done his lesson, step by step, following all the rules. It's just that the answers kept coming out wrong.

It was the attitude of the group. They treated him like a kid, too. Of course, he was only twenty-three and fresh out of school. He had tried to be friendly and he had assumed that they would realize increased production was as much in their interests as it was in his. Maybe that had been his mistake. After all, why should he have expected people who get paid a straight hourly wage to understand that? They were taking advantage of him. Well, he'd just have to put the screws on them; make them work harder. If Phillips was going to be tough with him, he'd have to be tough with them. Greg Horning was not going to get boxed in. He broke his pacing in the middle of a turn and strode out of his office into the shop.

The men were all at their machines. Helen and Jeannette were just coming in. Phil Martello jerked his head around when Greg's office door slammed.

"I'd like your attention for a moment. I have something I want to say to you." The girls stopped, immediately silent, just inside the door. Everyone looked at Greg and he realized that he had spoken louder than was necessary. He began again, more slowly and quietly.

"I don't know whether or not you know it, but our department is doing very badly. Our job is to get the work out and we're not doing it. Production's going down, in fact. We've dropped 5 percent since I've been here. You've got to work harder and get more out. Maybe you don't realize that or maybe you're trying to make me look bad. I don't know. But we're all out of jobs if we don't keep up with the competition."

Greg looked at the faces of the workers. They were all as passive and expressionless as the turned-off machines in the room. Just like when he had come in that first day. Phil Martello was opening and shutting his mouth in an elaborate yawn and Rick Cohn was nodding slightly but regularly to some rhythm that was going through his head. What was the matter with them? Couldn't they understand anything?

"Okay if you don't care, I do," Greg snapped. We're going to increase the output of this department and we're going to start doing it now. Now, let's all get back to work."

Greg strode back to his office and slammed the door again. The group outside his window watched him for a few minutes before they returned to their machines. He was pacing back and forth in front of his desk.

Greg realized during the days following his talk to the group that it had made no difference in their performance. If anything, they were more openly hostile. Sometimes he regretted having said anything to them at all. Sometimes he wondered if taking a different tack would have been more effective. Sometimes—and this seemed strange to him—when he went back to that afternoon in his mind, all he could see was Rick Cohn's rhythmic head. That head, with all that hair, bobbing easily to some unheard beat. The boy irritated Greg, and yet he found himself intrigued by him.

Rick was unpredictable and inconsistent and Greg didn't understand what made the boy tick. But there was no denying that he was bright and that he could produce. Greg could remember several days when Rick had turned out a great deal over standard.

Gradually an idea began to form around the image of Rick's bouncing head. If only Greg could get him on his side, get him to set a higher standard for the group. That rhythm that Rick responded to—none of the others understood it any better than Greg did himself. Rick was less tied to the group than anyone else; he was the only one in there who was younger than Greg and he hadn't been in the plant too much longer than Greg either.

Greg decided that it was worth a try. He called Rick into his office one day, early in the afternoon.

"I've been watching you, Rick," he said with a smile that was tighter than he had planned, "and I think you've got potential. Those times when you've produced, *really* produced, I mean—don't think I haven't noticed it. It's the kind of thing we need around here. I know it's hard to keep it up all the time, especially with the relaxed pace of some of the others. But I think you can do it. No telling what it could mean for you. A bright boy like you, if he puts out, isn't going to stay with that machine for too long. There are places to move with this company, but I don't have to tell you that. Let's give it try—what do you say?"

Rick looked at Greg a long time before he said anything. It made Greg feel uncomfortable. Finally he began to speak, softly, and in time with the beat that sometimes moved his head.

"Gee, that's cool of you, man. I mean to tell me I'm good. A guy digs that, if you know what I mean. But I think you've got me all wrong. I mean, sure man, some days I really turn out the stuff. You know, some days you wake up and you feel great and you think you can do anything. So you get in here and here's this machine. So you say, 'O.K., machine, it's just you and me. We're really gonna make it today.' And you turn it out. But let's face it, man. It's a game. You know what I mean? And some days you feel like playing and some days you don't. Some days you wake up and you just know you're gonna win. But you don't make any promises. How do you know what you're gonna dig tomorrow? It might be a whole new thing by then. You know what I mean?"

"Well, I suppose I do, Rick," Greg answered. But there was more than a few years and a few inches of hair between these two young men. Greg had plans, goals, places to go, things to achieve. He didn't think it was all a game. He knew what he would "dig" tomorrow. He didn't know what Rick meant at all. Still, this was the closest he had come to anyone in the group. He just couldn't let him go without some kind of link being established between them.

"O.K., Rick, O.K.—it's like you say, but let's also say that starting next week you change places with Kilpatrick. Now, you don't have to make any promises. It's just that you've done good work and you deserve the break. And if you wake up next Monday and feel like winning, you do it big—for both of us. What do you say?"

"Well, O.K., man. That's cool. But who knows if I'm even gonna wake up Monday mornings. You know what I mean?"

Rick's response to his offer had not been what Greg had expected. Still, given Kilpatrick's track record, he felt it was a worthwhile move. What did he have to lose? He was putting Rick on a machine that had longer runs and fewer changes. A really good man could turn out a lot of work there. Even if he wasn't consistent, Rick would certainly produce more than Kilpatrick was. Kilpatrick was pretty old—almost retirement age—and he was inefficient. It was just as well to have him on a machine with shorter runs and more set-up time—a machine that would have lower output, anyway. Greg wrote up the notice of the change and went right out to put it up on the bulletin board.

After finishing a report later in the afternoon, Greg got up from his desk, stretched, and strolled over to the window. Out on the floor, he saw all the men, except Rick, grouped around Creegmore's machine. They were huddled together; Creegmore had his hand on Kilpatrick's shoulder; there were wide gestures and long looks toward Rick and toward him.

He started to go out, then stopped. They had read the notice. So what. If they wouldn't play ball with him, he wasn't going to play ball with them. Sure, Kilpatrick was an old-timer—but he just wasn't shaping up. None of them were, so they'd just have to take their lumps.

As Greg watched, the group broke up; shaking their heads and gesturing, the men went back to work. Except Creegmore. Greg saw him go over to Rick and take his arm. The boy stopped working, but he did not look up. Creegmore's hand was tight around Rick's arm and he bent his head forward as he talked.

Once again, Greg started to go out on the floor. If Creegmore was threatening Rick . . .

But as he got to the door, he saw their faces. Creegmore looked the way Greg had felt when he'd had Rick in his office. And Rick was smiling—the way he had smiled at Greg when he'd said, "But you don't make any promises. How do you know what you're gonna dig tomorrow?"

QUESTIONS

1. Why do you feel Greg's appeal to the group to turn out more work fell as flat as it did?

2. Using the terms developed in the chapter, how would you characterize the group Greg had to deal with? Why?

3. Do you think it would have made any difference to productivity if Greg had set a higher standard for the group?

4. How would you evaluate Greg's reasons for switching Rick and Kilpatrick?

IF YOU DON'T
COME IN
SUNDAY
DON'T COME
IN MONDAY.

THE
MANAGEMENT

4. Administering positive discipline

What do we mean by positive discipline? For a hint of the answer, consider two tales: one of savages and the other of civilized men.

Among the Xingu Indians in Brazil, there is no equivalent word for punishment; no one punishes, not even the chief of the tribe. Yet the tribe has its methods for dealing with those who violate its laws.

Take, for example, what happens when an Xingu steals something. The tribal elders send a man at dawn to make a speech in front of the thief's hut. His remarks are couched in general terms—no names are mentioned, and the thief is not identified. Then the speaker departs and the village is silent. The method is almost always successful: The thief returns what he has stolen. And if he doesn't, the punishment is left to his own conscience and his diminished ego. He is aware that the whole village knows he is a robber, although no one will breathe a word.

Our second tale concerns the Luddites, English textile workers who took to smashing power looms with heavy hammers as their way of protesting against the introduction of machinery during the Regency of George IV. The outraged establishment of the day—the year was 1813—passed a bill imposing the death penalty on Luddites caught destroying frames and looms. Byron protested that only two things were wanting to convict and condemn a man under the bill: "twelve butchers for a jury and a Jeffreys [notorious hanging judge of the late Stuart period] for a judge."

However, reluctance to enforce the decree was not caused by a deficiency of the legislation. What was erroneous was the apparent assumption behind it: that a sufficiently severe punishment would prevent the crime. Actually, in the English law of the period, the punishments were frequently more criminal than the crimes. Stealing a loaf of bread was a hanging offense and so were countless other acts that we would regard as minor crimes. What happened as a consequence of these punitive laws? The hangman worked overtime and a large proportion of the population so resented the savage punishments that they became accomplices to crime. But we lack any evidence that the penalties acted as a deterrent.

Our two tales encompass a couple of morals as well as a partial definition of positive discipline. The dual morals are pretty clear, we think. The first is that the prime function of discipline is not to make the punishment fit the crime but to administer it in a way that will prevent a particular offender, at least, from committing the crime again. The second shows that the effectiveness of the discipline has nothing to do with the severity of the punishment. If anything, the ratio is inverse. Incidentally, there's more in Webster than lexicography: The last definition given of discipline is "punishment."

You may feel that our analogies are farfetched. What do the Luddites and the Xingu's have to do with constructive discipline in an office or plant in the 1970s in the U.S.A.? Quite a lot, we feel. We confess that we deliberately chose our exotic examples, at least in part, to illustrate the universality of our points. However, let's turn to something more familiar and consider a typical case of how a disciplinary situation evolves in a company setting.

A FEW SHORT BEERS

"That damn Reardon must have stopped off for some beers again at Croning," Rickey Allen swore to himself, looking at his watch. It was seven minutes after the end of the lunch period and still no Reardon.

Rickey was in charge of the pickling operation in a midwest wire mill. Tom Reardon, who worked on one of the pickling tanks, was one of Allen's best men—except for one failing. He frequently had lunch at a neighborhood bar. And when he did, he took his time getting back on the job.

Just then Allen was called to the phone. When he came back a few minutes later, he spotted Reardon all right—with a big grin on his face, shooting the breeze with Joe DiBona on number four station.

Rickey wasted no time in getting within earshot of Reardon and DiBona. "Quit the yacking, Tom, and get back to work," he ordered. "You're ten minutes late already."

The grin on Tom Reardon's face froze and a flush crept up his cheeks.

"Lay off, Rickey. I put in a hell of a morning's work and I'm entitled to a little break."

"That's not the point, Tom, and you know it. You're making a habit of coming back to work with half a load on, goofing off, and holding up the rest of the guys—that's the point."

"The hell you say," Reardon shot back. "You can't crucify a guy for having a few short beers. It's a free country and if I want to have a couple of beers with my lunch that's my business."

"And it's my business to see that you're at the pickling tank and working when you're supposed to be," Allen retorted. "Now get over to that tank—pronto."

Reardon didn't budge. He just jutted his jaw out as the flush deepened toward purple.

"Wait a minute, Rickey, just you wait a minute! You're making a big production about always being where you're supposed to be. The way you talk you'd think that you were always around when we needed you. When we had trouble with that 380 wire last week, we had one hell of a job flushing you out. It seems you were with your buddies in production control—probably settling the affairs of the nation," Reardon added sarcastically after a short pause.

"I was there on department business—and you know it," Allen shouted.

"I know no such thing," Reardon roared back.

"You're insubordinate, Reardon. Get your gear and check out. I'm suspending you for the rest of the day. Maybe that'll get the message through your thick skull about who's running this shop."

Commentary on "A Few Short Beers"

One message of our little vignette is that Rickey Allen wasn't running his department by the end of the conversation. He had abdicated control and let his temper take over. The case is an all too typical escalation of the disciplinary situation. The boss observes a laxity, usually (as with Rickey Allen) not for the first time. And of itself, the offense is not earthshaking. Reardon was, after all, only seven minutes late coming back from lunch. He wasn't drunk, just talkative. And he was an outstanding worker who had done his customary good job all morning.

Yet, as often happens and for reasons that usually defy rational analysis, this time the supervisor, in this case, Rickey Allen, flipped. His approach to Reardon was emotional and harsh, while Reardon's resentment was instant and equally harsh—a kind of emotional reflex. His resentment, in all likelihood, had three bases: He naturally resented Allen's approach; it was apparently the first time he had been reprimanded for coming back a little late—the first time is not the time to talk tough; and finally, Reardon knew he was good, and good men know they don't deserve to be on the receiving end of this kind of treatment.

From here on, things went the only way they usually go under such circumstances: Anger begets anger, accusations lead to counteraccusations and to a conclusion in which both parties are losers. In our case, of course, as the man who started the chain reaction, Rickey Allen was primarily at fault—the real spree was his. We say "primarily" because, ideally, Tom Reardon should have returned a soft answer and (with luck) turned away wrath. But in the real world, seldom does it happen that way. The burden of guilt rests with the man who strikes the first blow, hurls the first insult, raises the initial provocation.

Like most supervisors caught in a similar dilemma, Rickey Allen had a second chance—all it takes to succeed are magnanimity, common sense on both sides, and luck. If Rickey came in the next morning and sincerely apologized to Tom for losing his temper, assuming Tom hadn't quit already (part of what we meant by luck), and if he was willing to discuss, calmly and rationally, two questions (Tom's occasional tardiness after lunch and his own absences from the department), the situation just might resolve itself satisfactorily. In a union plant, however, the whole sorry mess would probably be beyond redemption. Tom Reardon would have immediately contacted the steward, who would have been delighted to file a grievance he was bound to win. To accuse a subordinate of "having half a load on," with no proof and in front of a third party, is to ensure the reversal of whatever penalty the supervisor imposes. However, the fact that Rickey had his emotions on so loose a leash indicates that he was probably functioning in a nonunion setting.

We dwelt, in our case, on the negative side of positive discipline (negatives are always more dramatic), on an instance where the offense was minor, the penalty excessive, and the manner of handling it calculated, if not guaranteed, to make the offender both repeat the particular offense and broaden the scope of his offenses. In short, our case was a distillation of what the supervisor shouldn't do.

CONDITIONS OF COMPLIANCE

Let's reverse the coin and try to be constructive. How can the supervisor administer discipline in a way that motivates, not demotivates—that is positive, not negative. In other words, to return to our basic theme, how should the supervisor behave when discipline is called for and he wants both to stop whatever laxity has occurred and to maintain his subordinate's overall performance at its current level or improve it? He has accomplished little if his manner of handling the problem has convinced his subordinate that it's altogether too risky to repeat the offense if he wants to keep his job, but at the same time has motivated him to seek out more protected areas in which he can play saboteur. This is a fairly frequent outcome of a disciplinary encounter.

TIMING

To suggest a few guidelines: To start off, the supervisor shouldn't procrastinate in administering discipline. The longer he postpones reproof or punishment after he has observed the violation, the more likely he is to get a "who—me?" reaction from the violator. Sure, he's done something wrong. Nonetheless, he's almost certain to resent his superiors playing a cat-and-mouse game with him.

Take Charley, who has been warned by his boss, not once but several times, to keep the guard down on his machine. However, because he has a "it-can't-happen-to-me" outlook, the guard never stays down much longer than the boss remains in clear view. However, the day comes when the boss catches him unawares but says nothing. Therefore Charley concludes he hasn't been noticed. Not so. The boss hasn't quite made up his mind what to do—besides, it will do Charley good to "sweat it out." At the end of the shift four or five hours later, the boss lowers the boom with a two-day layoff. Not too harsh perhaps, under the circumstances, but that's not how Charley looks at it. The delay has given him a chance to build a case, in his own mind, that the boss bears him a grudge, otherwise he would have looked the other way or acted on the spot.

Like most useful guidelines, this one has its exceptions. For example, if the boss breaks up an argument between two of his men and he knows one of them is a wise guy and a bully, that's not the correct psychological moment to talk to him. The man is in no condition to listen, and things are almost certain to get worse as he responds to the boss's words with threats or abuse. Furthermore, as we saw with Rickey Allen, if the boss is angry, it's no time for him to talk over a problem with an employee. He should wait until he cools off before talking. Also, sometimes the man's guilt isn't clear or it takes time and consulation to establish the penalty. What's the proper course under these circumstances? The supervisor should notify the man on the spot that he's well aware of what's going on, but it's going to take a little time—spelled out, whenever possible (twenty-four hours, forty-eight hours, or whatever)—to determine the facts and to fix the punishment.

TONE

The next prerequisite is to administer discipline impersonally.
A tall order, certainly. The disciplinary interview is inevitably
an emotonally charged situation in which the violator tends
to feel resentful even if guilty, and the supervisor feels angry
or at least righteously indignant, in part to protect himself
from any guilt feelings at having to hurt someone else. The
best that he can do is to approximate the impersonal, that
is, to administer discipline in a way that will do minimum
damage to his future relations with his subordinate.

He shouldn't hesitate to speak in very specific terms of
what the man has done wrong. If he's hesitant to discuss the
matter, he'll probably fog the issue or even raise doubts as to
its existence. And he shouldn't be apologetic about either the
rule or the penalty he's going to impose for breaking it. Even
if he has reservations about the rule, the least appropriate
place to lobby against it is during a disciplinary interview.
The apologetic approach is bound to be interpreted in ways
that will defeat the purpose of the discipline. His subordinate
will conclude—and correctly—either that he doesn't agree
with the rule, that he's being hypocritical in enforcing it, or
that he simply lacks the guts to back it up, or possibly all
three.

In setting the tone of the disciplinary interview, the supervisor wants to avoid personalities as he would the plague.
Phrases such as "I've really gone out on the limb for you"
or even worse, "How could you do this to me?" have no
place in this discussion. They get across a dual and dangerous
message: He's judging the whole man, and things between
them are never going to be the same again.

How does the supervisor set the stage for the relatively
impersonal disciplinary interview? First, he states the problem
as clearly, precisely, and unemotionally as he's capable of
doing. Then he encourages his subordinate to take as much
time as he needs to tell his side of the story—not of *why*
it happened but of *how*.

Once he's heard him out, he imposes the penalty, again in
the lowest key of which he's capable—no histrionics. Then
he sits back and listens to the employee's objections as to
why he's being unreasonable, unfair, arbitrary, and otherwise
unethical. If he has done his job properly, the boss can
afford to disregard the substance of the objections and take
them in stride as a necessary, even salutory case of "blowing
off steam" and a precondition of accepting the penalty.
People complain about the penalty when their real grievance is
at being caught.

The next, and most important, stage is where the supervisor abandons impersonality and reverts to his customary helpful role. Let's assume that he's just given a two-day layoff to a man who offered no better explanation for his habitual tardiness than a faulty alarm clock or a poor memory about setting it. He wants the tardy worker to suggest a plan for getting to work on time—get up a half-hour earlier every morning, join a car pool, move closer to the plant, buy a new and noisier alarm clock. If the man comes up with his own solution, he's more likely to follow it. Of course, if he has no plan, then it's up to the boss to come up with one.

FOLLOW-THROUGH

The supervisor isn't out of the woods yet. Once he has disciplined a subordinate, it's crucial that he treat him as he did before his reproof. The boss may feel like avoiding him for several days after the interview. That's only human. But he shouldn't succumb to the temptation. Instead, he should go out of his way, if necessary, to find some occasion to be friendly, to get across the message: "It was the act I was punishing; you, I like and respect. The past is past, and the only things that matter are the present and the future."

In talking of positive discipline, we should perhaps define it a little differently. It is discipline that simultaneously reinforces the rule and motivates the violator to comply with it and the other company rules in the future. As we have seen, it rests on a good deal more than the fairness of the penalty. Timing, tone, and manner are a large part of the battle. The boss who takes a morally superior tone or who plays judge and treats the penalty as a reprisal is not administering positive discipline. Above all, the supervisor must remain impersonal. As Cummings and Sholl wrote in *Personnel*, "There is all the difference in the world between falling down on the job and being accused of being a loafer, of committing an unwise act and being told you're a fool. The employee will remember and instinctively resent any downgrading aimed at him personally."

The Problem of Consistency

Part of the problem is that, among various punishments, the most that can be argued is that some are more unfair than others. Obviously, it's unfair when one supervisor, all other things being equal, imposes a penalty harsher than that imposed by another supervisor in the same plant for the same offense. And it's a common occurrence, at least in many non-union plants where the grievance procedures and practices are rudimentary and the communications flow is constipated, that rules are made on high by managers with little or no understanding of the informal standards that exist at the level where the rules are broken and presumably are enforced.

We use the words "presumably are enforced" because, when a lot of people feel a rule or a law is unreasonable, they will refuse to obey it—witness our experience with the not so noble experiment of prohibition and our present problems with people smoking pot. At the same time, a division of opinion usually arises among the law enforcers over a law or a regulation that is widely held to be unreasonable. To some, a rule is a rule and it's their duty to enforce it, in sorrow and anger perhaps, but enforce it they will. Others will either ignore the violation although they are aware of it, or recognize the violation but somehow neglect to impose the penalty even when it is mandatory.

Consider, for example, what happened during a simulation session at one of the Bell System's operating units. The instructor described a situation in which a supervisor caught a man working on a telephone pole without a safety belt. The official penalty for the violation was a layoff. Twenty-five percent of the foremen in the session said they would look the other way and ignore the violation. In 60 percent of the simulated cases where the foreman discussed the violation with the man, he admitted it, but in only 15 percent of these cases did the foreman lay the worker off. Obviously, the rule had broken down. Most of the foremen felt that either the rule or the penalty was unreasonable and they refused to enforce it. However, we believe that, in real life, the percentage of foremen who would prefer not to catch the violator would be much higher than it was in the simulation exercise. This way, they would minimize the possibility of getting into hot water with higher management for not punishing the offender.

Also, in real life the grapevine would have been at work exposing inconsistencies in the enforcement of the rule and contributing to a vicious cycle. The greater the inconsistencies of application, the less respect for the rule itself and the fiercer the resentment at those who followed the letter of the rule. In the end, we suspect, higher management would face two choices: either to set up a system of continuing surveillance to make sure that a largely discredited penalty was enforced, or to yield as gracefully as possible and modify the penalty. In the meantime, there are three lessons that an employee caught violating the regulation and punished as prescribed might learn from the episode: (1) He must not repeat the violation, (2) he must be sure not to get caught again, and (3) his supervisor is unfair and unreasonable. We think lessons (2) and (3) are the ones the average employee would learn from the experience.

What's the Matter with Punishment?

Let's look a little deeper at the problem of penalties and punishments. When we maintained that all punishments are unfair, we meant that it's important to recognize that a penalty is not the consequence of violating a rule but, instead, of being caught violating the rule. The distinction is crucial. Getting way with murder is difficult in the literal sense because of the resources the community brings to bear on a capital crime, but this is not so with most lawbreaking or rule violation. The relationship is like that between the total iceberg and the visible portion—with two-thirds submerged and unseen. And it's one big reason why discipline is so difficult to administer. More often than not, it appears to be punitive even when it isn't—and in terms of consequences, appearances count more than reality. The employee interprets the punishment not as the end result of the remorseless turning of wheels by an even-handed justice but as a personal act based on his superior's desire to get even with him, to show him who's boss, or simply because "he's got it in for me." This is rationalization, of course—for every boss who is unfair, ten appear to be. Punishment, in other words, contains within itself inherent elements of unfairness that cause the penalizer to appear unjust because, for the few who are caught and disciplined, the many who are equally guilty but undetected go scot-free.

Are we building up to the conclusion that, because all punishment contains an element of injustice, all punishment should be discontinued because it contributes nothing to positive discipline? In fact, its contribution is negative: Largely due to the aspect of unfairness, any punishment breeds resistance, encourages subterfuge, and undermines the employee's willingness to make future contributions to the organization.

Would that it were possible to dismiss the case for discipline or even the occasional imposition of penalties for wrongdoing. With all the problems involved, some of which

were just considered, discipline and punishment still play a
necessary role both in the community at large and within the
corporation.

What Discipline Should Accomplish

What does discipline accomplish? Why are penalties sometimes
necessary? The manager who disciplines a subordinate accomplishes four things:

1. He strengthens the rule and expresses his confidence in jt
by his enforcement. Rules, like muscles, atrophy through
disuse.
2. He corrects the individual's breach of the rules and warns
him that he must comply with them in the future or face more
serious consequences.
3. He reminds the man's coworkers of the existence of the
rule and of the gravity with which it is regarded. Occasional
references to the possibility of discipline help some people
to obey the rules of the game. As one man put it, "If you can
sneak nuts and bolts out of the plant in your lunch box, you
start trying to take spare parts and accessories out next.
It's much better if you know that they are going to check
your lunch box every night and you can't take out the
smallest thing. Then you don't get into bad habits."
4. Finally, disciplining the violator reassures the vast majority
who respect the rules not because they fear punishment but
because they believe in doing things right. Time out for
introspection. Haven't you ever resented the overly lenient
superior who let someone else get away with murder, though
it didn't happen to be your particular temptation? And
haven't you ended up breaking the rule yourself when he
persisted in his indulgence?

   We know of a case in an advertising agency where a
particularly sharp copywriter took advantage of his presumed
indispensability and started coming in thirty to fifty minutes
later each day than the other copywriters on the staff. But
not for long. After waiting for a few weeks to see whether
their coworker was going to be disciplined and brought into
line, the other copywriters felt free to break the rules too.
Now all the copywriters arrive at least a half-hour after the
nominal start of the working day. The moral is obvious: If the
violator isn't disciplined, the rest of the group, out of resentment at management or a natural desire to improve their

lot, will imitate him. An illegal perquisite is still a perquisite—with its currency undevalued.

Most people in an organization tend to obey most of the rules most of the time. The supervisor's role would be insupportable if they didn't—he would have to spend four-fifths of his time and energy spotting and correcting infractions. On the other hand, as we have suggested, the way of the transgressor seems to exert a real pull on many people—all they need is tangible evidence that other people have gotten away with it. D. H. Lawrence quipped that "mankind invented sin in order to enjoy the feeling of being naughty." Rulebreaking perhaps affords analogous attractions.

John Quincy Adams confided, somewhere in the five thousand or so printed pages of his interminable diary, that the principal social utility of religion is to keep man law-abiding. In his dismal view of humanity, it is fear of retribution in the next world—hell's fires, no less—that intimidates man into towing the line in this one. Whatever operative effect this sanction had in the days of Adams has vanished by now. If fear is going to be a motivator, then we must have recourse to more immediate penalties.

ALL TOTALED . . .

We have seen the case for punishment: Without the felt presence of other worldly sanctions, the existence of formal rules and the occasional imposition of penalties perform a therapeutic function, not in terms of what they accomplish in reforming the rulebreaker but in terms of what they do to prevent more dutiful employees from succumbing to temptation. In short, punishment does fulfill a preventive function, although not the one usually ascribed to it.

On the other hand, we're acutely aware of the deficiencies in any punishment. It is almost always resented, it frequently does permanent damage to the relations between superior and subordinate, and it very infrequently results in a change of attitude by the employee toward the offense for which he was punished. He merely redoubles his precautions against being caught again.

THE "HOT STOVE" APPROACH—PREDICTABILITY, FLEXIBILITY, IMPARTIALITY

One possible way of restating the problem of how to achieve positive discipline is to determine the conditions under which the employee feels the least resentment toward punishment. Some we have already dealt with in talking about the tone and manner in which discipline should be administered. These and others were incorporated into what the late Douglas McGregor of M.I.T. called "the hot stove rule." The process of effective discipline is similar to what happens when you touch a hot stove—the reaction you get is immediate, without warning, impersonal, and consistent.

The last conditions are the most important. When a superior enforces discipline, he must do it in such a way that the act and the discipline seem almost one. The employee therefore feels that the discipline is directed not against him but against the act—hence the need to administer discipline impersonally and impartially. If the boss does a good job, the employee will still feel resentful, but he will also feel somewhat guilty and foolish about his resentment—akin to the man who kicks the stove that has burned his hand, and his animosity probably will be neither deep nor lasting. He will feel, after a time, that the boss was performing a reluctant duty and only doing what he was paid to do—enforce the rules.

One element in the hot-stove rule deserves closer examination. It is consistency. The supervisor, of course, doesn't administer discipline in a vacuum. Other managers are handing out penalties to their subordinates for similar violations. We believe that managers should have a good deal of leeway in the kind of penalties they prescribe and we're against drawing up and posting standard and compulsory penalties for each violation. Carried to its logical extreme, for example, a mandatory discharge for stealing would mean that the employee who takes a box of paper clips would receive the same penalty as someone who rifles the safe. In short, no two offenses are really the same, nor are any two offenders.

On the other hand, in the interests of fairness and consistency, managers should get together among themselves and agree on a range of punishments. Any manager who goes outside the limits should be subject to severe discipline himself. But what if managers can't or won't agree on the same penalties? Then top management may feel that it's necessary to extend the list of fixed and formal penalties to include every infraction in the book. Consistency isn't perfect justice, but it's still justice.

Consistency contains the seeds of possible injustice, but it appeals to a strong need in almost every individual. Most of us want to know the limits of permissible behavior. And most of us tend to be unhappy and insecure in a situation where we are unsure what is expected of us. Child psychologists, for example, have found that children usually are not happier when they are given absolute freedom. One reason they get into so much mischief is that they are trying to find out how much they can get away with. Many adults are obsessed with the same question—they have to know the answer to "How far can I go?"

Consistency doesn't mean, however, that you determine the penalty only on the basis of the offense and ignore the history of the man who committed it. Consider, for example, three men who have been caught shooting craps behind the machines instead of working. The first man, a two-year employee with a barely satisfactory performance record, was given a three-day layoff a few months before for the same offense. He's discharged. The second man is also a short-term, not particularly distinguished employee, but he has no previous gambling record. He gets a three-day layoff. The third man, also without a gambling record, is an above-average worker with fifteen years' service. He's given a written warning. A higher consistency has governed management's decisions here. The key point about consistency in handing out penalties is that if two men with approximately the same personal histories commit the same offense, they should be treated equally. In summary, the goal to be sought in administering justice with consistency is a blend of predictability, flexibility, and impartiality.

DISCIPLINE WITHOUT PUNISHMENT

With all its virtues, the hot-stove rule contains inherent weakness. Every time the manager follows it, he puts his future relationships with a subordinate on the line. At best, he minimizes resentment—but does not eliminate it. Let's revert once more to definitions. Punishment is the last definition of discipline given in Webster. What's the first? "Training which corrects, molds, strengthens or perfects." We'll risk a definition of our own: Discipline is the well-tempered reprimand, one that the object accepts without resentment and that conditions his future behavior. We've pretty much concluded that punishment doesn't pay and we're interested only in discipline that prevents future wrongdoing.

We mentioned John Quincy Adams and his famous diary.

Let's cite him again, this time in an illustration of the well-tempered reprimand. His grandson, in his autobiographical *The Education of Henry Adams*, tells the story of what happened when, one summer morning at six years of age, he vehemently objected to going to school. He was winning the battle with his mother when the door to the President's library opened and the old gentleman slowly came down the stairs. Putting on his hat, he took the boy's hand without a word, walked him all the way to school, and didn't leave him until he was deposited in his seat.

Sixty years later, looking back on the episode, his grandson reflected that

> The point was that this act, contrary to the inalienable rights of boys and vilifying the social compact, ought to have made him dislike his grandfather for life. He could not recall that it had this effect, even for a moment. With a certain maturity of mind, the child must have recognized that the President, though a tool of tyranny, had done his disreputable work with a certain intelligence. He had shown no temper, no irritation, no personal feeling, and had made no display of force. Above all, he had held his tongue. During their long walk, he had said nothing. He had uttered no syllable of revolting cant about the duty of obedience and the wickedness of resistance to law; he had shown no concern in the matter; hardly even a consciousness of the boy's existence.[1]

On one point we have no evidence: Did the boy Henry Adams ever try to get out of going to school again? We suspect no, certainly not when the President was within hearing distance.

We're not recommending the wordless reprimand as a model. What worked between the eighty-year-old President and the precocious boy who was his awestruck grandson might be a dismal failure if a manager tried a variation of it with a subordinate, although one element in the encounter, the absence of "revolting cant," is one we commend to every manager in any disciplinary encounter.

Our main point is different. Whereas in meting out punishment the manager has to remain impartial and impersonal in order to defuse a potentially explosive situation,

---

[1] Henry Adams, *The Education of Henry Adams*, Houghton Mifflin, Boston, 1918, p. 13.

in administering a reprimand the manager can and should tailor his approach to the personality of the man. Because his basic role is that of a counselor and not that of a judge, he has much greater freedom of action.

An Individually Tailored Approach

Let's consider several examples of discipline without punishment, with the only thing in common between them the fact that each one worked. Take Daredevil Dan, who operated his forklift truck as if the main aisle of the plant were the Indianapolis Speedway. One morning, what the manager had long been expecting happened: Dan dropped and ruined half a shift's work of finished material. The manager could have fired him or given him a stiff layoff. However, Dan, except for his speeding, was a first-class operator.

He could have embarrassed Dan by making a snide remark in front of the whole crew, such as "I think we're going to trade in your lift truck for a perambulator." Clever enough to get a yack from the boys and certain to wound a show-off like Dan. But the manager reasoned it would accomplish the opposite of his objective. Being a show-off, Dan would probably drive more wildly than ever just to show everyone that the boss's cracks didn't bother him a bit.

What to do? The manager got Dan in private and cut him down with a couple of withering sentences: "Everyone's been telling me what a fool I am for letting you run that jeep. But I've been insisting that you were going to grow up one of these days." He left it at that. He gave Dan the opportunity to "grow up" without making him feel that he had to prove to the rest of the crew that he was unaffected by criticism. Furthermore, the manager assumed that Dan had a better side and appealed to it by putting on record his previous expressions of confidence. Dan, happily, rose to the occasion and was content to prove his mastery of the lift truck without endangering life and property.

Another case was a clerk-typist we'll call Lazy Leona, whose problem simply was that she was unambitious and bridled at the suggestion of hard work. However, her basic skills were excellent and her supervisor, although sorely tempted, decided against firing her. Motivating her was practically out of the question, the supervisor concluded. Counseling, an appeal to Leona's sense of fairness and responsibility, was bound to fail—she didn't have any, and such a session would probably result in tears, resentment, and mutual recrimination.

Discipline in Leona's case consisted of a four-pronged attack on the problem: (1) The supervisor gave Leona plenty to keep her busy and checked her progress regularly. (2) She gave her additional chores that forced her to work harder, although no harder than most of the grils, to get time for her additional tasks. (3) She spelled out standards and set a time limit each time she gave Leona a nonroutine job. (4) She moved Leona's work station to a spot among a hardworking group who, by example and/or pressure, would probably help Leona to turn in a fair day's work. In short, the supervisor gambled on having Leona either shape up or quit and, in this instance, her gamble paid off.

Then there's Superior Sam, an intelligent man and first-class operator whose problem was that the job was too easy for him. He frequently got bored and his favorite way of relieving boredom was to go visiting other workers in his own department and some of his buddies in other departments. Something had to be done. Yet when he was working, Sam was tops. Obviously, the management had to crack down on Sam, but it had to do it in a way that would spare his feelings and not give him the impression that he was being singled out and persecuted.

Sam was a reasonable man—that was the core of insight on which the manager based his strategy. The first step was to get the facts. He took notes on the time Sam actually spent doing the things he was supposed to do. Next, he made up a facsimile time card showing how much time Sam would have lost for the week if the time card were real and the time he spent away from the job were being deducted. Finally, he confronted Sam and let the evidence speak for itself. There were no histrionics, no verbal accusations, and everything was played in a low key. And Sam being Sam and basically rational and responsible, the approach worked.

We recall another case where a manager had a similar problem with Gregarious George, an amiable, not too bright subordinate who spent a good deal of time visiting other departments. The manager could have built up a case against this man (incidentally, a good worker when he worked) and eventually thrown the book at him. He preferred to handle the case differently. Whenever he suspected where the subordinate was visiting, he tracked him down, sneaked up on him, and told him in piercing tones, "Go back to work!" Undignified? Yes. Time-consuming? Yes. However, the boss maintained good relations with the man. And after having been startled out of his wits on several occasions, the subordinate quit visiting around.

A Problem-solving Approach

Another alernative the manager should consider, particularly when he has several violators, is the problem-solving approach. We know of one example where tardiness among office employees had been averaging a high 10 percent. Management could have taken the route of cajolement, warnings, and eventual punishment of the outstanding offenders. Instead, the managers met with their employees and agreed on a tardiness target of 3 percent. During the next two years, the tardiness rate never exceeded that target. We doubt if any other approach would have accomplished as much—and this with no resentment or bad feelings among the employees. The target, after all, was self-imposed.

As we asserted at the beginning of this section, one advantage of choosing the path of discipline without punishment is that the supervisor can vary his repertoire. He may be gentle with one man and tough with another, or he may appeal to reason in one case and, with deliberate care, use emotion in a second. What works with the Superior Sams of this world will fail to make a dent on the consciences of the Gregarious Georges.

Obviously, the well-tempered reprimand—maybe it's more accurate to call it the tailor-made reprimand—doesn't always succeed. Daredevil Dan may continue to speed down the floor risking his life and limb. Lazy Leona may neither quit nor meet any of her deadlines. What then? Should the manager fall back on the traditional progression of penalties, oral admonition, written warning, layoff, and discharge, always bearing in mind the hot stove at each step?

CHESTER IRVING BARNARD (1886–1961)

Barnard was a rare combination—in the United States there has been no equal—of the extremely successful executive and theorist on the executive process. He was, at various times, president of the New Jersey Bell Telephone Co., Director of Relief in the state of New Jersey, president of the Rockefeller Foundation, and head of the U.S.O. during World War II (incidentally, according to him the most difficult post he ever held in his life). He wrote only two books, but one of them, *The Functions of the Executive,* from which the selection is taken, is for our money the most insightful and the most valuable book yet written on what it takes to be a twentieth-century manager. Barnard tells it the way it really is—and tells it in a way that the reader can use to enrich his own understanding.

Barnard was associated personally and intellectually with Mayo, and the work of each man complements the other. Mayo's accent, as dictated by his studies, was on the small industrial work group at the operator level. Barnard took the whole organization for his province but similarly stressed the importance of the informal organization. A quality that distinguishes Barnard from Mayo was that he had the subtler and the deeper mind. You have already read Mayo and you are about to read Barnard; obviously you can judge for yourself. But let's consider one more example—Barnard's discussion of leadership in his second book, *Organization and Management.* He defines leadership as "the quality of the behavior of individuals whereby they guide people or their activities in organized effort," by which he both denies the existence of leadership with a capital L and at least implies that leaders are made as much by conditions as they are by innate abilities. And he cautions us that leadership is a perilous undertaking for "that (selection) which is made by formal authority we call appointment (or dismissal), that by the informal authority we may call acceptance (or rejection). Of the two, the informal authority is fundamental and controlling." Working from that basic insight, Barnard lists the five qualities of leadership in descending order of importance—on first glance a surprise ranking—as (1) vitality and endurance, (2) decisiveness, (3) persuasiveness, (4) responsibility, (5) intellectual capacity. We haven't the space to summarize his discussion of the five qualities, and no summary could do it justice.

So far this has sounded like a fan letter for Barnard—and so far it has been. Barnard, let's admit, has his arid and unattractive side. The man himself was pompous; he had the self-conscious air of one who had walked with the captains and the kings. He wrapped his rare perceptions in the intellectual window-dressing provided by Pareto's theory, a process that added nothing to the substance of his thought and prevented many from understanding it. We suppose that Barnard, like many conservative intellectuals of the thirties, accepted Pareto as a refuge against Marx. George Homans, another conservative intellectual and a friend of Barnard's, can be presumed to speak for the rest: "I felt during the thirties that I was under personal attack, above all from the Marxists. I was ready to believe Pareto because he provided me with a defense."

Finally, Barnard was an elitist, one of those from Plato on down who felt that decisions on large and complex issues were the natural monopoly of a few who were qualified by experience and brains. For the proof, read his essay "Riot of the Unemployed" in which he describes how he manipulated the leaders of the unemployed into accepting his diagnosis of their problems and which he sums up with the words "I do not think I had ever before made a purely personal accomplishment the equal of this."

However, having redressed the balance, let's end positively. Barnard has less fire in his belly than Mayo or Taylor, much less humanity than McGregor, Rogers, or Bennis, and the least engaging style of any of our classic management thinkers; against this, he has one pretty potent advantage—he thought more deeply about management on the basis of more direct experience than the rest.

As for his books, first *The Functions of the Executive,* Cambridge, Mass., Harvard University Press, 1938: We recommend skipping Part I which is pretty much window dressing a la Pareto and likely to discourage anyone who isn't in a masochistic mood. Of the second, *Organization and Management,* Cambridge, Mass., Harvard University Press, 1948: We recommend especially chap. II, "Dilemmas of Leadership in The Democratic Process," chap. III, "Riot of The Unemployed," and chap. IV, "The Nature of Leadership."

The Theory of Authority*

The necessity of the assent of the individual to establish authority for *him* is inescapable. A person can and will accept a communication as authoritative only when four conditions simultaneously obtain: (a) he can and does understand the communication; (b) *at the time of his decision* he believes that it is not inconsistent with the purpose of the organization; (c) *at the time of his decision,* he believes it to be compatible with his personal interest as a whole; and (d) he is able mentally and physically to comply with it.

(a) A communication that cannot be understood *can* have no authority. . . . Now, many orders are exceedingly difficult to understand. They are often necessarily stated in general terms, and the persons who issued them could not themselves apply them under many conditions. Until interpreted they have no meaning. The recipient either must disregard them or merely do anything in the hope that that is compliance.

Hence, a considerable part of administrative work consists in the interpretation and reinterpretation of orders in their application to concrete circumstances that were not or could not be taken into account initially.

(b) A communication believed by the recipient to be incompatible with the purpose of the organization, as he understands it, could not be accepted. Action would be frustrated by cross purposes. The most common practical example is that involved in conflicts of orders. They are not rare. An intelligent person will deny the authority of that one which contradicts the purpose of the effort as *he* understands it. In extreme cases many individuals would be virtually paralyzed by conflicting orders. They would be literally unable to comply—for example, an employee of a water system ordered to blow up an essential pump, or soldiers ordered to shoot their own comrades. I suppose all experienced executives know that when it is necessary to issue orders that will appear to the recipients to be contrary to the main purpose, especially as exemplified in prior habitual practice, it is usually necessary and always advis-

---

* Reprinted by permission from Chester Irving Barnard, *The Functions of the Executive,* Harvard University Press, Cambridge, Mass., 1938, pp. 165–170. Copyright © 1938 by the President and Fellows of Harvard College.

able, if practicable, to explain or demonstrate why the appearance of conflict is an illusion. Otherwise the orders are likely not to be executed, or to be executed inadequately.

(c) If a communication is believed to involve a burden that destroys the net advantage of connection with the organization, there no longer would remain a net inducement to the individual to contribute to it. The existence of a net inducement is the only reason for accepting *any* order as having authority. Hence, if such an order is received it must be disobeyed (evaded in the more usual cases) as utterly inconsistent with personal motives that are the basis of accepting any orders at all. Cases of voluntary resignation from all sorts of organizations are common for this sole reason. Malingering and intentional lack of dependability are the more usual methods.

(d) If a person is unable to comply with an order, obviously it must be disobeyed, or, better, disregarded. To order a man who cannot swim to swim a river is a sufficient case. Such extreme cases are not frequent; but they occur. The more usual case is to order a man to do things only a little beyond his capacity; but a little impossible is still impossible.

Naturally the reader will ask: How is it possible to secure such important and enduring coöperation as we observe if in principle and in fact the determination of authority lies with the subordinate individual? It is possible because the decisions of individuals occur under the following conditions: (a) orders that are deliberately issued in enduring organizations usually comply with the four conditions mentioned above; (b) there exists a "zone of indifference" in each individual within which orders are acceptable without conscious questioning of their authority; (c) the interests of the persons who contribute to an organization as a group result in the exercise of an influence on the subject, or on the attitude of the individual, that maintains a certain stability of this zone of indifference.

(a) There is no principle of executive conduct better established in good organizations than that orders will not be issued that cannot or will not be obeyed. Executives and most persons of experience who have thought about it know that to do so destroys authority, discipline, and morale. For reasons to be stated shortly, this principle cannot ordinarily be formally admitted, or at least cannot be professed. When it appears necessary to issue others which are initially or apparently unacceptable, either careful preliminary education, or persuasive efforts, or the prior offering of effective inducements will be made, so that the issue will not be raised, the denial of authority will not occur, and orders will be obeyed. It is generally recognized that those who least understand this fact—newly appointed minor or "first line" executives—are often guilty of "disorganizing" their groups for this reason, as do experienced executives who lose self-control or become unbalanced by a delusion of power or for some other reason. Inexperienced persons take literally the current notions of authority and are then said "not to know how to use authority" or "to abuse authority." Their superiors often profess the same beliefs about authority in the abstract, but their successful practice is easily observed to be inconsistent with their professions.

(*b*) The phrase "zone of indifference" may be explained as follows: If all the orders for actions reasonably practicable be arranged in the order of their acceptability to the person affected, it may be conceived that there are a number which are clearly unacceptable, that is, which certainly will not be obeyed; there is another group somewhat more or less on the neutral line, that is, either barely acceptable or barely unacceptable; and a third group unquestionably acceptable. This last group lies within the "zone of indifference." The person affected will accept orders lying within this zone and is relatively indifferent as to what the order is so far as the question of authority is concerned. Such an order lies within the range that in a general way was anticipated at time of undertaking the connection with the organization. For example, if a soldier enlists, whether voluntarily or not, in an army in which the men are ordinarily moved about within a certain broad region, it is a matter of indifference whether the order be to go to A or B, C or D, and so on; and goings to A, B, C, D, etc., are in the zone of indifference.

The zone of indifference will be wider or narrower depending upon the degree to which the inducements exceed the burdens and sacrifices which determine the individual's adhesion to the organization. It follows that the range of orders that will be accepted will be very limited among those who are barely induced to contribute to the system.

(c) Since the efficiency of organization is affected by the degree to which individuals assent to orders, denying the authority of an organization communication is a threat to the interests of all individuals who derive a net advantage from their connection with the organization, unless the orders are unacceptable to them also. Accordingly, at any given time there is among most of the contributors an active personal interest in the maintenance of the authority of all orders which to them are within the zone of indifference. The maintenance of this interest is largely a function of informal organization. Its expression goes under the names of "public opinion," "organization opinion," "feeling in the ranks," "group attitude," etc. Thus the common sense of the community informally arrived at affects the attitude of individuals, and makes them, as individuals, loath to question authority that is within or near the zone of indifference. The formal statement of this common sense is the fiction that authority comes down from above, from the general to the particular. This fiction merely establishes a presumption among individuals in favor of the acceptability of orders from superiors, enabling them to avoid making issues of such orders without incurring a sense of personal subserviency or a loss of personal or individual status with their fellows.

Thus the contributors are willing to maintain the authority of communications because, where care is taken to see that only acceptable communications in general are issued, most of them fall within the zone of personal indifference; and because communal sense influences the motives of most contributors most of the time. The practical instrument of this sense is the fiction of superior authority, which makes it possible normally to treat a personal question impersonally.

THE SINGLE-PENALTY APPROACH

We would argue that each manager should consider the merits of what we call the single-penalty approach, under which the only penalty imposed on an employee is discharge. Put that way, it sounds as punitive as hell—but it's actually the reverse.

The approach, to our knowledge, was developed first in a Douglas fir plywood mill with several hundred hourly paid and unionized employees and a history of bad union–management relations and excessive recourse to arbitration. An analysis of all disciplinary cases over a three-year period showed not a single favorable result from any of the penalties imposed. This led logically to the conclusion that punishment doesn't pay and that a new system of discipline should be substituted for the old.

But what new system? Management wanted one that was oriented toward the future, not the past. It wanted to avoid future trouble, not to apportion the proper punishment for a particular violation. "We feel that if we condemn an individual we give up all hope of changing him," said John Duberman, industrial relations director of the mill at the time the new approach was developed.

The new policy consisted of five basic steps:

1. With the first offense, the foreman issued the employee a casual, friendly reminder on the job.
2. If there was another episode within four to six weeks, the foreman had the employee come into his office for a serious but friendly chat.
3. A further episode within six weeks involved a repetition of step 2, but with a difference: First, the foreman in charge of the shift was also present, and second, the possibility was raised with the employee that he might find the kind of strict discipline necessitated by the working conditions of a plywood mill distasteful. Also, he was reminded that vocational guidance was available at the personnel office. Afterwards, a summary of the conversation was incorporated in a letter sent to him.
4. Another episode within six to eight weeks of step 3, and the employee was called into the foreman's office, sent home for the rest of the shift with pay, and asked to mull over whether he thought he could live up to the company standards. At the same session, he was told that another occurrence

of the same offense within a reasonable time would lead to his termination. Duberman emphasized that "during steps one to four the employee is reminded of the requirements without any implication that if he does not conform, he deserves condemnation and punishment."
5. Termination without discussion.

Did the approach work? The answer is in the affirmative, at least during the period that Duberman reported on. In the first seven months, only three people went to step 4, of whom two quit after a period of a few weeks while the third saw the light and reformed. There were no terminations, and moreover, the morale of foremen and superintendents had measurably improved. Asserted Duberman: "For the first time they felt they had a strong, reliable and fair tool to deal with unsatisfactory work performance and breaches of discipline."

We're willing to accept Duberman's claims because the policy developed at the plywood mill meets so many of what we feel are the preconditions for positive discipline. We're only surprised that variations on the policy have not been more widely adopted. Apparently it takes the complete bankruptcy of the traditional disciplinary approach, plus the documentation of the bankruptcy, to persuade most managements to break the "cake of custom" and search around for a more effective alternative.

Achieving Positive Discipline

When we flag this policy as fulfilling the requirements for positive discipline, we have in mind principally four points:

1. The discussions between boss and subordinate in steps 1 to 4 put the emphasis where it belongs, not on fixing punishment and accepting blame but on the simple reminder of the rule, an attempt to understand why the employee violated it, and hopefully a statement from him of his intent not to repeat the violation.
2. The policy avoided souring the relationship between the superior and subordinate as long as there was any realistic possibility of salvaging him. We feel strongly that to forgo the intermediate penalty of the disciplinary layoff or suspension connotes a hard head, not a soft heart. The man who is laid off may return chastened and repentent, a mood that

usually passes quickly. More likely, he comes back to work in an even nastier mood than he had when he departed.

3. The policy postpones punishment until everyone, with the possible exception of the employee being dismissed, acknowledges that it's the only solution to the problem. We've seen the impact on the rest of the work force of what is regarded, wrongly or rightly, as an unfair discharge—transfers, quits, and silent sabotage by the remainder of the work crew are apt to follow. Every supervisor should remember that, even though the man he's dismissed is gone, the manner of his dismissal remains, perhaps to plague him.

4. The policy takes into account the existence in any work force of irredeemable troublemakers—admittedly, in another work situation they might not be beyond redemption at all—and the necessity of getting rid of them once their disruptive pattern has been established beyond doubt. In other words, every plant or office has its small quota of "rotten apples" who must be weeded out if the department is to remain efficient and the other employees are to avoid contamination by example. Justice Holmes upheld a Virginia statute requiring compulsory sterilization of certain mental defectives with the comment, "Three generations of imbeciles are enough." A similar ruthlessness in weeding out employees is justified after a certain number of sufficiently serious offenses.

DISCIPLINE HAS A CONTEXT

So far we have written as if the supervisor operated in a vacuum—as if the decision on whether or not to discipline and how much is his and his alone, and that he is a free agent in the disciplinary process with plenary power and responsibility. Such is typically not the case. The average manager, in imposing discipline, has limited discretion and is subject to being overruled. And, in many cases, the first-line manager has little or no power over certain categories of discipline. Under some circumstances, the only discretion he has is whether or not to look the other way.

What keeps the supervisor from disciplining any subordinate in any way he can think of? The first limitation on his freedom to administer discipline is internal—his own personality set. If this seems like a paradox, it's real enough. By and large, the aggressive, dominant supervisor, for example, belongs to the Papa Knows Best School and identifies very strongly with authority and the rules that buttress it. His attitude toward discipline tends, in turn, to be highly legalistic. To him, a rule is there to be enforced, irrespective of the consequences or what a less rigid personality would judge to be extenuating circumstances.

Other determining factors are the size of the supervisor's department and the state of the technology employed. The larger the number of men he supervises, the more likely he is to use the legalistic approach and settle for matching the letter of the penalty to the rule. He isn't necessarily more heartless or less aware of the dangers of distributing justice by formula. It's simply that he lacks any intimate knowledge of his subordinates' personalities as well as the time to pursue the path of the well-tempered reprimand.

The point about technology places the average supervisor in a shabby light. However, it's a point that must be made. Take the case of two supervisors. One is in charge of forty-seven spinners in a textile mill, doing unskilled, repetitive jobs that anyone can master within a week. Contrast this man with the supervisor in charge of a ten-man maintenance crew in a chemical plant, skilled craftsmen all, who have spent years mastering the intricacies of the complex, expensive equipment they keep in good working order. Which supervisor is likely to apply discipline without punishment, and which will meticulously fulfill the requirements of the hot stove rule? Make no mistake: Positive discipline takes time, patience, and plenty of thought. The easy way out always is to follow the letter of the law, and this is the way that comes naturally to many supervisors with employees whom they feel can readily be replaced.

MORE LIMITATIONS ON THE SUPERVISOR'S FREEDOM OF ACTION

In discipline, as in so many matters, the bosses call the tune and the lowly first-line supervisor has little choice except to dance to the tune set for him. If he has any leeway, he will tend to cultivate the disciplinary style that wins favor and approval from his superiors and avoid the style that results in disapproval or retaliation.

We remember the successful division head of a successful organization—in five years of his stewardship, the division had tripled its sales and quadrupled its profits. He reflected,

in a rare moment of introspection, "I've always thought of my
employees as the enemy." To be sure, he was seldom that
explicit about his views, but nonetheless they permeated the
organization. When an employee was suspected of any
offense, "guilty until proven innocent" was the attitude a boss
was expected to take, and if guilt was proved, the maximum
penalty was the mandatory one except on those occasional
instances when the division head reversed a subordinate's
verdict, abandoned consistency, and indulged himself in a
sentimental and quixotic gesture.

Finally, there's the situation, becoming less common over
the past decade but predominant in unionized plants, where
the supervisor has lost most of his power to administer
discipline. It was Georges Clemençeau, the principal architect
of French victory in World War I, who quipped, "War is too
important to be left to generals." In many corporations,
higher management takes a similar position: discipline is too
important to be left to supervisors. Serious cases of discipline
in the union plant—those involving work standards, frequent
garnishment, work stoppages, organized gambling, and similar
problems—are the province of the labor relations specialist,
armed with suitable training, an overview of the situation,
and, purportedly, greater objectivity. Even in areas like in-
subordination, absenteeism, and careless workmanship, where
he has nominally more leeway, the supervisor is frequently
obliged to consult with his superiors, perhaps the general
foreman or the personnel man, before making a decision.
And when his decision coincides with theirs, it holds. In
rare cases (usually when union–management relations resemble a truce between the Montagues and the Capulets),
discipline is housed in a straitjacket. The only hope of preserving the always fragile contract is to fall back on an
exhaustive enumeration of violations and penalties, with
no discretion left to anyone. Justice without mercy or common
sense, which is what this approach is all about, sometimes
keeps the peace.

We are aware that we have listed these last limitations on
the supervisor's freedom of action as if they were hateful.
And no wonder—that's the way we feel about them. However,
we recognize that they are sometimes necessary. In the normal plant or office setup, the supervisor with tact, patience,
and judgement can accomplish much more by applying
discipline without punishment, by postponing punishment
until the time when discharge is the only alternative, or, as a

minimum, by following the requirements of the hot-stove rule.

The trouble is that this procedure requires time, patience, the willingness to be reasonable, the ability to compromise— and on both sides. The totally intransigent employee, whether badly advised or hostilely motivated, will frustrate the efforts of the most determined supervisor. If it's only one or two men who are at fault, the effort justifies the failure. However, when the basic agreement, the implied contract to work, has broken down and what you have is a continual conflict between what the boss can exact and what the employee can get away with, it takes an autocratic, uniform hand to achieve even minimum results. Our only caveat would be the feeling that past supervisory laxness, indifference, or over-severity probably have had a lot to do with bringing about the conditions under which other supervisors have lost their power over discipline. The sins of the fathers—it's an old, old story . . .

ORDER GIVING

Why do we write about order giving right after discipline? What's the association? Is it simply that disobeying orders frequently gives rise to discipline?

Not at all. The similarities run deeper and are more subtle and more significant. We have already seen that much discipline fails in its avowed purpose—to motivate the employee not to repeat the offense. In turn, many orders fail in their avowed purpose—to motivate the employee to do what his superior wants him to do. Punishment alone seldom suffices to motivate the worker to mend his ways, and his obligation to obey is frequently insufficient to make him accept an order from a superior. Punishment and obedience are flimsy crutches for the same basic reason: They ignore the realities of human nature and rely on fear to the exclusion of any other motivator—and fear cows one man at the cost of inflaming five. Whatever it may do for the ego of those who choose to use it, as a motivational tool fear is a demonstrated failure.

That order giving is a complex process is something many managers, especially those at the first level where the content of the order itself appears direct and unambiguous, fail to appreciate. Their reasoning is simplicity itself: "It's part of my job to give orders to my subordinates, and it's part of their job to carry them out—that's what we're both paid for."

A lot of research and observation, as we have suggested, tells a different story: Subordinates do not automatically obey an order because it comes from someone with the authority to issue it. Between obligation and obedience, other forces supervene. Many orders are tacitly accepted only to be so radically changed in their execution that the boss can scarcely recognize his brainchild in the end result.

Guidelines for Complying with Orders

To what forces are we referring? What happens in the interval between the giving of the order and its execution? Why do employees, on occasion, resist and twist orders? About forty years ago, Chester Barnard, whom we mentioned earlier as a rare combination of practicing theorist and successful operating executive, laid down four conditions that must be met before an employee can carry out any order from his boss.

1. He can and does understand the order.
2. He believes that it is consistent with the purpose of the organization as he understands it. In other words, the employee will resist in some fashion an order that he perceives as bad or stupid from the organization's viewpoint.
3. He believes that the order is compatible with his personal interests as a whole.
4. He's physically and mentally capable of carrying it out.

Points 1 and 4 are obvious, although they have contributed their share of headaches to many managers. Let's concentrate on number 3—it accounts for the most serious instances of noncompliance with an order and is by far the most difficult point for most managers to comprehend and cope with. Yet, until a supervisor has grasped something about the circumstances under which a subordinate will subvert an order despite the usually considerable risk involved—(the boss sooner or later will discover that his order has been flouted), he can attack the problem only with threats that are sometimes successful but more often impotent. One frequent cause of resistance to an order is that it contradicts a subordinate's own idea of what constitutes a fair day's work. Let's consider the case of a group of trained crewmen handling 150 trains a day. By taking a number of shortcuts, they completed the work in six hours—with the remainder of the time being devoted to loafing and sleeping. When management found out what was happening, the decree went out: Handle 200 trains a day. It's not difficult to guess what happened next. The crew resorted to the rule book and followed each rule to the letter. They worked a full eight hours but somehow only processed fifty trains. Common sense triumphed: Management gave up its notion of 200 trains a day, and the crew went back to its old and comparatively productive ways.

The Indifference Zone

Of course, in this example, the members of the crew drew courage and strength from collective action. A solitary employee would be far less likely to engage in so blatant a defiance of the intent behind management's order. Nor do we wish to exaggerate by claiming too much for the similarity between punishment and the obligation to obey. Punishment, as it relates to the goal of discipline, is almost always self-defeating because it is almost always resented. Not so with the obligation to obey and the goal of order giving. To explain the difference we will use another concept of Barnard's—"the zone of indifference." Once the employee has accepted the authority of the organization, including that of his immediate superior, in exchange for certain material and/or psychic benefits, he carries out many orders. He obeys, first, because he recognizes his general obligation to accept orders, and second, because the specific order doesn't challenge his sense of personal interest—it lies within his zone of indifference. Also, he weighs, consciously or subconsciously—and we suspect the process is usually subconscious—his feelings of attraction, repugnance, or indifference to the order against his overall satisfaction with his position in the organization.

Let's look, for example, at the matter of overtime. To the secretary with a very active social life and no pressing need for extra cash, overtime may be a fighting word. It's well outside her zone of indifference and she will use every stratagem she can think of to avoid it. To another secretary, overtime may be an unappreciated chore but her hours after five aren't that full—besides, she was warned that there might be overtime before she accepted the job. It's within her personal zone of indifference. Therefore, she makes no special effort to esccape it.

About one thing we can be fairly certain: Any order that changes the employee's frame of reference about what constitutes a fair day's work is likely to be resisted. Suppose that an office manager suddenly told his office boy to clean the copying machine every two weeks. The boy had been accustomed to cleaning it every two months—that's what it said in the manual. It was a messy, unpleasant job and one that he regarded as cruel and unusual punishment—to be ducked at almost any cost. We suspect that he might quit rather than conform to that particular order. Of course, if the circumstances were different, his reaction might have been different, too. Let's say that a service man from the manufacturer had just inspected the copier and had recommended that it be cleaned every two weeks, a suggestion based on his company's experience with thousands of similar machines over several years. Let's further suppose that the manager had called in the office boy and let him listen to what the service man had to say. The office boy probably would have accepted the order—and if he hadn't, it would indicate that there was something radically wrong in the relationship between him and his boss—which leads to an important point.

The process which determines where a particular order falls in the employee's zone of indifference—outside, within, or on the line—is subtle and complicated. Many factors enter into it: The employee's conscious and rational perception of his self-interest, his respect for the boss and his faith—or lack of it—in his credibility, his interpretation of what the boss says to him in giving him the order which, in turn, depends on how he relates the boss's words to his own past experiences and concepts. Here is an example, actually over simplified despite its length, of supervisor A endeavoring to get his subordinate supervisor, B, to understand a problem and comply with an order.

A SIMPLE LITTLE PROBLEM

Supervisor A: (*saying*) Good to see you back. How are things going? It's been a long time—
(*thinking*) *I've got to warm him up a bit before getting down to business.*
Subordinate B: (*interpreting received meaning*) *I wonder what's up.*

(*saying*) Oh, O.K., I guess, not much new except people pushing you all the time. You're lucky, Allan, being in that nice office.

(*thinking*) *I am sure he didn't drop by to pass the time of day and get away from that nice office. I'd better let him know I'm busy and not very happy with this job.*

Supervisor A: (*interpreting*) *There he goes, complaining again. I wonder if I should soft-soap him a little or get down to business.*

(*saying*) That's the way it is. They want those files right away and don't care who came first and how busy the other guy may be. But what are you going to do—that's just the way people are. I've got to get over to see the big boss soon, but first I wanted to get you started on setting up a special file for these accident cases involving minors. Remember we talked about it last week? Now I think I know just how we should do it. This might be a good day for a dry run and I can stop by tomorrow to see how it's going.

(*thinking*) *Much of what I give you comes from the big boss, so don't blame me. This is really an order I am giving you, you know I never just say "do this" or "do that." Dip into your memory and bring out what I said before, because what follows relates to that.*

Subordinate B: (*interpreting*) *There he goes again, throwing his status around. Now let's see what he wants. Oh, yes, I remember that discussion last week and how he wants a duplicate file by both age and sex for those under twenty-one.*

(*saying*) Shoot! I remember. But don't forget I've got to fit this into all the other things I am doing today, so don't expect miracles. This could be like last Tuesday, when I promised to get those lists done but never got to them.

(*thinking*) *I hear you and I remember—so go ahead. But don't hold me to a time schedule. Get your random-access memory working too and associate this extra task to the extra task I got last week. I'll do what I can, but no miracles performed here.*

Supervisor A: (*interpreting*) *Oh, boy, another excuse. He's getting ready to let me down.*

(*saying*) Sorry to say this, Beck, but this really is rush. I've got to get the forms printed after we see what the files are like and all that has to be done by next Monday. You know I get you out of as many unnecessary things as possible. You and I really talked them out of converting everything to hanging files. That really was a great battle and we won it because we stuck together on it.

(*thinking*) *I'm not just a fink. We've been through a lot together and I believe in reasonable work loads. We stick together on a lot of things—after all, this is our department, yours and mine.*

Subordinate B: (*interpreting*) *Allen is a pretty good supervisor— we really showed what a fighting pair we could be in the hanging file matter. Boy, that was a good battle! It showed the rest of this organization that this department is nobody's patsy.*

(*saying*) O.K. Give me the word on this.

Supervisor A. (*saying*) You recall that system of filing by age and sex we tried out last year, don't you? This is just a slight modification, using a lesser number of categories. Here, I've put them on this sheet—

(*thinking*) *Shift your thinking to that system you finally mastered a year ago that unfortunately we had to discard because we needed the file space. If you can remember that, all the rest will be easy because this is going to be exactly like that, with a few very simple modifications.*

Subordinate B: (*thinking*) *I guess we did do something like this last year, but I'll be damned if I can remember anything about it. That was nine or ten months ago at least, maybe longer.*

(*saying*) Yeah, I guess I remember.

Supervisor A: (*saying*) Well, on second thought maybe we'd better go over the whole thing.

(*thinking*) *That was a pretty weak yes he gave me, so I guess I'll have to start from scratch—he's dubious, I can tell.*

Subordinate B: (*interpreting*) *I am glad he has the good sense to be clear on these things. I know how angry he gets if anything is done wrong, even if it's his fault for not making it clear in the first place.*

(*saying*) Let me sit down and get some paper out to make notes, and give it to me *slowly*.

(*thinking*) *Remember, you're usually rushing off some place and don't take the time to give me a full description.*

Supervisor A: (*interpreting*) *I wonder if he just wants to make a big deal of this, or is he really trying to take it seriously?*

Comments on the Case

We can see how far removed this dialogue is from giving instructions to a computer. There are lots of anticipated and unanticipated byways and there is the need for redundancy and for analogy. The listener is tying in what he hears with what he already knows, and, if the sender listens carefully, he is revealing what he doesn't know.

The superior, supervisor A, made one big error when he invoked the wrong symbol—the big boss—in an effort to get off the hook on the order. Subordinate B interpreted the remark in an entirely different way—as an attempt on the boss's part to throw his weight around—and it made him feel more negative about the boss and more resistant to the order. The turning point in their interaction came when the boss's reference to the joint battle against the hanging files invoked the symbol of past solidarity and changed the emotional climate between them. After that, the subordinate was willing enough to accept the order. What was required, and fortunately was supplied, was the boss's perception that the subordinate's "I guess I remember" meant the reverse of what he said on the surface, that it would take a detailed clarification before the subordinate understood and could comply with the order.

One missing element in the case is any reason for the order, any explanation as to how the change embodied in it would benefit the unit, the overall organization, or the employee himself. The subordinate is free to conclude that it's simply a case of management caprice at work, of change for change's sake—at his expense.

As a general rule, to give an order without explaining why breeds resistance. Even in the military, things have changed since the Light Brigade and "Theirs not to reason why." Take the by now classic tale of "boiler scale" on a destroyer during World War II. Even in a danger zone, the captain could never get a much-needed five knots over the maximum rated speed because of the mysterious boiler scale. He got the needed knots only when he dramatized the importance of extra speed by having a blow-by-blow description of each engagement sent over the public address system to the men in the engine room. Once they knew the reason why, the boiler scale disappeared and the captain got his five knots.

One final point about the case: The supervisor was conscious of not giving his subordinate a direct order. The closest he came to it was his statement, "I wanted to get you started on setting up a special file" and so on. What about this approach? We would say that it was about right. Manners do count. Most subordinates appreciate an order couched as a request—not a blunt "do this" or "do that"—and few fail to perceive that the request has the force of an order. Some managers go to the other extreme: They present their orders as suggestions and are surprised and unhappy when their subordinates disregard them. Part of the confusion springs from an honest misapprehension: The subordinates took the suggestion at its face value. Part of it comes from the fact that many subordinates do not respect the boss who pussyfoots in giving an order. As Professor Whyte of Cornell points out, "Most men have no respect for the supervisor who gives orders timidly and with uncertainty." Of course, the context in which the order is given counts for something. A request that would be readily understood as an order (although not necessarily accepted) when made by a bank officer to a subordinate would be completely ignored on the docks if it passed from a loading boss to a stevedore. In the latter case, the request would probably have to be a direct order—with a few obscenities to underscore the point.

CONCLUSION

In our discussion of discipline and order giving, we have seen that each manager should begin by discarding any illusions he may have about the rationality of man—although he might well search for consistencies in man's irrationality. Rationality and self-interest would indicate that the employee who's been laid off for three days for excessive absenteeism should turn over a new leaf—yet, typically, he won't. Rationality and self-interest would indicate that the office boy will start cleaning the copying machine every two weeks, once his failure to follow orders has been found out. Yet the chances are probably fifty-fifty that he will continue to defy the order.

Discipline based on punishment fails 99 times out of 100 because the employee resents the punishment and therefore rejects the efforts to reform him. Order giving, based on the subordinate's obligation to obey a higher authority, frequently fails because it, too, is based on fear of the consequences of *not* following the order. Most orders receive a measure of compliance because they fall within the individual employee's zone of indifference. But when we examine the factors that determine the zone of indifference, we uncover a potpourri of emotions and attitudes—perceived self-interest, loyalty to the superior and to the organization, belief in the

credibility of the superior and respect for him as a man
and a technician, plus literally dozens of other elements,
tangible and intangible, that contribute to that general state of
mind known as job satisfaction.

In other words, success in handling discipline and order
giving is something no manager can take for granted. All it
takes is intelligence, intuition, prolonged and patient observation of men and events, a horror of easy answers and quick
solutions, a reputation for credibility and fairness, a strong
dose of humility—and a lot of luck.

SELECTED REFERENCES

Barnard, C., *The Functions of the Executive,* Harvard
University Press, Cambridge, Mass., 1938, chap. 5.

Feinberg, M., *Effective Psychology for Managers,* Prentice-
Hall, Englewood Cliffs, N.J., 1965.

Miner, J., *The Management of Ineffective Performance,*
McGraw-Hill, New York, 1963.

THE EDUCATION OF GREG HORNING: FEBRUARY 21

Apparently, Rick had not felt like winning when he woke up
on Monday—his output had been below standard. But since
he'd been on the new machine, he'd consistently turned out
more than Kilpatrick had. Greg had kept his eyes open—
the others seemed to be leaving Rick alone—and Kilpatrick
had been working slowly and sullenly, but without too much
griping at his new job. By yesterday, Greg had decided that
they would all adjust to the changes without a lot of trouble
and that everything would be all right.

But when he came back from a late lunch this afternoon,
he found all work stopped. Everyone was standing around
Kilpatrick's new station, looking at his machine, handling
malformed pieces which were supposed to be spools, and
talking at once.

"What's the matter? What happened?" Greg yelled, rushing
over.

Creegmore, who had been bent over examining the temperature dials on the machine, straightened up and answered
Greg. "Ted's just had a little trouble with his machine, that's

all. Helen had to go over to check something with Jeannette for a minute and Ted was watching the machine until it jammed . . ."

"Jammed! You mean the machine's not working at all? What's going to happen to the shipment we're supposed to get out by tomorrow?"

"They'll just have to sit on their asses and wait for it, that's all." Phil Martello volunteered this sarcastically. "Look. We'll have to get maintenance in here to fix it and you know those guys. We'll be lucky if they get it going in a week."

Greg looked at the pile of faulty spools lying beside the machine. "My God, Ted! How could you let that much stuff come off your machine without seeing it was no good?"

Kilpatrick just stood with his hands in his pockets, saying nothing. Again, it was Creegmore who answered. "All right, now, Greg. Take it easy. It wasn't his fault. You know we don't stop to check each piece. Besides, it's Helen who does the checking, and I told you, she had to step away for a minute. Now, if you'll just calm down, I can tell you what happened." He took Greg by the arm and drew him aside, explaining the situation slowly and in a low voice.

It seemed that the main temperature knob, which was supposed to be pre-set, had been loose for months. They had complained that it needed to be fixed, but maintenance never would cooperate. Today, the vibrations in the room had finally caused the control to shift to a high enough temperature to grossly deform the pieces. One of them had gotten stuck and caused the back-up, so that now the machine was not working.

"But why didn't Kilpatrick catch it sooner?" Greg persisted. "I don't care what you say, Henry. It was carelessness. Pure damn carelessness."

"Now, listen, Greg . . ." But Greg felt that he had allowed Creegmore to patronize him long enough.

"Look, I've spent enough time listening to your excuses for Ted. Now get back to work and get the others going, too. We have to make up as much of that shipment as we can. Send Ted in to see me."

Greg started toward his office. Creegmore seemed about to follow, then changed his mind. Instead, he went over to say a word to Kilpatrick, who, with his hands still in his pockets and his head down, followed his supervisor into his office.

The two men, both standing, confronted each other across

Greg's desk. "Well, Ted, what do you have to say for yourself?"

"It wasn't my fault, Greg. That control's been ready to go for months now. Henry knew it, and I remember the old foreman, before he left, he . . ."

"Never mind that, Ted," Greg interrupted impatiently. "You were supposed to be watching the dials."

"Yeah, but, Greg. You can't have your eye on everything at once. I was watching the other settings because it was a new batch of polyurethane I'd just put in. That dial that went—that's not supposed to change and . . ."

The older man went on with his explanation, but Greg was not really listening. When he had gone out to the shop, his first thought had been that the men had manipulated the dial purposely to sabotage the shipment. But that didn't make sense. If they had planned it, Kilpatrick wouldn't have been the scapegoat; they would have rigged Rick's machine. No, it had been an accident, all right and now Greg was pretty sure he knew why it had happened.

"Where'd you have lunch, today, Ted?" he asked abruptly.

"Huh? Why I went over across the way. I always go to that place across the way with the other guys. But what's that got to do with . . ."

"That place across the way—it's a bar, isn't it, Ted?"

"Well, yeah, I guess so. A bar and grill. But . . ."

"Look at you, Ted. You're all red in the face and you stink of liquor. This whole office stinks. I think you drank your lunch and you came back here drunk and didn't know what the hell you were doing!"

"Now, wait a minute, Greg. I . . ."

"That's it, Ted. You're lucky I'm not firing you. You were drunk and you were negligent—knob or no knob—and there's no excuse for it. I'm giving you a three-day layoff so you can go home and sleep it off. Now get out of here. I don't want to see you again 'til next week."

Kilpatrick's face had been red; now it was redder. His mouth worked open and closed without any words coming out. Then, his hands back in his pockets, he slumped out.

Greg went over to the window. Kilpatrick had gone straight to Phil Martello, who was listening with his mouth tight in anger as Kilpatrick talked. Creegmore started over to them, but Martello was already striding toward Greg's office. He threw open the door.

"Look, kid, I don't know who you think you are, and what's more, I don't give a damn." Martello spoke quietly, but his anger seemed to make the words reverberate in the small office. "We've got a union in here—in case you didn't know—and we're not going to stand for this kind of thing. You just try proving a charge of drunkenness. He had three beers—I was there, so don't tell me—I've seen him put away a dozen without missing a step."

"Now, hold on a minute, Phil . . ."

"You just hold on a damn minute, yourself, Ted Kilpatrick may not be the sharpest man in the crew, but he's been here over thirty years and if you think you can give him the shaft just because you don't like him, you've got another think coming."

"That's not it, Phil. He . . ."

"You just shut up and listen to me, buddy. I'm telling you this officially as a union representative and you listen to me good. We'll fight you on this all the way through. You'd just better forget this whole thing ever happened or you're beat before you've even started." Stopping to breathe hard, Martello glared at Greg. Greg ran his hand over his face.

"All right Phil. All right," said Greg very slowly, getting a grip on himself as he spoke, "We've all been angry. Maybe I should think about it a little more.

"Yeah. You think it over and you think it over right," Martello shot back, the door knob in his fist. "If you don't, I'll make you look like a jackass. And let me tell you—it'll be my pleasure." He slammed the door and was gone.

Greg passed his hand over his face again. Those union guys sure could put the pressure on. But he'd put the pressure on them too—maybe too much. Kilpatrick had a pretty unimpressive record, but he'd never had any accidents before.

"Yeah," Greg muttered to himself, "maybe I was too rough on him. Maybe he wasn't drunk, but he sure reeked of booze."

It might have been the kind of accident that could happen to anyone. Greg decided to call Ed Briscoe in maintenance and check it out.

"If that dial really could have gone out of kilter by itself . . ." Greg sighed deeply.

QUESTIONS

1. Why do you think Greg refused to accept Creegmore's explanations?

2. In talking to Ted Kilpatrick, at how many points did Greg deviate from the "hot stove rule"?

3. Do you feel that Martello's position toward Greg was justified? What about his tone?

4. What mistakes did Greg make in handling the situation?

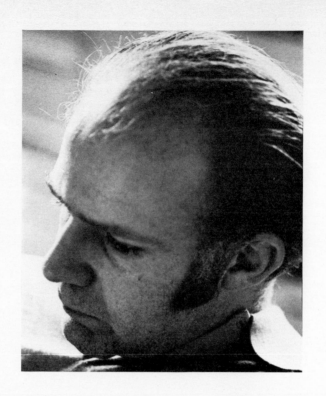

5. Controls, incentives,
and appraisals

Most new managers take as obvious what turns out to be one of their most difficult challenges. A critical element in every manager's job is assessing and influencing how well an employee is doing his job. This responsibility turns out to be a good deal more problematic than common sense might suggest.

Unfortunately, this element is made needlessly complicated by the different words and concepts that managers use for essentially the same problem area: influencing and appraising performance. Often this activity is regarded as a problem in *controls,* which managers at every level use to measure how well things are going. Such measures as production totals, quality levels, turnover, and absenteeism are designed to tell the manager how his people are doing.

But controls also involve *rewards* and *punishments:* Subordinates are usually rewarded, directly or indirectly, when they do well (in other words, are productive) and punished when they show up badly (when they show up late, for example, or not at all). Also, rewards are central to the general subject of *incentives,* that is, extra pay for additional performance. And, in the field of personnel administration, concern with making employee *appraisals* (often involving the filing of formal appraisal documents for each subordinate), giving *merit salary increases,* and deciding on *promotions*—all have their bases in management's evaluation of and influence on subordinates. After all, there is no point in going through all these procedures if you don't think that they will influence people to try to look better, to do those things which bring approval, and to avoid those things which are likely to be followed by punishment.

Thus controls, incentives, appraisals—what have you—all deal with getting employees to move away from undesirable work patterns in the direction of more desirable behavior. But to use any of these techniques, we must know the answers to these questions.

1. What is desirable job behavior?
2. Is the employee demonstrating this behavior?
3. How and when should the supervisor communicate his evaluations to employees?

Common sense is probably correct about one thing: the reason why assessment of performance is critical. We can look at this from the viewpoints of both the subordinate and the manager.

167

THE SUBORDINATE'S WORLD OF APPRAISAL: IMPLICIT CONTROLS

Every one of us in the world of work and in the community is deluged with requests, rules, temptations, and deterrents which influence what we should do with our time. At least for most people—again both at work and outside—there is neither time enough, energy enough, nor will enough to do everything we might do or are asked to do. Here is one employee's list of the decisions and choices she evaluates in expending her seven and a half working hours. (She is a claims adjuster in an insurance company.)

Management has told us we should handle twenty claims a day. One way I can reach this total is to avoid the really tough cases and shift these up to my supervisor.

My fellow employees often urge me to do less than twenty to prove to management we are overworked.

Sometimes if I hurry I approve or disapprove claims that I would settle differently if I had more time; I am not sure whether this makes much difference or not.

I am often asked by Accounting and our Customer Relations Department to answer inquiries, and I question how much time and energy I should devote to these outside requests.

If you want to do a really thorough job on some cases, it means a dozen phone calls, lots of checking in files, and even consulting with the more experienced adjusters. How thorough should I be?

I often am asked by those less experienced than I to help them, too.

I ought to spend some time reading some of the old files and policy statements here in the office to improve my ability to do this job. Also, I ought to be studying up on other subjects to qualify for a promotion.

I've been asked if I wanted to take over temporarily— while the girl who handles the job has her baby—a claim review job. It's hard work and very demanding, and I don't know whether it's worth it for a couple months.

The company wants you to keep your desk neat at all times and everything put away in files. If I do this, I work slower because it means constant filing.

You're only supposed to have one customer record out of Central Filing at a time. If I take several, I can work on another while I am waiting for some information on the first.

I have a typist working for me and I can let her fill in some of the more routine things, or I can meticulously spell out every detail.

I've got some ideas on how this job could be improved, and I wonder whether it's worth trying to get the company to listen.

This short list of one employee's choices could easily have been made longer if we had wanted to be exhaustive (in both senses of the word). But it is long enough to show that an employee's use of his or her day is obviously not dictated by some explicit job assignment. What you emphasize and deemphasize, what you do quickly or indifferently, what you concentrate upon, what rules or norms you follow and which you ignore, when you are responsive to the requests of others and when you turn them aside, when you seek to introduce improvements in the job or in yourself, and when you concentrate on the here and now—all are choices that you, as an employee, make. They are not predetermined by the organization or the definition of the job. Even on relatively programmed jobs, there will be a good deal of room for maneuver.

The Supervisor Provides Clues

While there are other influences on these choices (such as the informal group and the personaltiy differences that we have already discussed), one of the major determinants will be the supervisor's own actions. What does the manager emphasize or deemphasize? What does he reward or punish—or ignore? What does he watch closely and what, indifferently? Many times, managers are not aware of how they cue employees as to what is worth doing and what is not—in a world where you can't or won't do everything that conceivably might be done on any particular job.

A bank teller learns that, while his boss talks a lot about being pleasant to customers, the one thing that really makes him fuss is inaccuracy. So he is brusque at the window but spends a great deal of time counting his cash.

There is no workbreak scheduled during the day, but employees walk over to the cafeteria in threes and fours every day—and nobody says anything.

Chris Ames worked on his lunch hour and a little during the workday to develop a new fixture that would save setup time, but it wasn't successful. In the process, he broke a tool bit and the supervisor roundly criticized him for "wasting time and company property."

A salesclerk spent a great deal of time calming an irate customer who claimed that the store had shipped her the wrong size purposefully. The clerk was overheard by the buyer, who called her into his office to commend her. He also wrote a letter for Employee Records, indicating that this clerk handled difficult human relations problems with aplomb and dedication.

An engineer devoted a great many hours to preparing a special report and came up with some very startling conclusions that would save the company money. He even worked on it at home on his own time, concentrating harder than he ever had before. The report was two days late and he was sharply criticized. A few months before, he had done a perfunctory job on another assignment but turned in the report two days early. He was told he had done fine work.

A programmer notices that the people who get promotions appear to have several things in common: They don't wear "mod" clothes, they have reasonably short hair, and they use standard English. Their work in many cases is less good than that of others who aren't promoted.

In every one of these instances, it is not difficult to deduce the conclusion that will be drawn by the employee regarding what "really counts around here," what can be safely ignored, and what must be repressed if at all possible. Gradually, as an employees stays on a job, his performance will be shaped by these positive and negative reinforcements.

It may be helpful to conceive of a job as a large, shapeless, flexible mass of plastic which gradually begins to assume a fixed form as the employee receives "inputs" from the supervisor.

Unconscious Guidelines

And many of these inputs are not even consciously given: Often, a manager will be preoccupied with other matters when an employee shows him his solution to a particularly difficult problem. Contrariwise, a manager will be upset by other things when an employee appears to have ignored a rather minor rule or request. In the first instance, the absence of commendation and recognition may well teach the employee that real dedication doesn't count for much. From the second reaction, he is likely to conclude that trivial matters are more important than serious ones and that appearances count more than substance.

Therefore, a manager can't afford to let down his guard. He must constantly ask himself, "What is my action—or inaction—communicating to subordinates in terms of what is relatively most important to me (and their job future here), and what is of secondary or even no importance?" The manager cannot minimize his responsibility for shaping the highly amorphous, plastic "glob" of job requirements into a desirable job pattern. He can't afford to leave his explanation of these requirements to chance or to abstract written or spoken descriptions of the job. There are just too many possible bad choices, bad in terms of the overall welfare of the department, that can easily be made by the employee.

From the employee's point of view, working is a continuous learning experience which transforms an ambiguous environment into an understandable one. There are a large number of inputs coming from disciplinary actions, from promotion decisions, from merit increases, from the supervisor's frowns, smiles, and positive responses, and from many other things. The employee must make sense of this confusing array of "directions" by coming to some conclusions with respect to what's worth doing, what is better ignored, and what should be avoided at all cost. Then he is comfortable because his world is predictable, and most of us want to be able to predict the consequences of our actions (or inactions). Of course, we are also saying that what the employee perceives as the "real" world, what he has learned from experience— which always speaks in a louder voice than the supervisor's printed or verbal directions—may not be what the manager expects him to perceive.

Thus, nothing the manager does can be ignored because it is likely to affect this learning process, particularly during the more formative stage when either the employee or his boss is new and the worker is looking for hidden cues as to what is appropriate. The old cliché just happens to be true, "Do as I do, not as I say." Employees often ridicule management efforts to appraise their performance in the abstract. The following list of performance degrees for the factor "adaptability," taken from an "underground" employee-appraisal form, may illustrate our point about employee skepticism:

Far exceeds job demands: *Leaps tall buildings with a single bound*
Exceeds job requirements: *Must take running jump to leap over tall buildings*
Meets job requirements: *Can leap over a short building*
Needs some improvement: *Crashes into building when attempting to jump over.*
Does not meet minimum performance: *Cannot recognize building at all, much less jump*

Now let's turn to the other side of the equation: the supervisor's problem with assessing and controlling performance.

THE MANAGER'S WORLD OF APPRAISAL

We have been concentrating on the employee's efforts to "psyche out" his job world and make it predictable—to distinguish the real payoffs from the phony demands and requirements. The other side of the coin is even more critical—the manager's effort to find out what the employee is doing and how well he is doing it. Although such appraisal may appear easy, we shall see that it is not.

The process of appraisal is the subject of management controls, as they are formally called. Controls measure how well prescribed plans and activities and tasks are being performed. We shall look closely at how this is done, but first one ought to ask the question: What purposes are being served by these measurements, these controls?

Why Does the Manager Utilize Controls?

1. He knows that he is always in the role of a teacher or trainer, as we have seen. His communication to employees that he has seen something he likes or dislikes—in other words, his feedback—will affect significantly what an employee learns about the real job requirements.
2. He wants to know where work is progressing badly in order to be able to intervene, to do something to get the job or coordination or employee morale back where it should be. This contingency aspect of every managerial job is central to good supervision. There is the brighter aspect too,

that is, knowing where things are going well so that the manager doesn't have to spend scarce supervisory time on these situations and can devote his efforts to the problem areas.

Note that there can be a conflict here with point 1. Even though a subordinate is doing well and doesn't require the boss's attention, as we have seen, there may be need for the manager to tell him that he recognizes this good performance, and thus reinforce it.

3. The manager needs to be able to summarize the performance of his subordinates in order to make sensible personnel decisions on salary increases, promotions, transfers, and the like. These actions must be consistent with his continuous observation of performance or employees will feel there are serious injustices. Unfortunately, injustice sometimes does occur because managers haven't kept good records of what they have observed. Such an oversight also means they will have a difficult time justifying their personnel decisions to others. Furthermore, actual observations of performance are a good check on the effectiveness of management's selection techniques. Is the manager a good judge of employee potential? The answer is given when a supervisor compares his predictions, say before hiring, with what he observes later. Where there are major discrepancies, he had better change his selection criteria!

4. Under some circumstances, the manager may want to tie monetary rewards to the controls. Employees may receive a bonus based on how much they sell, how high they keep quality, how many units they produce, and similar achievements. These are called incentive plans and they depend upon the manager's ability to give quantitative dimension to job performance.

5. The manager also uses controls to spot undesirable trends. All human beings possess a well-known characteristic which is both a curse and probably a salvation: We are adaptive to our environment. Sit in a noisy room for a few minutes and you no longer hear much of the noise. Get a $35-a-week raise and in a few months the elation is gone and it seems as if you've had it forever. This same pattern of accommodation to conditions occurs in the work situation. An employee gradually arrives later and later, his work area gradually deteriorates, his performance gradually declines. If there were not reasonably objective standards, each of these trends, if it were gradual enough, might go undetected.

These, then, are five quite distinct managerial purposes

served by controls. All are important, needless to say, but we shall concentrate on points 1 and 2. Let's look at the first of these more closely:

Training Employees with Reinforcement

Psychologists speak about learning taking place as a result of rewards and punishments, positive and negative reinforcements. For example, if every time a laboratory technician thoroughly washes his equipment after finishing a test run, the supervisor remarks on that being a necessary and well-done procedure, this job pattern will become ingrained. Psychologists also refer to *one-to-one reinforcement,* meaning that the reward is forthcoming every time the behavior is demonstrated. Similarly, an employee can learn not to waste time thoroughly washing his equipment (assuming that step isn't necessary) if the supervisor rebukes him whenever he dawdles at the washing stage. This is an example of negative reinforcement, of course.

Unfortunately, forgetting—*extinction,* as it is technically called—also occurs quite quickly under one-to-one reinforcement. If the supervisor neglects to encourage desirable behavior and if the habit is clumsy or difficult to maintain, it may soon be forgotten, that is, extinguished. On the other hand, if the supervisor uses *random* reinforcement, extinction is very slow. By that we mean that the supervisor doesn't always smile or nod approval when a thorough washing job is done, but he does so when he happens to be walking by during this operation, say several times a week.

Sometimes we teach employees bad habits by random reinforcement without being aware of this. Take the case of the manager who complained that one of his key employees often forgot to lock up his drawing materials and files before leaving. On being questioned, he admitted that the man sometimes asked to leave things that way when he had been working right down to the last minute and had a pressing engagement downtown. In effect, the employee was learning that not locking up was all right.

ONE-TO-ONE OR RANDOM?

The major advantage of random reinforcement over one-to-one reinforcement is that extinction or forgetting is very slow even after the praise (or punishment) stops coming. So it is a good method of thoroughly and deeply ingraining a pattern of behavior. The disadvantage is that learning takes place much more slowly with its use. The obvious answer is to combine the two: use one-to-one at first when new behavior is being learned, and gradually shift over to random reinforcement. For example, to "fix" good typing habits, reward each perfectly typed letter for a few weeks, then sample the correspondence at random times after that.

An important note of warning here: one-to-one reinforcement will be ineffective if it requires the supervisor to stand over the employee and watch his every move. Such close scrutiny is overbearing and often interpreted as distrust. And, of course, the time required for the manager would make the process wasteful.

Managers, then, should remember the following principles of reinforcement: *One-to-one* means fast learning, fast forgetting; *random* means slow learning, slow forgetting.
There are two elements that we have neglected in this discussion of learning (sometimes called "conditioning theory"). They are the magnitudes of the rewards and punishments, and the differences between them.

MAGNITUDE

Supervisors often think that if a little is good, a lot is better. This is really not the case. In fact, overrewarding and overpunishing have deleterious effects associated with their use. There is a good deal of evidence that employees who receive excessive praise or very large salary increases grow uneasy as a result of feeling that they are getting more than they deserve. (Psychologists use the term "cognitive dissonance" to describe this effect.) They are not sure that they can live up to the high standards expected of them. Similarly, excessive punishment is deeply resented and may produce an opposite effect from the one intended, that is, a determination to get back at those responsible. (Recall our discussion in Chapter 4.)

Of course, magnitude is a subjective, not an objective, quantity that depends upon the employee's expectations. In regard to magnitude of reinforcement, we can talk about three different levels:

1. *Indifferent level:* The amount of reinforcement given is below some threshold of the employee's expectation, so he doesn't even recognize it. For example, after working for several weeks to finish a difficult assignment, the employee hears the boss say, "Thanks a lot, Charlie!" Or an employee earning

$200 per week is given a $5-a-week increase. Both these actions are too small to be considered rewards and may even cause resentment because they are below expectations. They certainly don't serve to reinforce desirable behavior!

2. *Normal level:* The affirmative and negative comments, encouragements, and disciplinary actions that follow employee actions are as expected. We have already described this level as part of the supervisor's training and reinforcement function.

3. *Excessive level:* The rewards or punishments seem so large that they cause the employee to become nervous or resentful because of their magnitude.

SUBORDINATE PERCEPTION: REWARD OR PUNISHMENT?

Individual expectations are so crucial to the way the employee perceives the action, of course, that the supervisor who intends to give a reward may be providing punishment or vice versa. A small reward may appear so unfair that the employee feels he is being disciplined in some way. On the other hand, an employee who gets only a mild rebuke for producing low-quality parts may figure "it's worth it" to avoid the effort of doing good work. (He has anticipated a major confrontation with the supervisor when the bad work was detected.) Thus he was given positive reinforcement by his superior, who thought he was doing just the opposite.

Another danger in excessive use of rewards is that employees become conditioned to expecting them and even expect more each time. (This is another element in favor of random reinforcement.)

Managers should also remember that rewards and punishments are not just equal and opposite. For example, punishments, when compared to rewards, are more likely to have undesirable by-products when used as learning prods. As we all know, they create hostility toward the giver and the desire to fight back at what is perceived as the enemy (as emphasized in Chapter 4).

Particularly when the threat of punishment is very great, the worker may even become paralyzed with fear and be unable to accomplish anything. This can sometimes be observed in very delicate craftwork where the employee knows that a slight mistake will ruin a very expensive die and might even result in his discharge. He may sit for hours before being able to resume work. The rule of fear is not usually a productive one. The same thing happens when a student is numb with fear of a final examination: The possible punishment (having to take the course over again with the same instructor!) seems overwhelming.

Further effects of excessive threats of punishment can be seen in many departments in which subordinates "fudge" data to avoid admitting job problems. Many managers are deceived as to the true state of affairs in their departments because employees can usually find ways to make the figures lie.

A department head had been relaxed about production quality in the die-casting group because it had not varied over several months. He learned later that the foreman had neglected to note the shift in the type of work being performed. The men were now producing very easy parts where the rejection rate should have been substantially under the 5 percent rate which had been acceptable when they were working on highly complex and intricate parts. He also learned that the same foreman was hiding rejected parts in paper scrap barrels. This behavior followed an announcement by middle management that any increase in scrap would have serious repercussions on the jobs of the supervisors involved.

A manager who is very much worried about a problem or anxious because his own boss is putting pressure on him is always tempted to threaten his subordinates with dire consequences if he doesn't get what he thinks is appropriate behavior. Aside from being rather childish, such threats may have the opposite effect to the one desired. Furthermore, the actual imposition of the penalty, should the desired behavior not be forthcoming, can have further repercussions. For example, if the employees are unionized, the union will likely have "a good case." Moreover, whether there is a union or not, penalties tend to unite work groups into a cohesive antimanagement force.

Now to turn briefly to the subject of how to evaluate employee performance.

OBSERVING EMPLOYEE BEHAVIOR—KNOWING WHAT TO MEASURE

The supervisor wants to assure himself that the employee is not doing things that are either unproductive, wasteful, or liable to cause later problems. Many times, it is necessary to observe the work in process because mistakes in work method or carelessness will subsequently be hidden from view. Slovenly filing, for example, may not show up until a document is sought. Poor welding or soldering may be spotted only in a later testing procedure, after much labor and material have been wasted in assembling the component.

To learn whether the employee is using proper methods and diligence, the supervisor makes periodic checks. Because employees are likely to behave differently under observation, and because it is very costly (as well as demeaning) to continuously watch subordinates, good supervisors learn to sample behavior. Rather than walking through the plant or office at predictable times, they adopt a random method of checking what people are doing and how they are doing it.[1] During their random appearances, they can note how many people are working, how many are idle, whether safety equipment is being properly used, if working instructions are being followed, and a number of other factors. Often work in process is scrutinized to see whether it is being handled properly. In the case of salesclerks, listening to the conversation between the customer and the clerk will give some idea of whether tact, responsiveness, and salesmanship are being employed.

But of course such watching and waiting is costly in time, and no matter how carefully done, it is somewhat abrasive from the point of view of the employee. This explains why workers seek work locations that are out of the direct line of sight of the supervisor's desk, prefer the night shift where the supervision may be limited, or take "outside" jobs like selling and landscaping where they are on their own a good deal of the time.

Some jobs and some industries inherently have good measures of performance which the supervisor can use in judging whether employees are doing a good job and which eliminate the need to watch them. For example, in retail selling the supervisor may be able to tell a good deal by the actual cash register and accounting records. He can tell what quantities of what kinds of merchandise a clerk is selling— perhaps even how much repeat business (does he have loyal

---

[1] This type of investigation is formally called the "ratio delay" method, and there are specific statistical tools that help a supervisor to know exactly when and how often to appear. Under a very precise system, he then records exactly what everyone was doing at that particular time. Using statistics, he can go from these records to a close prediction of the pattern total of the day for all employees.

customers?) and how many returns he has. Furthermore, there may be many employees in similar jobs both in his and other stores, so meaningful comparisons can be made in performance. (This is not true, of course, where a job is unique, a condition that makes appraisal very difficult.) Also, retail selling jobs often lend themselves to an incentive system whereby the employee is motivated to work hard (because of direct financial gain) without constant supervision.

The same may be true on a simple machining operation. The supervisor merely checks the records of the quantity produced and the number of rejects for quality and concentrates his attention on those workers who are exceptions (those employees whose work falls outside the acceptable quantity and quality limits).

Unfortunately, however, it is often more difficult than this to design controls which truly measure all aspects of performance in which the supervisor may be interested. For example, an employee may be careless about his work area, fail to maintain his machine, or devote all his efforts to relatively easy and straightforward tasks while he "goofs off" on the tougher jobs. But he produces excellent quantities on all the easy jobs. Measuring his performance is more complicated than simply counting!

Balance of Incentives

The amount of intervention required from the supervisor may also depend upon the balance of incentives in the situation. It may be instructive to contrast two types of industry in this regard.

In what has come to be called continuous-processing or automated plants (such as some chemical factories), employees work most when something has gone wrong. If they handle their jobs intelligently, foresee problems, diligently check the processing control records, and do good preventive maintenance, they may well have considerable time to themselves. Thus, for a good part of the time, the more they produce, the less they work! Both management and the workers are ahead when there isn't a great deal of effort expended.

Contrast this with a more traditional factory, where the harder the employee works, both the more fatigued he may become and the greater the advantage to the company. Here, the employee and the supervisor may have almost opposite incentives. The supervisor wants more work, the employee wants less. To make matters worse, in the automated plant, labor costs, as such, are a quite small part of total costs—

most of the expenses are for equipment. In the traditional factory, labor costs are very significant and management is much concerned with how hard employees are working.

Of course, there is an even greater extreme. Many professionals, such as doctors and professors, get such satisfaction from their jobs that they always push themselves to do more (even to the detriment of their health). Their internalized incentives (plus the early programming contributed by their training and experience) mean that they require almost no supervision from their superiors.

Elusive or Changing Measures of Performance

Some managers believe that employees work harder if they are kept guessing as to how they are being evaluated. So they keep changing their standards. This way, everyone is on his toes and can't relax thinking that he knows what to concentrate upon and what to ignore.

Such an attitude naturally destroys employee confidence in the supervisor and can also lead to a great deal of wasted time. Listen to this comment by a credit analyst:

Karl plays his cards close to his chest as to what he is looking for in these reports we are preparing. So every week we all get together and compare what he has said to each of us about our reports. We purposefully introduce a lot of stuff we don't think is useful to see how close he reads them and what he'll "bite on." They take a lot more time this way—much of it wasted—but believe me we're going to figure this guy out once and for all.

To see how destructive changing performance standards can be, it is worth looking at some studies of animal behavior. Scientists have shown that you can induce psychotic states in animals by using ambiguous stimuli which lead to reward or punishment. More specifically, psychologists condition an animal to know that jumping or pawing at a circle will give him a food pellet whereas jumping at a long oval will bring him a punishing electric shock. Gradually, the researchers change both shapes to a more elliptical one. Now it is difficult for the animal to discriminate between the stimulus that provides a reward and the one that brings punishment. At this point, the animal often "breaks down" and shows psychotic symptoms.

Management by Results

Managers have other relationship problems when they appraise employee performance. Our egos are easily bruised, and most of us resent and find fault with other people's evaluations of our work. It is easier to find excuses for poor results or to assume the evaluator is biased than to accept blame and admit our deficiences. Further, as we have seen before, many jobs do not have simply measured output standards. How does a supervisor evaluate a receptionist, a designer, an engineer?

To deal with both of these problems, many organizations emphasize management by results. Originally popularized by the two well-known management experts, Douglas McGregor and Peter Drucker, this approach to appraisal stresses:

1. Getting subordinates to set their own standards rather than having the manager establish goals.
2. Then periodically having the employees themselves evaluate how well they have achieved these goals.

Thus, to take an example in the clerical field. A secretary might decide that over the new several months she would:

1. develop a new cross-check type of filing system that would permit her to find any requested correspondence within a few minutes since they would be cross referenced to correspondent, company, and subject.
2. reduce the amount of photocopying charged to her department (by greater use of carbon copies) by 10 percent.
3. reduce present backlog of untyped reports by one-half.

Periodically, rather than having the supervisor judge the employees and assume a position of high authority and that of the disciplinarian, the employee herself is asked to compare her performance with her targets. The new goals are set and the process repeats itself. If done well, management by results taps the natural motivation of the employee to accomplish self-determined goals. It also serves to convert vague, subjective jobs into tangible targets. Since a large number of positions do not have "outputs" which can be associated with the skill and effort of a single employee, there is a need for some such method to provide a common (for superior and subordinate) frame of reference.

PETER F. DRUCKER (1909–   )

As professor at the New York University Business School, prolific author, constant lecturer, and peripatetic consultant, Drucker is very much with us. A principal reason for including him in our selections is the sheer celebrity of the man: he has written more words on management that have been read by more people than any living man. Yet it's not the only reason for choosing him. If we were compiling a selection of twentieth-century sermons, we would not include one or more by Billy Graham merely because he had reached so many people, including some in the highest places. Quality is our first criterion. And Drucker has it.

Yet writing about him is a puzzlement. Unlike all the other thinkers quoted in the selections, he has no central point of view, no unifying theory that he has pursued with more or less constancy throughout his career, no commitment to a specific method or discipline. Part of the answer lies in a paradox: Although Drucker is probably the best-known behavioral scientist, he is not, as he is the first to admit, a behavioral scientist at all. His formal training is in economics, but he classifies himself as a journalist—and what is sufficient for Drucker should be sufficient for us, too.

It is as a journalist that Drucker deserves to be understood and appreciated. He is critic, not creator; the man of uncommon experience and inspired common sense who exposes the fallacies or improves on the insights of minds more original but less balanced than his own.

We cited inspired common sense as one of Drucker's qualities. Here's an example, drawn from *The Practice of Management,* in which Drucker describes the limitations of operations research and all its techniques with these words: "They cannot determine what is the right question. They cannot set objectives for the solution. Nor can they set rules. Similarly, the new tools cannot make the decision concerning the best solution; they cannot by themselves make a decision effective. Yet these are the most important phases in decision-making."

There is nothing, or very little, that is original here. Most of the points have been scored separately by previous critics at inordinate length in the most constipated prose or reluctantly conceded by operations researchers themselves. What Drucker did was to state all the major reservations and do it with unequaled clarity and brevity.

In all fairness to operations research, let's add that Drucker went on to discuss the very real contributions that operations research could make to the decision-making process.

We hope that we have indicated something about the sources of Drucker's deserved popularity. For the rest, let us recommend you to his books. We have listed only four out of eleven, but they're all worth reading.

The Practice of Management, Harper and Bros., New York, 1954.
Managing for Results, Harper and Row, New York, 1964.
The Age of Discontinuity, Harper and Row, New York, 1968.
Technology, Management and Society, Harper and Row, New York, 1970.

Self-control through Measurements*

The greatest advantage of management by objectives is perhaps that it makes it possible for a manager to control his own performance. Self-control means stronger motivation: a desire to do the best rather than just enough to get by. It means higher performance goals and broader vision. Even if management by objectives were not necessary to give the enterprise the unity of direction and effort of a management team, it would be necessary to make possible management by self-control.

So far . . . I have not talked of "control" at all; I have talked of "measurements." This was intentional. For "control" is an ambiguous word. It means the ability to direct oneself and one's work. It can also mean domination of one person by another. Objectives are the basis of "control" in the first sense; but they must never become the basis of "control" in the second, for this would defeat their purpose. Indeed, one of the major contributions of management by objectives is that it enables us to substitute management by self-control for management by domination.

That management by self-control is highly desirable will hardly be disputed in America or in American business today. Its acceptance underlies all the talk of "pushing

---

* Reprinted by permission of the publisher from Peter F. Drucker, *The Practice of Management,* Harper & Row, New York, 1954, pp. 130–133.

decisions down to the lowest possible level," or of "paying people for results." But to make management by self-control a reality requires more than acceptance of the concept as right and desirable. It requires new tools and far-reaching changes in traditional thinking and practices.

To be able to control his own performance a manager needs to know more than what his goals are. He must be able to measure his performance and results against the goal. It should indeed be an invariable practice to supply managers with clear and common measurements in all key areas of a business. These measurements need not be rigidly quantitative; nor need they be exact. But they have to be clear, simple and rational. They have to be relevant and direct attention and efforts where they should go. They have to be reliable—at least to the point where their margin of error is acknowledged and understood. And they have to be, so to speak, self-announcing, understandable without complicated interpretation or philosophical discussion.

Each manager should have the information he needs to measure his own performance and should receive it soon enough to make any changes necessary for the desired results. And this information should go to the manager himself, and not to his superior. It should be the means of self-control, not a tool of control from above.

This needs particular stress today, when our ability to obtain such information is growing rapidly as a result of technological progress in information gathering, analysis and synthesis. Up till now information on important facts was either not obtainable at all, or could be assembled only so late as to be of little but historical interest. This former inability to produce measuring information was not an unmixed curse. For while it made effective self-control difficult, it also made difficult effective control of a manager from above; in the absence of information with which to control him, the manager had to be allowed to work as he saw fit. . . .

This should not be misunderstood as advocacy of low performance standards or absence of control. On the contrary, management by objectives and self-control is primarily a means to obtain standards higher than are to be found in most companies today. And every manager should be held strictly accountable for the results of his performance.

OTHER PROBLEMS WITH CONTROLS

Managers must be aware that employees are very sensitive to controls. They adjust their behavior accordingly, although the adjustment may not be what the manager hoped for. As we shall see, managers have to be very careful to select measurements that do not encourage responses that are destructive of the work organization. Inadvertently, many managers do, in fact, utilize such poor controls.

OUTPUT QUALITY MAY BE LOWERED

Here are some examples of destructive influences:

Certain employees were encouraged to produce as many units as possible by being told that their production was the primary measure of their effectiveness and by being offered extra pay (incentive piecework) for what they produced above a given standard. Gradually management discovered that the employees were becoming very careless about how much material they used, about keeping their equipment well-maintained and their work areas cleaned. Quality was a continuing problem because, in rushing the job, employees produced a great deal of marginal work.

Other organizational problems emerged. When management changed the material from which the parts were produced, the workers wanted the standard lowered (to enable them to get to bonus earnings more quickly), claiming that the new material was harder to handle and slowed down the machines. Also, when management attached new feeding devices to the machines (to lessen employee effort and make high production easier), the workers fought against management's raising the standard. When management argued that it wasn't fair to pay workers for the additional production that would be possible because of the new feeders (which were quite expensive), the employees charged that this was just a trick to lower their bonus.

In short there are dangers in poorly chosen controls and incentives. They may cause employees to neglect unmeasured or unpaid-for parts of their job. And they may create additional sources of antagonism between employees and their manager over what is a fair standard and what can be changed in the work environment.

COMPETITION VERSUS COOPERATION

There can be many other destructive results. An employee who is being measured and rewarded for doing a job in a certain way may become less cooperative with his fellow workers. If strongly motivated by the control and/or the reward, he may ignore their requests for help or for minor modifications in what he is doing that will make his work more consistent with their jobs.

Under strong incentives, employees can even begin to fight with each other over who gets the easiest or more lucrative jobs. A supervisor described his own experience like this:

I've had an awful time supervising these store clerks; they would kill each other if I gave them a chance to rush the big spenders who come in. At the same time, they all manage to be busy when a poorly dressed customer comes in and argue whose turn it is for fear that they'll be wasting time and losing commission. Each blames the other for not taking time to straighten up stock because they're too busy trying to write up sales.

In clothing plants, one can even see hair-pulling and fist fights over the distribution of new work, since some sewing jobs are slightly easier and permit more bonus earnings. Employees, like the managers themselves, are under strong controls, and they learn to pass the buck.

I got sore when those parts didn't fit—those guys were speeding so just to make bonus—so I didn't see anything wrong with throwing them in the tote box and letting the next group down the line sort them out. After all, I lost time because of the machinists' selfishness and I can't be expected to worry about the next group.

Among salesmen, one finds high-pressure tactics to make the sale and indifference to customer-servicing needs after the sale that result from supervisory pressure for higher performance. Several years ago, the telephone company found that carefully measuring how many connections were made by central-switchboard electricians (who did the rewiring for changed telephone numbers) spurred them into making more connections, but at the expense of quality. The old wire, from the previous connection, was not removed effectively, and after a few months, the back panels of the switchboard became so filled with old, unconnected wire that extra manpower was necessary just to clean it out.

Managers are not immune to this single-purpose emphasis. On production lines, the typical end-of-the-month competition to meet production quotas often encourages managers to "bleed" the line—to push everything in process through and leave nothing in the line to begin the next month's work. They also engage in what is called "balloon squeezing"— trying to prove that costs ought to be assigned to departments other than their own.

I was putting great pressure on my key men to keep welding costs down. I discovered that they were having the welders paint over weld defects that then wouldn't show up until the assembly or test operations—someone else's department. Then the other department's budget would get socked for the rework labor cost and my men would come out smelling like a rose.

GOOD CONTROLS TAKE TIME

An old-fashioned and fallacious view of bonus and incentive plans is that they relieve the supervisor of a good deal of time-consuming responsibility. This view assumed that the employee, motivated to earn extra money, would now take care of both himself and his work. But it doesn't work out that way, as we have seen, because incentives create their own supervisory problems.

Employees emphasize the most "profitable" parts of their job and ignore other aspects which may be critical to the flow of work and coordination between jobs. They argue with one another and with management over who has the most lucrative assignments and they are reluctant to accept any procedure, equipment, or materials changes which may injure their earnings potential. There are really more, rather than fewer, supervisory problems with incentives.

This does not mean, however, that incentives have no value. There may be a number of routine jobs that can be very well defined, that are highly autonomous (others don't depend closely on them) and that the employee cannot easily distort. Under these circumstances, the constant reward-reinforcement provided by "beating quota" can and does encourage greater productivity. Then the worker learns that greater productivity is rewarding personally, and he tends to repeat his behavior. Also, incentives may provide some job satisfactions that would be nonexistent on many dull, routine types of jobs. There can be on-the-job pride and pleasure coming from the sense of winning economic payoffs. But there may be fewer such jobs than the manager imagines or hopes, as we shall now see.

OUT-OF-CONTROL CONTROLS

Sometimes managers become angry when they detect that employees are finding ways of "beating the system," that is, of looking good under the control being utilized but hurting the job. Rather than admit to poorly chosen controls, the supervisor blames the employee. Then he starts issuing more and more rules to circumscribe what an employee can do. They require time to enforce and complicate the work situation.

Incentive workers, in an effort to produce more, were wearing out tool bits at an extravagant rate. The supervisor decided that an employee would have to sign a special form to get a tool bit from the storeroom. Also, if he got more than one bit per day, the form would have to be countersigned by the supervisor himself. In a short time, employees complained that the standard rate on the job should be loosened because there was always a line filling out forms at the storeroom. Also, there were long arguments over whether the excess wear on the bits was due to poor maintenance on the machine, poorer quality steel, or just employee carelessness. The supervisor found himself embroiled in these discussions and in approving tool-bit requests to the point that nearly one-third of his day was devoted to this process, which had required no intervention on his part before the incentive plan was introduced.

It is often worthwhile to reconsider whether the right controls are currently being used before instituting more complicated rules and procedures. Furthermore, employees are

very adept at finding their way around almost any new
rule or procedure, if you make it advantageous for them to
do so.

A SYSTEMS VIEW OF CONTROLS

Essential as controls are, we should be alert to the difficulties
of both establishing and using them. If they go awry, they
can be detrimental to the overall organizational system and to
individual production. We have already described two
tendencies relating to their use:

1. Managers are likely to employ, as a measure of job performance, aspects of the job which are easiest to count
objectively. They are apt to ignore aspects of the job that are
more difficult to measure. Unfortunately, many of the latter
job elements contribute to coordination and cooperation
between jobs and to real productivity as distinct from individual "scores." This is a systems view of jobs and of
controls.
2. Employees are quick and alert to sense where the real payoffs are and to respond accordingly. These responses to incentives and controls can introduce very real distortions into
the organization.

What must managers do to avoid these destructive aspects
of controls? Think carefully about the jobs being appraised in
terms that we dealt with in Chapter 2. Rather than starting
with what is available to measure, what is countable, start
with the job and all its interrelationships. Is the employee
performing a job which is truly an independent one or a job
that relates closely to the jobs being performed by others?
What are the most critical elements in a job which will
affect the total performance of the work system for which
the management is responsible?

In most cases, the supervisor will find that a job requires
more diverse behavior than can be measured by a single
yardstick or single number.

In some cases there may not be neat, objective measures
available, for example, in assessing an employee's helpfulness
to those around him. However, the worker needs to know
that his behavior is being observed, and he should be able to
detect positive reinforcement from the supervisor when he
acts commendably in this area. In other cases, managers may
shift their measures from the individual to the group. It may

be better to encourage cooperation by measuring the group's total production—thereby stressing collaboration—than to set up competition and fighting among its members.

Often a manager emphasizes effort when he should emphasize accomplishment. Maintenance workers in one plant were measured in terms of how many repairs they made per week. Later, the measure was shifted to how little downtime there was for the equipment. Now, maintenance employees were encouraged to keep things going. Often, in the past, a worker would see a minor malfunction in a piece of equipment that was still operating satisfactorily. He would get credit, however, not for preventive maintenance but only for fixing a broken machine when he was asked to do so. Now, however, if he spent a few minutes adding oil or tightening a belt or removing an obstruction, the equipment might not break down at all! In effect, he worked less hard by using intelligence and alertness, and management got more overall production than when employees were measured on the basis of how hard they worked.

On college faculties, teachers who have to obey the "publish or perish" commandment tend to neglect teaching. Even though teaching performance is harder to measure objectively, there are a variety of ways to sample student opinion and to detect the teachers whose classes are either readily filled up or consistently avoided. When the professors know that teaching also is being measured, they devote energy and care to this part of the job.

Controls and the Introduction of Change

Another aspect of a systems view of controls is the manager's use of his own time. As we have said, the manager depends upon his controls to tell him where something is going wrong which may require his attention. Quality is falling off on the stitching machines, absenteeism is climbing among the younger men in his department, squabbling is increasing among employees over job assignments. Each of these measures should bring him into action to get the system back to its normal operations: quality up, absenteeism down, intragroup squabbling down. Sometimes he must seek out a deeply buried problem (using good interviewing techniques). At other times, he may just give an order such as "Send that machine down to the repair shop and transfer the work to that idle equipment." The important thing is that he take action to get the system going.

The good manager also keeps track of where he is spending his time. How often must he talk with John about absenteeism? How often is that machine breaking down? Where he finds problems that are taking his time consistently and that seem to recur again and again each time he thinks he has them solved, he should take them as a signal that there is a more fundamental problem in the situation.

In a sense, the manager learns from this type of control. It measures his own use of time and shows that his intervention is not working. Perhaps the employee is unsuitably placed or the equipment is the wrong type for the job. These time-consuming areas require a major investment of work hours to solve once and for all. The manager may have to initiate a series of discussions with the employee, with the Personnel Department, and even with the union steward concerning a transfer of the wayward employee. Or he may have to undertake many long talks with his boss and the chief engineer to convince them that the machine is the wrong type for the work required of it.

Many managers are loath to invest extra days or even weeks in problems that have already cost them a great deal of time and effort. Yet, these are just the problems which require significant organizational changes if they are to stop being a drain on the supervisors' scarce time and energy resources.

Therefore, the good manager seeks out, by the systems type of control, the real trouble spots in his department. He then initiates, difficult as it may be, the process of organizational change, to rid himself of the time drain caused by recurring problems. Every manager, even those at the bottom of the executive ladder, has a responsibility to keep changing his organization as these recurring problems show themselves. Identifying and solving them is the mark of the successful manager.

CONCLUSION

New managers are often told that employees resist change. As we have seen in previous chapters, there are a number of instances in which they do so. But managers also need to remember that human beings are enormously flexible. They are constantly learning—that is, they are adjusting to the rewards and punishments that they find in their environment in such a way as to improve their lives. An adage of learning theory, called "the law of effect," is worth emphasizing:

Behavior is repeated which proves rewarding and tends not to be repeated when it is punishing.

Thus employees are very responsive to the rewards and punishments they find on their jobs. In fact, they engage in a great deal of "search behavior" to smoke out the real (as distinct from verbalized-by-the-boss) rewards and the real punishments. After all, the job situation is very ambiguous. The employee is typically asked or told to do many things that he doesn't have time or energy to do thoroughly. There are countless rules, norms, and practices (initiated by the company or the work group) which may not be mutually compatible. So he has the problem of finding his way in this maze.

Unfortunately, managers tend to forget that everything they do communicates rewards and punishments to employees. In the employee's eyes, formal controls, appraisals, salary increases, promotions, discipline, incentive pay, words of praise and criticism—all are summed together. From all these, employees deduce what is worth doing, what must never be done, and what they can get away with. A manager must always keep in mind the total impression he is communicating.

On the other side, the manager has to find ways of adequately assessing employee job behavior in order to accomplish a number of distinctive management responsibilities. These are:

1. To train employees through adequate reinforcement
2. To determine where his own supervisory intervention is required
3. To have the knowledge necessary to make personnel decisions on such actions as merit increases and promotions
4. To pay equitable bonuses or incentives when appropriate
5. To detect undesirable trends before serious damage is done

For all these purposes, he needs realistic information about employee performance. Naturally, perhaps, there is a tendency for managers to look only at those aspects of a job which are easiest to measure or appraise. They may neglect aspects of the job that, though more difficult to measure, may contribute significantly to total systems performance. This can lead to serious distortions as employees seek to "look good" in terms of what is being measured and slight those aspects of their jobs which are not measured.

From a managerial point of view, the controls that a manager uses to appraise employee performance thus become one of the most critical determinants of that behavior. In effect, managers have much more influence over employee behavior than they sometimes imagine. They can change this behavior more easily than they think—by changing controls.

What we have been describing is not much different from what happens in the classroom where there is an overemphasis on grades produced by a final examination. Rather than learn the material in the course, the student may spend all his time trying to figure out the instructor's special interests and the questions is he likely to ask. Everything he does has to help him "beat" that exam. Still worse, when students are told that the class will be graded "on a curve," meaning that one student's grade will go down if someone else does better, they won't even help each other learn. Every teacher and student faces the problem that some objective measure of performance is useful feedback and provides a summary of accomplishment needed by both sides. Yet overemphasis on a single measure, say a final exam grade, produces deleterious effects on both classroom and out-of-the-classroom behavior. This is one reason why, in recent years, there has been growing emphasis on programmed self-instruction in which there are built-in continuous feedback and reward and punishment directly related to the total learning process.

The manager must be careful, then, not to use as a primary control or measure of performance the most convenient statistic or objective measurement in the situation. This type of measure often neglects the total system in which the employee's job is embedded and fails to motivate him to do his total job. The manager must therefore find a number of measures of performance to give adequate weight to all the duties and responsibilities associated with a given employee. These measures are essential to employee motivation.

SELECTED REFERENCES

Whyte, W. F., et al., *Money and Motivation,* Harper & Row, New York, 1955.

McGregor, D., *Leadership and Motivation,* MIT Press, Cambridge, Mass., 1966.

Hampton, D., *Modern Management: Issues and Ideas,* Dickenson, Belmont, Calif., 1969, pp. 396–446.

THE EDUCATION OF GREG HORNING: MARCH 4

Greg's call to Ed Briscoe hadn't proved anything one way or the other, but it had made Greg think of something he hadn't been aware of before. Those knobs could loosen up by themselves sometimes, Ed said, but whatever it was, he wasn't going to let his crew get stuck with the blame. They had too much to do—they couldn't be expected to run all over the plant every time a knob rattled. Ed's loyalty to his crew struck Greg. He'd been expecting his group to support him; now, he suddenly saw that it could work both ways.

Still, if he reversed his decision, he'd look awfully foolish. Maybe he should check with Al Sykes, head of personnel. By the time Sykes finished raking him over the coals, Greg conceded he deserved it.

"You just don't pick someone who's been with the company for over thirty years as a fall guy," Sykes told him. "Not when there's a union in the shop. These men stick together—and with the amount of proof you had, you'd have to be out of your mind to think you could make it stick. You'd better do something to get yourself out of this mess—and fast."

So the morning after the accident, Greg had called Kilpatrick at home. He admitted to being hasty in his judgment and apologized for having accused Kilpatrick of being drunk. He told Kilpatrick to forget about the layoff, but since his machine wasn't functioning he might as well take the day off. Kilpatrick surprised Greg by saying, no, he'd rather come in. His wife had him doing odd jobs around the house anyway, and if he was there he could at least work with one of the other men and help make up for the lost time.

The reactions of the others surprised Greg, too. They'd pitched in making up the time on that rush order—they'd only lost a half a day getting it out. Greg had appreciated that and he'd told them so. During the next few days, Helen had called him over a couple of times to check pieces with him. They talked a little and she told him about her son who was majoring in business administration at college. "He's just about as pigheaded as you," she'd said, and they'd both laughed. Then there was that morning when he'd come in with the new tie—a wide one, with red, white, and blue stripes. Jeannette had called out to him in the same teasing tone she used with the men on the floor, "Hey, boss! You getting Rick to buy your clothes for you?" He blushed and grinned and they all had laughed.

Gradually the crew was becoming more friendly and relaxed. Greg found that he was relaxing too. Furthermore, he was beginning to see that there were better ways of tackling his big, unsolved problem—increasing production by 25 percent.

As the crew was starting back to their machines after the mid-morning break, Greg came out on the floor.

"Before you get back to work, I thought we might have a talk." He felt a little nervous, remembering the other "talks" he had had with his crew, but they had interested expressions on their faces and some of them were looking around for a place to sit.

"Sure, Greg. What'd you have in mind?" Phil Martello said.

"Well, Phil. I'll tell you. You all know the trouble I'm having with the big boss upstairs about our output. He's really on my neck for more production from this department, and I thought you people might have some worthwhile ideas about how we can get more out." He looked around the group, waiting. Martello was the first to speak.

"Gee, Greg. I don't know. I just don't know. We work damn hard. Now I don't know what more we could do. Of course, the materials they give us these days aren't what they used to be and there's always something going wrong with the machines. I mean, look at what happened with Ted's a couple of weeks ago . . ."

"And what about the materials handlers?" Helen cut in. "You know how they're always putting the tote boxes in the wrong place. And can you ever find one of those guys when you need them?"

"Well, you know I've tried to talk to them, Helen," Creegmore said. "They just won't cooperate. Now that I think of it, the mixing department does whatever they can to mess things up for us, too. Like you say, Phil, the plastic they been sending us is lousy quality."

"Okay. Let's back up a minute." Greg put in with evident exasperation. "So far all the complaints have been with other departments. What about what goes on right here. Every thing can't be the fault of another department. What can we do ourselves to get more work out?"

"Well, as I was saying, Greg,"—this was Phil again—"we do a fair day's work for a fair day's pay. In fact, we probably do a hell of a lot more than we get paid for right now. I don't see how we can do any more."

"Besides, Greg," Jeannette added, "what's the good of the men turning more pieces out when Helen and I—we get backed up with the flashes and the sorting and packing and all of that. If you put too much pressure on the men, they get careless, and that means more work than we can handle. See what I mean?"

"Now wait a minute, Jeannette," Phil broke in. "Don't you start blaming us. As I say, we do a fair day's work. And if we're more careful about the rough edges we'd have to slow down. Henry and Rick, now, it'd be easier for them to turn out more where they've got the larger machines."

"Hold on, now, Phil," Greg said. "No one is *blaming* anyone. We're just trying to figure out where our problems are so we can get rid of them. As far as the other departments go—I'll get to work on them and see what I can do. But what about us—that's the big point—we've got to cooperate too. Right?" He looked around the group. Creegmore and Alfred shrugged their shoulders, but the rest nodded or smiled.

The crew went back to work and Greg returned to his office. Not that the meeting went out of his mind—for the rest of the day the same questions about the crew's complaints kept popping up. How much of it had been buckpassing and an attempt to duck the pressure? How much of the griping was legitimate? And even if it was, what could he do about it? Most important, under these conditions, could they really do anything much to speed up output without sacrificing quality? It looked like a real can of worms.

QUESTIONS

1. It is easy for most employees to convince themselves (and to try to convince others) that they are working very, very hard (regardless of how hard they are working) and that their supervisor doesn't realize how conscientious they are. Is Greg here helping to give his people an overinflated view of their own accomplishments?
2. How can Greg reinforce positively their accomplishment associated with "pitching in" and getting out that rush order without agreeing with everything they say?
3. Are there any "internal" incentives on these jobs, associated with the way the work is done, that Greg is not

conscious of that either encourage or discourage good performance?

4. Given the nature of this work group and the work they are doing, what elements of employee performance should be discussed only with individuals and what elements should be discussed with the group as a whole?

6. The communications problem:
dimensions and solutions

MISS OTIS REGRETS

"Helen, there are a few things I want you to do while I'm away," said Charley Pringle. "First, there's that hydraulic pump for Drysdale Oil. Call Tom Watkins, the company's plant manager, and remind him that I promised speedy delivery on the Drysdale order. It's a big account, and if we ever lost it . . ."

"Yes, of course I'll call Mr. Watkins," replied Helen Otis. "Just how do you want me to put it?" she added in a tentative tone.

"Oh, by the way, before I forget, there's a little favor. It's Mrs. Pringle's birthday on Thursday. Call up the florist and order a couple of dozen roses—come to think of it, she likes amaryllis—claims they go with the living room rug. Get that, Helen? I'll be in the doghouse if you forget."

"Oh yes, Mr. Pringle."

At this point the telephone rang and Charley Pringle had a couple of minutes' conversation with a salesman about some of his problems. Miss Otis sat silent meanwhile, with her pencil poised in mid-air.

"Where were we? Of course. The Drysdale order. When you call Tom, remind him, in case he's forgotten, just how important Drysdale is to us. No, maybe you'd better not. If you put too much pressure on Tom, he really gets his back up. That man cares more about keeping to his schedules than he does about satisfying customers. A good engineer, but no businessman."

Miss Otis nodded her head sympathetically.

Aftermath

A week later, Charley Pringle came back, after a swing around the Northeast, to find a telegram from the Drysdale company requesting immediate delivery of the hydraulic pump and threatening to cancel all its business unless it received the shipment within forty-eight hours. Charley pressed the interoffice buzzer till the blood ran to the tip of his index finger.

"You rang, Mr. Pringle," said a distraught Helen upon entering.

"Yes, I rang, Helen—just to see whether you were alive and alert," Charley added sarcastically. "What happened to the Drysdale order? Didn't you call Tom Watkins and tell him to give top priority to that order? Drysdale had to have that pump."

"I called, of course. But I'm sorry—that wasn't quite the message I got across. I said you were concerned about the order and would appreciate whatever Mr. Watkins could do to get it out."

"That's what you said!" Charley leaned back in his chair and groaned.

JACK HENNING PUTS THINGS STRAIGHT

"You're probably wondering, Henry, why we're taking the chrome off the valve and making a few other changes," said Jack Henning, twenty-eight years old, an industrial engineer, with a buttondown shirt and a reputation for being whip-smart.

"Yes, I've been curious," replied Henry Schmidt, aged forty-three, a production foreman, with a plain white shirt and proud of his department and of his own competence.

"Well, I'll keep it short and sweet. We ran the whole process through the simulator—computer, I mean—and found that by substituting plastic for chrome, we could make big cost savings at a very small decrease in performance. A slight increase in the obsolescence factor would have been desirable too, but that we decided to forgo—at least for the time being," added Jack, brightening a little.

"Okay, I've got it," replied Henry. "We make something cheaper and we make more money."

"That's not really it, Henry. We've cut out a few features, but mostly the chrome, which was really an administrative circumstance in the first place. And our market researchers have checked—chrome doesn't count. Nine out of ten customers have indicated a willingness to accept plastic as a substitute, particularly if it means a price reduction, which it can." Henning underscored his words. "Got the picture?" he ended, with uplift in his voice.

"Got the picture," answered Henry.

Aftermath

Henry faced the crew. "What's the score, Hank?" asked Roy Le Blanc, the senior operator. "Yeah, what are they trying to put over on us?" chimed in George Williams, another operator.

"Well, it's like this," Henry began slowly and with some reluctance. "We had it pretty much figured. They decided to make more money out of the valves and found out that they could get away with it by making them poorer. Wish I could read it any other way. Any way you look at it, the company comes out ahead," finished Schmidt glumly.

"Are we going to get some of the dough?" Roy asked.

"Yeah, what about that?" a chorus arose from the rest of the crew.

Schmidt shrugged his shoulders.

HOW IMPORTANT IS COMMUNICATION?

Sound exaggerated, these two caselets? Yes, but not by much. Both situations are repeated not once, but hundreds of times—not every week but every day. The boss is disorganized, distracted, contradictory, and ambiguous, as he was in "Miss Otis Regrets," or arrogant, remote, uncomprehended, and uncomprehending, as he was in "Jack Henning Puts Things Straight."

Do breakdowns in communications such as these matter? To any manager, at any level, the answer must be yes. The typical manager spends at least 60 percent of his time communicating. One manager, observed for a period of thirty-five days, for example, had only twelve periods when he spent fifteen minutes of his time *not* talking, while another study found that in one English company, executives spent, on the average, 80 percent of their time talking. In short, communications count.

Drucker drives the point home: "The manager has a specific tool: information. He does not 'handle' people, he motivates, guides, organizes people to do their own work. His tool—his only tool to do all this is the written or spoken word or the language of numbers. No matter whether the manager's job is engineering, accounting or selling, his effectiveness depends on his ability to listen and to read, on his ability to speak and to write—in other words, on his overall abilities as a communicator."

For the manager, the communications process involves much more than simply expressing his ideas accurately and precisely, difficult as that may be on occasions. Nine-tenths of the time, when he communicates on the job he's not gossiping—he's working. What he has to say is a prelude to action—telling someone what to do or trying to persuade him to do it. Or else he's on the receiving end of some instructions or some persuasion. In all these cases, the communication is intended to have a direct consequence.

That's why it's so important for any communication to be understood correctly and that's also why understanding is never enough. To be effective, a communication must fulfill three requirements: It must be *understood*. It must be *believed*. And, finally, it must be *accepted*.

Therefore, when we talk, in this chapter, about barriers to communications and what the supervisor can do to overcome them, we will consider in turn the three types of barriers: barriers to understanding, barriers to credibility, and lastly, barriers to acceptance.

Now that we've established the importance of communications to the supervisor—and for that matter to every level of manager, let's go back to our cases and analyze what went wrong in both of them, how the communications barriers present could have been bridged, and what the cases tell us about communications barriers in general.

The Communication Barriers in the Otis Case

Our sympathies to Miss Otis. As a communicator, Charley Pringle was an abysmal failure. He made just about every mistake in the book. In the initial formulation of his instruction, he committed the always fatal error of making the key word ambiguous. Disraeli wrote that "words are but empty vessels into which I pour meaning." Fine—but what Charley Pringle meant by "speedy" might mean something else to Miss Otis and something else again to Tom Watkins, the plant manager. When Miss Otis pleaded for clarification— "Just how do you want me to put it?" was a distress signal born of confusion if we ever heard one—Charley ignored her and digressed to a totally different topic, ordering flowers for his wife's birthday. When he finally got back to what Miss Otis was supposed to say to Tom Watkins, he told her one thing, only to retract the instruction in the next sentence. Finally, when Miss Otis had relayed her version of the communication to Tom Watkins and failed to obtain the result Charley Pringle intended, he gave way to self-righteous indignation based on his fanciful recollection of his conversation with her. As with many of us, Charley's memory served as a defense mechanism that absolved him of any responsibility. What he should have told Miss Otis was that she and he and Tom Watkins could divide the blame between them.

Our little tale has several morals, first among them being the importance of avoiding ambiguity in communications. Don't use slippery words with multiple meanings, such as "speedy," "faster," "slower." Instead, use phrases with unmistakable meanings. "Give this order top priority," was what Charley Pringle remembered after the fact as his message to Watkins. "Give top priority to the Drysdale order" was much more calculated to get action on the order than the "speedy delivery" of his spoken message. Still better—more urgent and less ambiguous—would have been "I promised delivery on that pump within forty-eight hours." Maybe Watkins would have ignored the communication, but certainly he would have understood it. To take another example, if a foreman were dissatisfied with the pace of a grinding-wheel operator, he would stand small chance of the operator's achieving a satisfactory rate by merely telling him, "Go faster." However, if he expressed his goal to the operator in revolutions per minute, the operator might or might not make it, depending on his aptitude, attitude, and other factors, but at least he would understand the goal the foreman had in mind.

The other morals to be drawn from "Miss Otis Regrets" are simpler and more obvious: Not only say what you mean, but mean what you say. In other words, a supervisor compounds his chances of being misunderstood if, like Charley Pringle, he contradicts himself and changes his communication in midstream. As a corollary, it's important for the manager to plan any communications in advance: (1) to make sure that he knows his major theme, (2) to minimize the chances of having to contradict himself because he hasn't thought out the impact of his communication, and (3) to help insure that his communication will be clear and that he won't leave anything out.

A Simple Instruction?

Maybe this strikes you as much ado about very little. However, experience has shown that managers, and the rest of us, too, have difficulty in getting across even relatively simple instructions. To dramatize the point, one midwest corporation conducted the following exercise in its management-training program. The trainer drew five squares on a sheet of paper and kept the paper hidden. Then he asked one of the executives to draw square 1. Next he described where square 2 was in relation to square 1 and repeated this with squares 3, 4, and 5, the object being to have the executive draw the five squares to look exactly like the ones the trainer had drawn himself. What happened? The trainer repeated the experiment many times. But only in a small minority of cases was he successful in communicating a simple picture of five squares. In short, never underestimate the difficulty of communication.

One final moral from "Miss Otis Regrets": Don't interrupt

a communication with irrelevant digressions. Of course, interruptions are frequently unavoidable. The supervisor is the
man in charge of putting out fires. His phone keeps ringing,
people keep breaking into whatever he's doing to report on
emergencies—in brief, interruptions are part of his working life. At least he can avoid what Charley did and not be
responsible for interrupting the communication himself!
When Charley Pringle launched into his digression about his
wife's birthday flowers, he further compounded the confusion
of an already rattled Miss Otis. It would have served him
right if Tom Watkins had gotten an amaryllis plant!

PSYCHOLOGICAL BARRIERS TO
COMMUNICATION

The basic psychological barrier to communication is inherent
in the nature of language itself. Strictly speaking, we can't
convey meaning. All we can do is convey words. And as for
the words, they are what John Locke called them three hundred years ago—"merely arbitrary signs for certain ideas,
chosen by historical accident and liable to change." The real
meanings of words are in the minds of those who speak them
and in the minds of those who hear them, not in the words
themselves.

The implication, then, is that the full meaning of any word
or any communication (a communication being merely words
strung together in sequence) never appears until it is placed
in its context. And what do we mean by context? Nothing less
than the total personality and experience of listener and
speaker—their experience of the language, their knowledge
of one another, the frame of reference from which they view
the communication, their mood at the precise moment when
the communication is formulated and received. Looked at in
this way, successful communication appears to be what it in
fact is—a real achievement!

Our communications-receiving apparatus (sense organs)
and brain works like a combination converter and filter.
Instead of hearing what people say, we hear what our minds
tell us they said, which may be the same thing or may be
something very different. That we convert what we hear into
something relevant to our own past experience—and our
recent past at that, and not the speaker's; that we filter what
we hear through layers of bias shaped by group, class, age,
race, education, and occupation; that we distort or filter out
altogether everything that doesn't fit in with our preconceived
notions; that we continually convert sentiments into logic—

all give some measure of the problems involved in communicating.

Are you skeptical about people interpreting messages differently according to their past experience? Try a little experiment with yourself. Pretend you're a supervisor and further pretend that you're observing a group of your subordinates laughing heartily. You don't know the cause of the laughter—all you know is what you see and hear. What message comes across to you? There are three common reactions to such a situation, and yours may be one of them:

To the manager who believes work must be unpleasant in order to be productive, the laughter communicates to him that time is being wasted, and that maybe the assignments are too easy.

To the manager who believes that contented employees work harder, the laughter communicates that he is succeeding as a manager.

To the manager who is personally insecure, the laughter communicates the likelihood that the men are making fun of him.

Even if your reaction is different, we think you will concede the point: The same simple situation could convey very different messages, depending on what the listener brought to the situation.

Here's a simple example. The manager tells an employee that the company has lost some important jobs. The employee filters the message through his own experience. In the past, whenever his company has lost business, he has been thrown out of work. So what he hears the manager say is "You can expect to be laid off in the near future." When he comes in two weeks later and announces that he has taken a job with a competitor, the manager is shocked and surprised to hear that he thought his job was in danger.

What Happened to Jack Henning?

Our second little case, "Jack Henning Puts Things Straight," offers an example of communications block at the psychological level. When Henry Schmidt agreed that he had gotten the message, he wasn't consciously trying to deceive Jack Henning. It was just that the message he received was not the one that Jack was trying to convey. There were two messages, not one, and they differed greatly from each other.

Why the difference? Why couldn't Jack get through to

Henry? What were the barriers to effective communication between the engineer and the foreman?

A simple answer goes a long way toward explaining the problem. Jack and Henry belonged to different groups (what the psychologists call reference groups), identified themselves with different values, and shared different perceptions.

As an industrial engineer, Henning belonged to a group that traditionally has been obsessed with efficiency. To find a way of making any product that will (1) save substantial amounts of money while (2) diminishing the utility of the product only slightly as well as (3) having no negative effect on the sale of the product—this is the goal of every industrial engineer. Schmidt caught Henning in a moment of full professional pride.

From his perspective, Schmidt viewed the situation very differently. His pride was in his job, not the company. He identified with the work group he headed, not the overall organization—an identification common to most first-level supervisors. He was proud of doing quality work and he wanted to keep doing it. When Henning said that "chrome doesn't count," he obviously hadn't polled Schmidt or his crew. To them, the use of chrome had an emotional—if you will, a symbolic—significance. It meant, among other things, pride of product, aesthetic satisfaction from the job, the determination to be best even if it cost a little more. What Henning dismissed—the use of chrome—in a patronizing specimen of jargon as an "administrative circumstance" was something that had added to the self-esteem and contributed to the job satisfaction of Schmidt and his men. They cared little about what the market researchers said and even less about the computer's judgment. The message they received was that their jobs were being diminished and they were being involved in short-changing the customer with no hope of profiting themselves. We would wager that under these circumstances, Schmidt and his crew would see to it that not all of the savings anticipated by Henning were realized. Similar situations in industry have frequently led to similar disappointments.

CLOSING THE COMMUNICATIONS GAP

So far, we have emphasized the difficulties and complexities of communication, and we're not going back on anything we said. However, we also don't want to give the impression that most communications are inherently destined to be misunderstood and that communication is always a frustrating and usually a futile process. It doesn't always have to be that way, as almost every effective manager has learned. Feedback is what makes most of the difference between an effective and an ineffective communicator. What do we mean by feedback? How does it make such a big difference?

Using Feedback

A large group of management trainees listened intently as a trainer gave them elaborate instructions on how to arrange five dominoes in a certain pattern. But they were not permitted to ask him any questions. In another room, trainees received the same instructions, and they were allowed to ask the instructor as many questions as they pleased.

What happened? In the first room, only three trainees were able to arrange the dominoes correctly. In the second room, only four trainees did *not* arrange them correctly. What do you think accounted for the difference in performance? The answer is pretty simple: Feedback, the term adapted from engineering, refers to the ability of certain machines to check on their performance and to correct it, if necessary. The thermostat, for example, regulates the amount of furnace heat on the basis of feedback, in this case, the temperature of the room.

Norbert Weiner, who did some of the key pioneer work in applying the principles of electronic communications to human communications, observed in words that deserve to be writ in gold, "I never know what I said until I hear the response to it." In other words, you can't really know what you've communicated until you've gotten the feedback. What was true for Weiner is true for all of us. Only feedback can tell us what we're communicating or, in fact, whether we're communicating at all. Maybe the listener is tuning our messages out.

There are two prerequisites for successful feedback. A little feedback, of course, is better than none at all. But the more feedback the better. If the supervisor wants his listener to repeat what he thinks the manager said, he shouldn't limit him to yes or no responses, but instead should encourage him to say as much as he feels inclined.

Maximum feedback also requires face-to-face communication. Only when the manager can experience direct feedback from the receiver can he really know what the receiver is hearing and what he is failing to hear. He can catch the telltale gesture, the nervous cough, the turned-down corners of the mouth that alert him to the existence of the real meaning the receiver is giving to his words. There's a world in a wink, while memos can't frown. Written communications generally leave much unrevealed and unsuspected.

Let's return for one last look at our two whipping boys, Pringle and Tom Henning. Neither bothered to get any feedback, and therefore neither one had any way of being sure that he had communicated what he meant to say. Of course, the motivations underneath the failure to communicate were different. Charley was simply a well-intentioned bungler, or at worst a self-satisfied egoist. When Helen Otis plaintively inquired, "Just how should I put it?" Charley ignored the distress signal and went on to the next subject that absorbed his attention, the flowers for his wife's birthday. He assumed, as many managers have done, to their subsequent distress, that Helen understood what he said, the connotations as well as the words.

Tom Henning was different. His failure to communicate, together with his failure to obtain any feedback, was rooted in the same sentiment: indifference born of intellectual arrogance. Basically, he didn't care what Henry Schmidt thought of the change. If he agreed with it, maybe it would make a little difference on the shop floor, but the change had already been approved by the unbribable tribunal—the computer and the market researcher. Henry's opinion, in Tom Henning's context, was relevant but trivial.

Is feedback the complete answer to surmounting the barriers to communication? By no means. It's the biggest part of the answer, but as there are other facets to the communication problem, so too are there other solutions. Actually, two additional problems are interrelated with feedback.

The Medium and the Message

One is the problem of medium: Should the supervisor communicate orally or in writing? In one sense, we recognize that the question is immaterial. Several studies have shown that the supervisor communicates orally dozens, sometimes hundreds, of times daily in situations which leave him with no choice as to whether the communication should be oral or written. We'll restrict ourselves to the limited opportunities where the choice exists. In our discussion of feedback, we've already indicated that nothing, but nothing, can take the place of verbal communication. Yes, but on occasion it's imperative to reinforce verbal communication with a written follow-up. On what kind of occasion? Thereby hangs a story.

A manager we know put a certain price tag on his worth—

a combination of self-esteem and his reading of the market-place. A job turned up which fitted him, but there was a problem: The salary was short—within the target range of his goal, but still short. He made a clean breast of it to his prospective employer, confessed his deep interest in the job together with his hesitation because of the salary. In response, as he understood it then and later, he got a commitment to a salary figure upon employment, plus a raise six months later, that would bring him up to his concept of the going rate for his services. Six months later, no raise. The problem wasn't the quality of his work but contingencies. His raise was "dependent upon how well the company was doing," a consideration which had either never been made or which he had filtered out. In disgust, he quit. And no wonder, given his belief that his boss had reneged on a promise.

The lesson of this little tale? In matters which are important to the subordinate and therefore particularly susceptible to misinterpretation, the supervisor should follow up any verbal communication with a written confirmation. Of course, there are other circumstances when a supervisor should reinforce an oral communication with a written follow-up: When the communication is so lengthy, complex, or technical that the subordinate with the best will in the world would be likely to forget or misinterpret it, even if he understood it on first hearing. The supervisor, in preparing the written version, can take advantage of the feedback to get the full message across by stressing the elements he found people had difficulty in understanding.

Directing the Message

Another communication problem related to feedback is the question of layers of communication: How many intermediaries can there be between the communicator and the eventual recipient of the communication before the message is twisted and lost? An experiment conducted a few years ago at Bell Telephone Company sheds light on the probable answer.

Six men took part. The first man viewed a picture, received two minutes to memorize the details, and was then told to describe what he had seen to a second man. The process was repeated with the third, the fourth, and the fifth man. By the time the message came through to the sixth man, it was almost impossible to recognize the picture from his description of it.

Given man's propensity toward inattention and his capacity

for misinterpreting one part of the message and filtering out another part, the only sensible rule for the supervisor to adapt is this: If the communication is important, tell it to the man directly affected and tell him to his face so you can get immediate feedback. Put even one person between yourself and the recipient of the communication and you are asking for trouble. Like every rule, it has its necessary exception— time is short, the need to communicate is urgent, and other communications have a higher priority. Even so, the supervisor should follow up at the earliest possible opportunity to make sure that the other party has in fact received the message he intended him to get.

THE NONCOMMUNICATION

As a final barrier to communications being understood, let's consider the case of the message that was never understood because it was never delivered in the first place. Lest you think we're talking nonsense, we quickly add that we're talking about communications dictated by necessity and common sense but withheld by subordinates from the bosses who needed the information. The machine looks as if it's headed for a major breakdown, the man doesn't like the partner whom the boss has hired for the job, the secretary sees a better way of batching the work—all are matters which the boss need to know but frequently never hears. One study of a business organization concluded that it was common for most subordinates, particularly among the nonmanagement ranks and the first two levels of management, to withhold large amounts of need-to-know information from their superiors.

THE STATUS BARRIER

What's the explanation for this wholesale failure to communicate? Obviously, different subordinates have different reasons. One factor, however, is present in every situation: the status barrier. The supervisor worries so much about what the boss is thinking that he gives minimal attention to what his subordinates are thinking. His subordinates, for their part, care what the boss thinks, all right, but the status barrier inhibits their initiation of any contacts that aren't compulsory. Several studies have shown that bosses continually over-estimate the number of meaningful contacts they have with subordinates. And since information channels have never really developed, subordinates are naturally reluctant to communicate anything which could in any way have a negative effect on their relationship with their bosses. In some cases, obviously this reluctance is increased by other factors such as dislike and distrust of the boss, dissatisfaction with the overall job situation, or the influence of norms established by the group. It's significant that a study of boss–subordinate pairs found the fullest and most accurate communications occurred between a boss and a trusting subordinate who didn't want to get ahead.

THE OLD CREDIBILITY GAP

Getting communications understood correctly, as we have stated previously, is only part of the story. For any communication to be effective, the recipient must also believe and accept it. We subscribe fully to the words Whyte wrote a number of years ago in the book *Is Anybody Listening?* "Only with trust can there be any real communication, and until that trust is achieved, the gadgetry of communications are so much waste effort. Study after study has pointed to the same moral: before employees will accept management 'facts' they must first have overall confidence in the motives and sincerity of management."

How does the supervisor acquire a passport of credibility? Rigid adherence to two principles will carry him most of the way: He should tell the truth in his communications, and be sure that his actions support his words. There can be short-range advantages to lying or at least in not telling the whole truth as he knows it. However, sooner or later he is almost certain to be found out. And once lost, a reputation for credibility is almost never reclaimed.

Credibility is independent of position. Union members sometimes will believe in management pronouncements; people will believe even their enemies in war once they've established their reputation for credibility, as the British Broadcasting Company demonstrated in World War II. During the bleak years, the BBC had given the whole grim tale of defeats and disasters to its listeners. When the tide turned, Europeans of all nationalities tuned in to BBC and accepted its claims of a German rout—a well-deserved bonus of establishing a reputation for credibility.

The second point is just as obvious and just as important: What the supervisor *does* communicates to others more strongly than anything he says. To the extent that his actions contradict his words, he will be judged by others as a cynic trying to manipulate people or a man without integrity in whom no one should put any trust.

CARL R. ROGERS (1902–   )

Professor of psychology successively at Ohio State, Chicago, and the University of Wisconsin; now Resident Fellow at the Western Behavioral Sciences Institute; practicing psychotherapist for two generations; and through the medium of several books and numerous articles, therapist to mankind—that would be a fair measure of Carl Roger's career.

Yet it would be far from a full measure of what he has accomplished. More than any man living—and probably dead—he has taught people the meaning of communication and a good deal about how to achieve it. The principles and practices he first developed in order to help the neurotic and the disturbed to accept themselves, to grow, and to change, have proved equally valuable in breaking down the communication barriers between more normal people to help them to accept each other, to grow, and to change.

Rogers wrote that the therapist is most effective if he (1) is transparently real in his relationship with his client, (2) accepts the client as a separate, distinct person, and (3) is empathetic in his understanding, sees the world through the client's eyes. Substitute supervisor or manager for therapist and employee or worker for client, and the same criteria are equally valid for any meaningful communication between boss and subordinate.

That communication between managers and subordinates has made substantial progress in the past generation (and we believe it has) and that many managers have learned the value in sensitive situations of nondirective counseling and the nondirective interview, of "listening with a third ear" (listening for the implied as well as the stated meaning of what is said), is directly due to Carl Rogers and his techniques. As such, a generation of managers stands profoundly in his debt.

Still we haven't done Rogers complete justice. There is more to his thinking than an attitude toward communication and a hatful of communication techniques for overturning barriers and establishing mutual understanding, valuable as that certainly is.

Rogers, in the most profound sense of the word, is a social philosopher, a man who has assigned to himself no less a task than battling with the nature of man as defined by two millenia of Christian thinkers—original sin and all that—and buttressed by Freud with his bleak concept of the id and substituting in its place the scientific finding that the innermost core of man's nature is "basically socialized, forward-moving, rational and realistic." It is possible to applaud the effort, even if one is not convinced by the evidence.

As a social philosopher and practicing humanist, Rogers is preoccupied with the current and future role of the behavioral sciences, which he sees as a great force for good or evil. Here's the choice as he sees it: "We can, if we wish, choose to make men submissive, conforming, docile or . . . we can choose to use the behavioral sciences in ways which will free, not control; which will bring about constructive variability, not conformity; which will develop creativity, not contentment; which will aid individuals, groups, and even the concept of science, to become self-transcending in freshly adaptive ways of meeting life and its problems." Rogers, of course, comes down on the side of the Angels.

As for his books, the best known, the most available, and probably the best is *On Becoming a Person*, Houghton Mifflin Company, Boston, Sentry Edition, 1970. Also recommended is *Client-Centered Therapy*, Houghton Mifflin Company, Boston, 1951.

Dealing With Breakdowns in Communication— Interpersonal and Intergroup*

I would like to propose, as an hypothesis for consideration, that the major barrier to mutual interpersonal communication is our very natural tendency to judge, to evaluate, to approve or disapprove, the statement of the other person, or the other group. Let me illustrate my meaning with some very simple examples. As you leave the meeting tonight, one of the statements you are likely to hear is, "I didn't like that man's talk." Now what do you respond? Almost invariably your reply will be either approval or disapproval of the attitude expressed. Either you respond, "I didn't either. I thought it was terrible," or else you tend to reply, "Oh, I thought it was really good." In other words, your primary reaction is to evaluate what has just been said to you, to evaluate it from *your* point of view, your own frame of reference.

Or take another example. Suppose I say with some feeling, "I think the Republicans are behaving in ways that show a lot of good sound sense these days," what is the

* Reprinted by permission of the publishers from Carl R. Rogers, *On Becoming A Person*, Houghton Mifflin Company (Sentry Edition), Boston, 1970, pp. 329–334.

response that arises in your mind as you listen? The overwhelming likelihood is that it will be evaluative. You will find yourself agreeing, or disagreeing, or making some judgment about me such as "He must be a conservative," or "He seems solid in his thinking." Or let us take an illustration from the international scene. Russia says vehemently, "The treaty with Japan is a war plot on the part of the United States." We rise as one person to say "That's a lie!"

This last illustration brings in another element connected with my hypothesis. Although the tendency to make evaluations is common in almost all interchange of language, it is very much heightened in those situations where feelings and emotions are deeply involved. So the stronger our feelings the more likely it is that there will be no mutual element in the communication. There will be just two ideas, two feelings, two judgments, missing each other in psychological space. I'm sure you recognize this from your own experience. When you have not been emotionally involved yourself, and have listened to a heated discussion, you often go away thinking, "Well, they actually weren't talking about the same thing." And they were not. Each was making a judgment, an evaluation, from his own frame of reference. There was really nothing which could be called communication in any genuine sense. This tendency to react to any emotionally meaningful statement by forming an evaluation of it from our own point of view, is, I repeat, the major barrier to interpersonal communication.

But is there any way of solving this problem, of avoiding this barrier? I feel that we are making exciting progress toward this goal and I would like to present it as simply as I can. Real communication occurs, and this evaluative tendency is avoided, when we listen with understanding. What does this mean? It means to see the expressed idea and attitude from the other person's point of view, to sense how it feels to him, to achieve his frame of reference in regard to the thing he is talking about.

Stated so briefly, this may sound absurdly simple, but it is not. It is an approach which we have found extremely potent in the field of psychotherapy. It is the most effective agent we know, for altering the basic personality structure of an individual, and improving his relationships and his communications with others. If I can listen to what he can tell me, if I can understand how it seems to him, if I can see its personal meaning for him, if I can sense the emotional flavor which it has for him, then I will be releasing potent forces of change in him. If I can really understand how he hates his father, or hates the university, or hates communists—if I can catch the flavor of his fear of insanity, or his fear of atom bombs, or of Russia—it will be of the greatest help to him in altering those very hatreds and fears, and in establishing realistic and harmonious relationships with the very people and situations toward which he has felt hatred and fear. We know from our research that such empathic understanding—understanding *with* a person, not *about* him—is such an effective approach that it can bring about major changes in personality.

Some of you may be feeling that you listen well to people, and that you have never seen such results. The chances are very great indeed that your listening has not been of the type I have described. Fortunately I can suggest a little laboratory experiment which you can try to test the quality of your understanding. The next time you get into an argument with your wife, or your friend, or with a small group of friends, just stop the discussion for a moment and for an experiment, institute this rule. "Each person can speak up for himself only *after* he has first restated the ideas and feelings of the previous speaker accurately, and to that speaker's satisfaction." You see what this would mean. It would simply mean that before presenting your own point of view, it would be necessary for you to really achieve the other speaker's frame of reference—to understand his thoughts and feelings so well that you could summarize them for him. Sounds simple, doesn't it? But if you try it you will discover it is one of the most difficult things you have ever tried to do. However, once you have been able to see the other's point of view, your own comments will have to be drastically revised. You will also find the emotion going out of the discussion, the differences being reduced, and those differences which remain being of a rational and understandable sort.

Can you imagine what this kind of an approach would mean if it were projected into larger areas? What would happen to a labor-management dispute if it was conducted in such a way that labor, without necessarily agreeing, could accurately state management's point of view in a way that management could accept; and management, without approving labor's stand, could state labor's case in a way that labor agreed was accurate? It would mean that real communication was established, and one could practically guarantee that some reasonable solution would be reached.

HOW DOES THE SUPERVISOR ACQUIRE CREDIBILITY?

We'll discuss the full ramifications of the problem in Chapter 8, when looking at boss–subordinate relations. Suffice it to state here that the boss should always bear in mind the barrier that status erects to open channels of communication between superior and subordinate. The responsibility for initiating most communications is his—by necessity and by default.

Employees have eyes and ears. They can judge, usually with a high degree of accuracy, the fit between what the manager says and his previous actions. Take, for example, the supervisor who had always looked the other way where safety violations were concerned, believing (rightly or wrongly) that following the safety rules to the letter would interfere with meeting the production quotas on which he was really judged. Suddenly, he holds a safety meeting in which he talks tough— threatens to throw the book at safety violators. What message gets across to his subordinates? Probably not that he means what he says but that he is going through the motions because someone upstairs is concerned about the department's safety record. Furthermore, there will be real surprise and resentment if the supervisor proceeds to ferret out the violations at which he has previously winked and to punish the violators.

The irony is that this same lack of credibility can attach itself to quite sincere efforts on a manager's part to improve his relations with his subordinates—and sometimes thwart the efforts. We cite, for example, a manager of accounting, known behind his back as "the calculator" because of his cold, standoff manner in dealing with subordinates and associates. He was packed off for five days to a sensitivity-training program in which he learned the virtues of involvement with other people and of openness in dealing with them. The experience took, and he returned determined to remake his attitudes in dealing with people.

And he gave it the old college try, soliciting the reactions of people whom he had previously ignored, giving frank and full explanations of why he favored a particular course of action, being genuinely friendly and interested. The trouble was that no one met him halfway. His overtures were greeted with suspicion, his explanations were regarded as symptoms of previously unsuspected weakness, and his requests for advice were pretty much ignored. After a short time, he reverted to his old mode of action, thereby confirming the suspicions of those who felt all along that he was up to something. Of course, the story could have had a different ending if some of his associates had also participated in sensitivity training or if the manager had persisted longer with his changed behavior. Over time, his associates would have found the new look credible and accommodated themselves to it—with gratitude and mutual profit.

Tone—Words and Gestures—Expresses Attitude

We won't attempt a variation on McCluhan and contend that the tone is the message. But the *tone* of any communication, whether verbal or written, has a lot to do with whether or not it is believed and accepted.

Sometimes we even communicate, without words, things we don't mean. If the manager has been stopped by a policeman for speeding on his way to work, his general irritability toward any subordinates unlucky enough to come into contact with him—at least for the next hour or so—may "tell" them that he's dissatisfied with their work. Of course, that isn't his intention. But a raised eyebrow, a cold manner from someone who is usually warm, the measured tapping of fingers on a desk top—all convey a message just as surely as words do.

Humor in communications is also a risky device. Disraeli quipped that "the British People being subject to fogs and possessing a powerful middle class require grave statesmen," which helps to explain why he was so often in opposition and so seldom in power. Successful communication in the modern business organization doesn't require the solemnity of a Victorian statesman. But the manager still has to be sure of his ground in advance. Otherwise, he runs the risk of having people feel that he doesn't take the subject seriously—or a much graver danger—that he doesn't take them or their interests seriously. In either case, the message will be discounted.

Emotionalism and the appeal to fear are also dangerous in a communication. They're likely to boomerang and have the exact reverse of the desired effect. Consider the results of a study in which three different groups of high school students listened to three different lectures on dental hygiene. The first lecture pointed out the consequences of neglecting teeth in harrowing terms and stated that neglected teeth led to "pain, disease and body damage." The second lecture was moderate in tone, while the third avoided any reference to unpleasant consequences. All three lectures contained the same basic information and recommendations. The first lecture may have caused the most worry, but the third got results. The first group apparently resisted or resented the threat and tuned out the message—a phenomenon that sheds light on the relative failure, to date, of the campaign to intimidate the American public into giving up cigarettes.

LET THE FACTS SPEAK FOR THEMSELVES

By contrast, a sober and low-key presentation of the facts will help to create a climate of credibility. There's no scope for the talents of a Horace Hill, even minus his seventy-six trombones, on the plant or office floor. When the office supervisor, for example, announces the details of the company's new major medical plan, he's well advised not to tell employees how generous the new plan is but, instead, to let the facts speak for themselves. The employees have a pretty good idea of what similar and competing companies offer. If it's generous, they can see it for themselves, and if it isn't, the attempt to make it appear so will add an unappetizing dimension to an already unhappy situation.

The manager who makes a policy of letting the facts speak for themselves sooner or later is in for a bonus. He will face a situation, on occasion, in which he lacks the facts or can't disclose them, but assuming the condition is temporary, he can fall back on the mechanism psychologists call "transference." In this case, belief in the facts will be replaced by belief in an individual—the supervisor involved. "If he says it, that's good enough for us" will be the collective reaction from his subordinates.

One final word on tone: Arrogance is an enemy of credibility. We know a man with ability, a big reputation in his field, and considerable powers of articulation, but somehow many of his communications, even when they are correct, are disbelieved by the people whom he is addressing. The explanation is the arrogance of tone in his communication, conveying to the listener that his opinion is not worth considering, that his views, whenever they diverge, contain not a shred of substance. No matter how right our friend is, the egos of his listeners compel them to reject the message. We're reminded of a remark made to Ben Franklin at the close of a discussion in which he had been on the winning end, "Thee hath won thee an argument, but lost thee a friend."

Projection and Credibility

Any manager who wants to get his communication believed
would boost his chances if he put himself into his listener's
shoes and tailored his message to fit the vocabulary, values,
and interests of the listener. Take an obvious case: You're a
plant manager announcing an expanded production schedule
to the work force. You don't talk, in the message, about
bigger profits for the stockholders, higher salaries for management, and more promotional opportunities for the executive
staff. Instead, you will talk about more job security, the
opportunity for overtime, and the chance to acquire new and
valuable job skills. In other words, you tailor your message
to the interests of your listeners.

What happens to the manager who fails to practice projection in his communications? Consider, for example, a
young college-trained foreman who was having great difficulty getting his instructions across to the old-timers in his
work crew. He would hand out very specific instructions
and then discover, when he checked later, that the man had
done what he asked him to do—but that was all. The rest of
the job, which the foreman assumed quite properly the man
knew all about, wouldn't be done at all. He thought his way
out of this dilemma by using a little projection: He put
himself in the place of the old-timers and concluded that he
would resent getting detailed instructions from someone half
his age, particularly when he, as an old hand, had a basic
understanding of the job. When he applied this insight and
started making his instructions as general as possible, his
problems with half-finished jobs were over.

Of course, projection won't always turn up the answer to
getting a communication believed and accepted. But we
recommend its use to any manager, preferably before and
certainly after delivering a communication whenever he's
having trouble getting believed and accepted. Happily, most
communications permit a second chance.

Credibility and the Grapevine

What about the grapevine? How does it affect the credibility
of the manager's communications? First off, let's concede
that the manager has to live with the grapevine that is a
feature of every business. Actually, there's not one grapevine
but, depending on the size of the establishment, dozens or
even hundreds running up, down, and across. These grape-
vines, in turn, are rooted in large part in the nearly insatiable

curiosity of employees generally to know the answers to questions which management has answered but is unable or unwilling to disclose, the answers to questions which management has not yet answered, and the answers to questions which management hasn't even asked. As such, the collective grapevine fulfills an important function in informing people who are isolated from crucial information about the business—information to which they feel they're entitled. Furthermore, it has a generally unrecognized function in pressuring top management to come up with answers to problems or to ask questions about problems which were exposed to the top levels of the organization only via the grapevine itself. One study of a business organization purported to show that the grapevine transmitted more information than the formal systems. We are skeptical about the possibility of measuring the volume of information carried by the grapevine, but we concede that it is an important vehicle of communication. And it's here to stay.

The grapevine presents a problem to the supervisor when he has to communicate something which is at odds with what has previously been disseminated through this medium. Problem, you say? Isn't his the official word, and if he has a previous record as a truth-sayer, what's the problem? It isn't that simple. Experiments have demonstrated that a person is less likely to believe an official announcement if, prior to its issuance, he has heard a contradictory or conflicting rumor. However, if he gets the official words first, and the rumor second, he'll accept the former. That is, a message is more likely to be understood and accepted if it's not competing with another, and potentially conflicting, message. This was, of course, the basis for brainwashing in the Korean war. Some of our captured soldiers were isolated from their buddies and exposed to repeated anti-American slogans. A milder application of the same principle occurs when executives gather for an important policy meeting at a mountain-top conference center: Without the interference of normal communications, they would be more likely to "hear" the full message of the conference.

The implications for the manager are clear. In the words of General Nathan Bedford Forrest, "Get there fustest with the mostest." As soon as the supervisor is aware of an impending announcement, which all too often he himself hears first through the grapevine, he should pressure his superiors to get all the facts out in the open before the rumors begin. There's no other way of beating the grapevine.

CREDIBILITY IS NOT ENOUGH

We don't want to equate credibility with acceptance, to con anyone into thinking that once you've established the credibility of your message, you've insured its acceptance. As Pascal observed, "Habit is but a second nature." When the contents of a communication conflict with the habits of a lifetime, the communication will be believed but ignored. In an experiment on delegation involving a large number of middle managers playing the role of first-line supervisors, they all received pointed instructions to reveal some time-study data to their subordinates—but 54 percent of them ignored the instructions. They handled themselves according to their prior conceptions of the job and their customary styles of management. In other words, those who were generally permissive and democratic followed the instructions which the majority ignored.

Also, we sometimes reject the speaker's message out of hand because we suspect his motivations. "If he said it, it can't be so." The classic example of disregarding the message because of the source occurs in labor relations. Some union members interpret every company statement as an attempt to deceive them. Similarly, some managements regard every union grievance as a cynical maneuver to strengthen the position of the union leadership among its rank-and-file members.

One researcher clipped a cartoon from a union publication entitled "The Four Goals of Labor" and added a caption indicating that it had come from a publication of the National Association of Manufacturers. When a group of union members saw the clipping, they were, to a man, critical of it as an unfair, biased representation of labor's goals. We suspect that if you reversed the coin and clipped a statement of management's goals from an NAM publication, represented it as coming from a union source, and showed it to a group of managers, you would get a similar reaction. The supposed source would dictate the response to the communication.

Compromise and Goals

Probably nothing could have swayed the middle managers we described from sticking to their rut. Other situations, however, offer more promise that a communication will be accepted. In most cases, there's a central goal of the communication and a preferred, not obligatory, path for reaching it, unless the communicator is too much of an authoritarian or a perfectionist to recognize it. When the sender has feedback, especially from a sensitive and sensible receiver, the sender will understand that he has reservations about the communication—or at any rate about accepting it unless he can influence the sender. Unraveling what the receiver's resistance owes to ego and what to substance should best be left to Penelope or anyone else with twenty years for the task. The manager's job is clear. First, he must recognize that if he doesn't modify the communication, it will probably be rejected or given lip service, which amounts to the same thing. Second, he must determine the ways in which he can change the communication without damaging its substance.

Take, for example, the district sales manager who faced his salesmen's resistance to a new system of compensation and reporting on several counts. They objected that the new system, by paying higher commissions on high-volume, high-profit business, would force them to neglect business that had yielded steady commissions in the past. They also asserted that the new system would put them at the mercy of a few big accounts and that the reporting features of the new system were needlessly complicated and time-consuming. Finally, they complained that their views hadn't been sought in advance. The district sales manager, facing a real revolt in the ranks and the prospect of losing some of his best men, recommended to the home office that the objectionable reporting features of the new system be simplified. The core of the new system was the revamped compensation scheme; the reporting changes were a secondary feature not worth pressing for in light of the resistance. The home office accepted the recommendation and the communication was accepted, although reluctantly, by the salesmen—partly, we think, because it had been modified to meet some of their objections. The restatement of the communication incorporated some of their reservations.

We have stressed throughout this chapter that effective communication requires more than understanding. To be effective, a communication must be believed and accepted as well as understood. Whether or not the particular communication wins this kind of reception depends primarily on the sum of all the communications that have preceded it, on whether or not an atmosphere of mutual trust and respect has developed between the manager and the people with whom he is communicating. Where there is mutual confidence and regard, a clumsy communication will somehow muddle through. Where there is distrust and suspicion, technique alone will never suffice.

The reason is simple enough. Man is a rational being who learns from experience. Cherry compares the brain to a giant totalizer at the race track that accepts the tokens (money) from the outside world (bettors) and calculates the odds on various hypotheses (horses) to give the greatest expectation of goal attainment (profit) according to assumed standards of utility. Before a man decides which horse to bet on, he consults the horses' racing history and the track records and lays his bet accordingly. He is certain to pass up a horse whose record is spotty and whose performance is undependable. Similarly, the employee will neglect, ignore, or reject a communication from a boss with a bad track record for veracity and dependability. Lastly, there is the matter of self-interest. The employee will resist, reject, or, at most, pay lip service to any communication whose contents run contrary to his self-interest as he understands it.

THE OTHER SIDE OF THE COIN: LISTENING

In the remainder of the chapter, we're going to talk about the other half of the communications process—and the more difficult half: listening. Certainly, getting messages across to other people is difficult enough. However, we would argue that receiving messages from other people is even more difficult, if we mean by this finding out what is really on their minds.

A large part of the problem is that people don't spend enough time listening. They think that they are communicating with other people when what they really do is talk a lot and take the time to get the feedback to what they said. In fact, they take the echo-chamber approach to communication and settle for the illusion of it. They hear only themselves as their words are thrown back to them by the listener. Feedback, as we have stressed, is important, but there's much more to listening than that.

We agree with Whyte that "the art of listening remains one of the most overlooked tools of management," and we would add, one of the most important. The reasons why people spend so little time listening are fairly easy to identify. Some are too self-centered; it is impossible for them to concede the importance of what anyone else has to say. Some are too insecure; they're afraid that, if they listen long enough and hard enough, they will discover unpleasant truths about themselves. Some are pressed for time; they recognize that listening is a time-consuming process and they feel the return doesn't justify the investment. Finally, some shy away from listening because they feel it is an art which they haven't mastered.

Listening and Understanding

Many of those with reservations about listening as an un-mastered art are correct. Effective listening is an art which involves the development of a certain attitude, the skilled control of a definite strategy, and a set of techniques. Once the manager has all these under his belt, intense concentration, repeated practice, and a high degree of intuition will do the rest.

Listening with a "third ear" comes under the heading of concentration and even intuition. It sounds formidable but it's simply the recognition that there's a hidden content in many communications that can only be inferred by the listener. But how does the manager listen with a third ear? He's no psychiatrist, but actually, all he needs is a hunch. The other man's statements somehow don't sound convincing. He senses a buried meaning, so he probes for it. Joe might come in to quit because he was "just fed up with the job." But he didn't seem able to give any details of his dissatisfaction. Under these circumstances, the manager would search for clues, asking himself such questions as "Was his chance of promotion really the issue? Family troubles? Me as a boss?"

As we have discussed, symbols sometimes block effective communication. One case occurred in a large manufacturing company, when a new sales manager asked his salesmen to compute certain correlation coefficients on the basis of their sales records. The job was easy, but the reisistance to doing it was terrific. How come? After a lot of digging—that is, listening—the sales manager found out that, three years previously, an authoritarian and thoroughly disliked supervisor had tried to introduce the same technique. Ever since then, it had become a symbol of oppressive supervision to the salesmen. Once he had solved the mystery, the sales manager withdrew his request temporarily and waited for his men to develop confidence in him. Then he reintroduced the technique and met with no opposition.

How can the manager tell when symbols may be blocking communication? If there is extraordinary, unexpected resistance to a proposal, for example, it's a tip-off to look for some symbolic meaning.

As for the attitude the effective listener needs to develop, take the case of Tim Hardy, a cool, dependable lathe-operator who had demonstrated over the years his ability to juggle a number of rush jobs at once. Suddenly, all this changed. Hardy started performing like a robot, stopping his machine and changing his specifications each time he received a high-priority order even if there were only one or two pieces remaining on the earlier job. The result, after a time, was a huge backlog.

Hardy's boss was tempted to try for a quick solution: ball him out for not using more common sense and tell him to get back on the ball, or else. It could work, but on the other hand, it could lead to mutual name-calling and the kind of defiance which would leave his boss with no choice except to discipline Hardy or even fire him.

Instead, his supervisor took time out for insight. He kept his cool, determined to find out what was underneath Hardy's behavior, and ultimately got to the truth. Hardy felt, and with justification, that other operators were getting long-run orders which could be run automatically. He felt discriminated against, and in retaliation he practiced a form of malicious obedience that raised havoc with production schedules. The story had a happy ending. The unfair work split was unintentional—Hardy's boss had been handing out assignments by quality and quantity and neglecting complexity. Once the inequities were corrected, Hardy's performance returned to its previous level.

What do we mean when we contend that Tim Hardy's boss adopted the right attitude for effective listening? On the surface, Hardy's behavior was outrageous, indefensible—you name it. Yet the boss managed to rid himself of any preconceived notions, to suppress the natural temptation to harangue Hardy. Instead, he kept his cool and determined to get at the facts even when they pointed, as they did, to his own shortcomings as the root of the problem. Of course, effective listening alone is not enough. There would have been no happy ending unless Hardy's boss had straightened out the inequities which lay at the base of Hardy's actions.

THE NONDIRECTIVE INTERVIEW

Hardy's boss was actually using some of the techniques involved in the nondirective interview, a form first practiced in industry by researchers during the Hawthorne experiment. Since then, it has been used by legions of personnel men and line managers to get at the reality underneath the surface of what people were saying and doing.

What is the nondirective interview? How does it differ from the usual interaction between boss and subordinate that is our major focus in this book? And what functions does it perform? The interview is called "nondirective" because, by contrast to most boss–subordinate exchanges, the initiative lies with the employee, not with the boss—with the man being interviewed, not the interviewer. The employee does nine-tenths of the talking and the boss does the heavy listening.

What does the nondirective interview accomplish, for example, that can't be accomplished in the typical boss–subordinate interview? How does it differ from the one where the boss begins with a set of assumptions, poses a set of direct questions framed to confirm or modify these assumptions, and concludes with a decision or solution based on his initial assumptions plus whatever additional facts the questions have uncovered?

The primary uses of the nondirective interview are threefold:

1. It is a uniquely effective device for getting at what is really on someone else's mind. The direct-question approach may produce honest responses but they are bound to be partial and they are likely to be constructed with an eye to pleasing or at least placating the boss (if he is the interviewer). In other words, the direct-question approach never gets at the whole truth and infrequently achieves only the truth.

There are also many occasions when a manager recognizes that he has no ready-made set of assumptions. All he knows is that he has a problem with an employee. The cause of the problem is something to be determined during his interview with the subordinate. Under these circumstances, the manager has no choice but to practice patient and prolonged listening.

2. The nondirective interview forces the man being interviewed to think out loud about his problems, to organize them more clearly, and to think about them more deeply than if he would if he were merely turning them over in his mind. "I've never really thought of it that way before" is a phrase that often comes from an interviewee who has achieved new insights in the process of reorganizing and redefining his problems.

All this has great significance for the interviewer. He's

hoping—really, he's betting—that the subordinate will work his way through to his own solution and that it will be one that, as a manager, he can live with. He knows the truth of what Bobbie Burns wrote: "He who is convinced against his will, is of the same opinion still." Therefore, he would vastly prefer a solution reached by the subordinate to the one he might feel compelled to dictate himself.

3. The process of getting things off his chest frequently enables the subordinate being interviewed to achieve what the ancient Greeks called "catharsis"—a feeling of relief when a channel has been provided to funnel off frustrations even though the basic cause of the frustrations may remain.

Conducting a Nondirective Interview

So much for functions. Now let's talk about the nondirective interview itself and the three stages characteristic of each one: feelings, facts, and solutions. Almost every employee goes into a nondirective interview emotionally worked up. The interviewer should give him plenty of opportunity to blow off steam, partially, as we suggested earlier, to let him experience catharsis and partly because feelings color facts. The manager is not likely to reach a satisfactory solution of any problem until the employee can look at the facts rationally.

Of course, feelings themselves are facts and, on occasion, constitute the essence of the problem. We know of a case where the number one reason for the slump in a typist's performance was her intense dislike of the office manager. The causes of the dislike remained murky, but her feelings were very real and very strong. About all the manager could do, when the interview disclosed her feelings toward him, was to tolerate her hostility without responding to it and to discuss the possibilities of a transfer in the near future.

FROM EMOTIONS TO SOLUTIONS

The previous paragraph suggests an obvious point. The three stages of the nondirective interview are not watertight compartments. Feelings are facts, and the factual stage of the interview is scarcely devoid of emotion. Both stages hopefully build toward a satisfactory solution in the third stage. What distinguishes the stages from one another is the emphasis in each one and the differing degree of initiative played by the interviewer—in our discussion, the boss—in each one.

In the first stage, the manager plays a primarily passive

role. He has little or no idea of what will be forthcoming. He listens, accepts what the employee tells him, and urges the subordinate to keep talking. In the second or factual stage, his role becomes somewhat more active. Building on the indicators provided in the first stage, he seeks additional facts from the subordinate, his criteria being those facts that point to a viable solution of the problem, or he takes the initiative and provides facts drawn from his own knowledge. In the third, solution-reaching stage, the manager's role differs widely. As we now know, ideally the subordinate reaches a solution on his own which the boss has merely to approve. It is not always possible for the boss to be that nondirective, however. Sometimes it is imperative for him to step out of character because the subordinate is unwilling to come up with a solution with which the manager and the organization can live.

Let's assume, for example, that the problem under discussion is habitual tardiness—Jones is thirty minutes late almost every day. (Remember the discussion of *tone* in Chapter 4, which looked at this same problem.) The facts are: no alarm clock, unpredictable bus schedules, and insufficient sleep. For management, the only acceptable solution is for Jones to get to work at least roughly on time. Among the means toward that end are: Jones buys an alarm clock, Jones joins a car pool, and Jones makes a practice of getting eight hours a night sleep. Because Jones won't accept the latter two suggestions, he doesn't buy the solution. At this point, the manager would have to be directive—to assume charge and indicate that Jones has no choice but to take steps (the particular steps are up to him) that will solve the problem in a way satisfactory to management. Our example, happily, illustrates the exception, not the rule. In most cases, the subordinate does reach—with a subtle assist from his boss—a satisfactory solution to the problem.

LISTENING TECHNIQUES

The professionals who first developed the nondirective interview built into it a few techniques (gimmicks, if you will) which they found helpful in getting people to speak freely and fully, techniques from which many managers have profited.

SETTING THE STAGE

The first it not really a gimmick but an exception to the rule that the boss should be nondirective in the early stages of the interview. It's up to the manager to set the stage, to define the subject which the interview will cover. Otherwise, time is likely to be wasted in pointless discussion or aimless small talk that only increases the tension, anxiety, and frustration level of an already overwrought subordinate. If the reason for the discussion, for example, is that Ted's production record last month was down by 20 percent, the manager should begin with the simple statement, made in a non-emotional, unthreatening way, "Let's talk about your production record." On the other hand, once he's focused on the subject, this may be about as lengthy a remark as he will make for the next twenty to thirty minutes. He wants to give Ted the chance to air his feelings and to state all the facts of the situation as he sees them.

At the same time, the boss can't sit numb and dumb while Ted talks on. His responses should be limited but carefully thought out, and he should rely heavily on the psychologists' advice on the use of two devices, the reflective summary and the probe.

THE REFLECTIVE SUMMARY

In the reflective summary, the boss or any other interviewer summarizes the gist of what the interviewee has told him or has been trying to tell him, being careful to avoid any words or phrases that would imply a judgment, favorable or un-favorable. For example, the boss might say something to Ted like "You say the speeds on your machine are hard to con-trol." The simple statement accomplishes several things: (1) It shows Tom that the boss in listening, (2) it reassures him that the boss has passed no value judgments on what he has told him, (3) it gives him a chance to correct the boss if he has misunderstood what he has heard, and (4) it shows Ted he's interested and encourages him to go on with his story.

THE PROBE

The probe serves a different but related purpose. It en-courages the employee to tell the boss or interviewer more about something he's said, even if he appears reluctant to expand on his remark. In other words, the interviewer's antennae alert him that he may have hit pay dirt, and he wants to hear more.

Let's assume that Ted has had his say about the defective speeds on his machine. The boss has said nothing, although he's convinced he's still to hear the real explanation for the decline in his subordinate's production. Then he hears Ted tack on the comment that "It wouldn't be so bad if everything else around here worked." He has dropped a clue, and whether or not his boss ever gets to the root of the problem may depend on what he does with the clue. An indignant "Where do you get off—'if everything else around here worked' " would cause Ted to clam up, become defensive, and effectively terminate the interview. The most helpful follow-through would be to repeat, "If everything else around here worked," in a neutral tone of voice and wait for him to pick up the ball. If Ted ignores the invitation to expand on the remark, the manager still can't ignore the clue. He has to resort to something more direct, such as " 'If everything else around here worked'—tell me what you mean. I'm interested," and hope for the best, by which we mean Ted's honest answer to the question, not his politic one. What may be gnawing away at the employee may be the fact that he was overlooked for promotion to a job in which the boss wasn't even aware he was interested. Ted is bottled up—to himself and to others—and the boss is so removed that it might take an hour or more and the peeling off of several layers of meaning and feeling before they could arrive at the truth of the situation. Once they hit bedrock, they may or may not solve the problem, depending on the boss's ability to provide the opportunity for Ted to be considered at least for an adequate substitute position or on his persuading Ted that he will be best off staying where he is. Perhaps Ted needs recognition as much as he needs a promotion.

THE MANAGER AND HIS "THIRD EAR"

Listening is a basic tool for every first-level manager. But listening alone is not enough. The manager must not only convey that he is listening sympathetically and closely for the implied as well as the stated meanings, listening with the third ear. He must also set his listening in a framework wherein he both gets the truth and can help the employee to reach his own solution to the problem. Hence, the nondirective interview.

This type of interview, in turn, depends on skills that are painfully acquired. Practice a little introspection and consider the moral attitude requisite for a successful nondirective interview. To abandon preconceived notions, to take in facts without attributing praise or blame, to accept personal criticism without fighting back or even betraying annoyance, and to stand patiently by while a person slowly and painfully works out on his own a solution that you reached three days previously—doing all this tests the temper and tries the soul. Yet, it's part of the formula for conducting a successful non-directive interview.

The other requisites for the effective nondirective interview don't sin so much against doing what comes naturally—they're just hard work and they require extraordinary concentration. The manager must use reflective summaries and probes to make sure the facts are all in before he attempts to help the employee reach his own solution. If that doesn't work, if the employee can't or won't recommend on his own a solution satisfactory to the manager and the organization, the manager has to try for a joint solution. And as a last resort, after listening as carefully as possible to catch the cadences and gradations of reservation, the manager has to dictate the organization's solution—and hope the subordinate will live with it.

Almost ninety years ago, William H. Vanderbilt, in response to a reporter's question about the public's reaction to a move he was contemplating, replied, "The public be damned!" On any honesty index we would rate Mr. Vanderbilt tops. And he got away with it—there were no strikes, no rider boycotts of his railways. He died a few years later, the richest man in the United States, unloved but unchallenged.

Today's manager is in a very different position. Even if he felt like William H. Vanderbilt, he couldn't say, "The employee be damned." He has no choice but to listen—to listen hard and sympathetically—and to catch the subtleties of what his men are telling him so that he can retain and motivate them. In short, listening is a crucial skill for every manager, and the nondirective interview is a general-purpose tool that every manager should master.

SELECTED REFERENCES

Cherry, C., *On Human Communication*, Wiley, New York, 1957.

Krech, D., R. Crutchfield, and E. Ballachey, *Individual in Society*, McGraw-Hill, New York, 1962, chaps. 7–8.

Leavitt, H., *Managerial Psychology*, Univ. of Chicago Press, Chicago, 1964, part III.

Weiner, N., *Cybernetics,* Wiley, New York, 1961.
Whyte, W. H., Jr., *Is Anybody Listening?* Simon and
Schuster, New York, 1952.

THE EDUCATION OF GREG HORNING: MARCH 5

Still wondering about the gripes from the crew, Greg received
a call the next morning to report to Steve Phillips' office.
Production had come back up that 5 percent, Phillips told
Greg; in fact, the group was now doing 87 percent of
standard. That was better, but it was only a beginning. Now
was the time for Greg to really crack down on them—with
enough pressure, he could get them up to standard and over.

Greg knew that production was inching up a little, and he
was pretty sure it was because he'd eased up with the group.
Pressure just didn't work in that department; Phillips was
wrong—but he was such a difficult guy to talk to. Greg
hesitated. He could just go along with Phillips—agree, then
go back and do what he wanted with the group. As long as
he got results, Phillips wouldn't give a damn how he got
them. Still, there were those complaints. Greg couldn't bring
the other departments in line, but Phillips could.

"Well, I don't know if it's as simple as that, Steve," he
said finally. "They're working pretty well now, but they've
got a lot of gripes that sound sensible to me."

"Ah, the hell with the gripes. Those guys always have
a beef. If something goes wrong, it's always the other guy's
fault. Just don't pay any attention to them. Crack down.
They'll shape up." Greg ignored the sound of dismissal in
Phillips' voice and plugged on.

"They tell me that maintenance and materials handling foul
things up for them. They refuse to put things where we need
them to do the job right. And the machines aren't kept in
good repair—when they break down it takes days to get
somebody over to fix them. And then there's the plastic mixing sends us . . ."

"My God, Greg!" Phillips had been fingering through some
papers; now he threw them down on the desk. "They must
really be having a field day in there with this bright-eyed,
bushy-tailed patsy they've got! What's the matter with you,
anyway? Can't you see they're just selling you a bill of goods?
Now, you go back down there, and the hell with all these
excuses. I want to see the goods—you tell them to get off
their fat asses and work.

There was no point trying to argue with a man like Phillips, Greg thought as he went back to his office. His mind was set in concrete. Greg was sure he was wrong, still it made things damn difficult when . . .

"Oh, Jeannette. Hi. You want me for something?" Pacing back and forth in front of his desk, Greg had not heard Jeannette come in.

"Yeah. You see, Greg?" She held out a piece that looked all right, except that the edges were extremely rough. "This is what I was telling you about yesterday."

"Yesterday?"

"Yeah. Remember how I said if the men went faster the pieces came out all right but there was an awful lot of flashing to do on them?"

"Oh. Yes. I see. But that's a good piece, Jeannette. I wouldn't reject that piece."

"Well, that's what I mean, Greg," Jeannette said, her voice becoming more insistent. "It's too good to reject, but see how much extra time a piece like that takes—for Helen and me. It's because the men are going faster. It slows Helen and me down. If they could just be more careful. I mean, if we can't keep up with them, there's no sense in their going faster."

"Yes, I see. But I don't know what we can do about it," Greg answered vaguely. "We can't start rejecting perfectly good pieces."

"Well, I know that," Jeannette said, exasperated now and ready to leave. "Oh, never mind. This is just a waste of time. I have a whole batch of boxes to move around before I can get to doing these pieces, anyway. The handlers dumped them at the wrong end of the floor again. I just thought maybe you'd . . . oh heck—forget it."

Coming up in the elevator on his way back from lunch, Greg ran into Frank Granto from the industrial engineering department.

"You got a minute, Frank?" Greg said, putting his hand on Frank's arm. "There's something I've been wanting to ask you about."

"Yeah, Greg. Just about a minute. What's on your mind?"

"Well, it's about this materials handling business. My people have been griping about how they're always putting things in the wrong place and how that slows them down. Does it really make that much difference?"

"Are you kidding?" The elevator stopped at Greg's floor

and the two men got out together. "Do you know how much time a crew can waste just lugging boxes around to where they need them?"

"It's really important, then?"

"Listen, Greg. Those guys can make you or break you—let me tell you. It's one of the biggest keys to an effective work flow." They were at the door of the molding shop now. Frank had his arm on Greg's shoulder. "I'm really pleased that you've recognized this point, Greg. You're one of the few guys outside of our department who does. We're always trying to hammer it into the supervisors' heads, but they never listen."

"Yeah. Well, I guess that's a big problem everywhere, Frank," Greg said, smiling. "Everybody talks and no one listens."

Frank smiled back. "You've got a point there, too, Greg. Well, listen. I've got to get going. If there's anything else I can help you on, let me know."

"Thanks, Frank. See you."

Greg started into the shop, thinking. Maybe if Jeannette didn't have those boxes to move, she'd be able to keep up with the flashing. If her gripe was legit, maybe the others were too. Obviously Phillips wasn't going to help. Greg would have to see what he could do on his own.

Phil Martello stopped Greg as he went by: "Got a second, Greg, I want to talk to you."

"Sure, Phil, what's up."

"It's Ted Kilpatrick. You know he's a pretty old guy and some of the rows are getting to be too tough for him. What about if we change machines when the going gets too rough for him?"

"I don't know, Phil. I appreciate your wanting to help out, but . . ."

"I know how you feel Greg, about people doing their own work but this way you would be getting more production— I would be taking over the jobs that Ted is the slowest on."

"I see what you mean," said Greg after a minute's hesitation. "Okay—let's give it a try."

"Sure thing, Greg."

"One other thing, Phil. I appreciate your thinking of production as well as Ted. That's something we can't have enough of around here." Greg put his hand on Martello's shoulder and smiled. Then he went into his office to call Ed Briscoe in materials handling.

QUESTIONS

1. What connection do you think there is between Phillips' handling of Greg's complaints and Greg's handling of Jeannette's complaint?

2. How would you describe Jeannette's message to Greg as he heard it?

3. What's the significance of Greg's conversation with Granto for the first case?

4. Why was Greg able to communicate effectively with Granto but not with Phillips or Jeannette?

7. A balance theory of supervision:
using interaction to solidify leadership

Here, we are going to present another way of viewing the supervisor's job. The emphasis will be on *how* you do it rather than *what* you do. The method grows out of a great deal of social science research on what is called "interaction theory." Simply stated, this is a well-documented theory about individual personality and behavior, and its major finding is that human beings like a reasonable balance in their "inputs" and "outputs." (Figure 7-1 illustrates this concept.) When there is this balance, it is accompanied by a feeling of well-being. When there is an imbalance, say the inputs far outweigh the outputs, the employee (or the supervisor himself) feels cross, imposed upon, or even angry.

But what are these inputs and outputs? Human relations, the basic building block of our work and nonwork lives, involves the interaction of people: give and take, talking and listening, initiating and responding. When you watch people at work, at a party, or at home, this is what you see. Individuals are seeking someone to listen to them and to be responsive to them. If this requirement is to be satisfied, it is of course necessary to find another person who will be the complement, that is, who will listen and be responsive to the first person. It is as though each of us has, building up inside him, a reservoir of interactional energy that is seeking to flow toward other human beings. We want to be attended to and responded to by other people, that is, others willing to listen and to give us an appropriate human response.

Similarly, each of us has the capacity to take just so much of this initiation by others, these interactional inputs. We want to be on the giving side some of the time ourselves. And, in fact, if there are too many inputs to us or too few opportunities for us to do the initiating, we grow restless, even hostile or explosive.

BALANCING INTERACTION BETWEEN MANAGER AND EMPLOYEE

Since work is such a significant aspect of the waking day for most people, we can anticipate that people will seek to utilize their reservoirs of interactional energy on the job. To be specific, the supervisor has to be aware of his own efforts to balance off inputs and outputs and, even more important, the needs of his subordinates.

Thus, many of the things we have been saying about order giving, change, communications, discipline, and other administrative problems have interactional implications. The

Figure 7-1   Input and output

manager who is giving orders, raising questions, and communicating new policies is using up some of his own output reservoir—and perhaps getting a good deal of satisfaction in the bargain. But he is also draining off some of his subordinates' input capacity. And the reverse is also true: When the boss stops to listen to an employee's complaint or suggestion, seeks out his opinion, and lets him talk, he is providing a much-needed outlet for that employee (which may help to even out the balance in his relationship with the boss).

So the wise manager seeks to provide some rough balance in his relationship with each of his subordinates. This doesn't mean he precisely counts every time he takes the initiative in making a request of the subordinate and compares this with the number of times he allows the subordinate to make requests of him for information, for help, or just for a sympathetic ear. But he does make himself aware of the rough balance involved.

Thus, many supervisors find that it is much more useful to ask their subordinates questions than give them direct orders. At least with a responsible, committed subordinate, you don't have to tell him precisely what to do and, as we have seen, there are good reasons not to do so. Quite different responses are elicited by "How did things go with the Williston Company back order yesterday? Are you having any luck getting that pump motor fixed?" compared to "When you see the Williston representative, be sure and find out how they liked our last shipment. Don't forget to put that pump repair ahead of everything else you are doing."

But these are initiations too. Although less than direct orders, they still require the individual employee to respond. So the supervisor must take them into account in assessing his inputs, perhaps giving them less weight—say than a direct order—when calculating his outputs that need to be balanced off.

RESPONDING

The boss seeks to balance off these initiations by encouraging
the subordinate to initiate to him. How does he do this?
It's really not very difficult at all: He makes himself approachable. It's easy to talk first about the opposite type—un-
approachable supervisors. They're easy to spot. Whenever
you try to speak to them, to stop them for a question or
comment, it is obvious that they're very, very busy and
preoccupied, and they clearly communicate that they wish you
hadn't interrupted them at such an important moment.

The opposite is the supervisor who appears to welcome
employee inputs, who doesn't limit his conversation only
to the times he has something to say. Even when the employee
is interrupting something—most supervisors are pressed for
time—and even when he has a silly request to make or is
quarrelsome, the supervisor hears him out *responsively.*

All of us can distinguish between a responsive listener and
one who isn't interested in us. The responsive person lets us
do a good share of the talking, he appears to be concentrating
on what we have to say, he nods frequently or says, "Yes, I
understand," and shows by his questions and comments that
he is following our train of thought and not simply pursuing
his own. He is willing to go along with the way we want to
lead the conversation and is not pushing us to think solely
in his terms. This fragment may illustrate the difference.

With the *responsive* supervisor, the scene went this way:

Subordinate:	No matter what I do today, I can't seem to make things go right, I don't know if it's me or this equipment or the heat in here.
Boss:	There are those days—I have them myself. What's gone wrong?
Subordinate:	Well, first thing his morning I called up ...

With the *unresponsive supervisor,* this was the pattern:

Subordinate:	(same opening remark as above).
Boss:	You know that reminds me, I don't think you've been paying enough attention to those special orders.
Subordinate:	I know I sometimes forget, but let me tell you first about what happened this morning when I called ...
Boss:	Never mind this morning, let's be sure

you've got that procedure down cold that
we talked about yesterday.

Subordinate: But can't I just tell you . . .

Sure, what the employee had to say may not have been of
any great consequence. He may have wanted to complain
just to get his annoyance off his chest, to brag about his
conquest of a pushy clerk from another department, or even
to ask for the supervisor's help because he doesn't know how
to handle situations like the one that happened this morning.

The point is not only that the boss will never know what
was being expressed. More important, or at least just as much
so, he will have lost an opportunity both to let his subordinate initiate to him and to show him that he is willing to
be responsive to him. (Techniques of encouraging a person to
talk are discussed in Chapter 6.) To be responsive means
following the employee rather than leading him, listening
rather than dominating, being interested in other persons
rather than preoccupied with yourself.

Through the day, one will have the opportunity to allow
and encourage this type of initiation. Walking at a leisurely
pace through the department and having an office with the
door open—and where one doesn't always need an appointment to get in—making yourself accessible—these are
among the keys.

Note also that balancing off your inputs does not depend on
why the subordinate wants to contact you. Actually, the
motivation may be mixed, and even after hearing him out,
you may not know for sure. More important, if you are adequately responsive, you may not need to know. As an
example, let's hear out the subordinate we cut off above:

So I called up to ask Repair Service when we were going
to get that typewriter back we had sent last week, and the
first thing I knew they were giving me a hard-luck story
about how busy they were and how every department
expects its work to be done first. So I told them that we're
already one machine short, our work was being held up
and they had received it four days ago. They said they
would look into it and get back to me this afternoon, but
you know how reliable they are. . . .

Can you tell what he is really saying? Perhaps he wants to

brag to you that he was vigorously defending the department's needs. Perhaps he wants your sympathy because he has had a hard day. Perhaps he wants you to express appreciation or confidence in him or to help him deal with the outside repairman. But most important, he wants to have you be responsive to his initiation: his story about that morning's problem with the repairman. Even though that may be the *last* thing you are interested in and it really isn't a crucial problem no matter how or when it is settled, you are letting him take the initiative for a short period and get you involved in his life and his world. In the process, you will have earned "points," so to speak, that will make him more responsive to your next inquiry or request of him.

Personality Differences

The supervisor will have also to be aware of some differences among employees with regard to what they require in the way of responsiveness. Here are two typical cases.

Al Forter is always seeking you out. He has a hundred different things a day that seem to require your attention, or at least he thinks so. Even when you're talking to someone else, he'll butt in to get your attention. Your problem with Al is to keep him from monopolizing your time and to get him to restrain his impulse to initiate to you. That means at times you'll tell him you're too busy and perhaps you don't walk into his area any oftener than you have to. Otherwise, some of your other subordinates will begin to think you and he "have something going"—and favoritism ruins morale. Of course, he'll need some of your attention to satisfy that strong craving for a responsive ear, perhaps somewhat more than others but not as much more as he wants.

Henry Incerelli is very quiet. If you leave it to him, you'll never see him because he has no social initiative. But that's bad because, without such contact, your relationship will deteriorate. So you have to go out of your way to make it easy for him to take some initiative—stopping by his work area, calling him to show him something and then encouraging conversation.

Thus the supervisor seeks to develop a balance for different personalities, always being aware that some will demand too much and some, too little. And he must take the responsibility of making his total exchanges come out relatively even.

Internal and External Balancing

Note that this balancing involves both the initiation of the contact and the internal structuring of the conversation. The manager has to learn something about how different personalities carry on a conversation if he is going to be able to deal with them effectively on a face-to-face basis. Will he be confronting a granite rock or a Niagara Falls of chatter?

The key concept here is *synchronization*. Internal synchronization is much like the external balancing of inputs and outputs that we have been describing. Individuals want the sense of easy, smooth interactions with other human beings. That is, they don't want either long periods of silence or competition with another person for the chance to talk. The experienced supervisor learns to size up each person he will have to deal with and to make minor adjustments in his own pattern of interaction to complement the interaction habits of that person.

Thus, with some people who are rather long-winded, he will have to restrain himself because he is likely to keep cutting them off or interrupting before they are through. Other employees may be very laconic, and after the supervisor has said something or explained a new process, he will receive only a grunt or a few words in response. Again, if he is not careful, there won't be a synchronization because he will not be prepared to fill in the gaps. With short-winded people, the supervisor has to be able to speak frequently to avoid those uncomfortable (and stressful) silences when neither is speaking and both become strained. (Synchronization in conversation is diagrammed in Figure 7-2.)

INTERACTION AS A CONTROL MEASURE

Once the manager becomes sensitive to these differences in required patterns of interaction among his subordinates, he is all set to measure their morale in a rather direct and unobtrusive fashion. A man who is angry or disappointed nearly always shows his feeling in his interactional behavior. Of course, precisely how he shows that he is upset is distinctive

(1) Synchronization

Supervisor A --------- ------ --- ----------
Worker B ----- ---------- ------ -----

(2) Absence of Sychronization
Silence Periods

Supervisor A ------ ------ ---
Worker B ------ ---------- ----------

(3) Absence of Synchronization
Overlaps of Interruption

Supervisor A ------ ---------- ------------
Worker B -------------------- --------------

*___indicator speaking.

Figure 7-2   Synchronization patterns in conversation

with the individual—people differ substantially in this. But each person changes consistently when his emotions change. Therefore, although his words may seek to cover up his feelings, the observant manager can penetrate the verbal facade to assess the true emotional feelings. Most of us have done the same thing (although we may not be conscious of it) in assessing the feelings of our friends and close associates. We instinctively feel when they are relatively happy as compared to when they are upset.

All that is being said here is that this "instinctive" assessment can be made more precise and self-conscious. Listen to this supervisor explaining how he does it:

I know the minute I approach Heyfritz whether or not it's going to be a good time to add one of those extra jobs to his work load. If I more or less have to drag every word out of him—if he hardly responds at all when I speak to him about some trivial matter like the weather or how things are going—I know he is brooding about something. If I try to deal with him on a serious issue when he is like that, it is likely to lead to an argument because he'll hardly answer me and that, in turn, upsets me, and I start to speak more strongly and he'll mumble something about being pushed and I'll get even more hot under the collar. This way, if I deal with him on difficult subjects when I can tell he's in good shape, there are unlikely to be any of these repercussions which involve me in a disciplinary problem.

Now, Callahan is just the opposite. When he's disturbed, I have all I can do to keep him away—he wants to blast my ear off with talk. I ask him a simple question or pass the time of day, and I get a lecture! He's not that way normally—only when something is eating him. So when I've got to go and show him a mistake he's made in filling out an order—assuming I haven't been able to catch it immediately—I wait until I can *hear* that he's back to his normal give and take.

Thus some people become more voluble, others more reclusive, under stress. For still others, the difference between equilibrium and tension consists of more subtle changes in the way they handle interaction. In talking with them, the supervisor will notice that they are just somewhat less responsive—that is, there will be lulls or blank spots in the conversation. These are caused by the subordinate's failing to respond immediately when the boss pauses in his conversation. For others, the boss will notice more interruptions— he won't be able to quite finish saying something before the other person breaks in. Normally, these same people are easy to talk to—their inputs are nicely synchronized with the supervisor's inputs. It is the absence of synchronization that is the red light indicating that there is trouble brewing!

Another useful aspect of having interactions as one of the supervisor's control tools is this: He may be able to ferret out problems that would otherwise have remained buried and continuously damaging to the work situation. If the supervisor can detect that something is wrong even if he doesn't know what it is, he can start investigating. Furthermore, most supervisors are fooled into thinking everything is all right just because there are no visible problems. But when key employees are repeatedly under stress—and showing it by changes in their interaction patterns and their ability to deal with colleagues, associates, and outsiders, their feelings will eventually result in serious productivity and cost consequences.

A Manager's Self-control

There are some implications here for the manager's controlling *himself*. The same principles apply. When the manager is under stress, is angry, or tense, his own interaction pattern changes. That is, he starts to do to others what men like Heyfritz and Callahan have done to him. He may be sullen or unresponsive to the normal questions and comments of subordinates, or he may start "talking them to death." In turn, this upsets subordinates and quickly leads to their being less responsive. Also, they may perceive their boss, under these circumstances, as disliking them or expressing lack of confidence in them. In one man's words, "Sure, I know the boss has got it in for me now. I just went up to him to ask when those papers would be ready for me to check and I had a hard time getting a word out of him. He must be sore at me—he would hardly talk to me." (As we saw in Chapter 5, these implicit punishments are as important in "teaching" employees as the manager's explicit and purposeful rewards and punishments.)

After all, we test another person's respect and liking for us by asking ourselves: Is he responsive to what we're saying—in other words, to our inputs? And when the boss is under stress himself he may become less responsive or more easily "riled." His subordinates don't know whether he—or they—may have been struck by the seven plagues of Egypt. Here is one employee's description of a bad morning: "All I did was say I thought that machine was running too hot and he gave me a long lecture on what I don't know about engineering and leaving those kinds of worries to him and the engineers and how I have lots of other things that ought to keeps me busy, and on and on to a dozen different subjects. I had all I could do to get away from him, and I got so angry the more he talked at me, particularly since he didn't give me a chance to answer back."

So the manager, when he feels upset, should give himself a simple treatment: As much as possible, he should avoid trying to undertake contacts with subordinates (or peers or superiors, either, for that matter) while he is in a state like this. Even when he thinks he has himself under control, his interaction pattern will give him away. To make matters worse, the person or persons he inflicts himself upon will not know whether his tension reflects his assessment of them, something they have done, or his plain "rotten disposition."

There is added danger in that stressful patterns of interaction are contagious. When one person has to deal with another who is unresponsive, keeps interrupting, talks too much or too little, he himself becomes upset by the experience. Lack of synchronization in human relations—the absence of easy give-and-take conversation—is a major source of distress. And the newly infected person can spread the "illness" to still others. This is one of the major reasons why small problems become large problems in most organizations. The individuals originally affected by the difficulty begin interacting with others while they are still upset. Their behavior injures the normally easy and good relationships they may have had with others and creates a whole new set of problems.

Christy came steaming in here yesterday to ask for help in getting those displays done. He started talking like he owned the place; there was no way of turning him off. I used to think he was a pretty nice guy and I probably would have offered to lend a hand myself or give him a couple of my people for a few hours, but the way he carried on, I guess I was wrong about him. He's just another one of those fair-weather friends who will browbeat you the minute he feels that you don't jump to when he so much as says boo! I've *had* it with him and I told him so.

Of course, what this man didn't know and couldn't be expected to know is that Christy had just been let down with a vengeance. One of his best people, one he felt he could always count on to do good work, had forgotten all the special instructions he had received on a rush order and done it the wrong way. Christy was so upset with this man's failure to follow clear instructions that he could hardly contain himself.

Of course, that was the worst possible time to go outside his department to seek aid or to solve a problem, or even to deal with his own people. A manager has to quarantine himself, after he has been stressed, until he is able to engage in what is, for him, normal interaction.

This requires strong self-discipline. The very time you are most anxious to see someone, perhaps because he has let you down or because you need something from him, may be the time you are least able to persuade or negotiate or convince. Your interaction pattern—your inability to act normally and easily—gives you away.

A CONFLICT IN ENGINEERING

Two section heads in the industrial engineering department of a medium-sized company had been feuding almost since the day they were both promoted to their present positions two years before. Conflict, although not continuous, was never far below the surface, and the requirements of their jobs made the probabilities of trouble fairly high. One of the section heads was a methods engineer whose primary responsibilities were to develop new methods or processes in machine operation, to test them in the experimental shop maintained in the department, to figure cost benefits, and to turn the processes over to the installation section for testing in a pilot installation in the factory. The second man was in charge of the installation section. Whenever trouble occurred, the methods engineer believed the installation engineer changed the process or did not follow the method he specified. The installation engineer, on the other hand, was sure the basic idea was wrong or that the methods engineer did not take the practical requirements of the shop into consideration.

Because both men were good engineers and did their jobs well, the chief engineer did not want to transfer either of them out of the department. Yet he knew their disagreements were hurting production in the department. Further, both were bringing others into the feud. In an effort to solve the problem, the personalities of the two men were appraised, revealing interesting differences. The methods engineer had difficulty making contacts with others, and he was slow to take the initiative. Moreover, he was easily upset by criticism and withdrew and became petulant as a result. The installation engineer had a great deal of energy and initiative, and he liked to get things done quickly. He usually had little difficulty dominating others in the shop, but he was sufficiently flexible so the foremen with whom he worked got along well with him.

With the aid of the training director, the chief engineer tried to correct the situation. First, they discussed with the installation engineer the facets of his personality that disturbed his opponent. He began to realize he was too quick to take the initiative and dominated the methods engineer every time he raised an objection; in other words, his natural way of behaving, although effective in the shop, brought out instinctive unfavorable reactions in the other man. He saw that if he wanted to improve the situation he should try not to interrupt or take over the discussion when the methods engineer was presenting an idea but wait for him to finish. They pointed out to the methods engineer that one of his problems was trying to manage too many contacts during the day. They suggested that if he was under pressure or upset by other problems he should postpone seeing his "opponent" until the next day. They emphasized that everyone was subject to stress and that sometimes when he thought the installation engineer was being difficult, it might be that he, too, had had a rough day in the shop. In addition, the chief engineer worked out a schedule so each man could plan his contacts with the other rather than having the installation engineer go to the methods engineer every time he thought there was a problem.[1]

INPUTS—INITIATIONS—DIRECTION

The unwary reader may get the mistaken impression that the supervisor's job is largely one of receiving inputs from subordinates. Although responsiveness is critical to balance off supervisory initiations to subordinates, the initiations themselves cannot be neglected.

We have seen many supervisors who were reluctant to initiate to subordinates. They are the ones who are likely to say in front of a cluster of their employees, "I wish someone would clean up those scattered piles of reports waiting to be bound." They avoid direct orders and appear to assume that a right-minded subordinate will always know what he has to do. Similarly, they may be reluctant to give criticism or show an individual what he is doing wrong.

Feldman had a group of commercial artists working for him who prepared the visual aids for department meetings and planning sessions. Each artist would be given the raw data from which he was expected to develop an attractive, communicative chart. When he completed a chart, he would send it to Feldman who had to approve it before it would

---

[1] Eliot D. Chapple and Leonard R. Sayles, *The Measure of Management,* Macmillan, New York, 1961, pp. 106–107.

go to the requesting department. Feldman was loath to call an artist in and criticize his work. It always seemed too unpleasant, too time-consuming, even too embarrassing to tell the artist what he should have done, where he went wrong, and how to handle a given problem. So Feldman simply sent the sketch back to the artist by his secretary with a note attached saying something like this: "Sorry, I don't think this quite makes the point or shows off the data to best advantage."

As a hardly surprising result, subordinates, like the artists, didn't learn much in Feldman's department and they weren't sure what his standards were. In addition, a lot more work was generated because without real feedback, everybody was wasting time on a great many false starts.

So a manager has to be willing and able to take the initiative with subordinates. This means contacting them, calling them in for discussions, giving orders, discipline, instructions, and feedback on their performance. Too little initiative, too few contacts can be as serious a handicap for the manager as too many.

Moreover, a manager has to demonstrate to subordinates that he can and will take the initiative and so get them accustomed to accepting his direction. This is often a problem for the new manager, particularly if he lacks experience and obvious years of service. How, then, does he begin to win acceptance for himself as a source of direction?

As we have seen earlier, he may seek to legitimatize his managerial position. In other words, he demonstrates his right to be the boss in terms of his skill, judgment, knowledge, coolness under pressure, or other criteria acceptable to the work group for giving status and assigning leadership. (For a further discussion of this, see Chapter 3.) The job is not easy. To find out, assume that you have just been moved from a desk job to a machine shop. How could you legitimatize your leadership position, although you don't know much about the actual work?

At the same time, a good manager avoids giving directions in areas in which he is obviously ignorant or which involve controversy. The new manager, for example, can make a fool of himself by telling a subordinate how to fix an instrument when the employee knows much more about it than the boss. Similarly, he is likely to have his leadership challenged if he

knowingly or unknowingly overturns well-established customary practices. Mrs. Czovich, a new supervisor of receptionists, got a cool response when she instructed the girl who
had always handled the front-office reception area to take
over the back-office mail desk (also part of the receptionists's
jurisdiction). All the girls knew you worked your way up from
the mail desk to division reception areas to front office, and
now Mrs. C. was demoting somebody! But Mrs. Czovich didn't
realize that since she had only been on the job a few days.

Therefore, the supervisor gives orders at the outset about
matters that he or she is relatively sure about. He seeks to
accustom people to his leadership role by making requests
that are relatively obvious, that do not push into ambiguous
areas, and that concern situations which, as all can see, appear
to call for the supervisor's decision. As subordinates become
more accustomed to receiving and accepting initiations from
the new boss, he can begin asking more difficult things and
moving into areas with less clear-cut subject matter.

Of course, he also has to be willing and able to deal with
nonresponse where a direction is challenged or an order
ignored. (Such situations are more fully discussed in Chapter 4,
"Administering Positive Discipline.") If he fails to come to
grips with those who ignore his initiations, there will be
gradual but sure disintegration of morale. His leadership position will be undermined, and he's on his way to the down-
chute. No leader can survive direct flaunting of his orders.

Subordinate Challenges

The acceptance or rejection of a superior's orders raises a
frequently misunderstood point regarding the nature of organizations and leadership: Should a subordinate knowingly follow an instruction or a policy that he believes to be wrong?
Here is how one highly effective manager handles the problem:

My employees know they can't explain a botched job by
saying, "I was only following orders or company policy."
They know it is *part of their job* to endeavor to get orders
or policies changed which they believe are wrong or
inappropriate. This doesn't mean that they can simply
ignore what has been told them, but rather that they have
a responsibility to try to convince me why it is wrong
in general or at least in a specific case.

This kind of behavior requires a good deal of energy and perseverance. Orders and rules don't change themselves easily. One author has observed the efforts of a large Federal agency, employing a great number of engineers and scientists, to get an adjustment in civil service regulations drawn up largely to govern personnel administration in agencies that do not employ such highly trained people. A great deal of initiative and perserverance is required to convince people that a change is necessary. Too many subordinates (and managers alike) find it easy to say, "Well, what can you do? That is the way things are done around here." But almost everything is subject to change or modification if one is effective in presenting reasoned arguments and persistent in initiating to those who have the power or the position to facilitate the change.

DISCOVERING INITIATIVE

The supervisor has to distinguish those subordinates who can demonstrate this kind of initiative from those who respond with blind obedience. Note, pointing out real weaknesses is not the same as constantly wrangling that this or that won't work or isn't fair or doesn't seem right. The employee willing to explain and persuade, to take initiative when he feels strongly the situation (as distinct from himself) will be hurt if he simply follows the rules, can be effective within the modern organization.

Here is a description by William F. Whyte of just this kind of behavior:

Suppose a man is working under an autocratic boss. Is it necessary, under these conditions, to surrender one's independence and become a yes-man in order to get ahead?

First, we should question the pragmatic effectiveness of yessing the boss—at least in many situations. Much as the boss may enjoy that crisp "yes" when he hears it, he may find that its repetition is not quite enough to build up his faith in his subordinates. The autocrat is not necessarily a stupid man. He may have just as good an eye for results as the next man. If he finds the personal relationship with the subordinate pleasant but the performance results poor, we may find the boss beginning to complain that his subordinates are weak individuals who don't have the initiative and the drive necessary to do the job.

Two qualifications to this statement should be noted. The flourishing of yes-men may depend in part upon the ease with which results can be measured. Where performance results are exceedingly difficult to measure, the man who can be consistently agreeable to the boss has the greatest opportunity for capitalizing on this talent. Whether the measurement of results will undo the agreeable but mediocre individual should also depend on the extent to which decisions and instructions from his boss will be reasonably adequate to cover the situations that a subordinate meets on the job. If they are, although the subordinate may appear to be getting the results, it is his superior who is really achieving them.

This discussion of yes-men has only scratched the surface of a complex subject. My purpose here is simply to raise questions about a commonly held assumption: that yessing the boss contributes to advancement in the business organization. I have sought to point out that agreement pays off in some situations more than in others and that, in any case, it is hardly safe for the ambitious executive to assume that conformity, per se, will help him to get ahead.

Suppose our man serving under an autocratic boss wishes to increase substantially his own freedom of action—and still remains within the organization. Can he do anything about it?

The case of Wes Walsh suggests that he can. Walsh was superintendent of a plant of about the same size as John Dyer's. He came in under a works manager widely known in the company for his type of autocratic control. Furthermore, the offices of the two men were within a hundred feet of each other, so that although the boss was also responsible for other plants in the area, he could keep a close watch over Walsh. Nevertheless, Walsh was able to manage his plant very much according to his own notions, with little interference from above. How did he do it?

The previous superintendent had been constantly at swords' points with the works manager. He advised Walsh to keep away from the manager's office. "The less you see of that son of a bitch, the better you'll get along." Though Walsh and his predecessor were good friends, Walsh decided to disregard the advice. If it hadn't worked for his predecessor, why should it work for him? Instead, Walsh saw to it that he had frequent contacts with the boss—and contacts that were initiated primarily by Walsh himself. He would drop in, with apparent casualness, to report progress or to seek the works manager's approval on some minor matter, carefully selected so that the boss could hardly veto it. Walsh was getting his boss used to saying yes to him!

Major matters required longer interaction between the men, carefully prepared and staged. Consider the problems of the materials-reprocessing unit.

With increasing volume of production going through the plant, it had become apparent to Walsh—as indeed it had to his predecessor—that this unit was inadequate for current requirements. It was too slow in operation and too limited in capacity. This condition seriously hampered production and created a storage problem in the plant. Materials awaiting reprocessing were strewn about at one end of the operating area.

Walsh's first step was to propose to the boss that he pick a time when he could spend a couple of hours with Walsh in the plant, so that they could look over some of the problems the plant was facing. The manager set the time, and the two men spent the hours together on an inspection tour. To some extent the physical conditions the works manager saw spoke for themselves, but Walsh also supplemented these visual clues with an account of the way in which the inadequacy of the materials-reprocessing unit hampered his operations. The boss had to agree that the condition was undesirable. Eventually he asked, "What do you propose?"

Walsh was ready with a carefully worked-out proposal for the purchase of a new type of reprocessing unit at a cost of $150,000. After a brief discussion of the impact of a new machine on costs and production, the works manager authorized the purchase. It is noteworthy that essentially the same proposal had been made more than once to the works manager by Walsh's predecessor. Made no doubt in a different form and fitting into a different context of interpersonal relationships, the good idea had received simply a flat rejection.

So effectively did Wes Walsh handle his superior that he won a large measure of freedom from a man known throughout the works as an autocrat. And the works manager was more than happy with the relationship. In fact, several years later, after his own retirement, he was boasting to others about how he had discovered and developed Wes Walsh! . . .

Walsh suggests these rules for approaching a big decision
with an autocratic boss:

1. Prepare the ground carefully; don't just spring it on
the boss.

2. Don't present the problem and the proposed solution
at the same time.

3. Present the problem in stages and in such a way that
no solution will be immediately apparent to the boss. This
will help to assure you that he does not commit himself
before you have had a chance to make your full case.
Once an executive of this type has committed himself, it
is almost impossible to get him to reverse his decision. If
you can bring him through all phases of the problem with
the solution still unclear in his mind, then your chances of
getting your solution accepted are greatly improved.

It is not my purpose to suggest that Wes Walsh has discovered *the* way to deal with an autocratic boss. That would
be a gross oversimplification. I cite his story only in order
to show that a skillful and imaginative executive can win
himself considerable freedom of action from bosses whom
many would consider intolerable autocrats.[2]

Participation and Interaction

Wes Walsh's story has some implications for what we say
about participation and supervision. There can be misunder-
standings with respect to what is participation. At times, it is
conceived of simply as the number of decisions made by
subordinates as compared with those made by their boss. In
many instances, however, subordinates get the same sense of
participation by being able to criticize directly, and contribute
to, proposals made by their boss. When the supervisor shows
flexibility—willingness to modify and adjust plans in the light
of legitimate objections—subordinates display greater readiness to accept the decision as well as receiving a sense
of having participated in its formation.

I told the men that it looked to me as though we were
going to have to put in overtime for the next three days if

---

[2] Leonard R. Sayles, *Individualism and Big Business*, McGraw-Hill,
New York, 1963, pp. 170–173.

we were going to finish this new big job. There were groans from the men because this was the beginning of the deer-hunting season. One suggested that we could get things done a lot quicker if we combined the packing with the labeling. Another suggested that several pieces could be handled together if a larger pallet could be gotten from Stores. I figured that all of these suggestions might save us five or six hours at most so I eliminated the overtime for the first night, said we would work only one to one and a half hours at most the second night and I was sure we wouldn't need the third, if everyone did his job effectively.

Who made that decision? We don't think it's clear because a number of people participated and everyone felt satisfied that he had received a hearing (a response) for his view. It should also be noted that getting a hearing doesn't mean being told yes. A supervisor can allow criticism, hear out suggestions, and clearly be alert and flexible to new ideas and problems—without always agreeing. Most subordinates can easily distinguish between the boss who listens and weighs and then says no and the one who pretends to be allowing discussion but whose mind has already been made up and who sees this as just an exercise in good human relations.

Again, it goes back to balancing inputs and outputs. A supervisor who is seen as being responsive, as sometimes changing his mind when good contrary evidence is presented, is more likely to get his difficult orders accepted. It isn't a matter of giving up one to get one. But a boss who is receptive to initiations from subordinates finds that he can initiate to them a good deal more often than bosses who are unresponsive. Even minor concessions reveal responsiveness. Here is an example.

I find that I can ask my people almost anything and if it's reasonable—even if it's not part of their job, they'll do it. Now I do things for them too. Yesterday, for example, I asked Miss Cleary to run over to the downtown office to get some more legal forms. She said that she thought she was getting a cold and that the bitter weather might make it worse. Well, she is good about doing extra things and I could see that she looked tired and I said, of course, I would ask someone else this time.

ELIOT D. CHAPPLE (1909–   )

Eliot D. Chapple, in the early 1930s, worked with Elton Mayo (and Fritz Roethlisberger and Lloyd Warner) in Harvard's Department of Industrial Administration that conducted the famous Western Electric studies and other pathbreaking research in industrial human relations. But he disagreed with Mayo's research methods, and, to this day, Chapple's insistence on objective, operational measurements has made him an acerbic critic of a great deal of human relations research. Since he studied anthropology at Harvard and has broad interests extending over most of human culture, it is not suprising that he, probably more than any other student of management, has introduced a systems approach to leadership, organization structure, and job design.

Dr. Chapple has devoted most of his career to moving the study of man and his organization toward the natural sciences. He has done this by pioneering work in the objective measurement of human behavior. His interaction chronograph provides a split-second analysis of the precise way in which people interact with one another. As such it gives a truly scientific view of personality as represented by how a given individual expresses himself with other people. The same interaction measurements can be used to define differences in technology and in the requirement of given jobs. Thus management can be told that a given managerial position requires a specific pattern of interaction, and they can then assess whether a particular personality is likely to be able to perform that job effectively.

Dr. Chapple's work has emphasized that attitudes and feelings, which he believes cannot be measured objectively or precisely, are only by-products of various interactions. When two people interact easily, without stress, and complement each other's respective styles, this produces a feeling of well being, of mutual liking, and even of happiness. The opposite feelings of anger or hostility are created by stressful interaction patterns in which people interrupt each other, dominate each other, or fail to respond to one another.

Chapple's basic theories of human behavior have been adopted by other management theorists who have extended his work. These include Robert Guest at Dartmouth,

William F. Whyte at Cornell, and Leonard Sayles at Columbia. All seek to study the interactional requirements of
the organization. Rather than using attitude questionnaires,
they observe actual behavior in real organizations.

Dr. Chapple for many years headed his own management
consulting firm and more recently he has become principal
research scientist at Rockland State Hospital. Here he is
applying his methods and concepts to helping mental
patients adapt to their ward life and to outside jobs, and
he is matching therapists' interaction styles with patient
requirements.

Chapple was instrumental in founding an interdisciplinary
association, The Society for Applied Anthropology, in the
1940s. This group brought psychologists, economists,
sociologists, anthropologists, and business administration
experts together to seek to apply modern social science
methods to the solution of the problems of contemporary
organizations. For many years he edited their journal,
Human Organization. In addition to a large number of
articles, his works include *Principles of Anthropology,*
(coauthor), *Measure of Management* (coauthor), and
Culture and Biological Man.

Why People Behave the Way They Do*

Every person has a characteristic way of acting with other
people. He may be talkative or taciturn, aggressive or
timid. In different situations and with different people
his behavior may seem to vary to a considerable degree.
Nevertheless, it remains fixed within fairly definite limits,
and what a person will do can be predicted with com-
parative ease and accuracy.

The problem of the foreman is to learn how to predict
what his employees will do in given circumstances. To do
this he must be able to recognize the different kinds of
personalities and temperaments, and he needs to learn
how each individual will react in different situations.
He also must know how he himself should behave so that
each of his employees will work well and effectively.

* Reprinted by permission of the publishers from Eliot D. Chapple
and Edmond F. Wright, *How to Supervise People in Industry,*
National Foremen's Institute, Inc., Deep River, Conn., 1946,
pp. 8–13.

For reasons stemming from physiology,—from the way we function as human machines,—each of us brings with him an inherent type of activity when he comes into contact with other persons. Among other indications, this is shown by the amount an individual likes to talk or act, and in the speed of his "give and take" in each relationship. During any day the amount of such activity and the rate at which it appears is nearly constant. This rate can be estimated by adding up the length of time of all contacts and calculating the relative proportion of activity to inactivity displayed in each contact. If for any reason an individual is prevented from letting out his activity at his accustomed rate, he will take some other time during the day to make up for it. We have, in other words, a normal balance in our activity, which is principally expressed through our behavior in our relationships with others.

Not only do we have this need to operate within prescribed limits of activity; we also become accustomed at an early age to initiate a certain proportion of these contacts. Some of us find it hard to establish contact with others, and there are those who like to start up contacts with one and all.

Once a contact has begun, further difficulties may get in the way of fully active expression. Each of us is prevented from always getting the activity our system requires because of training. We are brought up from earliest childhood to carry out a smooth "give and take," to wait our turn until the other person is through. With some people we can restrain ourselves easily, but when we encounter a person who differs quite a lot from us in the amount he likes to talk and in the speed of his conversation, someone has to give way. One or the other has to inhibit his natural self to some extent, and try to adjust to the other fellow's behavior. Again, as a result of our early experience, we differ individually in the ability to make adjustments. Some people seem to be able to vary their behavior quite a lot, others find it difficult to adjust to any but a particular type of person.

When adjustment fails, behavior may take several forms. We may find ourselves interrupting the other person and trying to out-talk him so that he will be silent while we continue, or we may become more and more silent till we finally are no longer quick to respond when the other person stops talking. Furthermore, even though we may be able to adjust to another person for a brief period, we may find it hard to keep it up and even harder to continue in such a relationship. The person who likes to hold the floor compels us to be silent. If we dislike being squelched in this way, and, hence, try to take the conversation away, we are liable to get into a fight. Even if it does not come to that, our normal balance is still disturbed with such persons, and consequently we have to find an outlet with some individual for the activity which the talkative one suppressed in us. The reverse is also true, of course. When we feel like talking to someone and the person replies only in monosyllables, our attempt to strike up a conversation is frustrated,—unless we are natural talkers and need nothing more than the presence of another person to encourage us.

It is important to realize that whenever we happen into situations which upset the normal balance of our behavior we feel emotionally disturbed, and simultaneously our outward behavior changes. The disturbance, under ordinary conditions, may be very small,—some flicker of disappointment or annoyance, which is quickly compensated for in our relations with others. But, if disturbances of this sort happen too often, or if the adjustments required are too extreme, we experience all the internal discomfort of apprehension, anger or disappointment. On the other hand, when we are with people whose rhythms of speech and behavior fit our own, we experience a feeling of pleasure. This pleasure varies in intensity as the experience is prolonged or repeats itself at regular intervals.

One other point should be made. The degree to which our basic needs for activity and adjustment are being satisfied in our relationships with others produces not only the emotions we experience but also the changes in our behaviour. To illustrate: when we become angry, besides feeling anger, we also act in an angry manner. We lose our ability to have a free "give and take" and act in a way, that of "being angry," in which we pay practically no attention to what the other person is actually doing. . . .

We can, therefore, determine whether a particular person's balance is unsatisfactory for the job, and whether the amount of activity, of initiative, of adjustment he is getting is insufficient for his emotional needs. We can estimate what will happen to a person if we have to change his contacts with others. We can do this because the reactions described above operate invariably and differ from person to person only in number and type of contact. Some persons get mad easily and others will "blow up" only after a much greater number of emotional upsets. For practical purposes, these differences can be measured relatively accurately, and each individual can be classified in terms of the amount of activity, of initiative, of speed of acting and response, and of ability to adapt to others' behavior.

The foreman's job is to find out the score for everyone in his department and for those who come in contact with it. He can do this by keeping figures on contacts as part of his regular records; how long each contact lasts, who initiates it, and something about its general character. By keeping up these records every day, he is in a position to see how fluctuations in each individual's contacts affect his performance on the job. He can thus see for himself how the figures for output and quality are dependent upon his figures for the human relations on the job. This takes the guesswork out of supervision and enables him to regard each person as he would one of his machines,— as having tolerances within which effective operation is possible. These tolerances are fixed by the capacity of the individual to adjust to others within the limits of his basic level of activity.

The foreman should realize that each person requires a certain number of contacts a day. Some of these the individual wants to initiate himself, other contacts must happen to him, that is to say, must be initiated by others. When an individual likes to initiate contacts himself, but instead finds himself always on the receiving end, he will compensate,—by going to the foreman with complaints, by grousing to other workers, by making up occasions to leave his work to talk to others. If his job fails to give him the outlet for activity he needs, he will be emotionally disturbed. What he does by way of compensation he does because he is compelled to by the laws under which the human body operates. The supervisor who wishes to secure an effective working group must learn to use these laws of behavior for his own benefit, otherwise they may work against him.

REPRESENTATION

Having covered two major supervisory behavioral patterns, initiating (or directing) and responding, we have to complicate the picture by adding a third: representation. By representation we mean the supervisor's action in getting the attention of outsiders to the problems of his subordinates. That is, the supervisor is the interface between his group and the rest of the organization. A good many of the orders he gives and the demands he makes on his people flow through this interface. That is, his superiors expect him to transmit instructions and directions to his people. Similarly, other department heads make requests through the supervisor.

Significantly, the reverse flow is watched very closely by subordinates. Does their boss give as good as he gets? Does he defend and protect their interests, resist unfair demands, and seek to use his interface position (and his status and power) to protect his people? Here are just a few descriptions of bosses who do this:

We would do anything for Miss Cary because she really takes care of us. If someone hasn't been given a new uniform on time, doesn't get a merit increase when she deserves it, is given a hard time by another supervisor, you know that within five minutes Miss Cary will be up in the front office telling them that they can't do that to "her girls." She's a real fighter when it comes to anyone trying to take advantage of us.

Garfelli is a pretty tough supervisor. If you do anything wrong he tells you about it in no uncertain terms, and his language isn't always what they teach you in school. But most of us couldn't care less how much he shouts at us because we know that when the chips are down—when the big bosses try to forget our needs—Garfelli is right in there punching. When you work in his department you know you've got somebody who watches over your interests. So he never has to worry about his men backing him up when he asks a favor; they know he has never let them down yet. He's a real scrapper.

Most subordinates know that it is a lot easier for a boss to concentrate on channeling *downward* what upper management wants than it is for him to channel *upward* what they want. Many managers therefore appear to their subordinates to knuckle under to the status system—to press hard downward and soft upward. They don't fight when upper management says no to a request. Many of the key decisions that affect their welfare (such as basic wages increases, work loads, clothing allowances, and some disciplinary actions) will be made outside their own departments. So they cannot expect to have a very affluent future when their boss is weak-kneed and unwilling to press their demands to outsiders. Thus supervisors need to bring into balance their internal initiations and eternal representations, as Figure 3-3 suggests.

Employees recognize that an organization's resources are limited and that everyone can't win. The departments that have the best working conditions, the best jobs, and the best earnings are usually those with strong-willed bosses who spend some of their energies initiating upward. Another department may be just as deserving, but if it has too meek a supervisor, its people get less.

To be sure, a supervisor's ability to do this is dependent not simply upon his own energy and the personal courage needed to buck the status ladder, but also on the kind of boss he himself has. (See Chapter 8.)

If the people at the next level of management are unresponsive, unwilling to let the supervisor initiate to them, he will appear impotent to his subordinates. Thus upper management can help make or break a supervisor. If his superiors are reasonably responsive when he says, "I need this for my people," he will be much more influential with his group. If they consistently turn him down, the manager will have trouble appearing as a real leader to his people.

Of course, the supervisor has to use good sense in per-

Figure 7-3   Balancing internal and external interactions

forming his role of advocate. He has to distinguish good causes from poor causes and learn to make an effective case when he is representing his department. If he goes upstairs frequently unprepared, uninformed, or as the defender of "bad" cases, his demands will be more and more discounted or ignored altogether.

A manager needs to remember that people working for him are good judges of his willingness and ability to act as their representative.

SUMMARY

There is another way of looking at all the things a supervisor handles: discipline, order giving, communications, dealing with groups, and the rest. That is, he needs to look at the overall pattern of interaction involved in his relationship with subordinates both in the group and as individuals. Subordinates will respect and follow a boss who devotes as much effort to *representing* their interests to outsiders, particularly upper management, as he does to handling internal matters. Also, they expect his *responsiveness* to them to be roughly comparable to the amount of *direction* he gives them. That is, he should allow their intiating to him as well as his initiating to them. These three major behavioral patterns (representation, responsiveness, direction) need to be in equilibrium if motivation and morale are to be retained.

Managers also need to be aware of individual differences in both the need and capacity of subordinates to initiate and seek responsiveness. Some subordinates will seize every opportunity to monopolize the supervisor's attention, by demanding more than their share of his time and too much responsiveness. Others will be reluctant to initiate a contact. The supervisor has to even out these differences to some extent by rationing those who initiate too much and making himself more available to those who are unlikely to take the initiative.

These personality differences, expressed in interaction terms, also affect the way subordinates handle their own jobs. Knowing something about the individual's personality helps the manager predict the way a job will be handled and also to detect when an individual is under stress. Anger, fear, or hostility is shown when an individual changes his interaction pattern, becoming more or less active. These behavioral differences are a more reliable guide to feelings than the actual words spoken or sentiments overtly expressed.

SELECTED REFERENCES

Chapple, E., and L. Sayles, *The Measure of Management,* Macmillan, New York, 1961, part 2.

Lawrence, P., *The Changing of Organizational Behavior Patterns,* Harvard Univ. Graduate School of Business, Division of Research, Boston, 1958.

Sayles, L., *Managerial Behavior,* McGraw-Hill, New York, 1964, chap. 9.

Whyte, W. F., *Organizational Behavior,* Irwin-Dorsey, Homewood, Illinois, 1969, part V.

THE EDUCATION OF GREG HORNING: APRIL 7

"Now, you see, Henry. It's very tricky here and you'd better go very slowly until you get the hang of it." Greg was out on the floor with Creegmore. The engineering department had developed a new mold which they were testing out on Creegmore's machine. It would eliminate one step in the process, but it was still in the early stages. Until they could iron out the bugs in it, it tended to break very easily. "When they demonstrated the process to me, they suggested that you hold it right here, just before it's time for the piece to come through. See?"

Greg looked up at Creegmore. "Yeah, yeah. I see," Henry said and nodded. But he was frowning and the corners of his mouth were pulling down. He obviously didn't buy engineering's suggestion.

"Unless, Henry," Greg went on, "you can think of a better way. I know you know a lot more about the actual operations than I do."

"Well, now. Let's see." Creegmore's face suddenly came alive. He bent forward to examine the new operation. "It seems to me, if you just eased it through here instead of holding it at all, the piece would come through nice and smooth. See? Like this." Creegmore demonstrated his idea. It worked nicely—and it was faster besides.

"Say, Henry. That's fine. Better than what the engineering guys said. Let's try it your way a while. If it works out, I'll tell them we've got a better method down here."

"Okay, Greg," Creegmore said, looking pleased. He started back to the job he'd been doing, but Greg stopped him.

"You know, Henry. I've been thinking about that talk we had several months ago when I first came," Greg said.

"Yeah, what about it?" Creegmore asked, his face suddenly tight again.

"Well, I think maybe you were right. Maybe industrial engineering doesn't have all the answers."

"You're damn right, they don't," Creegmore answered warmly.

"Well, look, Henry. If you can take a minute, come in and let's talk about it. I'd like to have some of your ideas."

"Now?"

"Yes. That'd be fine—if you've got the time."

"Well, sure I have, Greg," Creegmore answered quickly with a smile. "Be glad to."

"Now, for instance," Henry said, when they were settled in Greg's office. "There's the process we do on the gears. Now the job description says we're supposed to set the temperature gauge at one point and leave it that way through the whole process. But if you do that you begin to get more and more warp on the pieces when you've got a long run. Now if we vary the temperature while the run's going on— just a hair up and down—the pieces come out more regular. You see what I mean?"

"Yes, Henry. That sounds sensible. But what about the time it takes? You feel it's worth it?"

"Oh, it doesn't take up any more time. Attention—now that's another thing. You've got to watch it pretty carefully, but that's another story. And, of course, you've got to know what you're doing."

"Well, that sounds like a good idea. But what about..." But Creegmore was all wound up now. He went on enthusiastically.

"And then look at what we do when the machines aren't working good. We can't get maintenance in here every time something is a little off. You know how they are—never get hold of them, anyway. Now before you told us to stick to the rules, we used to use a prod on the runners when they got out of line. It was something we developed ourselves. But we stopped using it now. But it saved us a lot of pieces. Now we either get more rejects or we have to stop using a machine sometimes and wait and have it regulated. See, these machines are almost like people—you know what I mean?" He looked at Greg, who nodded. "They all have little quirks that make them different. Those engineers don't know anything about that. Only we do—we know our own machines and we know the different things you have to do on each one to get the best output. You see what I'm getting at?"

"Yes, I do, Henry," Greg answered. "But that's one of the points of the job description, Henry. You each have *one* machine and you get the feel of it and know all the fine points of how it works. Now these refinements of yours sound good to me. I'm 100 percent for your using them." Henry smiled and started to comment, but Greg had not finished. "But this business of one man spelling another. Now that's something else—I've let Phil help you but that's a special case. If you each know your own machine another man can't get as good output from it as you can. That day Alfred came in here and you were supposed to be watching his machine . . ."

"He had a good idea there, Greg," Henry broke in. "You ought to get him to tell you about it some time."

"Well, I will, Henry," Greg went on. "I'd like to hear everyone's ideas. But that's not my point. Now you were supposed to be watching his machine and you were way over across the room arguing about something. Now, that's what I mean, Henry. That kind of thing is bad." Seeing Henry look pleased with himself, Greg paused.

"You know, I agree with you there, Greg. But can I tell you something? I was doing your job that day. Of course, you were just fresh in here and you didn't know the ropes yet, but I shouldn't have to be haggling with the materials handlers all the time. You're the boss and you're supposed to clear all that out for us. We shouldn't have that kind of problem with them."

Greg smiled wanly. Creegmore could always make him feel a little defensive. "Let me think about that, Henry."

"Sure, Greg. You're the boss. You've got to stand up for your crew with the other departments. Take the problem we're having with the mixing department right now. They're storing more and more of their stuff in our area. Pretty soon we're not going to be able to go anywhere in here without falling over a sack of plastic pellets. It's disgusting."

"I didn't know about that."

"Well, you've seen those damn bags all over. What'd you think they were there for—decoration? They're taking advantage of us and if I were supervisor I wouldn't stand for it. You should do something about it, Greg," Henry finished, leaning over toward Greg. "They're making you look like a damn fool—letting them get away with it."

"Maybe I look like a damn fool—maybe I don't," said

Greg, reddening slightly. "But you've got a point and I'll see what can be done. Thanks for the advice."

"Now the suggestions I made . . ."

"I think we should try them. We're sort of playing it by ear—whatever works is good for the department."

"Right, Greg. I guess we see more eye to eye than I thought. I'll be getting back now. Don't forget those pellet sacks."

"No, Henry," and Greg managed a small smile. "Whatever works is good for the department," he said to himself.

The pellet problem turned out to be a bigger ball of twine than Greg had expected. When he saw Joe Barber, head of the mixing department, he found out that his predecessor had given them permission to use some of molding's space to store their plastics. Steve Phillips had also approved this allocation.

If he made any static about it, he risked causing trouble with Phillips and friction with mixing—but he had to keep good relations there. On the other hand, if he did nothing, Creegmore would think he was a coward—and the rest of the crew would probably share his feelings.

QUESTIONS

1. Point out the places in which Greg is being very responsive to Creegmore and the effect of this on Creegmore's attitudes.
2. What appears to happen to the amount people talk—the quantity of words—when the give and take is easy in conversation? Is Greg ever too responsive?
3. Can you identify any parts of the dialogue in which the easy give and take breaks down?
4. What should Greg do in relation to Creegmore if the pellet problem isn't solved? Does this mean he is not representing his group effectively?

8. Initiating upward:
the supervisor faces the boss

Today's supervisor lives in a complex world. He must maintain good relations with his own subordinates. Between them there should be mutual feelings of trust and respect. He must perform his duties to the satisfaction of his immediate superior, who is his prime source of punishments and rewards. He must deal on occasion with direct pressures from levels further up the hierarchy—with the expectations and demands of his superior's boss or someone even higher. Then, too, he has frequent relations with other line and staff departments—some on the same status level, others *nominally* on the same level but actually in a position to give him orders—all of whose cooperation the supervisor needs to discharge his duties effectively.

These relationships would present fewer problems if the goals of the various individuals he depends on and the groups of which he is a member were the same. In the broadest sense, all management groups are committed to the goal of maximum profitability for the organization. But this over-reaching goal permits striking and frequently bitter divergences of opinion about how the goal can best be achieved, as well as endless power and status conflicts between managers. In these conflicts, the supervisor is frequently a witness or a victim.

Among the groups with which the supervisor is most intimately connected—the work group that he leads and the higher management group that he immediately represents—there is not even an agreement on ultimate goals. True, few rank-and-file workers want to destroy the enterprise that employs them. They feel a stake in its survival to the extent that it fulfills their personal goals—good wages, a pleasant working atmosphere, the opportunity to do challenging, high-quality work under conditions over which they exert some control, a guarantee of security for the future, and other satisfactions. Reasonable goals—all of them. But goals that, if fully realized, would clearly conflict with the overreaching corporate goal of maximum profit.

THE MAN IN THE MIDDLE

More than twenty-five years ago, Fritz Roethlisberger of the Harvard Business School, in a classic article, described the foreman—the description would apply equally well to the first-line office or engineering supervisor—as "the man in the middle," endlessly subject to conflicting pressures and grievances from higher management and his own work group. Roethlisberger's description is valid for the supervisor. He is still the man in the middle.

The *effective* supervisor mediates successfully between his work group and management and discharges the obligations of his dual loyalty—to his subordinates and to his boss. The *ineffective* supervisor is caught in the crunch between the conflicting forces, sinks into inaction or succumbs to the pressure from one side or the other, and becomes useless to the organization.

The picture is the same as it was when Roethlisberger wrote about it in 1945, yet it is also altered. Wherein lie the changes? Actually, there are two differences: The controls, largely statistical, which higher management can use to check up on the performance of the supervisor and his work group are now more sophisticated, and the pressures the first-level supervisor can bring to bear on his subordinates are different and generally less effective.

HOW DOES THE HIERARCHY LIMIT THE SUPERVISOR?

In most plants and offices with more than five hundred employees, higher management receives, on a weekly or daily basis, computer-processed data covering every quantifiable aspect of the supervisor's operation—pieces of paper processed by categories or components manufactured, lost time, absenteeism, scrap, rejects, tardiness, overtime, and every other production factor. Each item is meticulously flagged to call higher management's attention to any deviation from a predetermined standard of acceptability. True, twenty years ago higher management was receiving some of the same records. But it received them monthly or less frequently, if at all, and the records themselves were neither as comprehensive nor as accurate. The computer, with its ability to handle fantastic numbers of interrelated computations without man and without error, has tightened higher management's controls over its supervisors. Doomsday comes every Monday.

AFFLUENCE LESSENS THE SUPERVISOR'S POWER

The supervisor's position is further complicated and weakened by the decline in the economic pressures he can exert on his work group. Admittedly, these pressures have been exaggerated. The supervisor has always had to come to terms with the production-line workers, office girls, and engineers who do the actual work of the organization. They have always had the tacit power, by practicing malicious obedience (obeying his directions too literally), slowing down, wasting materials or spoiling work, and a hundred other subterfuges, to increase the supervisor's costs and make him look bad in the eyes of his superiors. To ensure output at a satisfactory level, the supervisor has made deals and guaranteed concessions to his work force, few of which would pass muster with higher management.

The difference is that in a period of comparatively full employment and affluence among workers, the supervisor's ultimate weapon—dismissal or the threat of it—has lost most of its past clout. Certainly, supervisors can and do fire employees. But we would guess that for each man fired today, five are retained only because the supervisor can't face the task of finding replacements for them. Threats, in other words, are out—way out—and persuasion is way in, as a means of maintaining production. But there's a problem: The concessions many supervisors must make to keep the men working, we suspect, are greater and frequently more difficult to grant because of the sophisticated controls available to higher management.

HELP IS ON THE WAY

The picture has a compensating side. Higher management doesn't exist in a vacuum, and it is aware of the changes in the relative bargaining position of the supervisor vis à vis his work force. Roethlisberger commented that "the foreman was painfully tutored to focus his attention upward to his immediate superiors and the logic of evaluation they represented, rather than downward to his subordinates and the feelings they have." The statement, largely true in the 1950s, would not be true today. The supervisor has been taught and encouraged to empathize with his subordinates and even to feel loyalty toward them. Much of this new emphasis reflects the findings and teachings of behavioral scientists over the past two decades, but some also reveals a recognition, usually unacknowledged, of the supervisor's weakened bargaining position.

We recall a conversation with a senior vice president of a large New England bank, a man who skillfully concealed any inner warmth he possessed. He described with considerable satisfaction the stratagems employed by the bank to make its employees more productive, including paying 10 percent more in each job classification than its competitors. The goal of this effort: a 60 percent workday—that is, the bank's clerical force would do 60 percent as much work as the time-study people had determined they should be able to do without overexerting themselves. The vice president reported the success of the program and added complacently that other bank employees in the city were working a 50 percent day. The time-study engineers may have been mistaken—that's not important. The attitude of the banker is, and it's symbolic of the attitude among higher management generally. The big bosses don't expect the same level of production among rank-and-file employees as they did previously, and their diminished expectations have in turn lessened the pressure upon the supervisor.

THE WINNING SUPERVISORY STYLE

The implications seem plain. Said Machiavelli to his prince, "It is better to be feared than to be loved." But today's supervisor is hardly a sixteenth-century prince. He instead faces a situation in which it is very difficult for him to make his employees (subjects) fear him. And he had better be loved if he is going to do a good job. In other words, the supervisor must master the arts of persuasion, and the ability to inspire the affection, or at least the respect, of his employees, if he wants to motivate them to a level of performance that will earn him the confidence and approval of higher management.

The winning supervisory style—one that would please bosses and subordinates alike—would appear to be a compromise. It would force subordinates to conform strictly to quantitative performance goals explicitly set and rigidly monitored by top management, but allow them maximum leeway in planning how to reach those goals and in most other aspects of plant or office behavior. For example, the quota for answering inquiries from correspondents is set at sixty a day, but the correspondent can decide whether she will plod along like the proverbial turtle and take a half-hour for lunch or will work at a breakneck clip and then spend two hours and a half out shopping.

The Supervisor as Imitator

Would that it were that simple. Several factors complicate the picture, of which the most important is that nine supervisors out of ten—we suspect the proper figure is 99 out of 100—imitate the style of supervision practiced by their immediate superior. If he is dictatorial and distrustful, always specifying each instruction to the last detail and forever checking to see whether his orders are being followed, so are the supervisors under him. If the superior is permissive and confident, allowing his supervisors to work within broad directives and interrupting only when something has gone wrong, so are they.

CLOSE OR GENERAL SUPERVISION?

Imitation the sincerest form of flattery? Maybe not. A question that leads into a semantic bog. But among supervisors, imitation of their bosses is a form of flattery almost universally practiced. Those supervisors who are on the receiving end of *general* supervision are likely to practice it themselves. If they receive *close* supervision, they will supervise their subordinates closely.

Chris Arygris described, for example, a brilliant plant manager, the outstanding performer in a multiplant operation, who was constantly interceding, constantly checking, constantly controlling his supervisors. All of them respected him, all of them feared him, most of them—perhaps surprisingly—liked him. And all of them did their best to act like him, including those who failed because his style went against the grain and they weren't good actors. Even the failures shared in the informal agreement that whoever first saw the plant manager in the morning would tell the rest what he's "hot on, today," and in turn they all would be "hot on" their own men and take the necessary steps to see that the manager would not "catch us with our pants down."

In exoneration, one point must be stressed. Even those supervisors whose natural style of supervision differed from the plant manager's were not guilty of unadulterated sycophancy. The plant manager was a rare composite of energy, intelligence, and devotion to work, obsessed with accomplishment and committed to rewarding it. With such a leader, supervisors will apparently forget their resentment over being closely controlled and even the general antagonism of the led toward the leader (a natural burden of leadership). They will compete fiercely for recognition and praise through the only medium the leader recognizes and rewards: excellence of performance.

Of course, imitation in an organization begins at the top. It's the total corporate climate that sets the style from which the supervisor's boss takes his cues, and which the supervisor, in turn, copies. However, it is not merely a process of imitation, conscious or otherwise. If higher management be-lieves in tight controls and continual surveillance over opera-tions far down the line, the supervisor will find himself loaded down with paperwork. The constant reporting will compel him to exercise close supervision over methods of output and deny him the leisure he needs to build up a consulting relationship with his subordinates.

Process and Position of the Work Group

Other factors, always closely related to the dominant man-agement style of leadership but sometimes opposed to them, are the nature of the work and the strategic position of the work group. Close supervision is the appropriate and effective style for some types of work and work groups, whereas general supervision suits other work and other groups. Within the same organization or even the same office or plant, the same dominant style, whether permissive or close, may be just right in one area, tolerable in a second area, and destructive in a third. As Professor Leavitt of Stanford University put it, "The degree of latitude or control that is applied to a particular function is being selected more and more in order to expedite that function. Large organizations cannot be managed as unified wholes with a single managerial strategy equally appropriate for its varied subsections."

IS THE JOB REPETITIVE OR CREATIVE?

Let's apply this to a couple of supervisors and the different functions they perform in the same level of job. Brad Mason is a hatch foreman working the piers in Seattle. Every ship that ties up presents different problems. The winches, hatches, booms, and tackle, even the men down the hatch—all are different with each shift. Getting the cargo unloaded calls for a quick undogmatic mind and a method of getting things done by showing people what has to be done and then giv-ing them the proverbial rope. The tasks are unique, ill-defined, and dispersed. Brad Mason practices general supervision—otherwise, he's dead.

Ed Epstein has a quite different job. He is in charge of customer inquiries for Helpers A–Day, a large credit card organization. Nine-tenths of the inquiries fall into relatively few categories and are answered with a form response. Any other approach would lead to inconsistencies, spiraling costs in handling, and general chaos. Ed knows the rules and makes random checks on a set schedule to make sure they're being followed. He's got the job laid out in front of him and follows it every step along the way. He doesn't ask for advice because he doesn't need it. Ed Epstein practices close supervision—otherwise, his job makes little sense.

Obviously, we have indulged in hyperbole. Few people have jobs that dictate a style of supervision as precisely as those of Mason and Epstein, but the point still holds. Most supervisors have subordinates whose work falls somewhere between the two broad categories: repetitive and creative. In the repetitive job, the employee repeats the same task over and over again for extended periods of time. His tasks are usually routine and unchallenging, and the emphasis is on perserverance and discipline, self-imposed or otherwise. In the creative job, an employee applies his skills to more demanding tasks that are usually varied, challenging, and longer in duration. Contrast, for example, the typical assembly-line worker versus the electrician in the maintenance department. Would anyone argue that the same style of supervision will be equally effective with both?

HOW MUCH STATUS DOES THE JOB HAVE?

Here's another important distinction—a matter of power and status. The assembly-line worker has little pride of workmanship, feeling of importance within the organization, or even sense of self. His relatively small self-confidence comes from his sense of mobility, but within limits he still can be bossed and even pushed around. Not so your maintenance electrician. His superior economic position, his sure knowledge of the scarcity of his skills, and his pride in his craft combine to give him a firm sense of his strategic position within the organization—and generally a determination to exploit it for whatever it's worth. Few supervisors would attempt to practice close supervision with a maintenance electrician—and almost none could succeed.

DETERMINING SUPERVISORY STYLES

Supervisory styles are determined by a confluence of factors, the most important of which is the style of management at the top, and the least important the supervisor's own natural style and preference.

Top management, as we have said, plays the dominant role in determining leadership style for reasons that are partly psychological and partly strategic: Each level in a typical business tends to imitate the style of the level immediately

above it. Managers are an imitative class, even what Walter
Bagehot called the British middle class of a century ago,
a "deferential" class.

The second factor is the one of controls. A top management that hoards all the decisions worth making unto itself—
and surprisingly, this feat can be accomplished effectively in
large organizations—obviously expects underlings at the
various levels down the line to tread warily and interpret all
policies and rules as literally as possible. Freedom exists only
in the areas not covered by directives.

In a highly centralized organization, however, the supervisor is not likely to take advantage of even the limited
opportunities for initiative. Instead, he will tend to play safe:
When in doubt, don't. In an organization where many important decisions are delegated to levels below top management, the effect is similarly contagious. Managers at lower
levels, including first-level supervisors, will show both
flexibility in interpreting policies and initiative in handlng
matters not covered by the rules. Whether or not they practice
a general style of supervision will depend on the interaction
between the requirements of the work situation and their own
natural style. At least the option will be open to them.

Whether they *should* practice general supervision is a moot
question. In any employee popularity poll, all the evidence
indicates that it would win hands down. For example, a survey,
conducted several years ago by Scott Meyers among more
than thirteen hundred managers of all levels at Texas Instruments, showed an overwhelming preference for a developmental manager (roughly, one who practiced general supervision) over a reductive manager, regardless of the manager's
values or style of supervision. The same survey also revealed
that, of the managers rated as highly motivated, one-half
had developmental bosses and only 8 percent had reductive
bosses.

Yet we have seen that autocratic management and supervision can obtain outstanding results, at least in terms of
production and what Emerson called "the unimpeachable
judgment of an unbribable tribunal, the account of profit and
loss." In a book written by Marrow, Bowers, and Seashore, a
trio of experts prominently identified with the cause of
participative management and general supervision, even they
concede that the " 'goodness' of any particular social organization and of any particular set of guiding principles for
social progress lies not so much in its own inherent merit
as in its utility for the effective use of work facilities and work
process resources." In other words, the decision to employ

general or close supervision should depend on the requirements of the particular work situation. Unfortunately, the decision is usually determined by the collective temperament of top management, which may match the requirements of the job, but frequently does not.

A LITTLE MATTER OF INFLUENCE

More important than the supervisor's style of leadership in getting ahead with his bosses is his influence. Do other levels of management respond positively to his requests and recommendations? Does he have the skill to make effective presentations to his boss and to other managers within the organization? In short, can he sell himself and his ideas?

Incidentally, we feel that the supervisor who practices general supervision but has little or no influence with his superiors is almost certain to destroy his influence with his subordinates. For example, he calls a group meeting to discuss the problem of how to deal with excessive absenteeism. Then he takes his group's recommended solution to higher management, only to have it rejected out of hand. The experience is repeated several times with the same result. The group sinks into frustration and cynicism, becomes hostile and disrespectful to the supervisor. His position is barely tenable once his impotence has been exposed.

What gives a supervisor influence with his bosses? Performance is one part of the answer. Suppose a supervisor fails to measure up to the statistical indices used by top management to monitor and reward performance down the line. He is almost certain to be the subject of a confrontation between his boss and higher management—a confrontation from which his influence will emerge diminished or destroyed. Communication is also an important part of the answer. Success here lies not so much in the supervisor's manner of delivery or expertise in organizing the subject matter of his presentation as in the substance of his communications—what he tells the boss, and of almost equal importance, what he conceals from him. In subordinate–boss communications, the substance is still the message.

Maintaining Credibility

As a basic maxim of communication between subordinate and boss we commend: Tell him what he needs to know, not simply what he wants to hear, even when he has given unmistakable signs that he doesn't want to hear all the facts. We know of a case where the machinery on a conveyer line had become too light for the production load, causing frequent breakdowns and the replacement of bearings, drive belts, sprockets, and other parts. The supervisor knew a major installation was in order, but each time he approached the plant superintendent he got the Typhoid Mary treatment, and eventually he subsided. Production was being maintained at the expense of excessive overtime when the day of reckoning arrived. The plant manager called for an accounting and the supervisor was on the spot. Should he take the blame, or should he be disloyal to the superintendent, his immediate superior? He "took the count" and hoped that his superior would repay his loyalty. Who can say that he decided wrong? He owed his job to his boss. And besides, he had to balance the temporary gratitude and protection of the plant manager against the possibility of permanent hostility and continuing retaliation from his immediate superior.

We weren't surprised to hear the results of a study made to determine why some boss–subordinates communicated and others did not. The finding of the study? The most accurate and extensive communication took place between a boss and a trusting subordinate who didn't care about getting ahead.

Empathy Works

Most bosses want the truth and appreciate it, at least in the long run—the previous case nothwithstanding. In another situation with which we are familiar, the superintendent steadily resisted pressures from quality control for a lower scrap-and-reject rate on two grounds, one explicit, the other hidden. He didn't want to add the expense of hiring more inspectors to his budget, and he feared that higher-quality work would mean lower production—and production was the *idée fixe* of his boss, the plant manager. The easy position for the supervisor was to sympathize and agree with his boss. "If we went along with those goddam perfectionists in quality control, nothing would ever get out the door." However, the supervisor said nothing of the kind. He *empathized* with his boss instead of *sympathizing* with him, and recognizing that more inspectors would contribute to the company's—and the superintendent's—good, he took a stand in favor of adding them. In time, his pressure was influential in persuading the superintendent to modify his position. The superintendent probably never thought fondly of the supervisor for standing up to him. But he respected his integrity and recognized his credibility. People—and bosses are people too—have a deep and well-founded respect for someone who sticks to what he believes is the truth and who shows he is interested in nothing less.

Empathy Can Boomerang

Not all bosses can tolerate openness. Sometimes the truth hurts too much to accept. Take the case of the direct-mail supervisor for a magazine-publishing company that sold some of its periodicals by means of premium booklets on subjects assumed to be of interest to potential subscribers. The publisher of one magazine was a man who preached quality to his subordinates, but who at the same time impressed his bosses by repeatedly demonstrating how costs could be cut at the expense of quality—with little or no loss of sales.

The two most recent premiums, written by hacks at bargain-basement prices, had been judged unusable by the publisher. The direct-mail chief saw his opportunity and seized it. He wrote a memo to the publisher in which he stated the case for higher-quality premiums in the strongest terms of which he was capable. Among his statements were these:

Evidence suggests we are not competitive. We should commission premiums from people who know their subjects thoroughly, but at our rates the experts won't write for us.

Premiums obtained at our price have been money thrown away. I can't resist quoting Ruskin's warning. "But when you pay too little, you sometimes lose all, because the thing you bought was incapable of doing the thing it was bought to do!"

The publisher never answered the memo or even alluded to it in any future contacts with the supervisor. His answer came in a red-faced tirade addressed to another supervisor who had tactfully submitted a much milder document on the same general topic—the need to improve quality. (This is a wonderful example of displacement.) Apparently the publisher didn't trust his own self-control enough to risk a direct confrontation with the first supervisor, who had challenged his self-image so painfully. At any rate, the direct-mail supervisor's days of influence with the boss ended abruptly with the delivery of his memo.

The Uses of Deception

Through a frequent and painful paradox, the supervisor is required to limit his communications to his boss in order to maintain his influence with him. There are things the boss would like to know, that he may need to know, that policies and regulations require that he know. But sometimes these things must be withheld from him so that the performance level in the supervisor's operation can be maintained at a satisfactory level. Obliged to make a choice, the supervisor has to balance his fears. If he conceals the facts, the boss may discover the deception and penalize him—a real but indeterminate fear, since both the risks and the penalties are difficult to calculate. If he tells the truth, the price of his honesty will be the impaired performance of his work group, the almost certain loss of influence with the boss, and penalties once the performance drop becomes obvious. Faced with this dilemma, most supervisors opt for deception.

Take the supervisors described by Dalton. They were under intense pressure from higher management to increase production and driven into various departures from official procedure in order to retain influence with their bosses and win their approval.

The pay rate varied with the product specifications, and several supervisors through an informal deal with their work groups, rearranged the order sequence to permit the higher-paying orders to be run first, regardless of the scheduling. The deal, of course, was in direct violation of company regulations and threw the supervisors into conflict with production planning, which had worked out a rigid sequence for processing orders based on delivery deadlines promised to customers.

We would assume that the supervisors couldn't get away with an evasion so bald-faced. Not so. Production planning threatened the supervisors involved, who first played dumb and then contrived elaborate excuses to conceal their departures from schedule. What happened when production planning confronted higher plant management with evidence of what the supervisors were up to? Very little. Higher management condemned the supervisors' actions for the record but enforced no penalties, and the practice continued. Of course the supervisors' deal was contrary to the rules, but one fact overshadowed any other consideration: Total production in the departments that had broken the rules was much higher than it had been before.

Perhaps the supervisors had anticipated the tacit approval

of higher management when they circumvented the rules, although we doubt it. Instead, when faced with the pressure for higher production, they made a deal with their workers that ensured it, then crossed their fingers and prepared to take the consequences if and when their arrangements were disclosed to higher management.

The Indispensables

Not every case of deception involves the supervisor's concealing facts from his boss because of pressures from his subordinates. Sometimes it's the supervisors themselves who take advantage of their strategic position and apply pressure on their bosses to circumvent the rules. We're familiar with one case involving two copy supervisors in the Cleveland office of a New York advertising agency. The agency is notorious for the strictness and minuteness of its regulations, and the resident vice president is equally notorious for his zeal in enforcing them. One motto of the organization is that "there is no such thing as being a little bit late." Obviously, one of the V.P.'s responsibilities was to uphold the no-tardiness rule and discipline violators.

The two supervisors systematically began to violate the rule, coming in first a few minutes late each morning, then gradually extending their tardiness to a half-hour or forty-five minutes. The V.P. closed his eyes to the practice (after all, these were his most valuable employees), but after several weeks he took reluctant cognizance. The senior of the two laid it on the line—he would resign rather than obey the rule—and the V.P. promptly caved in.

That's not the end of the story. The two supervisors continued to do good work, thus keeping their end of the silent bargain, but the extent of their tardiness reduced the rule to a travesty. Being an hour late became standard operating procedure. Other supervisors and employees imitated the two copy chiefs, feeling that the V.P. would not crack down on them either, and they were correct. There was one curious side effect. Out of fear, guilt, or a combination of both, the V.P. became more unrelenting than ever in rigidly enforcing every last petty regulation in the shop, apparently seeking to compensate by his zeal in other areas for his backsliding with tardiness.

Bypassing the Boss

Another practice calculated to endanger relations with the boss, but one that supervisors sometimes feel justified in, or even driven to, adopting is bypassing the boss. Sometimes quick action is imperative and there just isn't time to contact the boss, or he's out of town or otherwise not available. One supervisor described his strategy this way: "I am always in a position of getting people to waive the formal requirements. Recently a manager said he couldn't do it without the authorization of my boss. I told him I could sign for my boss. I just had to get that approval that day. Of course, as soon as I could I went to my boss to make sure he was in agreement with my action."

Another innocent and necessary form of bypassing the boss is cutting the red tape involved in going through channels. For example, in a small manufacturing company the accounting department was located directly across the hall from research and development. Everyone recognized that scientists and engineers kept odd hours and everyone accepted this practice. What the clerks in accounting wouldn't accept and repeatedly griped about to their boss was that the clerks in R and D felt that they too were privileged characters with no obligation to keep regular hours.

What could the accounting supervisor do about the problem? If he followed the rule book, he would report the matter to his supervisor. It would travel on up the line (doubtless with the facts being distorted in the process) to the common superior of both accounting and R and D, and then down the line again till it reached the presumptuous clericals in R and D.

In this situation we suspect nine supervisors out of ten would cross the hall for a face-to-face talk with their opposite number and try to resolve the problem on the spot. Going through channels would be the last resort. It always takes time and frequently complicates the problem. Think of what would happen in a hospital if, say, an oxygen tank goes out of order. If everybody always followed channels, the nurse would report to the head nurse, she to the chief engineer, and he to the repairman. The patient would probably be dead before the equipment was fixed.

Of course, the supervisor who cuts red tape always runs the risk that what's decided upon at his level will be over-ruled by his superior at one level of the hierarchy or another, sometimes on the merits of the case and sometimes out of someone's pique at being "short-circuited." However, it's a risk most supervisors feel is worth taking.

FRITZ J. ROETHLISBERGER (1898–   )

Roethlisberger, along with Mayo, is generally described as the father of the human relations movement. But when he talks about the human relations movement, he does not mean the plethora of canned programs and panaceas assembled by the naive and the greedy under the banner of human relations that sought to claim descent from the Hawthorne experiment and the research conducted by Mayo, Roethlisberger, Whitehead, and others. By the human relations movement he does not mean the alleged discovery—it was, in fact, *not* demonstrated by the Hawthorne studies—that relations between the supervisor and the worker depended on the supervisor's skill and that these relationships, in turn, determined such key factors as job satisfaction, morale, and productivity. In fact, Roethlisberger has devoted much time and energy over the past four decades to disclaiming the parentage of Hawthorne for what he describes "as the ball of wax that came to be known as human relations."

What is the legitimate scope of the human relations movement as it has appeared to Roethlisberger? What is the principal legacy of the Hawthorne studies—which is almost the same question? We have seen something of what Hawthorne meant to Mayo, and we would argue, although he might disagree with us, that Roethlisberger views the lessons of Hawthorne differently. To him, Hawthorne was a justification of the clinical approach to studying men at work; that there was no substitute for the slow and laborious task of observing how workers actually behave in the shop; that no generalization holds water unless it has taken into account the work group as a social system; that for the investigator to ask about the morale of our plant is about as sensible as for the physician to ask about the health of the patients in our hospital. Roethlisberger emphasized that the satisfactions and dissatisfactions of the individual employee were always relative to the demands he brought to the particular situation along with the demands that the particular situation made on him.

Beyond that, he saw the principal lesson of Hawthorne as the importance to the employee of being listened to and paid attention to. And of the two, he would stress the importance of counseling to the manager, what he defined as "listening with understanding," of listening for the little things that made the big difference. In other words, Roethlisberger saw that human relations skills must always exist and be developed within a particular organizational setting in which the manager by patiently observing himself as well as observing and listening to others becomes in time—and usually it takes a long time—proficient at promoting cooperation and participation. Roethlisberger was only secondarily concerned with generalities, what he calls "the search for simple uniformities"; his emphasis, instead, is on the clinical investigatory approach—on the close study of unique situations.

Most of this may strike you as commonplace and obvious, which is but one proof, and probably the most convincing proof, of Roethlisberger's status as a classic management thinker. It is the fate of the most perceptive insights of one generation to become part of the intellectual folklore of the next. So it has been with Roethlisberger. The more responsible practitioners of the human relations movement have shared his perceptions and preached and utilized his approach for a generation.

As for further reading, the following are important to any understanding of Roethlisberger's ideas: *Management and the Worker* (with Dickson), 1939—*the* book on Hawthorne; *Management and Morale*—a better written book (obviously, Roethlisberger was the stylist of the team) but of much less significance; and *Man in Organization* (1968), a collection of essays written over a forty-year period, of which the best, such as "The Foreman: Master and Victim of Double Talk," are very good indeed.

The Foreman: Master and Victim of Double Talk*

It is in his new streamlined social setting, far different from the "good old days," that we must learn to understand the modern foreman's anomalous position. The modern foreman has to get results—turn out production, maintain quality, hold costs down, keep his employees satisfied—under a set of technical conditions, social relations,

---

* Reprinted by permission from Fritz J. Roethlisberger, "The Foreman: Master and Victim of Double Talk," *Man in Organization*, The Belknap Press of Harvard University Press, Cambridge, Mass., 1968, pp. 37–42. © 1968 by the President and Fellows of Harvard College; all rights reserved.

and logical abstractions far different from those which existed 25 years ago.

For one thing, he has to "know" more than his old-time counterpart. Any cursory examination of modern fore-man training programs will reveal that the modern fore-man has to know (and understand) not only (1) the company's policies, rules, and regulations and (2) the company's cost system, payment system, manufacturing methods, and inspection regulations, in particular, but also frequently (3) something about the theories of production control, cost control, quality control, and time and motion study, in general. He also has to know (4) the labor laws of the United States, (5) the labor laws of the state in which the company operates, and (6) the specific labor contract which exists between his company and the local union. He has to know (7) how to induct, instruct, and train new workers; (8) how to handle and, where possible, prevent grievances; (9) how to improve conditions of safety; (10) how to correct workers and maintain discipline; (11) how never to lose his temper and always to be "fair"; (12) how to get and obtain cooperation from the wide assortment of people with whom he has to deal; and, especially, (13) how to get along with the shop steward. And in some companies he is supposed to know (14) how to do the jobs he supervises better than the employees themselves. Indeed, as some foreman training programs seem to conceive the foreman's job, he has to be a manager, a cost accountant, an engineer, a lawyer, a teacher, a leader, an inspector, a disciplinarian, a counselor, a friend, and, above all, an "example."

One might expect that this superior knowledge would tend to make the modern foreman feel more secure as well as to be more effective. Unfortunately some things do not work out the way they are intended. Quite naturally the foreman is bewildered by the many different roles and functions he is supposed to fulfill. He is worried in particular by what the boss will think if he takes the time to do the many things his many training courses tell him to do. And in 99 cases out of 100 what the boss thinks, or what the foreman thinks the boss thinks, will determine what the foreman does. As a result, the foreman gives lip service in his courses to things which in the concrete shop situation he feels it would be suicidal to practice. In the shop, for the most part, he does his best to perform by hook or by crook the one function clearly left him, the one function for which there is no definite staff counterpart, the one function for which the boss is sure to hold him responsible; namely, getting the workers to turn the work out on time. And about this function he feels his courses do not say enough—given the particular conditions, technical, human, and organizational, under which he has to operate.

Curiously enough, knowledge is not power for the modern foreman. Although he has to know a great deal about many things, he is no longer "the cock of the walk" he once was. Under modern conditions of operation, for example, there seems to be always somebody in the organization in a staff capacity who is supposed to know more than he does, and generally has more to say, about almost every matter that comes up; somebody, in addition to his boss, with whom he is supposed to consult and sometimes to share responsibility; somebody by whom he is constantly advised and often even ordered.

To the foreman it seems as if he is being held responsible for functions over which he no longer has any real authority. For some time he has not been able to hire and fire and set production standards. And now he cannot even transfer employees, adjust the wage inequalities of his men, promote deserving men, develop better machines, methods, and processes, or plan the work of his department, with anything approaching complete freedom of action. All these matters for which he is completely or partially responsible have now become involved with other persons and groups, or they have become matters of company policy and union agreement. He is hedged in on all sides with cost standards, production standards, quality standards, standard methods and procedures, specifications, rules, regulations, policies, laws, contracts, and agreements; and most of them are formulated without his participation.

Far better than the old-timer of 25 years ago the modern foreman knows how much work should be done in what length of time; how much it is worth; what the best methods to be used are; what his material, labor, and burden costs should be; and what the tolerances are that his product should meet. But in the acquisition of all this untold wealth of knowledge, somehow something is missing. In some sense, not too clearly defined, he feels he has become less rather than more effective, less rather than more secure, less rather than more important, and has received less rather than more recognition.

INTERACTIONS WITH MANY PEOPLE

Let us explore further this feeling of the modern foreman. Not only does he have to know more than his old-time counterpart about the "logics" of management, but also he has to relate himself to a wider range of people. In any mass production industry the foreman each day is likely to be interacting (1) with his boss, the man to whom he formally reports in the line organization; (2) with certain staff specialists, varying from one to a dozen people depending on the size and kind of organization— production control men, inspectors, standards men, efficiency engineers, safety engineers, maintenance and repair men, methods men, personnel men, counselors; (3) with the heads of other departments to which his department relates; (4) with his subordinates—sub-foremen, straw bosses, leadmen, group leaders, section chiefs; (5) with the workers directly, numbering anywhere from 10 to 300 people; and (6) in a union-organized plant, with the shop steward. Exploring the interdependence of each of these relationships as they impinge in toto upon the foreman makes it easier to understand how the modern foreman may feel in his everyday life. A diagram may help to make this clear.

Foreman-Superior

In the modern business structure there is probably no relation more important than that of the subordinate to his immediate superior.[1] This statement applies straight up the line from worker to president. It is in the relation between a subordinate and his immediate superior that most breakdowns of coordination and communication between various parts of the industrial structure finally show up. It is here that distortions of personal attitude and emotional disturbances become more pronounced. Why this relation is so important could be indicated in any number of ways. But it is clear that any adequate analysis would go far beyond the confines of this article, since it would involve a critique of modern business organization and the individual's relation to authority and, in part, an examination of the ideologies held by the leaders and executives

---

[1] See B. B. Gardner, *Human Relations in Industry* (Chicago: Richard D. Irwin, 1915).

of business.[2] It is enough that the importance of this relation and its consequences in terms of behavior, particularly
at the foreman level, are matters of common observation;
and it will be at this level of behavior and its associated
feelings that we shall remain.

Personal dependence upon the judgments and decisions
of his superiors, so characteristic of the subordinate–
superior relation in modern industry, makes the foreman's
situation basically insecure. He feels constant need to adjust himself to the demands of his superior and to seek
the approval of his superior. Everything that he does he
tries to evaluate in terms of his superior's reaction. Everything that his superior does he tries to evaluate in terms of
what it means or implies about his superior's relation to
him. Everything that his subordinates and workers do he
immediately tries to evaluate in terms of the criticism it may
call forth from his superior. In some cases this preoccupation with what the boss thinks becomes so acute that it
accounts for virtually everything the foreman says or does
and all his thinking about what goes on around him. He
will refrain from doing anything, even to the point of
dodging responsibility, for fear of bringing disapproval from
the boss. Hours at work and at home are spent in figuring
and anticipating what explanations or reasons he will need
to give the boss. And the boss's most innocent and unintentional acts—failure to say "good morning," for instance—are taken perhaps to imply disapproval.

It is hard to realize how much those who are interested
in improving the efficiency of industry have neglected this
area. If the man-hours spent by subordinates both on
and off the job in preoccupation about what the boss thinks
were added up, the total hours would be staggering—not
to mention the results this phenomenon has produced in
nervous breakdowns and other forms of mental anguish.
Stranger still, it almost appears as if modern industrial
organization, which prides itself so much on its efficiency,
has aggravated rather than reduced the amount of this
preoccupation, with disastrous consequences for health and
thus for efficiency. All this applies to the foreman in particular.

The crux of the foreman's problem is that he is constantly
faced with the dilemma of (1) having to keep his superior
informed with what is happening at the work level (in

---

[2] See Chester I. Barnard, *The Functions of the Executive* (Cambridge:
Harvard University Press, 1938), pp. 161–184.

many cases so that his superior may prepare in turn for the unfavorable reaction of his superior and so on up the line) and (2) needing to communicate this information in such a way that it does not bring unfavorable criticism on himself for not doing his job correctly or adequately. Discrepancies between the way things are at the work level and the way they are represented to be to management cannot be overlooked, and yet the foreman feels obliged to overlook them when talking to his boss. This makes the foreman's job particularly "tough" and encourages him to talk out of both sides of his mouth at the same time—to become a master of double talk.

Each foreman, of course, resolves the conflict in terms of his own personal history, personality, and temperament. Some foremen become voluble in the face of this situation; others are reduced to stony silence, feeling that anything they say will be held against them. Some keep out of the boss's way, while others devise all sorts of ways for approaching him and trying to direct attention to certain things they have accomplished. And extraordinary are the skills which some more verbally articulate foremen develop in translating *what is* into a semblance of *the way it ought to be* in order to appease their superiors and keep them happy.

But, for the most part, the foreman, being loyal and above all wanting to be secure, resolves the conflict and maintains good relations with his superiors by acting strictly in accordance with his functional relations and the logics of management. In spite of what this may lead to in his relations to workers and other groups, his relations with his superiors at least are not jeopardized.

Thus the foreman, like each individual in the modern industrial structure, is in effect painfully tutored to focus his attention upward to his immediate superiors and the logics of evaluation they represent, rather than downward to his subordinates and the feelings they have. So rigid does the conditioning of supervisors and executives in the industrial structure become in this respect that it is almost impossible for them to pay attention to the concrete human situations below them, rich in sentiments and feelings. For them, this world of feeling does not exist; the territory is merely populated with the abstractions which they have been taught to see and the terms in which they communicate—"base rates," "man-hours," "budgets," "cost curves," "production schedules," and so on.

THE SUPERVISOR ACTS ON HIS OWN

Not at all innocent and extremely risky is the tactic used by the supervisor who makes decisions on his own, overruling the boss or ignoring him because he believes that his superior has decided wrong or would do so if he had the chance. A classic case involves the origin of the phrase "turning a blind eye." Lord Nelson ignored the instruction issued by his superior to break off his engagement at the battle of Copenhagen, clapped the telescope over his blind eye—and won the battle. The problem of playing this game is that it is almost as dangerous to win as to lose. There's no possible defense in case of failure, and the best that the supervisor can hope for if he makes the right decision is forgiveness from his boss—and grudging forgiveness at that.

What's the worst? Take the case of a general superintendent who was asked by his boss, the plant manager, to represent him at the monthly budget review. The plant manager warned him against accepting a recommendation for a lot of costly new equipment from Vince Reilly, superintendent of building Two, but added, "Don't get into an argument with Reilly if you can help it." The meeting came and Reilly made his recommendation, but here the general superintendent departed from the script. Reilly's arguments impressed him and the others at the meeting so much that he suggested, and the group approved, a decision to purchase a single item of the new equipment to help determine whether a major investment would be justified. A week later, when the plant manager was back on the job, he vetoed the purchase and fired the general superintendent, making the undeniable point, "I spelled out exactly what I wanted you to do. If I had wanted you to do my thinking for me, I would have told you so." Our sources tell us that Reilly was right and that the compromise initiated by the general superintendent was an intelligent decision, if he had been free to ignore the human element—his boss's prejudices and instructions. He wasn't—he did—and he paid the price.

Over the Boss's Head

Now let's consider the royal flush in bypasses: going over the boss's head and appealing to his superior or even someone higher up. Nothing could be more dangerous for a subordinate. His job invariably will be at stake. But under two circumstances, a supervisor may decide to proceed. When he feels his supervisor is incompetent and he has to secure recognition from someone else or quit, and when he believes

so passionately in an idea or project which his boss opposes
that he is willing to lay his job on the line for the chance
to win his point.

DOES IT WORK?

An example of the first occurred several years ago in the
advertising department of a large furniture company. A young
copywriter, ambitious, intelligent, and convinced of his
worth, found that his most original ideas and crispest copy
invariably landed in the boss's wastebasket. He had decided
to resign, but before leaving he tried a desperate strategem.
After all, what did he have to lose? He assembled several
of the advertisements the company had run together with his
own version of each ad, sent the package to the company
president, and awaited the results. He didn't have long to
wait. Within a week he was transferred to another supervisor,
and within a month his old boss had left the company.
Furthermore, he was never far from the president's eye after
that. Today, he's a senior vice president and advertising is
merely one of the functional areas for which he is responsible.

Another man who risked all and won was a young naval
lieutenant at the turn of the century, William S. Sims. He was
convinced that continuous-aim firing, introduced into the
British Navy in 1898, had revolutionized naval gunnery and
changed it from an art to a science. Obviously, the American
Navy had to follow suit. In thirteen official reports to the
Bureau of Ordnance and the Bureau of Navigation, Sims
documented the case for continuous-aim firing, supporting
his arguments with masses of factual data. The reactions of
the naval brass? Dead silence, followed by derision of his
claims and, finally, name-calling. In desperation, Sims wrote
to the commander in chief, Theodore Roosevelt, and presented him with the evidence. The President's reaction was
swift. He installed continuous-aim firing in the U.S. Navy, and
made Sims inspector of target practice, a position he held for
the last six years of Roosevelt's administration. Sim's personal
mark had been made. He rose rapidly, and capped a distinguished career by serving as chief of naval operations in
World War I.

THE BOSS IS STILL THERE

We have cited two instances where going over the boss's
head paid off spectacularly, and where the game was worth
the candle. These are the exceptions. In 99 cases out of 100,
the supervisor who makes an end run around his boss

finds that, even when he gets the decision he is seeking, he still has the boss to contend with. The price of his victory will be the permanent loss of whatever rapport existed between him and the boss—in the final showdown, the supervisor will have outsmarted himself. Anthony Jay, in his book *Management and Machiavelli,* quotes Bismarck's letter of resignation from the Prussian civil service: "A Prussian official is like a player in an orchestra . . . he has to play his instrument as the needs of the conducted piece dictate . . . but for my part, I want to play music such as I regard as good— or else not play at all."

Supervisors are not Bismarcks. Lacking his spectacular abilities and iron will, they are compelled to play the music as orchestrated by their bosses. Nor is this altogether undesirable. Most managers have good reasons for taking a different position from their subordinates. Suppose they are wrong sometimes—think of an organization's cost in time and efficiency if the supervisor feels psychologically free to go over the boss's head every time he disagrees with his decision. And think of the effect on the morale and self-confidence of the boss if his subordinates are ready and willing to undermine his authority whenever the spirit moves them. A degree of intimidation in subordinates, instilled by their bosses, is one price paid by a successful organization.

Reverse Bypassing

A variation of bypassing, and obviously one over which the supervisor has no control, is played by the big boss himself when he bypasses one or more levels of management to find out directly from the supervisor what is happening— for example, in the production shop or the field sales force. Top management is frequently dissatisfied with the quality of reports that filter up to it and wonders what is really going on, especially when it seems to be going on badly. We are reminded of Haroun-al-Raschid of *Arabian Nights* fame who, so the legend goes, would emerge from his palace at night dressed as an itinerant traveler, and mingle with his subjects to discover what they really thought about him and his regime. The same story told about kings and other potentates symbolizes an important fact: Status, power, and sheer size tend to isolate the top man from the truth.

In large organizations where the top men view operations mostly through the eyes of others, experience often leads them to distrust the evidence of those eyes. So they decide quite literally to see for themselves. Here is a description of a former president of Curtis Wright, who was famous—some say, notorious—for being his own chief troubleshooter.

He [Hurley] seldom moves through channels. He figures that the division manager doesn't have any more idea than he has of what is wrong or the figures would not have been negative in the first place. So instead of waiting for a briefing, Hurley moves directly to the spot, right down to the machine on the floor if that is the heart of the problem. Many a division manager has discovered hours later that the boss had been in his department and long since moved on. And many department heads have discovered that an important job has been given to an employee they hardly know and without consulting them. Hurley spots a man who seems bright and says you do it. That the job may be completely unrelated to the employee's work is of no concern to him.

EFFECTS ON THE SUPERVISORS

What's wrong with bosses like Hurley who cut red tape and get down to the grass roots by a direct approach to supervisors or even their subordinates? Given the way Hurley and others like him handle their bypassing of the channels of authority, a great deal. They give the responsible executive no time to take corrective action before they rush in and take over. They diffuse their energies and ultimately their authority too thin instead of saving these assets for the problems where it is appropriate to lay them on the line. The top manager who dashes in, unbriefed and unexpected, to take charge inevitably damages the organization from the standpoint of the supervisor. If the superior has the right answer or selects the man who can come up with it, the supervisor concludes quite logically that the big boss views everyone between himself and the supervisor as incompetent and to be ignored. If the big boss makes a mess out of the situation, if he doesn't have the answer or dumps the solution into the hands of the wrong man, his incompetence will undermine the supervisor's confidence in the whole organization. The subordinate has seen the clay feet and the image will never look the same again.

Bypassing can be a virtue, even a necessity. General Horrocks of the British Army, for example, described the circumstances under which bypassing is desirable, and his specifications can easily be translated from the military to a business organization when the pressure is on in an emergency or when important plans are being formulated or results analyzed. Bypassing gives the man at the top a chance to evaluate the quality of younger managers, to get authentic information, and to obtain proposals and appraisals firsthand from the men who generated them. And another specification of Horrocks which is just as important in business: Always invite the man's immediate superior to be present at any discussion.

What the top man loses in frankness and openness of communication is compensated for by what he gains in retaining the confidence and the position of the superior. When a confidential session between a supervisor and his boss's superior is really called for, it is time to consider whether one of them should not leave the organization or at least the organizational unit. If they're both valuable men, their relationship has deteriorated to the point where one man's potential is going to be better realized somewhere else—within the organization or outside it.

The Open Door

Finally, of course, the supervisor can himself be the victim of a bypass. Many companies maintain an open-door policy. The rank-and-file employee has the privilege of walking into the office of any manager in the organization, up to and including the president, and voicing his complaint or making his suggestions. In most cases, however, the open-door policy is a fiction. The door may be open but somehow the rank-and-file employee seldom crosses the threshold.

The reasons aren't hard to fathom. The social distance between the average hourly employee and typical higher management is too great. More important, just as the supervisor hesitates to bypass his boss because he is the prime source of all penalties and rewards, the rank-and-file employee hesitates before he bypasses the supervisor. He balances, usually unconsciously, the slim chance of winning anything from his appeal against the danger of losing a great deal.

Another limitation of the open-door policy, even in organizations that sincerely subscribe to it, is the natural reluctance of higher managers to make it too effective. They are interested in creating a viable appeal channel, but they are not interested in spending great quantities of time listening to petty grievances and trivial or worthless suggestions from every clerk or assembly-line worker.

Take the case of the man in the welding shop who read in a trade magazine about some new equipment. In his role as a stockholder in the company—he owned twenty shares—he wrote the president, recommending the purchase of the equipment. In return, the welder got a warm letter from the president, commending his interest, promising to investigate his recommendation, and concluding with an invitation to communicate with him whenever there was something he felt the president should be aware of. The president's polite gesture—at least we take it as that—triggered an avalanche of suggestions. The welder swaggered around the shop boasting about his buddy Frank in Chicago. Finally, one night while under the influence, he called Frank to describe in vivid terms what he thought of his immediate boss. The next morning saw the finale—an ultimatum from the plant manager: Quit bothering the president or get out.

That the case is extreme, we agree. But it illustrates an important and difficult problem for higher management: on the one hand, how to encourage the rank-and-file employee to bypass his supervisor when his complaint or suggestion is legitimate and significant, and on the other, how to discourage him from using the open door when the complaint or suggestion is small and has little merit.

What is the supervisor's attitude toward the open-door policy? Doesn't it worry him when his disgruntled employees go to higher management with troublemaking problems, false charges, or tales out of school? Obviously, although he's probably even more concerned when the tales are not only unfavorable but also true.

How the supervisor feels toward the open-door policy depends heavily on two factors: the degree to which he has removed himself from his own men, and the approach the big boss takes with his subordinates. Many times a subordinate bypasses the supervisor because he feels, "What's the use?" The supervisor has made it plain in the past that he has neither the time nor interest to listen to his subordinates' complaints or ideas. The supervisor who hasn't heard from his men recently about any problems may be the rare but lucky man whose department has no problems. More likely, he's the supervisor who has gotten the message across that he doesn't want to hear that anything is wrong in his department. He has only himself to blame if his men choose to forget that he is one of the channels through which they should go.

Making the Open Door Work

What does the boss do when he's approached by an employee with a gripe against his supervisor? Steer a delicate course between Scylla and Charybdis—between encouraging bypassing and sabotaging the supervisor's morale on one hand, and banning the bypassing thereby having a disastrous effect on the workers' morale, on the other. If the subordinate hasn't already talked to the supervisor, the boss's preferred course of action is plain: He should listen sympathetically but noncommittally, then refer the subordinate back to his supervisor. What if the subordinate has talked to the supervisor and his failure to obtain any satisfaction from him is precisely what has landed him on the boss's doorstep? What does the boss say then? Up to a point, he follows the same script, listening sympathetically but noncommittally, even if it appears obvious that the supervisor is at fault. At the end of the talk, he confines himself to a promise that he will talk to the supervisor and that the supervisor will, in turn, be in touch with the employee.

From there on, it is more difficult to prescribe the course of action. Too much depends on the men involved and the circumstances. An autocratic boss, confronted by a pig-headed and stupid supervisor, might find it a necessity as well as a pleasure to administer a brutal tongue-lashing. Nothing less would take. However, even under those circumstances, the boss should take great care to see that the rank-and-file employee knows nothing about how he handled the problem. It should be the supervisor who explains the change of position to the subordinate, not the boss, and wherever possible, the decision should be presented as a case of the supervisor's having changed his mind, not of having had his mind changed for him. Obviously the employee, knowing the stubbornness of his boss and his past opposition, will suspect the true story. But the continuing authority and prestige of the supervisor requires the big boss to maintain the myth that the supervisor made the final decision. Otherwise, his every decision could be challenged by anyone who disagreed with it and his position would become untenable.

Speaking Up for His Men

One final problem area in upward communications casts the supervisor in a position where frank speaking may get him into immediate difficulty with his superiors, and silence will get him into trouble with his subordinates and may ultimately undermine his effectiveness in helping management gain its objectives. We're talking about the supervisor's responsibility to protect his subordinates' interests and represent them to higher management. His is the duty to speak out on their behalf when higher management has made what he and they feel is a wrong decision.

Some supervisors fulfill this role admirably. Consider, for example, what one worker said about his foreman. "My present foreman is the nicest guy I've ever worked for. The other foremen respect him also. I saw him stick his neck out with the general foreman over work loads. He'll argue a point with the general foreman if he thinks he is right."

However, there is considerable evidence to suggest that this foreman is in the minority. One study conducted by the Opinion Research Corporation showed that only 12 percent of the hourly workers interviewed rated their supervisors as "good" in handling questions and complaints, and another study showed that nearly half the employees agreed with the statement that an employee who told his immediate supervisor everything he felt about the company would probably get into a lot of trouble. "Many employees believe," concluded Alfred Vogel, research director of the Opinion Research Corporation, "that their bosses are paid to block criticism from going up the line." Incidentally, supervisors had a very different perspective on themselves. In dealing with their employees' problems, most asserted that they "almost always" or "usually" take prompt action.

THE DILEMMA OF DUAL LOYALTY

What's the reason for the generally poor performance of supervisors in representing the interests of their subordinates to higher management? The easy answer is fear of retaliation from higher managers, the paradox being that the more credit a man gets from below, the less he gets from above. Credit from below comes when a supervisor questions every unwelcome decision from above and protests vigorously and repeatedly any time higher management has done wrong by one of his subordinates. The dilemma is real enough, but let's not exaggerate its importance. The supervisor, as we have seen, has dual loyalties—to both management and subordinates—but only the most Neanderthal of managements fail to recognize the existence of this duality or attempt to monopolize his allegiance. The more sophisticated managements know that his duality works to their advantage even when, or perhaps most when, the supervisor's loyalties are weighted in the direction of his employees. A study conducted by the Prudential Life Insurance Company indicated that out or eleven high-production supervisors, nine identified themselves more with their employees than with the company. Among low-producing supervisors, the reverse was true: Eight

of them identified themselves with the company and only
two with their employees. The same pattern was repeated in
the attitude toward separate dining rooms for supervisors.
The high-production supervisors reflected the attitude of their
employees and objected to the segregation, while the low-
production supervisors went along with it. The wage contract
apparently buys the minimum level of performance—conscience and fear motivate employees only up to a point.

Performance beyond this point is the result of many factors,
not the least of which is loyalty of the employees to the
supervisor and their desire to make him look good. Obviously,
he must earn this loyalty, and his most effective way of doing
so is by representing their interests to higher management.

RECOGNITION OF DUAL LOYALTY

As we have pointed out, most higher managements are
aware of, and even encourage the supervisors' dual loyalty.
But in some companies they don't recognize it: They rebuff
the supervisors' every attempt to represent their employees'
interests, frequently adding gall and wormwood by complaining
that the supervisor isn't acting like "a company man." Here,
we can end our search for the reasons why the supervisor
isn't doing a better job of speaking out for his subordinates.
He isn't allowed to, and if he persists, he probably will lose
his job.

The umbrella of top management's demands, however,
isn't broad enough to cover all circumstances where supervisors renege on their responsibilities of representing their
subordinates. Some rather ugly factors also enter into the
picture—to be specific, arrogance and a sense of social distance. Most supervisors have a low opinion of the capabilities
of the employees who work for them. A survey of five hundred managers showed that the managers in every group
rated their subordinates and rank-and-file employees well
below themselves, particularly on responsibility, judgment, and
initiative. When the supervisor fails to speak up for an
employee, he is showing him how little he thinks of him.
At the same time, he is reasserting and reinforcing his own
sense of superiority. After all, if the employee's judgment were
equal to the supervisor's, the issue would never have been
raised.

And the supervisor is doing something else: By showing
that he is 100 percent "a company man," he emphasizes his
social distance from his employees. We usually think of social
distance in terms more innocent or harmless—the supervisor

up from the ranks stops bowling with the boys on Fridays, drifts out of the social club where some of his men spend their spare time; or quits having a round of boilermakers at the shift's end. None of these are as dramatic as failing to speak up—this clearly emphasizes the message: "I've left the boys behind. I'm 'a company man' now."

Why should some supervisors be so compulsive on this score? Chester Barnard, in his classic study, *Functions of the Executive*, captured the pathology of their behavior when he wrote, "The nearer one in authority over workers himself stands to the workers in respect of origin, education, occupational capacity, and level of earnings, the more violently self-assertive will be the manifestations of his will-to-power, the more insistent he will be in a display of authority, and more sharply will he therefore come into conflict with the worker's sense of self-esteem."

What Barnard wrote we think applies only to a virulent minority, but with that minority, we subscribe to the indictment. Human nature wears many masks to hide from itself. Some supervisors who fail to represent their subordinates rationalize their failure as due to fear of retaliation from higher management when the real reasons are located deep and unacknowledged in their own natures.

Of course, as we noted before in talking about supervisory styles, the particular style of the supervisor has less effect upon his employees than whether this style has helped him win influence with his bosses and peers. His skill in this area is revealed when he speaks up for his men. Employees respect the boss who represents their interests, but if the representations almost always fail because the supervisor's low level of performance, ineptness in handling his other upward communications roles, or both have destroyed his influence with higher management, his repeated failures will in the end forfeit his employees' esteem. It is not enough for the supervisor to be a man of good will. Influence fosters respect; impotence destroys it.

WHAT IS GOOD SUPERVISORY PERFORMANCE?

We postulated that the superiors' influence with higher management depends largely on two factors: his personal skill in upward communications and his level of performance as recorded by a complex network of statistical controls. We have seen the delicate, even torturous course he faces in his communications with higher management. By comparison, his job of impressing his bosses with his superior peformance should be straightforward.

To determine whether or not the supervisor is doing a good job, all higher management needs to do is look at the figures covering key factors such as production levels, percentage of scrap and rejects, man-hours expended per unit of production, tardiness, and turnover. It's all down in black and white—and figures never lie. (Our discussion of supervisory performance will include relevant conclusions from Chaper 5.)

The Unmeasurables

Figures never lie, but sometimes they omit—and omissions frequently conceal the true facts of performance. Any attempt to measure performance through statistics fails to get at the whole truth because some elements of the supervisor's performance are very difficult to measure, and others, such as the supervisor's success in maintaining the morale of his department, resist statistical measurement. These inherent weaknesses of statistical controls have two consequences, both of them unfortunate for the supervisor and higher management. His superiors get a picture of the supervisor's performance that is distorted and that doesn't reflect his real value to the organization. The supervisor, in an effort to impress higher management, concentrates on those areas of his operation where success can be quantified and where it is certain to be recognized—and, he hopes, rewarded.

In most industrial operations, cost accounting has developed "standard costs" for every item produced. If the standard cost of an item is 45 cents and the supervisor's department can make it for 43 cents, he is a hero. But if he makes the same item for 49 cents, he is a bum. Sounds fair enough, and it would be, except for two things. First, cost accounting is far from an exact science—figures may never lie, but they're only as accurate as the input from the frequently fallible and occasionally devious industrial engineers who set the standards in the first place. Second, standards may be too "light" or too "loose" because of an error, or occasionally they may be too "tight" because the industrial engineer feels it's his job to build pressures for top performance into the standard. In these instances (and they're common), the supervisor is either penalized or rewarded by the defective standard, and higher management gets a false picture of his performance.

Then we have the areas, such as morale, that most supervisors tend to neglect—and for good reason. Because such areas are so hard to measure, higher management has no yardstick with which to judge the supervisor's performance. So it usually overlooks them completely when the time comes to hand out pay and perquisites. Good employee relations are something a supervisor may get around to worrying about when he's sure his costs are in line, his production is up to snuff, and his scrap rate is well within the allowable limits. Developing his men is a similar area. The personnel department exhorts supervisors to develop their men for positions of greater responsibility and usefulness, but we have never heard of a supervisor's receiving a bonus or any other form of explicit recognition for his developmental prowess. Until we do, we expect that supervisors will continue to gold brick on their developmental function.

Measurement: The Enemy of Performance

When statistical data are the prime means of evaluating success or failure, supervisors will sometimes go a long way to show up well on paper. Figures never lie but they can be "adjusted." In one department, men tossed defective parts into trash cans, with their supervisor's full knowledge and tacit approval. The reject count, naturally, was below average. In another department, the supervisor himself came back at night to collect the rejects and dump them into a local quarry. In the morning, there would be nothing to count in the trash cans.

And figures are juggled. An engineering supervisor in an electronics company, whom we know, recently submitted a quarterly budget that allotted many man-hours to a project that was nearly finished, and assigned only a few hours to a project, already way over its budget, that needed many more hours to complete. The supervisor's reasoning was obvious: The juggling wouldn't cost the company any more money, and unless higher management found out the truth (which he felt was unlikely), it would get him off the hook.

BUCKPASSING

Buckpassing is also endemic in operations which emphasize statistical controls. Whenever parts turn out defective, there is always controversy about which department should be charged with the cost or repair. And the bigger the charge, the longer and louder is the controversy. In a plant described by Argyris, for example, a dispute over one big error lasted two months. The supervisors of the departments most likely to be blamed waged a continuous campaign to prove their innocence. Each supervisor blamed the others, since no one wanted the error on his record. In consequence, the supervisors spent hundreds of man-hours arguing and debating among themselves. The big boss, unable to pinpoint the responsibility for the error, finally gave up and allocated it to "general factory loss."

The supervisor is limited in the degree to which he can fight excessive statistical controls by lying, buckpassing, and covering up, particularly now that we have the computer with its practically unlimited capacity to spew out data and instantly flag any deviations from the predetermined standards. In short, because the supervisor is almost certain to be found out, he has little choice but to attempt to meet the standards set up by higher management, even when the attempt may bring him into direct conflict with the standards set by the union or the work group, both of which have their own techniques of retaliation.

TRADING OFF

As we observed previously, the supervisor is the man in the middle, caught between pressures from above and below. How does he resolve the dilemma? Frequently, he trades off privileges in areas higher management isn't concerned about or won't discover for a production level higher than he could obtain from his employees without these concessions. For example, one supervisor in a welding department lets his men bring in transistor radios—the kind with an ear plug for silent listening. And he allows them to play cards on their lunch hour—contrary to company rules, and he even supplies, free of charge, day-old crullers from a local bakery to sweeten up their coffee breaks.

WHAT'S WRONG WITH STANDARDS

We're not against standards as such, nor against supervisors trying to meet them. Standards have a large and legitimate place in the pattern of controls and rewards in any organization. We take issue only when standards are arbitrary in makeup and excessive in number, and when complete compliance with them is the supervisor's major hope of influencing higher management. In fact, in an organization where top management makes a fetish of meeting standards and complying with the letter of each and every policy, rule, and regulation, such rigidity reflects its basic belief in the incompetence of lower-level management and the rank-and-file employees. Herman Wouk's definition of the U.S. Navy, in *The Caine Mutiny*, is valid for many companies as viewed from the fortieth floor: "an organization designed by geniuses, to be run by idiots." Small wonder that this type of organization breeds more than its share of Captain Queegs among its supervisors. That such supervisors are more to be pitied than censured is not too difficult to understand.

We maintain that, with certain qualifications, there is nothing wrong with using statistical standards as indices of supervisory performance. Our opinion of them depends on how they are determined, how they are used, and whether or not they are viewed in the proper context. Are the standards imposed arbitrarily by a staff department, or are they drawn up jointly by the supervisor and his boss, possibly with an assist from a staff department? Are they used as a means of identifying a defective supervisor—and setting him up for disciplinary action, or are they regarded as a means of pinpointing an area where the human and technical resources of the organization should be deployed and the supervisor helped to solve his problems? Finally, are standards regarded as the first, and practically the last, word on the supervisor's performance, or are they seen as a valid but partial measure of how well he is doing? If the latter part of each of these three questions can be answered with a yes, statistical standards are being used properly and the supervisor has a fair chance to impress his boss with his effectiveness in handling the technical side of his job.

The Context of Measurements

We want to emphasize the importance of placing statistical controls in the proper context, of not mistaking any part of the performance for the whole. Measure such items as production runs and reject rates—fine. But higher management should not neglect to measure, by means of turnover rates, attitude surveys, and direct personal observation, the *human* efficiency of the supervisor's operation too. Nor should it fail to measure the third element of any supervisor's performance—his personal contribution to the organization and his own growth potential. His superiors should consider and evaluate the suggestions he has submitted, the ideas he has contributed at meetings, the courses he has taken, the qualities of judgment and initiative he has shown in handling day-to-day decisions. All the communication skills of Shakespeare, Dickens, and Raquel Welch will avail the supervisor

little if his superiors, particularly his immediate boss, won't
evaluate him fairly on all the key components of his performance.

CONCLUSION

We have seen that whether or not the supervisor succeeds
with his boss depends upon a more or less happy concatena-
tion of factors, several of which he has little or no control
over. Take the worst of possible combinations: The supervisory style favored, in fact insisted upon by the boss, is both
uncongenial to the supervisor and unsuited to the requirements of the work process and to the stragetic position of the
work group. The statistical standards in the department are in
effect rigged against the supervisor by a hostile superior and
an overzealous industrial engineering department. The
supervisor, in turn, spends most of his time airing what he
feels are the legitimate complaints of the work group to a
boss with no inclination to consider its gripes sympathetically.
In such situations, the supervisor obviously can't and won't
win. That such a siutation is atypical is also obvious.

The more typical supervisor makes do through various
strategems: he uses empathy frequently with his boss; he tells
the boss everything he needs to know but omits those things
he doesn't have to know that would lessen his own influence;
he knows where and when to extend privileges and make
concessions to his subordinates to get the performance the
boss expects, and where to withhold them. He knows that
it is an important part of his job to represent the legitimate
gripes of his subordinates to his boss; he also knows the
importance of timing and delivery. In short, the successful
supervisor in relation to the boss plays many roles—counselor,
informant, diplomat and deceiver—and displays skill in all
of them.

SELECTED REFERENCES

Argyris, C., *Executive Leadership,* Harper and Row, New
York, 1953.

Dalton, M., *Men Who Manage,* Wiley, New York, 1959.

Guest, R., *Organizational Change: The Effect of Successful
Leadership,* Irwin-Dorsey, Homewood, Illinois, 1962.

Jay, A., *Management and Machiavelli,* Holt, New York, 1967.

Whyte, W. F., "Structural and Administrative Innovations
that Motivate People" in L. Sayles (ed.), *Individualism and
Big Business,* McGraw-Hill, New York, 1963, chap. 16.

THE EDUCATION OF GREG HORNING: APRIL 19

Jeannette told Greg just before four o'clock. They had done it. Not 110 percent—but for the first time the injection molding department had hit 100 percent of standard.

"Hey, that's terrific!" Greg said. "I think it calls for a celebration. No more work for today—what do you say?"

"Great! I'll go tell the others."

Greg was pleased—and proud of the crew. They were really shaping up. Creegmore, apparently, had passed the word after their talk a couple of weeks ago and it had made a lot of difference. They'd gone back to the refinements they used before Greg had enforced the rules and introduced Alfred's clamp and a few other improvements that Creegmore had come up with. If there was a little more job sharing than Greg would have liked, the results made him overlook it.

Greg had finally overcome the materials handling problem. Ed Briscoe had given him a rough time—his people just didn't have the time to go watching out for particular places to put every little thing. But Greg had fought. In the first place, by keeping their machines under careful check, his people saved the maintenance crew a lot of repair time. Perhaps Ed hadn't been aware of that. Well, he had noticed that Greg's department called for repairs less often than some of the others, but still . . . And when you thought about it, Greg had persisted, how much extra work was it for a man to carry something just a few more yards. When you measured that against the women having to stop in the middle of something, maybe lose count on a shipment, to jump up and run around trying to find boxes—surely, Ed could see his point. Well, maybe—he'd see what he could do. It had worked, and the improved delivery system had made quite a difference.

Yes, Greg was feeling pretty cocky.

"Hey, Greg! There you are!"

"Come on in, boss! Join the party!"

"Pretty good, huh, Greg? We'll be breaking records by next week."

"How about a coke, Greg?"

Someone had turned on a transistor radio and Rick and Jeannette were dancing. They'd come up with soft drinks and doughnuts from somewhere—the festivities were in full swing.

Greg was arguing with Phil Martello over who would win

the National League pennant, when he heard his phone ringing.

"Mr. Horning? This is Mr. Phillips' secretary," the voice said
when he picked up the phone. "He'd like to see you in his
office right away."

"Is that how you get your people to work up to standard?"
Phillips shot out at Greg when he came in. "Break for cock-
tails every afternoon? Why didn't you tell me? I'd have
called a caterer for you!"

"Now, just a minute, Steve," Greg answered quickly. "If
we were making too much noise and somebody complained . . ."

"Nobody complained. I went by myself and saw what was
going on."

"Well, if you'd have cared to come in," Greg said, his face
very red, "you could have congratulated us and joined the
celebration. We hit the 100 percent mark today. I thought
that was worth a small sign of appreciation from me and I . . ."

"All right. All right," Phillips answered more calmly. "I
guess I should have asked you before I flew off the handle
that way. But just the same, Greg, don't let it happen again.
It's a violation of company rules and if it got around, it'd
set a bad example for the rest of the plant. Besides, I think
you were a little ahead of yourself—after all, the goal's 110
percent, isn't it?"

"I know that," Greg answered, his resentment well under
control now. "But they've worked damned hard and I wanted
them to know I appreciated it. After all, all I did was let
them quit a half hour early and drink a coke with them."

"Okay. But, listen. Don't you let up on them now. The
target's 110—and don't you forget it. You hit that, and *I'll*
throw the party."

"No," Greg said, with a small smile. "I won't forget it."
He felt he'd been dismissed, but he had something else on
his mind. "Steve," he said, "as long as I'm up here, there's
something I'd like to talk over with you."

"Yes? What is it?" But Phillips sounded disinterested. He
glanced at his watch as Greg went on.

"Well, we're having a hassle with the mixing people. They
got permission from the supervisor who was here before
me to store their sacks of pellets in our area."

"Yes. I know about that—I okayed it. What about it?"

"It's beginning to get awfully jammed up with those sacks
and my crew is complaining."

"Your people are always complaining. Just tell them to do their work. If they don't like the decor, they can always go to work for *House Beautiful.*"

"Steve! Damn it—that's unfair. They're working hard and their morale's getting better all the time. You can't expect them to work in a pigpen."

"Oh! Don't be so melodramatic, for God's sake! It's far from being a pigpen."

"That's not the point. They think it's a pigpen, and if they think so that matters to me."

"Are you telling me you can't get more work out of them unless we take those sacks out?" Phillips said impatiently.

"Honestly—I'm not sure. But I know it lowers morale, for one thing. For another, they waste time beefing to me about it. And how can I expect them to listen to me when I tell them it's important to keep their work stations clean and then let them work in a mess like that?"

"Maybe you're right. But even if you are, we're short on space. There's no place else to put all that stuff." Phillips got up. Obviously, he was ready to quit for the day.

"Well, of course, I don't mean that it all has to go," Greg felt that he had to close in quickly. "We can keep about as much as used to be stored there before I came on the job. And the rest of it—well, I noticed an area in the mixing shop last time I was there. They've got old parts there now that they don't use. I asked one of the men. They could pile them into about half as much space as they take up now and the rest of the pellets could go in beside them."

Phillips was getting into his coat. "All right, Greg. We'll see. I'll look into it and let you know."

"Good, Steve. Thanks," Greg got up, too, and went toward the door.

"And don't forget," Phillips said, following him out, "no more parties until I send the invitations."

QUESTIONS

1. How would you explain the fact that the group reached 100 percent of standard?

2. Do you feel that Greg should have checked with Phillips before holding "The Party"?

3. How would you appraise Greg's handling of Phillips?

4. In his conversation with Phillips, Greg was performing a vital function of any supervisor. How would you describe the function?

9. *Lateral relations and external demands*

There should no longer be any lingering doubts: The manager's job is dealing with people. Many of these people are his own subordinates whose cooperation and motivation he must obtain. But many of those he deals with do not work under him. After all, he must work with his own boss, and there will be large numbers of people in other units who affect his own department. The duplicating department is getting prints back too slowly. The personnel department has not authorized a high enough salary for clerk-typists to attract a good person. The next-door department is putting excessive pressure on a key man, who therefore is threatening to quit. All these situations require the supervisor to initiate and maintain relationships with a wide variety of personalities and departments.

It is easy to make two common mistakes in dealing with other people. The most obvious is to assume they are just like yourself. "If I see that getting here five minutes late in the morning is a problem, it should certainly be apparent to Mary too. After all, she knows what responsibility means."

But when we stop to think about it, of course, such an attitude is foolish. Individuals differ enormously, one from the other, in their personal makeup and in their reactions to the work situation. We cannot assume that our feelings or needs are mirrored in other people any more than we can assume that everyone will work harder if offered more money or that all employees will take criticism equally well or poorly.

Some managers go to the opposite extreme. In effect, they tell themselves that the human element is just too complex to be comprehensible. In their eyes, every person is not only different from every other person and but also unpredictable. "One day Joe is as pleasant as can be to deal with, and the next day everything I say is likely to cause him to explode." Furthermore, since no two people are alike, it would appear to be an impossible task to try to understand enough about personality differences to make this insight useful in dealing with job problems. This philosophy causes many supervisors to give up when it comes to coping adequately with personality variations.

However, we have already seen that there are some common factors. For example, while individuals differ in the relative importance they place on various on-the-job sources of need satisfaction, we observed in Chapter 1 that they all have some measure of physical, egoistic, and social needs.

Obviously, working with other people in the organization is going to depend upon their different personalities. With Jim, for example, you know that you have to spend a long time beating around the bush before you tell him the problem. Frank is impatient and wants it straight between the eyes and no stalling. But working within an organization also requires understanding and predicting how an individual's reactions depend upon the *position* he is playing. Thus, as we shall see, as a supervisor you can come to expect certain behavior from a fellow supervisor who depends upon your department to feed him supplies for his department—regardless of the personality of that supervisor.

Greta Commins and Henry Krisky behave almost identically, although they are very different kinds of people. Both Greta and Henry are in charge of departments that service many other departments. Greta heads up the typing pool and Henry is in charge of maintenance. Both are constantly being called by other supervisors to rush their work, even to put it ahead of other supervisors' work. As service managers, they frequently become provoked at how selfish other managers are in trying to get their needs satisfied ahead of their colleagues.

Thus, whenever a supervisor approaches Greta or Henry, it will be useful for him to know that they both are frequently strained by these competing demands. He can easily evoke an angry, emotional response by putting on pressure to get his work out first. Other managers are also liable to try that maneuver. As will be clear later, these other managers also believe that either the service manager or their "competitors" are preventing them from getting fair access to service.

In this chapter, we shall describe various managerial "positions" that may surround the supervisor. We shall also seek to show what it's like for the supervisor to fill a given type of managerial position and what it's like to have to deal with him in that position.

YOU ARE NOT ALONE

While it might be a nice prod to the ego to think that you are almost totally on your own—at least within the confines of your own department, this is just not the case. The large organization employs a number of managers, experts, technical personnel, and staff aides with whom you will have to build a satisfactory working relationship. This relationship is not simply a matter of good fellowship or the sharing of common membership in the XYZ Corporation. No, the larger company has established its structure, its patterns of work, in such a way that managers must collaborate and interact with one another. And to carry out that collaboration effectively, the manager must know the names, numbers, and positions of the other players on the team.

In fact, the personnel in an organization are like an athletic team in that everyone is playing a unique position. You'll work closely with some managers and see others only in an emergency. Some are there to watch you, and others, to help you. Your success depends upon distinguishing who does what and knowing how to work with each one in different types of "plays."

The managers, aside from your boss, with whom you'll be spending most time are:

Those who precede and follow you in the flow-of-work
Those who provide common services for many managers
Those who are available for advice and counsel on difficult supervisory problems
Those who seek to "stabilize" the larger organization by limiting your decision making
Those who evaluate or "audit" your performance in your job

WORK-FLOW RELATIONSHIPS

Most supervisors are "in the middle" in more ways than one. Of course, they must accommodate the conflicting demands of boss and subordinates. In addition, most of them find themselves between a department or group that sends them work and one to which they send work.

For example, a bookkeeping or clerical department may receive data from one or several departments on their sales or costs or orders, and in turn, it prepares reports which go to other managers. Here, it is numbers or data that are moving between departments. Physical parts or materials also "flow": The parts machined in the grinding department go to a subassembly group and, when incorporated into the sub-assemblies, they are moved to the final assembly and shipping department.

But, knowing what we now do, we can predict the problems the supervisor will face in relating himself to these preceding and succeeding stages in the work flow without even knowing whether it is sales figures or steel parts that are moving. Each supervisor in the flow of work will be trying to persuade other supervisors to do their work in ways that will help him get his job done much as employees in a work group seek to modify one another's behavior so that they can work together easily and with minimum disturbance.

To simplify the problem, let's look at two supervisors, Homer and Chris. Homer is in charge of the receiving and storage area in a large store selling tools, hardware, toys, and general merchandise. His people also restock shelves in the selling area. Chris is in charge of the total selling area. Here are some typical problems they will face almost every day in maintaining a working relationship with each other.

FROM HOMER'S POINT OF VIEW:

I get a rush call from Chris that he is out of light bulbs. I've got two people out sick and the others are unloading a truck. He expects me to get the men out of the truck, get the truck driver to stay overtime, and start the men picking out light bulbs, when he could have noticed he was getting low yesterday.

Chris is always telling my people that they can't leave anything in the aisles. But how are they going to load up the shelves efficiently if they can't bring a number of cartons out at the same time? He wants them to bring out one at a time, which would probably increase my labor costs by 25 percent.

The way we store things, it is a lot easier to stock the shelves in the same order that we warehouse. In other words, I want my people to restock Chris's department by moving from light bulbs, to cleaning supplies, to small tools, and so on. But Chris always has his "special list." He wants us to move from one emergency situation to another, and my people complain that they have twice as much running around to do this way.

FROM CHRIS'S POINT OF VIEW:

I can't predict what my customers are going to buy. You suddenly get a run on some item or we run a sale and everything is grabbed up the first hour. Whenever I call Homer for help, he tells me that I am asking for things in the wrong sequence or his people are busy doing something else. After all, we're in business to please customers, not truckers or warehousemen.

When Homer's people are working in the selling areas, they are as sloppy as can be and they don't care how much they interfere with customers.

Homer has developed a system for restocking shelves that is fine for him, but lousy for us. Why can't he arrange his warehouse supplies to fit our needs, not his?

Raising the Pressure Level

From his own point of view, each is right. Each supervisor is making demands on the other to fit his own needs. How each supervisor does his work has an immediate and critical effect on the other supervisor—they are very much interdependent. How can that work-flow interdependence be converted into cooperative give and take?

In answering the question, it may be easier to look at the typical adjustments which guarantee the opposite: open conflict and mutual frustration. If Chris and Homer wish to frustrate each other, each will try to get the other to do his bidding by raising the pressure level. Since they are on the same organizational level, neither is the boss of the other—one can't just *order* the other to be more helpful or cooperative. But they can put on more and more pressure. This is always the first temptation when the other person is making it difficult for you to do your job.

Thus, Chris will be tempted to:

1. Go to his boss to put pressure on Homer, claiming that Homer is causing him to lose sales.
2. Collect evidence on the length of time he has had to wait for shelves to be restocked, the number of times he has had to get Homer's people to clear the aisles, and the number of times they have stocked the wrong items on the wrong shelves.
3. Call Homer or one of his men on the phone, saying a big customer is actually in the store and waiting for some piece of merchandise.
4. Try to get a rule or policy established that restocking should have priority over all other work in Homer's area.

5. Give orders to Homer's people when they are not doing
their jobs as Chris thinks they should.

And what will be the result if Chris thus succumbs to the
temptation to fight back? Of course you have guessed it.
Homer will retort in the same ways. Pleading with the boss to
defend him, putting pressure on Chris and his people, and
developing evidence to prove that Chris is tardy in getting
information to the warehouse—these are all methods available
to Homer, too. What's sauce for the goose . . .
    In many adjacent work-flow positions, this kind of open
warfare exists. Each person is convinced that the other is
selfish, uncooperative, and out to embarrass him. And since
supervisors may see less of each other than do employees who
work next to each other, it is easy for such conflict to per-
sist. In fact, it is highly likely because supervisors like Homer
and Chris tend to see each other only when one or the
other is upset with something. Under these emotional circumstances, it is easy to blow up at the other guy. Imagine
your best customer has just said she is never coming back
to the store because, for two days in a row, you've been out
of floor paste! And here you've called the storage area three
times for it. What is Chris likely to say to Homer when he
next meets him?

Improving the Relationship

But it is not that difficult to avoid these work-flow relationship problems—particularly when each supervisor recognizes the temptations and the pitfalls.
    Each must try to build a working relationship and not wait
to see the other supervisor when he is upset and aroused and
apt to be hostile. For example, if Chris knows he has just
placed a special on floor wax and that customer demands are
likely to be larger than usual, he can tell Homer *in advance*.
This allows Homer to make plans to accommodate the added
stocking job into the working schedules of his people in the
least disruptive way. In turn, if Homer knows he has some
trucks coming in which will require several hours to unload,
during which time his men will not be able to service the
selling floor, he can give Chris advance notice.
    Both can avoid seeking to force the other to cooperate by
using pressure tactics such as appeals to the boss, excessive
demands, and trying to prove the other is the villain. For
example, if Chris is out of some item, he might ask Homer to

bring over only enough items to get him through the day, or offer to send one of the clerks into the storage area if Homer will have the items ready to be carried out.

In a sense, each supervisor endeavors to build a *balanced* give and take with the other. That is, he knows he is going to have to respond to requests from the other about as often as he asks the other to respond to him. If he tries to "out-point" the other supervisor by making many requests of him or his people without being willing to accept demands himself, we can predict trouble. Shortly, if not at once, the "put-upon" supervisor will start to fight back, and when he does, the first supervisor will become more antagonistic. Soon the two will be engaged in open conflict.

So Homer and Chris will have to find ways of accommodating to the other's needs, avoiding contacts with each other during periods when they are under great stress or emotionally upset, and responding to requests as often as they initiate them.

SERVICE RELATIONSHIPS

In some ways, service relationships are similar to work-flow relationships. Managers are dependent upon service groups to get their work done. However, unlike work flow, "services" are pooled or centralized activities which handle requests from a great many line supervisors. In a department store, the receiving and ticketing department services many selling departments by providing them with new and priced merchandise. A maintenance group in a school or factory fills requests for repairs from all over the plant just as a typing pool responds to the clerical needs of a number of managers.

By putting yourself in the place of the manager of a service group, it is not difficult to imagine his troubles. Everyone wants his work given top priority and, as fate would have it, usually everyone comes around at the same time. It takes a great deal of personal skill and fortitude to manage the service or support group. The manager has many different people making demands upon him, but he has no one to make demands upon. It is very much a one-way street. As we have seen in other contexts, such unbalanced jobs, where all the demands flow in one direction, are most difficult to handle.

And to make matters worse, the manager always faces the tendency for any minor scarcity in his service area to become a major shortage. As many managers know, there is no such thing as "a little shortage." Again, imagine yourself as the manager dependent on getting some computer runs completed by the machine room in time to give you data for the reports that top management is on your neck to complete. You hear through the grapevine that the machine room is behind in its work or overloaded, and that people sometimes have to wait forty-eight hours to get material back. What are you likely to do?

Most managers are apt to increase their demands in the hope that they can thus satisfy their minimum requirements. If you need the data tomorrow, you will rush in with the punch cards today, first thing, and insist that this is a rush order and must be processed today. Further, if you know that you will need some work done later in the week, you'll take that along with you so that it gets an earlier place in line. But, of course, everyone else will do the same, the minute the word gets out that computer time is scarce. Everyone "ups the ante" in an effort to guarantee that he won't suffer delays and won't look bad to his boss because of falling behind schedule. The result is often an enormous logjam or bottleneck at the focal point of all these demands: the service group and the service manager. "The little shortage" becomes a major scarcity, with rationing just around the corner.

Service managers, for their part, may lose self-control and start arguing with their customers. "You aren't going to get this for a week no matter how loud you complain, and if you keep taking my time by complaining, it will probably take longer!" The manager who has expected service and not an argument is then tempted to fight back with threats of reprisal and the whole process may degenerate into a street brawl.

Planning versus Pressure

To prevent this, managers dealing with service groups have to recognize the psychological and organizational pressure which these people operate under. If you watched them closely, they would look like the harried waitress you have seen in a restaurant when everyone demands service at the same time and the kitchen can't keep up. Under those circumstances, many understanding patrons learn to help out. They don't add to the waitress's problems by demanding faster service, asking for a variety of extra things (more water, another kind of dessert, a special drink), and complaining of what they do get. Instead, they help make service easier.

When the waitress comes for the order, they are ready with their decisions and don't dawdle over the menu. They may pour themselves water and even pass the plates back and forth if the waitress has put the beef order in front of the guest who ordered fish.

For her part, the good waitress can take some pressure off her position by giving patrons a realistic view of the likely service. Also, she might say that items 3 and 77 on the menu are already prepared and can be served a great deal faster than the others (assuming the patrons are indeed in a hurry). She may also suggest that they order only a main dish or carry over a drink from the bar as a means of reducing the congestion in the kitchen.

These same tactics help in any service relationship where there is a scarce resource. The managers requiring its use can avoid the temptation to add pressure on top of pressure (and to encourage retaliation against themselves, at the same time) by improvising ways to assist the service group. They can give longer advance notice of their requirements, thus permitting more efficient scheduling. They can offer to handle some of the more routine parts of the job usually performed by the service group. For example, the production manager might tell the manager of the typing pool, "Don't bother collating and stapling the reports; we'll do it here when you send the typed pages back." And they can express understanding of the difficult job being performed during peak-demand periods.

On the other side, the service manager has to accept a reasonable amount of the stress and strain that are inherent in the position. But he or she can also take the initiative in showing other managers how they can facilitate their work by timing their orders carefully, preparing the work efficiently, and doing certain things for themselves.

Most managers are not prepared to wait in line or are always fearful that someone else is getting more than his fair share. Yet getting service work done within the organization is just as much a process of give and take, of using personal and personality skills, as getting an employee to accept a difficult and unusual assignment. It is usually not simply a matter of writing out an order—except in the most routine cases. So dealing with service groups becomes both a time and an energy requirement of most managers' jobs.

One additional note on the other side of the coin: inside the service group. Because of the pressures coming in from other managers, the service manager would be well advised to protect his own subordinates from undue buffeting. The manager himself, given his supervisory status, is much better able to stand up to overdemanding colleagues than is one of his subordinates. The subordinate is tempted to agree to everything, to promise too much, and to give unrealistic expectations to other managers. Such "cooperation" only makes the situation worse for the service group and for the requesting manager as well. The service manager can more easily take the initiative in getting demands reduced or modified, dealing as he is with his status equals, which the subordinate is not. (Consider how easy it is for the typical instructor to fend off eager students, all of whom want their papers graded yesterday!)

ADVISORY RELATIONSHIPS

Most organizations provide a certain number of experts to help the manager make difficult decisions. For example, the union claims the supervisor unfairly disciplines (with a two-day layoff) one of the men when he came in fifteen minutes late two days in a row. The personnel department is supposed to have expertise on handling both union grievances and disciplinary problems. The supervisor can go to the department and learn some of the implications of sticking to his original decision or of conceding that he was wrong, given the facts of the case and the current status of the union–management relationship. Or, with a mechanical problem, the supervisor may go to Engineering and get that department's opinion on whether a certain machine is worth repairing or ought to be replaced.

All this sounds both simple and highly useful to the supervisor, particularly in areas where he is inexperienced. Where do the difficulties occur in these advisory relationships? Maybe a supervisor's comments will suggest some of the problems:

When I went into personnel yesterday to ask them how to handle my worst troublemaker, Crouse, all I got was a lot of double talk, "ifs," and "buts." They said if I discharged him—these were some of the likely consequences, and if I kept him on—these were some of the other troubles I would have. I wanted them to give me a straight yes or no answer as to whether or not I could get away with sacking him. I left more confused than when I came in. Some help they are!

What has happened here to frustrate our supervisor with a personnel problem who is seeking a quick answer? It sounds to us as though the fault lies with him. He wants personnel, with which he has an *advisory* relationship, to make his decisions for him. Of course, they (that is, personnel) would then be responsible for the decision. If it backfired, if there were unpleasant ramifications that hurt production or caused major union–management troubles, the supervisor could say ingenuously, "Well, after all, it wasn't my decision, they told me to do it that way."

In a good advisory relationship, the adviser avoids making decisions for the line manager. This way, the line manager doesn't feel an outsider is telling him how to run his affairs, and he also learns how to cope with both responsibility and risk. After all, a good share of management consists of making decisions where the information is imperfect and the outcome is in doubt. A supervisor who hopes to grow in managerial stature must learn how to obtain technical advice— how to use the experience, know-how, and counsel of the adviser—and then sit back and make his own decision.

Carrying the Burden

Further, there will be times when he may get conflicting advice. His own boss may sometimes act as a consultant rather than a boss, and several staff departments may have different outlooks. Again, it is up to the supervisor to factor in these judgments with his own judgment and come up with a decision. If it is his decision, he will be in a better psychological frame of mind to handle any of the follow-up problems. On the other hand, if he feels someone has made the decision for him, he will be tempted to "pass the buck" for any undesirable consequences.

In the XYZ Company, the Employment Office doesn't just advise superiors on prospective job applicants—it actually selects candidates for supervisors. Crichot hired Oliphant this way after he was "advised" that he would be a good shipping clerk. When Oliphant began objecting to his work assignments the first week, Crichot got angry and refused to work with him and told his boss, "Look, I didn't want him in the first place. They put him here and I want them to take him out. I don't have the time to try to motivate him." Some weeks before, Chrichot had brought in a cousin of an existing employee. The man soon began exhibiting a good deal of tardiness, but that time, Chrichot felt responsible and worked with the new employee until he "came around."

The supervisor therefore ought not to expect an adviser to give him a final answer, but he can help substantially in coping with problem equipment, people, and procedures.

Eager Advisers: Unasked-for Advice

But some advisers want to go beyond the consultation role. In doing so, they can create, in effect, the opposite type of problem for supervisors. They pressure the supervisor to try out new procedures or take on new ways of handling employees when he may be content to continue with his old way of doing things. So the supervisor has to be able to handle the overly eager, as well as the reluctant, adviser. Let's look at an example of the eager-beaver type.

I keep having trouble with our procedures department. They want me to adopt a new filing setup and start using some new equipment they've found. While they claim it would reduce fatigue and increase my girls' output, I'm skeptical. In the first place, I would probably lose several days' work just having those girls retrained. And there would be no assurances the new techniques would work any better, and this way nobody in the department is complaining. New methods always result in lots of complaints. They want me to accept all of this new stuff because it looks good on their record if they can get improvements introduced. Only, how do I know it's an improvement?

Some managers complain that staff advisers look for trouble in their departments in order to justify their being called in to offer a solution. While such fears are not always justified, it is not easy to fill an advisory slot. Here you have to wait to be asked for help. If you aren't invited to give advice, you can't be active and you can't prove to your boss that you are doing a good day's work. Having such an optional status, it is no wonder that many advisory managers do try to drum up business for themselves by finding sore spots.

Many supervisors, moreover, are either blind to the availability of such consultation services or reluctant to try anything new because it would require some short-run effort on their part. Surely one of the important characteristics of the successful supervisor is his willingness to invest time and energy (and budget) in solving his persisting problems. A methods engineer tells this story:

Carlin was a reasonable supervisor, but I could never convince him to take the time to develop a method of equalizing the difficulty of the jobs in his department or to find a way that his employees would accept as equitable to exchange jobs. The result was that he was spending half his supervisory time arguing with workers about who had the tougher job or who should get some easier job that was coming up tomorrow or who was being favored and who discriminated against. Well, one day, he finally had a revolt on his hands; everyone just stopped working. Now his problem was so evident to him that he was actually looking for help. As a staff man, I know that when someone "is hurting," that's the best time to sell them on a new idea. With no production at all coming out, he called me up, and I got the people back to work by promising that we would do a major study in the department. Two weeks later, I prepared a number of options on sharing both the "good" and the "bad" jobs that were discussed by the whole department. The employees actually voted on the plan they liked best and there hasn't been a gripe since. Now Carlin probably had to spend three or four days working with our industrial engineers on this but he has saved himself ten or fifteen hours a week he used to spend arguing with his people. Some people take a long time to learn.

Thus, good advisers learn to begin selling their services and themselves by working first on areas in which the supervisor has obvious and real problems, rather than by trying to convince the supervisor he has a problem. If they do well solving these, they will be called back again and again for other, and perhaps less obvious, problems. When the supervisor wants to be an adviser to someone, even his boss, he uses the same principle: He works in areas where the other person has a major incentive to try something new and to give up the old.

GEORGE STRAUSS (1923–)

George Strauss was trained in human relations at MIT under Douglas McGregor, Mason Haire, and Alex Bavelas in what was then called the Industrial Relations Section. He also took work in social psychology at Harvard and with the group dynamics specialists that Kurt Lewin had assembled at MIT. Strauss was also trained in labor relations and industrial economics; he thus represents the interdisciplinary background that is very useful in management.

His early research was in the field of labor relations— how local unions functioned in various industrial plants and in the construction field. At this time he wrote *The Local Union* with Leonard Sayles. From labor relations he moved to the personnel administration field and then to general management. He has pioneered in the study of *lateral relations* within management. His most famous study concentrated on purchasing agents and their dealings with other managers who must make use of the purchasing department. He has also looked at the role of professionals in industry and at white-collar unionization (in government and education, particularly). He has been a vocal and respected critic of those students of human relations who feel that all work can be made intrinsically satisfying.

Dr. Strauss taught at Cornell and the University of Buffalo before moving to his present position as associate director of the Institute of Industrial Relations and professor, University of California at Berkeley. For a number of years he has also edited the journal *Industrial Relations,* and he is coauthor of two large texts: *Personnel* and *Human Behavior in Organizations.*

Given his remarkably diverse training and his eclectic mind, it is not surprising that his periodic reviews of the organizational behavior and management field are so highly regarded. He is one of those rare teachers who are also researchers and noted writers; he is also able to tie together the research and writing of others in both a sympathetic and critical fashion. He is as generous with praise as he is with his editor's red pencil.

Techniques for Dealing with Other Departments*
Normally the agent attempts to fill requisitions as in-

---

* Reprinted by permission from George Strauss, "Tactics of Lateral Relationship: The Purchasing Agent," *Administrative Science Quarterly,* vol. 7, no. 2, September 1962, pp. 165–167.

structed. The majority of interdepartmental contacts are handled routinely and without friction in accordance with standard operating procedures. Yet many difficult problems cannot be easily programmed. Other departments are constantly placing pressures on the agent, who must take countermeasures, if only to preserve the *status quo*. And if the purchasing agent wishes to expand his power aggressively, as many do, he will inevitably run into conflict.

Understandably, then, successful agents have developed a variety of techniques for dealing with other departments, particularly when they wish to influence the terms of the requisitions received. These techniques will first be summarized briefly under five general headings. . . .

1. *Rule-oriented tactics*   a. Appeal to some common authority to direct that the requisition be revised or withdrawn. *b.* Refer to some rule (assuming one exists) which provides for longer lead times. *c.* Require the scheduling department to state in writing why quick delivery is required. *d.* Require the requisitioning department to consent to having its budget charged with the extra cost (such as air freight) required to get quick delivery.

2. *Rule-evading tactics*   a. Go through the motions of complying with the request, but with no expectation of getting delivery on time. *b.* Exceed formal authority and ignore the requisitions altogether.

3. *Personal-political tactics*   a. Rely on friendships to induce the scheduling department to modify the requisition. *b.* Rely on favors, past and future, to accomplish the same result. c. Work through political allies in other departments.

4. *Educational tactics.*   a. Use direct persuasion, that is, try to persuade scheduling that its requisition is unreasonable. *b.* Use what might be called indirect persuasion to help scheduling see the problem from the purchasing department's point of view (in this case it might ask the scheduler to sit in and observe the agent's difficulty in trying to get the vendor to agree to quick delivery).

5. *Organizational-interactional tactics*   a. Seek to change the interaction pattern, for example, have the scheduling department check with the purchasing department as to the possibility of getting quick delivery *before* it makes a requisition. *b.* Seek to take over other departments, for example, to subordinate scheduling to purchasing in an integrated materials department.

STABILIZATION RELATIONSHIPS

The decisions of any one supervisor can affect many or most of his colleague–supervisors. If supervisor A grants a 20 percent salary increase to his secretary, supervisor B's secretary, who does the same work and who has been told she is one of the best secretaries in the firm, will want the same or even a greater increase. If supervisor X decides to provide 10 percent fewer parts this week (because of vacations), supervisor Y (whose department uses those parts to make subassemblies) is going to have cut back 10 percent whether he wants to or not. There are many such decisions that have a broad impact, and in such areas, the organization may establish a special department to control these decisions "for the greater good."

In this vein, personnel may have to approve all salary increases. Production control may have to approve weekly production schedules. Each supervisor will have to budget enough time and energy to work with these "stabilization" groups. For example, it may be very important to get a key worker a salary increase that at first blush will appear excessive to personnel. The manager has to be willing to explain, justify, and persuade why this case is special and why it should not set a precedent.

Obviously, the supervisor won't win all these arguments, but he will win more than if he simply doesn't try. Just as misguided is the manager who can't understand why any limitations are necessary:

All those guys know is what is down in the rule book. They're just there to tell you no, and get paid a lot for doing it. I never waste my time explaining things to them because they couldn't care less how I personally am being affected.

But the pont is that "they," meaning the managers who are responsible for these functions, do care. However, their job is the difficult one of balancing individual needs against the needs of the total organization. When they hear a well-presented, rational case and the individual need is great, they will often make exceptions.

The company's traffic department is supposed to keep us from overpaying on transportation charges. There is a firm rule: Everything gets shipped truck or rail express unless you can convince them that the world will come to an end otherwise. I did just that. We have a finicky customer in Sacramento and we had sent him the wrong style and he said he was losing business, being out of stock. It was a small order and not much profit involved, but I felt sure we would never see that store as a customer again unless we made up for the mistakes in the last shipment. I culled our records and could show that more than half our total sales come from small customers like him and that over five years he had spent $11,000 on our merchandise. By the end of the "data," they were approving air express and even special delivery charges.

So far, we've been assuming that these stabilization departments only deal directly with the supervisor. They may also come in contact with his subordinates. Under these circumstances, it's important for the supervisor to demonstrate that (1) he has some technical knowledge in the area, and (2) he has some power in the situation. If he simply abdicates when his subordinates are having trouble with the "rulings" of the stabilization department, he will lose the respect of his people.

Time Study and Rate Setting

In this connection, the role of time-study and rate-setting engineers provides a good example. These people are responsible for making sure that employees throughout the organization have comparable work loads and comparable opportunities to earn extra pay if the company is using incentive plans.[1]

Below is a typical exchange between an industrial engineer (time-study man) and a supervisor. Given this breakdown in

---

[1] Incentive plans, sometimes called piecework, provide that an employee is paid by the quantity he produces as distinct from the time he puts in. But to pay for quantity, it is necessary to have some standard or base line. Otherwise, one employee might be able to earn $25 an hour and another only $2 an hour. To assess what an average employee might be expected to produce per hour, many companies use industrial engineers who observe employees, time them, and estimate how hard they are working. Their results show up in the form of a "rate" for a given job. Thus, a pieceworker on a punch press might be given an extra half cent for each acceptable unit his machine produces over the standard of 750 per day.

communications and mutual trust, consider, as you read the dialogue, the impact on the relationship of the supervisor to his men; the relationship of the time-study man to the employees; and the attitude of employees toward the fairness of the rate-setting (that is, stabilization) decisions of the Time-study Department. Here is the scene: The supervisor has just received official notice as to what piece rate he can pay his employees on a new job. At this point, the time-study engineer who analyzed the job comes into the supervisor's office and the following discussion takes place.

Supervisor: It looks to me as if that rate is pretty tight and we are going to get a lot of gripes from the operators.

Time-study Man (to himself): How does he know; he hasn't even looked over the study—in fact, he probably doesn't even understand time study; he just wants to avoid any personal troubles with the men. *(to Supervisor):* Well, I've done a careful job, and I think it is a good standard.

Supervisor (to himself): Here is another one of those know-it-all kids who thinks he has learned in a couple of days what it took me 15 years to learn. There's no use trying to reason with them. *(To Time-study Man):* I've already heard a number of complaints from the men that they can never make out under this new standard. I wonder whether there might not be some factor that was overlooked in the study.

Time-study Man (to himself): Just as I thought, he doesn't have the ability to get his people to accept the new standard; they are so used to only doing half a job that tightening up seems unfair. *(to Supervisor):* If they would only give it a chance and really try it out, I know they could make it, but they prefer to gripe rather than work.

Supervisor (to himself): There is not much use even talking to him; he doesn't care about what happens *after* he sets the rate. In fact, he probably gets a pat on the back from his boss for the amount he increases the standard on the job; the greater the increase the more likely he is to get a raise himself. I'm left holding the bag as far as dealing with the men is concerned and with the new quality problems that are going to come up when they try to beat it and with more tooling breakdowns and costs which those guys never figure on. *(to Time-study Man):* O.K. We'll see what happens but I can tell you right now we are in for trouble on this.

Time-study Man (to himself): Sure, if that's the way the supervisor feels about the standard already, what can you expect from the men? We'll have trouble from them. *(to Supervisor):* If they'll only give it a fair trial I know it's going to work out.

Supervisor (to himself): They think they can never make a mistake! Everything was fine here until he came in. *(to Time-study Man):* We'll see. . . .[2]

Obviously, the supervisor finds himself in the middle, between the stabilization department (in this case, time study) and his men. To be successful and not be torn apart by these conflicting interests and points of view, he must be able to stand up to both and be responsive to both. He must show the time-study experts that he is willing to spend time to understand their methods, their studies, and their objective of organization-wide stability, not just departmental harmony. He is also willing to dispute them when he thinks they are wrong and ready to defend their rate setting to his employees when he believes they are right. As we noted in Chapter 7, he will be willing to represent his department to the time-study people when they have legitimate complaints and he will have the courage to initiate to his subordinates and get them to accept the rate when they have no legitimate complaints. By balancing this direction and representation, he proves to both his employees and to time study that he is fair and responsive.

AUDIT RELATIONSHIPS

Audit relationships are like the stabilization relationships just discussed in that they involve the supervisor with other reasonably powerful managers. Audit managers are those who evaluate or appraise the work of the manager periodically in order to tell his boss and/or upper management how well he is performing. For example, traditional auditors like accountants are used to telling management whether a given

---

[2] George Strauss and Leonard R. Sayles, *Personnel,* 2nd ed., Prentice-Hall, Inc., Englewood Cliffs, N.J., 1967, p. 665.

department has stayed within its budget or how closely it is meeting standard cost targets.[3] Personnel, by looking at turnover, grievances, absenteeism, and the like, will be able to assess whether or not a supervisor has been able to build both good relationships and a department of loyal employees. Quality inspectors appraise the quality of work completed by the department, and there may be other auditors looking at such things as safety records, housekeeping, employee morale, and the like.

But these, too, are not passive relationships. The manager may have to spend time and develop skills in explaining to each expert who is appraising his department why his group has fallen below some standard. In some cases, external conditions were changed—absenteeism was high because bus service was suspended during the heavy snow storm so several employees couldn't get to work. In other cases, the standard may just not be appropriate for the operation, and the manager has to try to convince the audit group to change it.

When our value engineers came up with these new plastic parts, we had to change the sealing material. We know it won't stand the same 140-degree heat test as the old sealant, but we think it doesn't have to because the plastic will never get as hot as that metal did in actual use. Now the engineering department never got Quality Control to change its test standards—say down to 125 degrees—so we've got to convince them, hopefully with the engineering department's help. Otherwise, our reject rate is going to look like the national debt.

Sometimes, appraisal groups will be mutually contradictory. A manager is told he must not use overtime for his people above a certain level and he is also told (by another department) that if any orders are delayed more than twenty-four hours, it will be considered a serious supervisory error. With extra orders coming in and no extra employees, he may have the choice of looking bad on one measure or the other. And here again, managerial decision making is involved.

---

[3] Standard costs, somewhat like piece rates, involve targets established by some expert as goals that the average supervisor ought to be able to hit. But here the target is the production cost per unit rather than the number of units produced. (See additional discussion in Chapter 8, pages 299–304.)

The experienced manager knows he may have to take the risk of falling below standards in some areas temporarily in order to meet standards defined in another area, which in the short run are more critical for the large organization. This is another reason why the supervisor's boss who misuses quantitative standards to evaluate subordinates is creating troubles for himself, as we saw in Chapter 8.

The manager has to learn to be adaptive and to shift his emphasis as one or the other of these standards appears to take on more importance. During a period of declining sales and profits, anything that cuts costs may have top priority even though some traditional standards are not met. When a company is growing in a highly competitive environment, getting and keeping new customers, sometimes almost regardless of cost, may take the top priority position.

Also, the experienced manager learns that many audit groups, if he is willing to take the time to learn from them, may well help him find ways of overcoming his poor performance. After all, they are typically expert in the area they are surveying, they have seen many, many other departments, and they frequently prefer to correct a situation rather than issue a negative evaluation.

We have some really great accountants. My costs were out of line and they did a complete evaluation of exactly where I was getting into trouble. I found some things that were easy to cut back and now my boss is happy as a clam. I used to think those accountants just tried to get the goods on you and couldn't care less what happened to your work or reputation. But when you take the time to sit down with them, it turns out they are very reasonable guys. I learned something about accounting too, so those reports just aren't a series of numbers.

Of course, the manager has to expect that each expert auditor thinks his subject and area are the most important and the ones that the supervisor can't afford to neglect, whether it's personnel or costs or safety or what have you. But this attitude is inherent in any professional group that devotes itself to improving a given field. The manager has to be the generalist who balances off all these experts, each of whom wants him to concentrate all his efforts on perfecting his results in the auditor's special area. So, as the balance wheel, the manager works with these various audit groups, both listens and explains, and strikes a reasonable middle course, depending upon the circumstances of the day and his own departmental situation.

WHAT KIND OF WORLD IS THIS?

The new supervisor's first reaction to these complications in his work life may be, "Stop! I want to get off." There will appear to be too many people making demands upon him in addition to his boss, too many people to please or to compete with for scarce resources. He will assume that if the organization were well managed he would be given all the resources he needs to get his job done and would control them absolutely. Furthermore, only his direct boss would be telling him what to do or making requests of him.

But this is *not* an upside-down world—or organization. It is created by the need of organizations for specialization. The modern firm and the government agency need specialists in purchasing, finance, industrial relations, safety, quality, and many other fields. Many of these experts will have an impact on the supervisor's immediate world and job. This is inevitable and consistent with good management.

Thus the supervisor's job becomes somewhat less simple, less obvious, less clear-cut. He has to deal with competing requests, with competitors for scarce supplies, with occasionally contradictory requests: "Watch quality," "We need extra output" "Use that new employee even if he doesn't do such good work," and "Put that rush order ahead of your regular work—but don't neglect your regular work."

The effective supervisor is one who doesn't get flustered or disgusted with these noisy—that is, contradictory or at least inconsistent—requests. He can balance them off and maintain flexibility. This week, he may have to emphasize labor relations and devote a great deal of time to the union steward and to working out job assignments. Next week, then, he will pay less attention to union requests and push for output. He may have to use up a good part of his monthly overtime budget (during a period when cost-cutting efforts are in full swing) to meet a rush order from an adjacent department. This may leave him with little overtime for his normal needs for the remainder of the month. However, this kind of flexibility is required if the supervisor is to be responsive to the ever changing needs and demands of the organization.

This doesn't mean that the supervisor always says yes to requests that are made to him. He often must say no or evolve a compromise with the other team: "Look, I'll give you half of what you need today if you let me have the remainder of the week to fill the rest of the order. This way, I can go to work tomorrow on handling the requests that I'll be neglecting today by helping you out."

Of course, such negotiations and compromises take time and the energy to engage in discussions. Thus, much of the supervisor's day is spent in negotiating with other supervisors who "surround" him in the work situation. The manager can't afford simply to agree or disagree. He must often take the time to work through an improvised, one-shot agreement to cover an immediate situation in which he is blocked by contradictory requests being made upon him. Furthermore, once he has gotten his colleagues to agree to a compromise, he may have to spend more time and talk on persuading other managers to go along with the arrangement.

I said we would work continuously and as long as necessary to get that accounting report out today. But then I had to call accounting and get them to agree to authorize overtime (which had been prohibited since last month). I also had to go next door and borrow back the two employees I had loaned the duplicating department when we had been short of work. And then I had to bring my boss up to date on all these deviations from our usual operating procedures.

The Manager—Mr. Dynamo

To the uninitiated, this may appear like going around in circles. Each new request or compromise requires a number of other supporting agreements. The manager must keep on the move, must keep improvising to accommodate to an ever changing environment. His job is not a static one in which he does the same thing every day and is successful as long as he follows instructions and keeps his own people responsive to his directions. Rather, his job is dynamic: He must keep finding new solutions to the new balance of forces that are impacting him.

A recent study of successful and unsuccessful supervisors in a very large industrial company shows clearly that those who got ahead were those who had this dynamic view of their jobs. The ones who failed were those who were always complaining that the company "is going to the dogs":

> "I don't have enough authority."
> "There are too many bosses pushing you around."
> "The service departments don't really support you."
> "Orders keep changing; people keep changing their minds."
> "Stop all this changing and this negotiation—"
> "I want to get off this merry-go-round!"

The reason for all this change and dynamism is that many of the problems of an organization are not soluble by a simple "do-this or do-that" decision. The decision depends upon different managers and different specialists coming to some kind of tentative agreement to modify what they are doing or to concede on something that they used to feel strongly about. All this takes a great deal of interacting, communication, and many supervisory meetings:

Our standard operating procedure is that every machine that goes out of here must spend two weeks in testing and also receive a final paint job. One of our best customers called and said he needed a machine to test out a new apparatus he was constructing. We had none available to ship him but the sales department said that "one way or another they would get him one."

They had called us in final assembly to ask what we could do to help out. The only machine we had close to completion was supposed to have an extra-large exhaust on it. It hadn't been finished, waiting for the exhaust to be fabricated. So I called the machine shop and asked if they could rush out a baffle to cut down the size of the exhaust that would allow us to attach the standard fittings. Normally they would take three or four days to machine something to order, but I know the chief machinist and he agreed, as a favor to me, to get one done this afternoon.

Then I told the sales manager that he would have to get testing and inspection to agree to waive both the final test and the painting requirement, or nothing else would be worthwhile. He did it, but then testing insisted that I sign a statement indicating that I knew no reason why the machine was not safe to operate, and I got them to come down and witness a sort of "rough and ready" test we improvised on the shop floor. Then sales and I both went to see production control. P.C. had to agree to change the production schedule that had come out on Monday.

They were reluctant to do so because the schedule reflected their efforts to satisfy all company customers while, at the same time, production costs were being kept down.

Rather than sending it over to shipping to be packaged, I agreed to let the shipping people work in my department constructing a container for the machine. I made sure that they knew this was a special concession and wouldn't be repeated because I can't get my work done if those men are working in my area—we're too cramped for space.

Count the number of contacts required to get that machine out. Which do you think involved difficult negotiation? Which contacts were easy? In how many did the supervisor take the initiative and when was he responding to other pressures? What kinds of relationships were the ones with advisory, auditing, work flow, stabilization? Who was ordering whom in these relationships? Which probably took the most time?

This procedure is much more normal in most organizations than a simple follow-the-leader, every-day-is-like-every-other-day activity. Managers spend a great deal of their time working out these lateral relationships because work gets done through other managers as well as through subordinates. Figure 9–1, showing the supervisor's pressures, does not exaggerate.

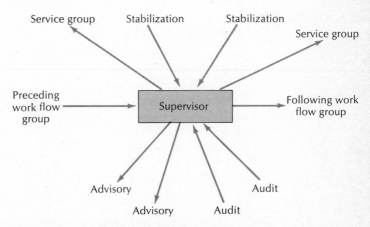

Figure 9-1 The supervisor's external world

CONCLUSION

The supervisor himself has to interact laterally to get his work done. His success in handling these horizontal relationships is just as crucial to job success as his vertical relationships with subordinates and superiors: These dealing with colleagues facilitate getting work done as information, assistance, and requests for modifications of one another's efforts are exchanged.

Now we can begin to understand how time is the very essence of the supervisor's job. He can't spend too much time directly observing or intervening with subordinates or he will have to neglect his lateral relationships. On the other hand, the demands of these relationships may be so greedy that he will have difficulty spending adequate time with his subordinates. Effective supervisors are very conscious of this need for balance and close budgeting of their time. They realize that the secret of their successful performance is their allocation of time: How much time can I afford to train employee A, to correct or discipline B, to observe C, to handle these lateral relationships?

One final note: The individual supervisor may play more than one position. Thus a supervisor may have a series of work-flow relationships with other departments. At the same time, he may have a stabilization relationship with another department. (It has to get his permission before it can change the specifications on the work it is performing.)

Because of the supervisor's technical knowledge, he may also be an adviser to one or more other groups in the organization when they get into trouble. This means that he has to have a number of "plays" in his repertoire. He is a little like a baseball player who shifts from playing third base to shortstop, then to second base. Unlike the ballplayer, however, the supervisor may have to perform these different roles on the same day, even in the same hour, as different problems occur in the organization.

Some of these positions have higher status than others. Also, it is much more fun to audit another manager than to have to provide him with service. It is therefore tempting to distort your job, ignoring its less prestigious aspects so that others will be more deferential to you. Obviously, if all managers did this, there would be little service work performed and even advisory and some work-flow relationships might be neglected. Every manager learns more skills and also learns the troubles of the other fellow by handling all the dimensions of his job.

The modern organization can be more frustrating because a great deal of the work involves persuading and negotiating with peers as distinct from giving orders to subordinates. But the reward is a much more fully developed range of personal skills that evolve from successfully meeting the high challenges of working with people at your own level.

SELECTED REFERENCES

Sayles, L., *Managerial Behavior,* McGraw-Hill, New York, 1964.

Walker, C., R. Guest, and A. Turner, *The Foreman on the Assembly Line,* Harvard University Press, Cambridge, Mass.

Whyte, W. F., *Organizational Behavior,* Irwin-Dorsey, Homewood, Illinois, 1969, part VI.

THE EDUCATION OF GREG HORNING: MAY 2

"This is for Aerotech, Inc. Rush it. They're one of our best customers. S. P."

The order came directly from Phillips and Greg took it to Creegmore and got him going on it. This kind of thing was no problem anymore—now that the workers were coordinated and the output was up, an emergency like this could be absorbed into the schedule without disrupting things.

But about thirty minutes later, Creegmore came in to see Greg. "I wanted to get into the job and make sure before I told you, but I'm going to run short of plastic before I finish this order."

Greg looked up, surprised. "But it's the same material you were using for the other pieces. A normal day's supply should be enough to get you through."

"Yeah. Well, a normal supply would have been enough, but those smart alecs in mixing gypped us today—I would have run out, anyway."

"Well, you get back to work. I'll see what I can do." Greg reached for the phone and dialed Joe Barber's number.

"Joe? This is Greg Horning. We've got a problem over here. It seems you delivered us a short supply today and we haven't got enough plastic to get through the day."

"That's ridiculous. We sent you what you always get." The mixing department head sounded clipped and cold.

"Well, I don't know how it happened, Joe. But my best

man was just in here and he said he was going to run out. Is there anything we can do?" Greg kept his voice firm but friendly.

"Sorry obout it, Greg. But we've been having troubles over here, too. Our large mixer is on the blink—maintenance has been promising to get to it for weeks, but you know how they are. Now that I think of it—we could have measured short, the way that machine's been acting up."

"Well, look. Couldn't you send over another batch right now? We've got this rush order on our hands—it's got to go right out today to one of our best customers. The orders came from Phillips this morning."

"Sorry, Greg. But there's nothing we can do. The crew's working on another plastic now; if they had to make a switch, we'd lose half a day's work. You know how that would look on the cost sheets. Cost us a fortune. Phillips would love that, huh?"

"Well, thanks anyway, Joe. I'll see what else I can do."

"Right, Greg. Good luck."

He probably enjoyed that, Greg thought, hanging up. There'd been bad blood between the two ever since Phillips had gone along with Greg's recommendations about the pellet sacks.

Well, I guess you can't win them all, Greg thought, picking up the phone again to call Ed Briscoe.

"Hello, Ed. This is Greg Horning."

"Hi, Greg. How's it going, kid?" Greg had been getting along quite will with Ed lately. There'd been a good deal of give and take between the two departments. Just last week, one of the materials handlers had spilled a couple of sacks of pellets in the molding shop when he'd been coming in with a delivery. He'd been behind schedule and hurrying and run right into them. "It's all right. You go ahead—you're in a rush. One of my men will take care of it," Greg had said. He'd gotten Alfred to clean up the mess and sent the handler off to finish his deliveries.

"Well, I'll tell you, Ed. We've got a little problem here. Maybe you could help us out."

"Sure, Greg. What's up?" Briscoe at least sounded willing to listen.

Greg explained the situation, then he asked, "I thought maybe you could lay your hands on some of that 616 grade plastic. That'd do the job and I thought if there's any of it anywhere in the plant, Ed Briscoe would know where it was."

"Well, as a matter of fact, Greg, we put some of that stuff down in the storeroom a while ago. But..." But Greg was ready. Before Briscoe could bring up the problems of getting it moved, Greg cut in.

"That's just great. Now what I thought was, if you could just lend me one of your men and a truck for an hour or so, I'll send some of my crew down with the fork lift to load it. How'd that be?"

"Well, I guess I could spare you a man. Yeah. We can manage that. I'll have someone down there in half an hour."

"Thanks, Ed. I really appreciate this. Listen. We'll have to get together for lunch real soon. What do you say?"

"Fine, Greg. I'll give you a call."

Greg smiled as he hung up the phone. You can't win 'em all; on the other hand, you don't have to lose them all either.

QUESTIONS

1. Could Greg have put more pressure on Joe Barber to send him that extra material? How? With what likely consequences?

2. Under what circumstances would Ed Briscoe's reaction not have been as helpful?

3. Does it make any difference in the handling of lateral relationships that Barber is in the work flow and Briscoe is in a service capacity?

4. What should Greg do if the shipping supervisor calls to say that they will need the Aerotech order in a couple of hours if it is going to be shipped today?

10. The supervisor
and the union

The odds are very good that a supervisor, at some point in his management career, is going to have to learn about and deal with unions. With 19 million unionized workers in the United States, even organizations which were once thought antagonistic to unions are finding that they must learn to bargain with representatives of their employees.

WHY UNIONS?

The rise of unions is not very surprising. Even though you may work for a well-established organization like a bank, a government office, or an insurance company, as an employee you are likely to experience a great number of situations where you think you've been unfairly treated. After all, how do any of us know what is equitable, fair treatment? Reflection will tell us that we all believe we work terribly hard, are underpaid or at least underappreciated, and often receive unfair assignments and even unfair reprimands. In addition to this all-pervasive sense of personal worth and personal righteousness, we always have the opportunity to look around and see others who are better off. The guy next door, who hasn't had as much education as you have, works in a similar company and gets 25 percent more pay. And at the office, there are the girls upstairs in the executive offices who have a lounge to take their coffee breaks while you have to walk over to a little, untidy cart, pick up a cup, and take it back to your desk with no chance to sit and chat for a few minutes.

Unions promise employees that they will both eliminate such inequities and provide workers with more benefits than they could get by themselves. An employee can be made to feel pretty impotent if he tries to bargain very hard with a whole company, unless he has very rare and valuable skills that are hard to replace. (There is a good deal of controversy among professional economists on whether unions actually have been responsible for increasing the earnings of American workers, but the important point is that most workers believe organized effort does help to raise wages.)

In addition, most employees have a deep-seated uneasiness about being given benefits, whether wages, improvements in working conditions, or so-called fringe benefits. They like the idea of *earning* or *winning* them. Of course, unions are not reluctant to say that they've helped workers win benefits from a not overly enthusiastic nor overly generous management. Further, employees in every organization have heard stories about the "girl in department 16 who had been praised to the sky by her boss, received merit increases, and then one day was fired for a minor infraction of the rules."

As we have described in dealing with other problems of supervision, we are all uncomfortable living in a situation where there is great inequality of power. This is why adolescents and young adults are likely to rebel when their parents say "you must." They feel such decisions ought not to be made solely by the older generation. When you are totally under the control of another person because he is bigger, stronger, or more powerful in any way—even when he is kind to you—you feel it is unfair. Implicitly, we recognize that where there is substantial power inequality, the good things can be capriciously and arbitrarily removed just as easily as they came.

So unions appear to provide a means of winning and holding on to benefits and of reducing the inequality in power between the individual employee and the organization. Unions also appeal as a means of dealing with difficult supervisors. They help in two ways. They bring the organized power of the group to bear against the supervisor's possible threats to discipline an employee with whom there is a disagreement. Moreover, the union provides a mechanism and a channel for getting beyond and around the supervisor and reaching the critical, decision-making upper management levels. After all, it is upper management that establishes most of the important policies that affect earnings levels and working conditions (such as prices in the cafeteria, amount of money available for salary increases, and the use of incentive systems). It is difficult even for a group of employees to walk into the office of the general manager or someone even higher and say, "We want to talk about company wage policy."

Of course, many workers join unions just because they have to. Sometimes, they are under social pressure from the group. More often, a union has established itself in the organization and has succeeded in negotiating a union-shop agreement. Under such contracts, all new workers, within a reasonable time, must join the union.

But whether reluctantly or enthusiastically formed, an existing union poses a number of challenges for the supervisor. What are these challenges and how can they best be handled?

SUPERVISORY CHALLENGES INTRODUCED BY UNIONS

From the supervisor's point of view, the existence of a union introduces two kinds of critical changes. It influences his decision making, and it affects his working relationships with subordinates and union representatives.

When a union is organized, it seeks to restrict management's freedom to decide a number of questions regarding employees. The union leaders therefore negotiate a contract which specifies such things as rates of pay for specific jobs, the order in which employees will be furloughed if cutbacks are planned, and procedures that must be used if there is disagreement between one or more employees and management. Thus, management cannot freely change job structures, move people from one job to another, or alter their pay and working conditions without negotiating with the representative of the employees—the union. Furthermore typical supervisory decision criteria (such as efficiency, equity, and eligibility for reward) have to be modified in the light of contractual limitations introduced by the union.

Impact on Decision Making

From the union point of view, these limitations on the manager's decision-making ability are needed to do two things: first, to protect employees from capricious and potentially discriminatory supervisors, and second, to protect the union's position and reputation. The union insists that its status is important because, in the long run, a strong union, with loyal members, will mean better working conditions for the workers. The following situations illustrate the most frequent and difficult types of decisions affected by the union.

EQUITY VERSUS PRECEDENT

George Hingham has been coming in late for several mornings now. You can tell he has been drunk the night before and has had a hangover. You've talked with him, and he has promised to do better. You know something about him—he comes from a broken home, grew up in a very bad slum, and has been struggling to kick a drug habit. From your point of view, the facts that he works reasonably hard when he is here and had a good attendance record his first week on the job mean that he is making progress. You would like to wink at the company policy that after a tardy worker is given a verbal warning, his next late arrival calls for a day off without pay—because Hingham is making some improvement. But you know you've got another problem employee whom you have also warned and who is now testing the limits. Your boss also is very strict on these matters. He constantly tells you, "Don't look at the individual—look at the rule. We've got a union here and if you make an exception for one member, it will force you to make an exception for all. You will have established a precedent. The next time you try to discipline an employee for a poor attendance record, they'll throw in your face that he isn't one of your favorites like Hingham was, so you're giving him the business."

ABILITY VERSUS SENIORITY

The company is hitting a rough period and your boss has told you to cut back at least two employees by next week. This means a layoff, of course. The man you would like to furlough is Albert Gorce. He has been goofing off for months now and does everything grudgingly. His work is just passable, so you can't charge him with anything. But the union contract is unambiguous on this score: At the time of a layoff, the man with the least seniority goes out the door first. Gorce has been around eight years. The irony of it is that the newest man, Kaufman, is one of your best employees. He is eager and bright and does fine work. If you lose him, you are going to cripple the department because he is the one man who can handle the really tough assignments with the very critical tolerances.

The same thing may happen when the opposite type of question occurs: Who is going to be promoted? The seniority principle is less strong here than in layoffs. But consider a typical case: Jane Adams is the best stenographer you have hired and now there is an opening for an executive secretary. You think that Jane would be great on the job, but she has been with the company only eight months. On the other hand, Christine Shametz has worked in the department for several years and has been reasonably good. The union contract reads that a promotion must go to the most able person unless there are several with approximately equal ability, in which case the senior one must get the advantage. In practice, in many companies this means that the employee with greatest seniority must be offered the job unless there is someone else who is head and shoulders—as they say—above him in ability.

So our supervisor faces a challenge: Can he (or she) prove beyond any reasonable doubt that Jane is superior to Christine? In most instances, there will be a number of ambiguities surrounding performance (as we saw in Chapter 5). Jane is fast and accurate and appears to be more alert (and is certainly more attractive). Christine can argue that she has shown her ability to handle a wider variety of assignments over the years, that she is loyal, and that she has more formal education. Furthermore, the union may imply that management is rewarding Jane because she is pretty and compliant while Christine is too skinny and has often spoken up when she has sensed unfairness.

Again the question is, can the supervisor prove with objective evidence that Jane has demonstrated substantially more ability than Christine?

COMPENSATION DIFFERENTIALS

Greg Carling has come along very fast since he was hired last year as a machinist, second class. He is very ambitious, takes orders well, and is eager to learn. You would like to reward him for his efforts, show him that you appreciate them, and try to ensure that he doesn't take a job down the street where wages are a little higher. When you propose an increase to your boss, he reminds you that the union has negotiated a rate for each job. A man gets a raise when the union negotiates an increase for everyone or when he is promoted to a higher-rated job. When Carling can qualify as a first-class machinist, he gets a raise. But, unfortunately, he can't yet do a number of things which are in the job specifications for first-class work.

Does this seem unfair to you? The union admits that everyone isn't equal in performance, but it argues this way: Management might use differentials to reward their friends (for example, those who don't object to violations of the union–management contract) and punish the vigorous union activists. So the union seeks to eliminate management's ability to make distinctions among workers in a given job category.

ALTRUISM VERSUS DUE PROCESS

A manager was in the habit of giving his employees a day off now and then during the deer-hunting season and when the fishing season opened as his way of saying thank you

for their help during the year. It was also his way of showing that he was "a good guy" and worthy of their respect.
But one year, everyone was officially told that the company
was facing some financial reverses and costs should be
tightened up right down the line.

When several of the men asked about taking off the first
day of the deer-hunting season, they were told that it would
be impossible this year. They said they had it coming to
them—it was a "holiday" that the department had always
"celebrated." The union got involved and pushed a grievance,
arguing that neither the company nor its supervisors can
unilaterally change employee benefits. The supervisor had
established a clear precedent by always giving off that day,
and if he wasn't going to continue the practice, the men
expected some other benefit in return.

EFFICIENCY VERSUS THE CONTRACT

You observe that the girls on two clerical jobs often help
each other with filing, proofreading, and running the copying
machine. Three of them are called copy girls and the
fourth is a clerk typist. You've often wondered what the
rationale is for having two different job classifications anyhow,
and you'd like to shift the duties around as the work load in
the department changes. So one fine day, you announce that,
in the future, the girls all will be called clerk-typists (which,
by the way, means a $4-a-week increase for the three copy
girls).

The union immediately objects that jobs can't be "eliminated" arbitrarily and implies that this is a way of reducing
employment in the long run (even though no one is being
dropped). Furthermore, the union representatives say that
"giving a raise without consulting the union" is a device for
impressing the workers with how generous the management
is and how the union is unnecessary. Even though proofreading work may be declining, they want to be sure that
the job isn't eliminated. "Since, in the contract, there is a
salary specified for that job, you can't eliminate the job
without bargaining with the union on it!"

NEIL W. CHAMBERLAIN (1915–   )

Neil Chamberlain has moved among positions in universities, foundations, and government. His career is a good example of the contribution of economists to management thinking. Like Whyte and Drucker, his work epitomizes the restlessness and breadth of the truly creative thinker. While best known for his analysis of labor-management relations, he has also sought to develop compact theories to explain the operations of the firm and management decision making. Central to much of his work is the concept of bargaining. While many of us restrict our application of negotiations to the labor-management field, Dr. Chamberlain has observed the extent to which organized groups within the firm (divisions, departments) seek to compromise their needs with the needs of the larger organization. Thus decision making, a central activity of the manager, typically involves bargaining, not simply the effort to maximize. He has also been interested in the planning process both within the firm and in government.

Some of his best-known books in these areas include *Labor, A General Theory of Economic Process, The Firm: Micro-Economic Planning and Action,* and *Enterprise and Environment.*

While serving as head of the Ford Foundation's business and economics program he was instrumental in helping business schools introduce more behavioral science into their curriculums. He has also been active in promoting greater understanding of American institutions and methods through the American Seminar in Salzburg, Austria, which gives a seminar for young executives drawn from European companies, trade unions, and government agencies.

Foreman and Steward*

But the balance is not all on the negative side. Collective bargaining can be made into an effective tool by the foreman who is willing to work with it. Normally we are inclined to think of the grievance procedure as a union device, as a protest technique. The human relations people have been quite right in suggesting, however, that the

---

* Reprinted by permission from Neil W. Chamberlain, *Labor,* McGraw-Hill, New York, 1958, pp. 248–249.

grievance procedure in its bilateral stages is only one example of the consultative technique and that the sophisticated foreman can avail himself of the grievance procedure, as a consultative technique, and make it a tool for his own use. The union has provided him with a steward, the union's intent being that the steward should act as the first-line check on supervision, ensuring that the rights of union members are respected. But once the union has provided him with a steward, there is no reason why the foreman cannot make use of the steward for his own administrative purposes. The union steward can become a useful tool of management. Let us see how.

The one effective curb which has always been exercised over leaders is the reluctance of their followers to comply with directions. At some point, on some issue, individuals will rebel against even so-called absolute authority. Even a Hitler and a Stalin, with all their power, could not completely ignore the feelings of their followers. To secure compliance, it is necessary not to ask too much. In order for authority to remain unchallenged, its exercise must be accepted by those to whom it applies. This simple homily is relevant to authority wherever found, including that of the foreman in his shop. The foreman's command may meet with an apathetic response that robs it of its intended effect. His decision may be translated into only partially conforming behavior by those to whom it is entrusted, whose interests may be involved quite differently from the interests of the foreman and whose actions are designed to protect as best they can their own interests which have been overlooked by the foreman.

Yet it is difficult, if not impossible, for any individual to predict the likely reaction of others to his assertion of authority. All of us have experienced surprise at one time or another at the kind of hornet's nest which we have kicked up by some decision or action of ours. But for every such overt display of resistance we can be assured there are many more covert manifestations.

Under the circumstances clues to the responses of others become important management aids. If the foreman improves his understanding of how his men are likely to react to his decisions, he can make his decisions more effective. The contemplated action which, he finds, is likely to make more trouble than he had originally expected can be modified to avoid that consequence. With respect to any change, the singleness of *his* objective may blind him to the multiplicity of effects on *others* and the accompanying protective responses evoked from others which modify or even nullify the results intended by the change. If he is made aware of these conditioning circumstances the proposed action can be reformulated to accommodate, at least in some degree, interests which had been neglected. As a result of such compromise, the outcome may be less desirable than had previously been *intended* but far more rewarding than it otherwise would have been *in fact*.

Within the context of this approach to the decision-making process, the union steward can play a dual function. Not only is he the leader of the opposition, the champion of those injured by the exercise of authority, the public defender; he becomes a consultant with whom the foreman may confer, whose advice he may solicit, whose opinions he may use as a sounding board.

In the hands of an inept foreman, this approach may lead to an abnegation of authority to the steward. At the point where consultation leads to a bifurcation of leadership, with a sharing of authority between foreman and steward, the foreman's effectiveness as a leader of his men suffers. From preliminary investigations, it would also appear that shop morale declines. Men prefer to work for a foreman who is not afraid to use the authority of his position.

Conclusions for the Supervisor

Thus we can make certain generalizations about the impact of the union in supervisory decision making. Obviously, the supervisor has to be familiar with the agreement (the *contract*) negotiated between company and union. More and more, his decisions will be restricted by this contract and he must be sure that what he does is consistent with this document. In a sense, his effectiveness is curtailed because the best decision (in his judgment) for the unique problem (such as George Hingham's tardiness) may be inconsistent with the general rules. He must consider past practice and precedent, too. If he does something today, will it come back to haunt him tomorrow? He can't consider individuals quite as much as he used to, but he must be more responsive to the group and even to the political needs of the union leader, as we shall see.

Obviously, some supervisors are frustrated by these restrictions and they see them as foolish barriers. That is both realistic and silly. There are all sorts of restrictions on a supervisor under the best of circumstances: his boss's pet ideas, an employee's personality limitations, an old building, a cranky machine, wage and hour laws—one could go on and on. The challenge of management is to get work done in spite of, and within, these constraints. Almost no one has a free hand to do what he pleases in any organization—or even in most aspects of life.

The union just adds another set of constraints that have to be considered before the supervisor moves on a number of issues. But the existence of the union also affects *how* he moves, the *process* by which he gets decisions implemented.

THE BARGAINING PROCESS

If you think carefully about all the supervisor's decision-making problems that potentially involve the union, it may appear that his job has been complicated beyond reason. It will certainly seem that way if the manager tries to handle every employee grievance and supervisory decision so that problems never develop. Given all the coercive comparisons, jealousies, ambiguities, and legitimate differences of opinion and interest in any work situation, the realistic manager must anticipate that he will have to devote time and effort to working through various difficulties. Only a very naive or foolish manager expects that, through cleverness and omniscence, he can avoid such efforts. The real key to successful supervisory–union relationships is an understanding of the *process* through which such differences are resolved. It is this process which prevents arguments and grievances from becoming major issues which might cause strikes or slowdowns. Thus, although no manager can avoid union problems, he can handle himself and his responsibilities in such a way that their number may be minimized and the problems that do occur will be resolved with a minimum of controversy and hard feeling.

This process involves both greater sensitivity to the need to document your decisions and actions and those of your employees—and an ability to learn to negotiate and come to terms with the departmental union representatives (the steward).

Records, Notices, and Warnings

Many union–management disagreements involve questions about the past. Did Helen Corelli actually receive a verbal warning for being late? Did the employees who handled carbon black always receive an extra twenty minutes of wash-up time? Were two workers assigned to the large mill *only* when the machine was running extra-long pieces? Managers have to keep much better records on what happens with whom, and when, where, and how often it happens. An employee may say that he was never warned about coming in late unless a supervisor keeps good records and can show that he has communicated the regulation clearly and unambiguously. If there is a rule that no smoking is allowed, it is the manager's responsibility to see that everybody knows it. He can't say, "Well, they should have known it. We've had the rule for years and, after all, it's obvious that's no place to smoke!"

Managers can't get away with vague statements like "I am pretty sure I did that" or "Anybody knows that." They must find ways of documenting their actions and those of their employees. Similarly, they must keep track of the frequency with which actions occur. If an employee is allowed to repeat questionable behavior or a benefit is granted consistently, the union can claim, with justification, that a pattern or precedent has been established which *must* be continued unless the company and the union can agree jointly to discontinue the practice.

It is always helpful if the union representative is notified when anything extraordinary occurs. He can then feel that the manager is not trying "to pull a fast one," that he is being kept informed, and that he has the necessary knowledge to do his job as a watchdog.

Handling the Union Representative

It should already be clear that patience and fortitude are required. There will be many problems which defy easy solution and require endless discussions which will try the patience of the manager. However, he has to be willing to listen to the complaints and arguments (even when he thinks he can predict exactly what will be said because it has been said many times before). Some of the listening is necessary to satisfy the union official that his status is not being ignored and that the supervisor respects his position. Listening also indicates an open mind and serves to fill the political needs of the union official, who must show he is alert and on the job. This doesn't mean, however, that the supervisor should allow endless harangues or should not terminate discussions after a reasonable time because some talkative union representatives seem to enjoy bargaining for its own sake—and many of these officials are relieved from work responsibilities while engaged in union business. There is a fine line between cutting off necessary expression and being taken advantage of.

Many times, a supervisor feels threatened by a union steward. This undesirable reaction stems from a number of factors. Many people become emotional when their decisions or actions are questioned, and some supervisors just panic when told, "You've made a serious mistake. You can't transfer that employee to another job. It's a violation of the union contract." They either feel intimidated by such a challenge or believe that their wisdom and honesty are in question.

Of course such reactions are naive because the modern supervisor never has complete autonomy or independent power anyway. There are always "outsiders" who can question his decisions: his boss, Accounting, Industrial Engineering, Personnel, Safety, and almost every other department. (His responses to this type of challenge are discussed in Chapter 9.)

The supervisor may also be intimidated by the relationships of the steward both with the group and with higher levels of the organization. One satisfaction of management and also a symbol of successful leadership, as we have stressed before, is initiating to subordinates, giving orders, and sensing ready responsiveness. The supervisor often feels that the steward interferes with or blocks his subordinates' respect for the legitimacy of the supervisor's position.

When I asked the men to help out the maintenance crew by moving all of the empty boxes out of the way, they said the steward had told them it wasn't in their job description, it was laborer's work, and they didn't have to do it.

I overheard the steward saying something to them about my having had trouble in my previous department getting along with people.

The steward came over and said I shouldn't put pressure on Bozo to work overtime; it was a man's own decision as to whether or not he wanted to accept overtime work.

There will also be times when the steward may know something that has happened in the higher echelons of the organization before the supervisor has been informed. The union chain of communications is (regrettably) shorter, more informal, and swifter than management's means of keeping everyone informed. Thus, the steward may learn that the company has just lost a critical order from one of its best customers and tell everyone he works with. When the supervisor is asked what he knows about the order and has to plead ignorance, he loses some status in the eyes of his employees.

It is easy to perceive the union representative both as a stumbling block to getting employees to respond and as a strong competitor for the loyalty of the work group. The supervisor may fear that the union actively *seeks* problems—even tries to catch him in some mistake—in order to dramatize to its members that it, the union, is on their side and that management is out to hurt them. In truth, however, many managers take pride in protecting their people and put a good deal of effort into representing them to outsiders. (As pointed out in Chapter 7, representation of one's subordinates is a necessary component of any leadership pattern.) Managers naturally resent any implication that they exploit employees or are indifferent to their welfare.

CONTROL EMOTIONS

How, then, can the supervisor handle this challenge to both his image and his authority? First, and most obvious, he needs to recognize and control the temptation to become angry and to lash out at the union for its "unfairness." Bitter denunciations, efforts to show up the exaggerations of the steward, and complaints about "ungrateful" subordinates who forget "all I've done for them in the past" only play into the hands of an aggressive union and its leadership.

The opposite tack is much more likely to be fruitful. Accept the fact that the union does make life different and that the union leader has to try to prove himself an active check on unilateral management decision making. Unionized workers are likely to suspect their leaders of not being forceful enough. They tend to worry that the leader will sell out to management and that they won't get their money's worth for their dues. So the union leader is also on the defensive a good deal of the time.[1]

---

[1] See Leonard Sayles and George Strauss, *The Local Union*, rev. ed., Harcourt, Brace & World, New York, 1967, pp. 131–142.

You can't wonder, then, that he's a pretty aggressive opponent, on occasion. Remember that, although your actions may appear perfectly logical, reasonable, and fair in your eyes, they usually are seen very differently by employees. Many times the steward is simply voicing what others may be timid about saying—that you appear to be acting unfairly or precipitously.

I really got the surprise of my life when the steward said I was browbeating employees to make bonus. Sure, I would talk to everyone who was below, but I didn't think they thought I was threatening to fire anyone who didn't get up there right away. I sometimes speak gruffly, but that's just my way. Well, it turns out that most of those young girls thought I was a regular Simon Legree, just waiting to get the goods on them.

RESPECT THE STEWARD

If the steward knows you are willing to listen to him when he is speaking sensibly and not just emotionally, he can provide you with a good sounding board on some of your actions. This assumes that he does have the respect of his group (not always the case, as we'll see), is a reasonably well-controlled personality, and is not seeking hostility for its own sake. And, as we have said, your discussions with the steward show him that you respect his position as the representative of the work group. Here is a very typical case.

I was having a great deal of trouble with O'Leary, who had a drinking problem. He would never be late and he was rarely absent, but there were many mornings when I thought he was a danger to himself and to the equipment. I had talked with him and told him that if this continued, I was going to have to take disciplinary action. When it didn't stop, I called Cabot, the steward. I told him how frequently this was occurring and that we were both going to be involved in a messy disciplinary case unless O'Leary came around. Cabot said he hadn't realized this had happened more than two or three times. Now he would keep his eyes open and check with a few of the boys and see what they knew. The next week I saw Cabot again, and he said that he had learned that O'Leary was in real financial trouble—lots of debt and a wife who thought there was no tomorrow—and he did, in fact, come in pretty hung over once in a while, but the poor guy "was hurting." I told Cabot that I couldn't be responsible for his killing himself or someone else in a machine and it had to stop. He asked me if I could find out whether the company credit union might help, and when I said I would and would hold off any disciplinary action for another couple of weeks, Cabot said he would have a long talk with O'Leary. I knew that he would tell O'Leary that he would have to straighten out or the union couldn't do much for him if he got booted out since the evidence was building up. . . .

Here is a good example of a complex bargaining process at work on a very informal level. The steward gets advance notice of a problem and the sense of being respected by the supervisor. He is forewarned and also gets the chance to forewarn the employee and to check out department public opinion on O'Leary's behavior. Thus his political position is recognized and protected and he gets a chance to be involved actively. (Most union leaders get some satisfaction out of activity and out of give and take, and management can therefore make good use of their energy and need to be involved.) There is also an exchange of favors: Both supervisor and steward have the satisfaction of getting the other to be responsive to him. The steward proposes a postponement of any definitive action to give him a chance to do some things, and asks the supervisor to check the credit union. The supervisor gets the steward to go to work on the recalcitrant employee.

The same process may work when a layoff is necessary, when transfers have to be made, or even when new equipment is coming in. Obviously, it won't always work and the manager shouldn't expect perfection. However, there is much more likely to be agreement *before* everyone in the department gets excited and draws up battle lines.

In O'Leary's case, for example, if the supervisor had fired the man precipitously—even with good and sufficient cause—everyone in the department might have felt sorry for him and banded together to protest "the cruel injustice." Whatever the steward's own opinion about the case, he probably would have been forced to oppose the supervisor vigorously. But the problem was handled so that every one was prepared and, had the counseling and aid for O'Leary not changed his behavior, disciplinary action would have less likelihood of being opposed.

Quiet, behind-the-scenes give and take solves many more problems than legalistic pro and con grievances. The supervisor has to spend more time and energy and invest more advance planning and forethought, but in the long run, it pays off in less lost time, less strife, and fewer open disputes. The latter are costly in terms of morale and relationships. There will still be times when there are strong conflicts of interest or when the steward will even have to fight for a case he doesn't believe in. But the intelligent supervisor understands that sound day-to-day working relationships with the union can withstand such interruptions.

WHO IS THE UNION REPRESENTATIVE?

So far, we've been rather vague about the union representative with whom the manager comes into contact. That was purposeful—to avoid that additional complication. Most unions have an elected representative for each major department or work area. He or she may be called a steward, committeeman (committee woman), or some other name. It's his job to try to settle problems that come up in that group with the supervisor in charge of the department.

If they can't solve the problem there, they may take it to the next upper level of management or to a higher union official (likely to be elected, also). There may be still higher union officials dealing with higher levels of management in large organizations. This step-by-step procedure by which unresolved problems climb the ladders of both management and union hierarchies is called the *grievance procedure*. (The procedure is diagrammed in Figure 10-1.)

Knowing that the steward has been elected, however, doesn't tell the manager much about his leadership position in the group. Sometimes an individual is elected only because he wants the job—he may not even be popular. There will be other, informal leaders in the work group whom the supervisor will also have to keep in mind because they are more influential in shaping group opinion or even in knowing group feelings. Some stewards are loud and bossy, getting a great deal of satisfaction in voicing discontent even when there isn't much of it. Others are very quiet, moderate people who speak up only when there is a real problem.

Obviously, the supervisor will learn to discount some of

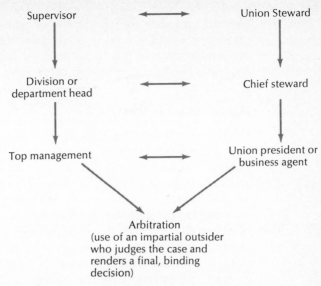

Figure 10-1   Typical grievance procedure

the loud clamorings of the troublemaker and to take seriously
the problems raised by the representative who is sober, is
himself an informal leader, or is on good terms with the
group's informal leader.

To make matters more complicated, there may be situations in which one clique is strongly represented by the union
steward while another clique is apathetic or antagonistic to
the union. There may even be two factions vying to elect
their respective candidates and seeking to embarrass each other
at the expense of the supervisor.

The men on the large drawing machines had never liked
those who worked the smaller drawers. The L.D.s said the
S.D.s had a soft job and they should get paid much more
for their heavier work than the few cents an hour differential they now received. The steward came from the L.D.
group. When management lost a big contract and had to
lay off some workers, the steward made it clear to the
supervisor that the first to go had to be men on the smaller
machines. "Ours is a higher-rated job and layoffs always
begin with the less-skilled men. Even if you need less of
the big machines, we can handle their jobs a lot easier
than they can handle ours." Of course the S.D.s were just
as adamant that they should stay if it should turn out that
some of the large machines were to be shut down.

Thus the supervisor was caught in the middle between two contending groups. He really would have been happy with any solution, but he had to be prepared for a long series of arguments because of the intergroup conflict.

Types of Union Leaders

At times, a steward who is purely destructive will be elected. He is anti-everything and devotes himself to proving that the manager is always wrong. Usually, such highly aggressive personalities are also unable to settle problems by negotiating with the supervisor. All they can do is complain. Although such negative pyrotechnics try the patience of the manager, if he can retain his "cool," the union members will eventually recognize that this kind of steward isn't able to accomplish much beyond providing an outlet for himself and perhaps for them. When they learn that he can't undertake the more painstaking job of working out settlements, they will replace him with someone who is less of a firebrand and more constructive.

Then the manager must be careful not to destroy the political position of the constructive steward by doing things which create the impression that the steward is too friendly with management. Too frequent contact outside of work, socializing, and excessive friendliness can be interpreted by suspicious rank-and-file employees to mean that the steward has sold out. In fact, the supervisor ought to avoid associating the steward's name with what are likely to be highly unpopular decisions (such as the discharge of an employee for good cause) even though the steward may concur with them privately. The union representative can then be free to object, albeit weakly, to the supervisor's action. The last thing the supervisor wants is a collusive relationship which may succeed in the short run but which will surely backfire in time. At best, the membership is suspicious of the motives of its leaders.

HOW DO YOU BARGAIN?

Skilled negotiation is an art which may take years of practice to acquire. Many books have been written about bargaining techniques, but there are a few things which every supervisor can learn quickly.

1. Remember that bargaining involves give and take. You

can't expect to win everything you want—even if you are sure you are right. Moreover, the union representative has to be able to show his people that he has been effective in defending their interests. Therefore, extreme rigidity and a take-it or leave-it attitude on the manager's part is bound to lead to an impasse.

2. Don't try surprises or trickery even though they may help win in a particular grievance. In the long run, the quality of the relationship may deteriorate to the point that there will be much more trouble on other issues.

Handler suspended an employee for selling "numbers" (gambling slips) during working hours to his fellow workers. The union argued that he just had it in for Krepps; there was no good evidence other than rumor that he sold "numbers." The supervisor refused to change his decision and the union pushed the case up through the grievance procedure over the next few months. On the last day of arbitration, Handler was present and showed a Polaroid picture he had taken which showed Krepps taking money with one hand while he had a fist full of policy slips in the other. Of course, the discharge stuck and the union looked foolish. But they vowed they would never trust Handler again. "No use even dealing with him since he doesn't put his cards on the table, but we'll make so many grievances in his department that his boss will think he's the worst supervisor in the plant."

Of course, the supervisor did nothing wrong in seeking evidence to substantiate the charge, but he should have presented it to the union at the outset. Union–management relations ought not to be conducted like the adversary legalistic proceedings in which both sides keep each other at arm's length. That's fine for Perry Mason, but not for the supervisor who has to continue to work with the union.

3. Try to narrow the differences by establishing as much agreement as possible on the facts in the case. "O.K.," a supervisor might say, "we'll agree that all employees have not been given that wash-up privilege in the past if you'll accept the fact that the grinders have been doing it for at least three years, and have always had at least fifteen minutes. So the issue comes down to whether it is fair for workers on just the dirtiest jobs to get this privilege." If you try to deal with everything at once, many problems are insoluble.

4. Seek to distinguish between what the union representative considers his most vital issues and the secondary problems. For example, employees and the union can get themselves very worked up over what they consider a matter of principle and the argument will be very difficult to resolve. On the other hand, there may be secondary or less crucial issues which can be settled amicably and easily. (Of course the same holds for management.) As one supervisor tells it:

Two employees were fighting and I first insisted on disciplining both equally; I didn't care who started it. They both were going to get a two-week layoff. The union guy at first said I was a tyrant and this wasn't the kind of first offense that ought to have such a stiff penalty attached. But in talking with him, I finally learned that everyone in the department thought that there ought to be a distinction made between the instigator and whoever was caught. Anything else violated their sense of fair play. Once I agreed to consider making some distinction in penalty, the rest was easy to wind up.

The generalization is that most people find it difficult if not impossible to compromise on principle or what they see as major symbolic issues (such as acceptance of the union, acceptance of management's "right to manage," and seniority). Also, there is a tendency for the union to ask for more than it knows it can achieve, and the sooner one sifts out the more from the less important, the quicker a settlement.

5. Try to overcome a stalemate by attempting to settle the easy things first—it sometimes helps. The simple decision provides everyone with a sense of successful bargaining and moves the discussion off dead center. Save the most difficult for the end. At times, it may even be necessary to postpone for an extended time the very sticky issues.

The steward and I tried to work out a rule that would govern who would get stuck with that messy clean-up job that comes in every week or two. It wasn't any good trying rotation because the employee whose turn it was might be tied up finishing a critical job or be taking that as one of his leave days. Everything else we tried either displeased the men or I couldn't live with it, so we agreed to disagree. I would of course continue to make the decision each time and they would protest if they didn't like it. If we had tried to settle on a formula we would have been arguing from now till next year.

---

6. Don't reward pressure tactics—show you can hold your ground. Many times an aggressive union official will threaten to call a wildcat strike, to go over your head to upper management (to "tell all!"), to make life miserable for you, or to disgrace you by other means. If you concede under these circumstances, it will encourage continued use of threats and even stronger tactics. It is an old principle of labor relations that the only thing worse than a wildcat strike is a successful wildcat strike. Prove that reasonable give-and-take discussions are much more rewarding (in terms of good settlements) than pressure tactics and don't bargain while employees are engaged in illegal acts.

7. Similarly, don't threaten the union leader with embarrassing him in front of his men or otherwise undermining him. As we have said, he is probably an elected official. He has to show his people that he is working hard for them and therefore has to gather in some "victories" or "winnings" to prove he is an effective negotiator.

8. Do not hesitate to conduct some bargaining quietly and in private. Many times, you or the union steward will want to try out some ideas without having either talk about it to outsiders. Some concessions the union steward may make only if they are arranged in private and if you don't quote him or embarrass him. "All right, we'll look the other way when you lay off Strickoff, if you'll agree not to push the disciplinary penalty against him. There's some justification for saying he broke his seniority during that two-year leave of absence anyhow, but that disciplinary thing would really hurt his employment record."

These kinds of trade-offs always sound illicit or even unfair if announced publicly. But bargaining does involve certain "giving in" and certain "admissions" which would prove politically unacceptable if widely announced. This is why, in international relations, negotiators insist on seclusion and often announce only the final results of their deliberations and not *how* they arrived at the settlement.

9. Try to pace your negotiations. It never hurts to spend some time in easy conversation with your union counterpart. If the debate gets too hot, it may be worthwhile to break off discussions because little of constructive value is done during periods of substantial emotionality and emotion is usually catching. Also, there may be value in giving the other person time to digest certain new information or a suggestion or even to check it out with others. In other words, don't expect an immediate yes or no on everything, and in turn, you may want to ask for time.

10. Don't give the impression that you can only say no to things, and that to say yes, everything must be checked with your boss. Under such circumstances, the union delegate rightfully concludes he is wasting his time negotiating with you and always should immediately bypass you with his requests.

USING THE UNION

At the very beginning of this chapter, we talked about reasons for unionization: the desire on the part of employees for recognition, participation, for control, and for more! Managers, if they are to be realistic, have to accept the fact of unionization. Even well-managed, generous enterprises come to be organized because no company can give its workers everything they want. Some things they *must* get—and *want* to get—for themselves through their own group.

But all this need not be solely a burden for the manager. Unionization can provide job satisfactions: an increased sense of job security, of respect and identity and assurance that one is getting a square deal. Furthermore, the supervisor can use the union in at least two important ways.

The Watchdog Effect

The union can be a kind of control system alerting the supervisor to hidden problems. Remembering that the union representative may exaggerate and may even not be a good representative of his group, there will still be many times in which he will bring the supervisor's attention to problems that might otherwise go unnoticed for an extended period. Often problems which are not promptly dealt with get worse and are therefore more difficult to solve than they otherwise would be. And they also hurt productivity during their festering period.

Within the laboratory technician group, there had been a story circulating for years that, back in the 1950s, technicians had received the same salary as test-cell mechanics.

But, as the story went, the head of the lab during the middle of that decade was a snob who believed that technicians were not much better than bottlewashers and he allowed their earnings to lag behind the increases granted the mechanics. Many technicians bore a real grudge and, particularly as their work load increased as a result of the expanded new product-development efforts, they resented and resisted all new job requirements.

The breaking point came when their present supervisor sought to eliminate the use of two technicians for certain procedures which he felt could be handled by one. By this time, there was a union in the lab and the union steward raised a grievance about a change in their work load, insisting that the change had to be negotiated through the union.

During the discussions between the steward and the head of the lab, this differential between themselves and mechanics came up. The lab director was surprised by this comparison; he had never heard of this "inequity" before. In checking the records it was found that indeed there had been parity back in 1953, but after that time the test-cell mechanics jobs had been changed substantially. Only employees with "technologist" degrees from junior colleges or special training programs could qualify and the work became substantially more demanding. The old test-cell work was gradually phased out and the new people took over tasks that had been performed by engineers.

When this was finally explained to the technicians they became much more reasonable about their own salaries, and the grievance over the two technicians was settled quickly by a mutually satisfactory compromise. During the more demanding procedures, the old methods involving two technicians would still apply, but in other cases one technician would handle the whole thing. However, the supervisor would have to expect that such a technician would handle less jobs per day.

It should be noted that this type of problem resolution is rather typical in union–management relations. The steps are often these:

Underlying and unexpressed problems are brought out into the open. (In the above case, the 1953 salary comparison came to light.)

The process of give and take between union representatives and employees gives workers a sense of having some control over their jobs and environment.

A workable solution is evolved which incorporates some safeguards for the workers and some for management. Neither side gets what it wants completely.

Both management and the union learn something about the other's needs. (In this case, for example, management learned that the technicians were also afraid that a trend was emerging which would make their jobs increasingly demanding.)

Through the settlement, and the give and take and the release of pent-up feelings which precede it, morale—and often productivity as well—is improved.

Accepting the Decision

The second contribution the supervisor can receive from the union is greater acceptance of certain critical decisions that might otherwise be resisted or considered unfair. In the case of the laboratory technicians, for example, the process by which union and supervisor negotiated technician work-load changes served to legitimatize the final agreement. One technician was heard to say:

You know I thought the company was really giving us the business: getting more and more work out of us for the same pay. But I think the rule that came out of that grievance is fair to both sides. I just know that on these special tests you would need at least four hands to do it yourself, but as long as I know that we're safe on those, I'm willing to try doing the routine ones by myself.

In effect, if the relationship with the union is a good one, the union representative will sell the grievance settlement to his fellow employees: "Look, guys, they [management] gave a lot on this and I know we can live with the agreement. You know that if any one tries to pull a fast one by sneaking in extra work on any of these jobs, we'll blow the whistle as we did last time. We got a good deal because, frankly, in the other labs in the other divisions, the work load is a lot higher than we've got."

Similarly, if the manager has forewarned the union representative and given him a chance to do his own investigating and perhaps cool off the hot heads in the group, he may well find that the union can serve as an effective channel of communication to employers.

Obviously, employees won't think that management is credible if they feel they are being "used." They need to be consulted in advance, to be given responsive answers to their complaints and inquiries, and to have their political needs accepted by supervision.

A LAST WORD

None of this discussion of management–union relationships should be taken to mean that the supervisor can thus neglect his own direct relationships with subordinates. While there will be times that he will communicate through the steward and use him as a sounding board or as an informal leader, there should be more times in which the supervisor continues with direct communications, counseling, advising, directing, and disciplining employees. If he relies entirely on the steward, he can both become a captive and lose his own status among employees. The union is an extra channel to be used. It is not a substitute for leadership and close, direct relationships with subordinates.

SELECTED REFERENCES

Chamberlain, N., *The Labor Sector,* McGraw-Hill, New York, 1965, chaps. 1–14.

Estey, M., *The Unions: Structure, Development and Management,* Harcourt, Brace & World, New York, 1967.

Sayles, L., and G. Strauss, *The Local Union,* Harcourt, Brace & World, New York, 1967.

THE EDUCATION OF GREG HORNING: MAY 24

The gripes from the crew about the night shift had been increasing. Greg's crew would often come in in the morning and find a lot of unfinished work left for them to do and the shop in a mess. Another gripe came frequently from the women when it came to inspecting work. The night shift had no one in particular to do their inspecting—the operators did it for themselves. According to Helen and Jeannette, they couldn't care less. They let a lot of shoddy pieces go through and the girls had to reinspect the night shift's work and flash a lot of their output before they could let it pass.

As a result, they wasted a lot of time redoing the night shift's work, and this really slowed the whole department's production. Greg checked the complaints and they were legitimate all right; if anything the mess was worse than they had claimed.

Greg had tried talking to the night supervisor about the problem, already, but it hadn't had any effect. He was in charge of the whole plant for the night shift, and he didn't have the time to keep a close watch on any one department. So he had no choice but to leave them pretty much on their own, hope for the best, and leave the problems to the day shift foreman.

Greg was not sure what to do. He could bring the problem to Phillips' attention, but he knew better than that now. Phillips would chew out the night people, maybe fire some of them as a warning to the others. It might make them shape up, but the bad feelings it would generate wouldn't be worth it. In spite of the fact that the night shift was causing his crew trouble, they'd all join together against him if he went upstairs. It would get back to his people through the union and they'd think he'd been a fink, running to the big boss instead of handling the situation himself.

The union! That was it. This was a problem that the union should be brought into. He'd better have a talk with Phil Martello.

Martello was not exactly enthusiastic when Greg called him in to talk about it.

"I don't like the sound of it, Greg. You're putting me in the middle of a very sticky situation."

"I know it's sticky, Phil, but you've complained yourself about the mess they make. They're the worst crew in the plant and we have to take the rap. Something's got to be done about it."

"You're damned right, Greg," Phil answered angrily. But he was being defensive. "But you're the one that has to do it. You're management. Why should I do your job?"

"Listen, Phil," Greg said carefully, trying to be persuasive. He knew how Phil must feel—he knew what it was like to be boxed in. "Think about it. What could I do? I could get some of them fired and it would stick—the union wouldn't like that much, would they? Or I could get Phillips to hand out a bunch of layoffs. Your people wouldn't like that much either. There's got to be a better way. That's why I'm talking to you."

Phil smiled reluctantly. "You sure have learned a few things in five months, damn you."

Greg laughed.

"But, honest, Greg," Phil went on, shifting in his chair. "I don't know what those guys do at night. Maybe they got it good—maybe too good—but I don't know what I can do about it."

"But you do know what this place looks like in the morning. And you do know how you gripe all the time about your machine being all fouled up with dirt."

"Yeah."

"And you know the men on the night shift," Greg persisted. "Now you can talk to them, see, where I can't. You can tell them how you guys feel—that you're not going to fight for them because you know they've been goofing off. And you can tell them what I'll do if they don't shape up. From you, it's a friendly tip. See. A word to the wise, that kind of thing. You know."

"Yeah," Phil said, a little more positively. "I guess I could try that. I know some of the guys from the union. We have a meeting next Thursday night. I guess I should tell them—they've been getting away with murder."

"You sure should," Greg said, closing in. "After all, it's our own men they're hurting. Our crew. It's not as though it was something that doesn't affect us. It does. It hurts our whole operation. And you can talk to them. You're a union steward. They'll listen to you."

"Well, all right, Greg," Phil said. But he was still doubtful. "I'll give it a try. Maybe they'll listen to me."

"Okay, Phil," Greg said. "I won't move on this until I hear from you. Let me know what happens."

"Yeah. I'll let you know," Phil said, nodding his head. "Yeah. I guess they'll listen to me. Anyway, it's worth a try."

QUESTIONS

1. Is Greg being realistic in hoping that the night shift will listen to the steward, Martello? (Are members expected to take instructions from their elected officials?)

2. At what point in dealing with the night shift could the steward best be brought into the picture?

3. What should Greg do if the steward tells him absolutely no, he won't cooperate?

4. How would you cope with Martello if he agreed to do this only if Greg would promise to get the day crew a fifteen-minute wash-up period in the afternoon?

11. Adjusting to change:
process and problems

Ours is an adaptive society. A cliché, but it encapsulates a truth that has consequences for everyone living in our world. The process of technological change, the mainspring of social change in general—which the philosopher Alfred North Whitehead described forty years ago as "quick, conscious, and expected"—has greatly accelerated in the two generations since he wrote these words. Change which had been arithmetical in his day has become geometric in ours. Time has telescoped: Once we could measure the progress of technology by a millenium or at least by centuries—there were five thousand years between the hand plow of Egypt's Middle Dynasty and Cyrus McCormick's reaper. Today, it's a strain on the imagination to visualize the advances of the next twenty years. And if we tried, we would probably be wrong. Future realities are certain to outstrip and confound present expectations. As Herman Kahn of the Hudson Institute observed, "A study in 1937 missed not only the computer but atomic energy, antibiotics, radar, and jet propulsion, nearly all of which had been around in principle and waiting for development."

The supervisor, particularly the supervisor in industry, finds himself peculiarly the victim or the beneficiary of change. We don't deny the facts of change in every type of organization from universities to political parties, and this change—as events at Columbia, Berkeley, and other universities throughout the United States have demonstrated—can be rapid, drastic, and violent. However, it is the industrial supervisor who finds himself in the front lines of technological change, for it is industry that has been both the catalyst and consequence of technology. "More even than machinery," as Galbraith expresses it in *The New Industrial State,* "massive and complex business organizations are the tangible manifestations of advanced technology." Industrial research and development budgets, the most accurate barometer of technological advance and of change within the industrial organization, have grown fourfold over the past thirteen years and will probably double over the next decade. It's reasonable to assume that the supervisor, who has been forced, along with the other members of the organization, to accommodate to the demands of a rapidly changing technology in the past, will have to make increasingly more drastic accommodations to meet the demands of a progressively accelerating technology in the future.

THE PARADOX OF PROGRESS

Technological change is equated with technological progress, and who is against progress? None of us, and the supervisor is no exception. He subscribes to the shibboleth as staunchly as anyone—but perhaps with an extra measure of conviction. If he works in a typical industry, he is supervising the manufacture of products, many of which were not on the drawing boards ten years ago. And they are made by machines which hadn't been invented twenty years ago. Furthermore, the supervisor is likely to be coordinating his efforts with a computer-based production-control system that was developed and installed within the past five years. The evidences of change—and progress—are all around him. The supervisor has seen that many of the promises of change have been fulfilled—the plant is more productive; earnings, including his own, are up. Change has benefited the overall organization, its stockholders, even society as a whole. The company may be selling an improved product at the same price or lower, with both developments being directly traceable to technological change, a familiar phenomenon.

What is the paradox? It is that the average supervisor who subscribes heartily to the idea of change and has seen the benefits accruing from it, has found himself opposed to many specific changes, including some from which he has derived tangible, and sometimes quite substantial, economic advantages. Where particular changes are concerned, his reactions have spanned the spectrum from violent opposition or passive resistance to indifference or enthusiastic cooperation. And in his task of facilitating the adaptation to change, he has encountered a similar range of reactions from his subordinates: At one time or another, most of them have responded to a proposed change with ready sympathy, sullen indifference, explicit hostility, and varying shades of emotion in between.

The Dynamics of Change

With each change, the picture is always complex and always different. The organization as a social system, whether it be an office or a factory, involves an ever shifting equilibrium of forces. The supervisor's own operation, in turn, is a miniature social system in itself, dependent on and interdependent with the larger organization, but also with its own unique and continually fluctuating equilibrium of forces. Any major change imposed from without on this miniature social system is bound to alter more or less severely the equilibrium of forces within. Of each major change, we can say what President Pompidou said of France after the general strike in May, 1969, "It will never be the same again."

The dynamics of change are also such that the supervisor, in evaluating specific innovations, finds himself at different times holding quite different opinions vis à vis his subordinates. Sometimes there will be essential agreement of attitude toward the change. More frequently, supervision is in the position of selling the rank and file on a change, decided upon by top management, understood and accepted at the supervisory level, but suspected by employees. Occasionally, we find the situation, a dangerous one for the organization, where supervision is in tacit collusion with the work force to oppose a change which it is formally charged with implementing. Among supervisors, a combination of lip service toward change and subtle sabotage is not uncommon.

WHY RESIST CHANGE?

Why does the same supervisor resist change on one occasion and embrace it on another? Why do we maintain that the opposite reactions may be equally rational and appropriate? Why do the supervisor and his subordinates take positions toward a proposed change that are sometimes in agreement, sometimes slightly different, and sometimes diametrically opposed? And how can their distinctive positions be equally justifiable?

Let's begin by describing, in some detail, the chief categories of reasons why supervisors—and their subordinates too—resist organizational change, conceding that the categories are not self-contained and that most employees oppose a particular change for reasons which encompass several categories.

Psychological Resistance to Change

Any change that affects an individual involves him in a loss of security. He is trading in the familiar, the routine, the more or less mastered, for the new, the unpredictable, the to-be-assimilated. The worker in a factory, for instance, derives part of whatever sense of security he has achieved from his sense of occupational identity. Let's assume he is a lathe operator, with a specific set of training and skills. Install a new machine which requires that he upgrade his skills—or worse and more frequent, which makes some of his previous skills redundant since it will automatically make the adjustments that he formerly made by hand—and you have undermined his sense of occupational identity.

Professor Elting Morison cites a fascinating case of pride of craft that spurred workers to resist change and thereby established the dominance of one firm over all its competitors. Between 1864 and 1871, ten Pennsylvania companies realized the superiority of the Bessemer process and imported it from England. All but one, the Cambria Company, also imported British labor. By the end of the seventies, Cambria had secured a commanding lead over its competition. How had this come about? The Bessemer process improved but the British laborers, proud of their craft and secure in their mastery of the original techniques, adopted none of the improvements, while "the Pennsylvania farm boys, untrammeled by the rituals and traditions of their craft, happily and rapidly adapted themselves to the constantly changing process."

The supervisor is even more likely to find himself in this type of bind. In one commonly encountered situation, for example, the supervisor has to adjust to a computer-monitored production-control system. This necessarily involves him in a kind of record keeping and continuous monitoring of operations that are quite different and distinctly more difficult than anything his job has demanded of him. His previous training and experience equipped him for his job as it was. The job changes have undermined his sense of competence and also his sense of occupational identity. It isn't the same job any longer, and even more unsettling, he may be unsure that he is up to his new responsibilities. Quite naturally, he does whatever he can to thwart the introduction of the new system.

Employees and supervisors have no monopoly on resistance to change based on feelings of insecurity. Dr. Donald Schon, in a stimulating study of technology and social change, cites a number of examples of underground opposition toward technical innovation among the same members of top management who formally and warmly endorse innovation as a prerequisite of the organization's survival and growth. Among his examples is a foundry under severe competitive pressure whose new products director had been futilely exploring new product possibilities for the past two years. The problem was not a shortage of ideas—twenty-five promising new suggestions had been developed—but the set of criteria specified by top management. They were so rigid and exacting that they made product innovation impossible. On the other hand, the company president was content to see the organization continue its essentially sterile new product activity. Dr. Schon summarized the informal, implicit attitude of many top managements toward technical innovation thus: "It's the enemy of orderly, planned activity. It changes everything about the business we are in. It hurts. Let us talk about it, study it, praise it, espouse it—anything but do it."

Changes Diminish Status

A closely allied reason for resistance to change is the feeling, whether justified or not, that innovation threatens the individual's status within the organization. Status is a matter of comparison, and one side affect, usually unintended, of most substantial organizational changes is the lowering of the relative standing of one or more units of the organization, and the elevation of the standing of other units. Quite naturally the personnel in the downgraded units are unhappy over the change.

We know of one case in a leading educational organization where the reporting relationship of the electronic data processing operation was shifted: Previously, the head of the EDP department reported to the head of accounting, but now he reports to a vice president in charge of administration. Incidentally, accounting and EDP both report to the same vice president, and the heads of the two separate but equal operations are on the same level. Obviously, the accounting and EDP departments will continue to work very closely together, and the new reporting relationship, while not so close as the old, should help.

What happened was a rapid and drastic decline in the previous pattern of cooperation between the EDP and accounting departments. There were instances of high-handedness by some of the systems men and programmers who were feeling their oats but the basic problem was that the personnel of the accounting department, from the top down, reacted to their loss of status and power by deciding that practically nothing the computer department did was turned out to the accounting department's satisfaction. To changes, large and small, proposed by the computer department and previously accepted by the operating departments involved, the accounting department raised one of two stock objections: "That's the way it has been and it can't be changed," or "We weren't consulted in advance." At last hearing, the conflict continues, and many changes that would be beneficial to the organization are stalemated while the accounting department and the EDP department are nominally trying to work out their differences.

One big reason why computers in general have not been used more effectively within organizations are the changes they engender in the status relationships between various levels of supervision. Consider banks where, traditionally, the men who deal with the customers on the rugs out in front monopolize all the prestige. The "back room" was for clerks and calculators with low-status positions. Enter the computer and the back-room operation took on a wholly different coloration. Highly paid systems men and programmers, the masters of a complex and esoteric technology, were soon competing for deference, status, and power with the men out front. Small wonder that, in many banks, the debugging operation has taken much longer and has proved more difficult than anticipated, and that some of the problems can be traced to resistance from managers and other personnel who resent the status changes brought about by the computer.

Change Threatens Economic Position

Many changes tend to depress the economic position of those involved in the change, either on an absolute scale or in relation to other people within the organization. Under some circumstances, violent resistance may be a logical, almost inevitable, reaction to the economic implications of the change. Frank Cousins, a prominent leader of the British Trade Union movement, commented on how appropriate the reaction of the Luddites was when they destroyed the looms over a hundred and fifty years ago. He observed: "The machine looms destroyed the jobs of thousands of hand loom weavers. They were introduced without consultation, without regard to human values, and they had dire consequences for the men directly concerned."

The Luddites, of course, faced unemployment and possible starvation as the consequence of change. Fortunately, with all the options open to employees in our society, we have no Luddites. But we do have many cases of workers resisting change because it threatens—at least they feel that it does—

their jobs or the size of their pay checks. The classic example is the introduction of new machinery that will increase output. In this case, unemployment is the big fear—or a change in the incentive system under which workers are paid. Speedups and lower wages are the threats perceived.

The reaction of workers to this kind of change will be largely determined by their experiences. If the introduction of high-speed or automatic machinery in the past has meant layoffs, it will be next to impossible for top management to sell employees on a different interpretation. The same holds true when previous changes in the incentive system have been followed by lower wages among incentive workers. The lessons taught by experience are usually indelible.

Resistance to technological change can be most effective. Take the case of a company, manufacturing hypodermic syringes, that developed a machine capable of increasing the production rate of the syringe bodies from 400 to 1,500 per hour. At least that's what the machine did in the manufacturer's plant. Then the union representatives looked at the new machines and predicted that they wouldn't increase production above 700 units per hour. The correctness of the prophecy should come as no surprise. The production rate of the new machines rose to about 700, leveled off, and stayed there. The environment of this story is crucial—a company with a record of poor union–management relations and of general mistrust and hostility between management and the work force. No reassurance from top management or supervision would have been believed, so the workers instead took the task of ensuring their job security into their own hands.

A POSITIVE REACTION

Another kind of reaction based largely on economic grounds looks at first glance like resistance, but is actually the reverse. It is not a true opposition to the change but a conscious determination to bargain about its conditions and to get the maximum advantages from it. Joan Woodward, in her insightful study "Industrial Organization: Theory and Practice," examined the process of change in seven firms and concluded that on the surface, the greatest opposition to change came from the most self-assured and successful individuals and groups—both managers and rank-and-file employees. However, closer scrutiny revealed that changes in the organization were viewed as opportunities to obtain either a reduction of effort, an increase in wages or both. Moreover, Miss Woodward found these efforts were successful. "Even where they [the operators] did not get all they asked for, they managed to get something, and resistance evaporated as soon as terms were agreed."

The supervisors carried on a similar bargaining process and were similarly successful. In every case, they made top management conscious of their importance, and in at least two companies their bargaining led to concrete gains at the annual salary reviews.

MANAGEMENT BUNGLES CHANGES

So far, we have concentrated on the intrinsic, the unavoidable, reasons, given the circumstances, why people resist change. Let's switch from human nature to human frailty. Many of the problems in introducing change and much of the resistance arise because top management doesn't understand the process of initiating change and makes a mess out of it.

A LITTLE TIME

What's the evidence? One proof is that management chronically underestimates the time necessary to implement a major change. When the airlines began developing a computer system for customer reservations, for example, they originally estimated that the whole reservations system would take three or four years to install. Actually, it was seven or eight years before the new system was working effectively. Joan Woodward found that implementing change was a very slow process. In one firm it took nearly eighteen months (twelve meetings held at four- to six-week intervals) to resolve a bottleneck problem by changing the manufacturing layout.

A LOT OF PRESSURE

Top management compounds its initial mistake by putting pressure on those people who, as seen from on high, are not working fast enough and not adapting fast enough. The result is frequently panic and almost always resentment by supervisors and employees. Management also draws the conclusion, from unrealistic estimates and consequent pressure, that the change was a mistake—or if not, it can't be made to work.

Top management obviously wants the change to succeed, so why does it habitually underestimate the time factor involved? One reason is that the big bosses and the supervisors themselves don't understand the give and take in jobs. They fail to see that most jobs require smooth, synchronized patterns of interworker and intermanagement relationships that take months to develop and months or years to restructure. For example, the U.S. Navy is able to train destroyer crews to use new electronic gear in a week or two if the ship is in port. However, because of the complicated human interrelations, it takes about six months at sea to learn to operate the equipment efficiently, smoothly, and harmoniously.

Actually, and as management usually doesn't recognize, there is no such thing as a change that's simple and compartmentalized. Changes ramify. Take the classic instance: Professor William Whyte's description of bartenders clashing with waitresses over who came first, what did you order, your handwriting is lousy, and other parries. The battle ceased when the spindle was introduced—a nail and a piece of wood on which the waitresses placed their orders. This meant that the waitresses didn't give their orders verbally to the bartenders and didn't have to compete with each other for preference, nor could the bartenders any longer resent the fact that their behavior was determined by actions initiated by the waitresses. The depersonalization revolutionized the relationship between the bartenders and the girls.

HOW TO FACILITATE CHANGE

If we have created the impression that it's natural and inevitable for supervisors and subordinates alike to resent and resist many changes, that is our belief and our intent. However, the problems of facilitating the introduction of change can be tackled and most of them resolved successfully by a top management with the right attitudes and the right techniques.

Let's take attitudes first. Management should never assume that it will in fact have anticipated all the problems. There's never been an organizational change of any magnitude in which anyone has predicted the full ramifications. Management should also expect that there will be resistance at all levels and that no timetable can realistically schedule its extent or the length of time necessary to overcome it. Any efforts we have seen have fallen far short of the mark in both regards.

As Joan Woodward stressed, the initiation and implementation of change is a very slow process. Furthermore, she found that, no matter how carefully and slowly the idea of change was introduced, the immediate reaction of both lower supervision and employees was to resist. Successful change requires a flexibility of mind, a patient appreciation of the problems involved, and a constant readiness to respond to challenges, criticism, and new ideas from the people who are most affected by the change.

None of these findings frees management from the necessity of doing a lot of hard thinking and careful planning before it institutes any major change. Management's inability to anticipate all its problems is no excuse for not trying to cope with as many as possible.

Change as a Total Systems Problem

What kind of advance planning does management need to do before the introduction of new equipment, new procedures, and new processes? Management must realize that change in any of these constitutes a total systems problem, to be evaluated on the basis of its full impact on all the jobs that may be affected. Management can't afford the shortcut of looking merely at what appears to be the focal point or the point at which change is actually introduced.

Alex Bavelas and George Strauss cite a vivid example of the difficulties management gets into when it neglects the total systems approach to change. The problem of how to increase productivity in the paint room of a toy factory was basically solved by giving the female workers control over their own work pace. The experiment succeeded and productivity zoomed, but in the end the solution failed because it succeeded too well. The experiment was limited to this one department, with the result that the semiskilled painters there were earning more than skilled workers in other departments. They protested so much that the superintendent revoked the new arrangements and went back to the old system. Management had forgotten that the factory, like any other organization, is an interdependent system. Incidentally, when the old system was reinstated in the paint room, production dropped drastically and within a month all but two of the eight girls had quit.

What Change Does to Job Behavioral Components

Another crucial aspect of planning any change is for management to think through the effects of the change on the behavioral components of jobs. What kinds of behavior are no longer required in the job and therefore have been removed or modified? What kinds of new behavior are required?

For example, in many automated factories the new technology has virtually taken away the supervisor's old function of giving out job assignments. Yet, in some plants, supervisors continue to give such orders because they are used to this pattern of relationships. It maintained their status—and they have no viable substitute. In this case, management should aid the supervisor in developing genuinely useful new relationships with some of the staff and maintenance groups. Thus it can spare him the need to keep to old routines that salvage his ego but are essentially irrelevant to the new technology.

Explaining the Change in Advance

The case for explaining a change in advance to all those who will be affected by it is so overwhelming that discussion of it seems almost unnecessary. We left it in because of the evidence that, although almost every management makes a stab at announcing changes in advance, many of them handle the job badly. Arnold Judson, for instance, in his book *A Manager's Guide to Making Changes,* tells the story of a group of girls who were told six months before their company's move to a new building that they no longer would be private secretaries or stenographers, but instead would become part of a secretarial pool. End of explanation! And end of staff: Before the move was completed, 70 percent of the group had resigned. Frankly, the part of the story that puzzles and depresses us is the tenacity of the 30 percent who stayed on.

The basic principles of explaining change are few—and simple enough. Top management, and supervision to the extent of its involvement, should try, once it has identified the probable consequences of the change, to empathize with the people affected by it. Bosses and supervisors should put themselves in the workers' shoes. Then they should make a reasoned and balanced statement, preferably in a face-to-face meeting with employees, of the pros and cons of the change from the vantage point of the interests—not of the company or of top management—but of the people at this meeting. In other words, management should use the same approach in selling change that successful salesmen have preached and practiced for generations: Tell the user what's in it for him.

Of course, there's a difference. In selling change: Overstatement is more dangerous and likely to boomerang, and the maintenance of credibility is essential. It's vitally important to reassure employees, for example, that no one is going to lose his job because of the change—if such is the fact. But God help the management which makes the statement, knowing that it's a lie.

Lastly, it's important to announce a change substantially ahead of its initiation. What's "substantially ahead"? We feel that depends on circumstances—on the magnitude of the change and the best estimates of how upsetting it's going to be. Certainly, far enough in advance for employees to get used to the change and to mull over its implications, and for the management to get ample feedback on their reactions, to consider their criticisms, and perhaps to modify the change in the light of these criticisms. The only thing we feel that management did right with the secretaries when planning its move to the new building was to tell them six months ahead of time.

The Case for Participation

The argument that management, in planning a change, should involve everyone who is going to be severely affected by it rests on two stools. The process of change generally calls for both an increase in orders and more frequent interaction between boss and subordinates. With these go the employees' growing sense of dependency on management and authority and their decreasing sense of autonomy and independence. In other words, the process of change threatens man's psychological security and motivates him to resist it, irrespective of the benefits it may confer on him.

However, if supervisors and employees are allowed to play a part in planning the change, their psychological security may actually be increased, and one basic reason for resisting the change will have been eliminated. In fact, they are likely to favor any change of which they were, even to a minor degree, the co-architects.

The other argument for participation is that the people who will be affected by the change have a lot to contribute.

They see the problems from a perspective different from management's, and they see them very closely. In fact, they will frequently spot bugs that management hasn't anticipated, and they may also see the solutions.

So much for theory. What evidence do we have that the theory works? A plethora of data is the short but accurate answer. Studies—at least the proverbial baker's dozen—are available. The role of participation in the management of change has fascinated the current generation of behavioral scientists, though it means different things in different studies.

CONSULTATION

Successful participation occurs at several levels. The lowest consists of consultation by the personnel in charge of engineering the change with those directly affected. We know of one company where management solicited criticism from employees after moving an assembly line from one part of the plant to another. Management was flabbergasted by the number and the quality of the criticisms. The workers knew much more about the problems of exchanging and moving materials than the engineers! They also knew that the new location of certain parts made an enormous difference in their ability to do the job. Many modifications, large and small, were made in the assembly line, incorporating the employees' suggestions, and they all represented improvements over the conscientious and professional efforts of the company's engineers.

Robert Guest, in his monograph *Organizational Change*, stressed the role of consultation in the success story of a plant manager who, in three years, converted a sick operation into one of the most efficient and profitable of the company's 126 plants. The manager's role in the first few months, as he saw it, was to ask questions and to dig out ideas for improvement from the group as a whole. The process of information gathering took several forms, the principal one being the manager's face-to-face conversations with his subordinates on the lower level, hourly workers, and union representatives. Ideas were then listed for the agenda of weekly planning sessions. The plant manager didn't share his power to make changes, but took extraordinary care to solicit ideas and suggestions from almost everyone in the plant before he initiated any changes.

LET THE EMPLOYEES MAKE DECISIONS

A more substantial degree of participation in the management of change is seen when the problem is defined from above but the subordinates develop the alternative solutions and choose between them. Bavelas, for example, describes an effort to change the productivity level of three groups of workers in a garment factory. Two groups were given the problem of production standards but were not required to make a decision. The third group had to make a decision—and, significantly, it was the only one that increased its productivity.

Rare, in business at least, is the situation where management allows employees who are going to be affected by the change to participate both in defining the problem and in choosing the solution. Yet evidence suggests that both these levels of participation help to facilitate the introduction of change and should be more widely employed by top management than they currently are. Larry Grenier, after surveying eighteen studies of organization change, concludes flatly that "successful change depends basically on a redistribution of power in the organization"—a redistribution in which top management shares more of its power with lower levels in the organization.

The Setting Is the Thing

We wouldn't go so far as to say that change should always be supported by redistribution of power. Sometimes previous experience renders participation sterile. Take the study in the footwear department of a Norwegian factory where participation in determining work methods made no important difference in production. The explanation was simple. Sixty-four percent of the workers, relying on their previous experiences, said that they knew the rates would be reduced when they exceeded a certain standard.

And sometimes participation is unnecessary. A case in point is the "Work Itself Program," conducted by AT&T over a period of several years with many different jobs. AT&T was seeking to enrich the jobs of both employees and first-level supervision by giving the employees more responsibility and control over their jobs, and by changing the supervisor's role from primarily that of a monitor-checker to that of a consultant-trainer.

The first experiment involved 120 girls, largely college
graduates, who handled inquiries from shareholders, and
their seventeen supervisors. The so-called achieving group,
twenty-eight letter writers and their supervisors, gradually
assumed more responsibility over a seven-week period,
beginning with the appointment of subject-matter experts in
the first week and culminating, in the last week, with the girls
being encouraged to answer stockholders' letters in a personal
way. As the girls took on more responsibility—for example,
in the third week supervisors cut the verification of letters
from 100 percent to 10 percent—the supervisor's role also
changed from that of mother hen to that of resource person.
Success was not immediate, but by the end of the fourth
month, the productivity and customer-service record of this
group was markedly better than that of the other three groups
with the same function—and it has continued to improve
since then.

The striking thing is that in this and eighteen other experiments, there was no participation by anyone directly affected
by the change nor was a word of explanation given. First-
level supervisors simply received a series of instructions and
transmitted them to their employees—instructions which
revolutionized the jobs of both supervisor and subordinate.
There was a minimum of resistance—one girl in the achieving
group quit because she wasn't getting more money for a
more responsible job. But the experiments have by and large
achieved their goals—making jobs more interesting and
employees both happier with their jobs and more productive.

What are the implications of the Work Itself Program for
the management of change? Apparently, when the change
improves the instrinsic nature of the job as the employee sees
it, the time, effort, and money spent on getting participation
or even on explanation are wasted. People know a good thing
when they see it. And there's a corollary implication: When
the benefits to those affected by the change are not so
obvious or when there are distinct negatives as well as pluses,
explanation and participation—at least of the consultative
variety—are justified and are usually necessary as a means of
minimizing resistance. Of course, there's the other justification
for participation—the valuable advice management receives
from employees. Even in the Work Itself Program, the
girls proved to be far better judges of who the true subject-
matter experts were, and the supervisors reshuffled many of
the initial assignments after consulting with them informally.

DOUGLAS McGREGOR (1906–1964)

Douglas McGregor began his career with a doctorate in experimental psychology from Harvard University, which might have directed him into a traditional psychology department. Instead he moved to MIT which just before World War II established an interdisciplinary department to explore the problems of people at work. He soon attracted a number of students by his original conceptions of authority, supervision, and management. Very early he was concerned with methods of motivating people to improve their performance, which depended upon their being able to satisfy their own personal needs by working toward organizational goals. His famous "Theory Y" was an effort to show that the human potential for effective performance was much greater than most managers assumed and that both people and organizations would thrive in a freer, more flexible and open supervisory climate.

When he was offered the chance to become president of Oberlin College, he accepted the responsibility as an opportunity to put into practice his theories of management. There he pioneered in academic administration with his efforts to get both students and faculty to assume greater responsibility for administrative decisions. He then moved back to his professorship at MIT, where his influence over students and businessmen grew. At MIT he brought together an outstanding group of young psychologists including Alex Bavelas, Harold Leavitt, and Mason Haire, who made outstanding contributions to the leadership field. Further the McGregor group attracted a number of young men who became teachers of management in their own right including Warren Bennis, George Strauss, and Leonard Sayles, whose work is represented in this book.

McGregor's most famous book is *The Human Side of Enterprise* (McGraw-Hill, 1960) where his famous "Theory Y" point of view was first developed. After his untimely death his friends and students put together some of his other work under the title *The Professional Manager* (McGraw-Hill, 1967). Through his teaching and contact with students, and his widespread consulting work and conferences with key executives, his seminal ideas on industrial leadership became an integral part of the management philosophy of literally thousands of executives in this country and abroad. It would be difficult to identify a more influential leader in this field. Interestingly, his influence was in large measure due to his own style of human relations, his giving of himself and his enormous respect for his fellow human beings. Everyone who knew him responded as much to his character as to his persuasive ideas.

Some Strategic Leverage Points*

PHYSIOLOGICAL AND SAFETY NEEDS

Man is a wanting animal—as soon as one of his needs is satisfied, another appears in its place. This process is unending. It continues from birth to death.

Man's needs are organized in a series of levels—a hierarchy of importance. At the lowest level, but preeminent in importance when they are thwarted, are his physiological needs. Man lives by bread alone, when there is no bread. Unless the circumstances are unusual, his needs for love, for status, for recognition are inoperative when his stomach has been empty for a while. But when he eats regularly and adequately, hunger ceases to be an important need. The sated man has hunger only in the sense that a full bottle has emptiness. The same is true of the other physiological needs of man—for rest, exercise, shelter, protection from the elements.

A satisfied need is not a motivator of behavior! This is a fact of profound significance. It is a fact which is regularly ignored in the conventional approach to the management of people. I shall return to it later. For the moment, one example will make my point. Consider your own need for air. Except as you are deprived of it, it has no appreciable motivating effect upon your behavior.

When the physiological needs are reasonably satisfied, needs at the next higher level begin to dominate man's behavior—to motivate him. These are called safety needs.

---

* Reprinted from *Leadership and Motivation,* Douglas McGregor, pp. 8–17, by permission of the M.I.T. Press, Cambridge, Mass. © 1966 by Massachusetts Institute of Technology.

They are needs for protection against danger, threat, deprivation. Some people mistakenly refer to these as needs for security. However, unless man is in a dependent relationship where he fears arbitrary deprivation, he does not demand security. The need is for the "fairest possible break." When he is confident of this, he is more than willing to take risks. But when he feels threatened or dependent, his greatest need is for guarantees, for protection, for security.

The fact needs little emphasis that since every industrial employee is in a dependent relationship, safety needs may assume considerable importance. Arbitrary management actions, behavior which arouses uncertainty with respect to continued employment or which reflects favoritism or discrimination, unpredictable administration of policy—these can be powerful motivators of the safety needs in the employment relationship *at every* level from worker to vice president.

SOCIAL NEEDS

When man's physiological needs are satisfied and he is no longer fearful about his physical welfare, his social needs become important motivators of his behavior—for belonging, for association, for acceptance by his fellows, for giving and receiving friendship and love.

Management knows today of the existence of these needs, but it often assumes quite wrongly that they represent a threat to the organization. Many studies have demonstrated that the tightly knit, cohesive work group may, under proper conditions, be far more effective than an equal number of separate individuals in achieving organizational goals.

Yet management, fearing group hostility to its own objectives, often goes to considerable lengths to control and direct human efforts in ways that are inimical to the natural "groupiness" of human beings. When man's social needs—and perhaps his safety needs, too—are thus thwarted, he behaves in ways which tend to defeat organizational objectives. He becomes resistant, antagonistic, uncooperative. But this behavior is a consequence, not a cause.

EGO NEEDS

Above the social needs—in the sense that they do not become motivators until lower needs are reasonably satisfied—are the needs of greatest significance to management and to man himself. They are the egoistic needs, and they are of two kinds:

1. Those needs that relate to one's self-esteem—needs for self-confidence, for independence, for achievement, for competence, for knowledge.

2. Those needs that relate to one's reputation—needs for status, for recognition, for appreciation, for the deserved respect of one's fellows.

Unlike the lower needs, these are rarely satisfied; man seeks indefinitely for more satisfaction of these needs once they have become important to him. But they do not appear in any significant way until physiological, safety, and social needs are all reasonably satisfied.

The typical industrial organization offers few opportunities for the satisfaction of these egoistic needs to people at lower levels in the hierarchy. The conventional methods of organizing work, particularly in mass production industries, gives little heed to these aspects of human motivation. If the practices of scientific management were deliberately calculated to thwart these needs—which, of course, they are not—they could hardly accomplish this purpose better than they do.

SELF-FULFILLMENT NEEDS

Finally—a capstone, as it were, on the hierarchy of man's needs—there are what we may call the needs for self-fulfillment. These are the needs for realizing one's own potentialities, for continued self-development, for being creative in the broadest sense of that term.

It is clear that the conditions of modern life give only limited opportunity for these relatively weak needs to obtain expression. The deprivation most people experience with respect to other lower-level needs diverts their energies into the struggle to satisfy *those* needs, and the needs for self-fulfillment remain dormant.

Now, briefly, a few general comments about motivation:

We recognize readily enough that a man suffering from a severe dietary deficiency is sick. The deprivation of physiological needs has behavioral consequences. The same is true—although less well recognized—of deprivation of higher-level needs. The man whose needs for safety, association, independence, or status are thwarted is sick just as surely as is he who has rickets. And his sickness will have behavioral consequences. We will be mistaken if we attribute his resultant passivity, his hostility, his refusal to accept responsibility to his inherent "human nature." These forms of behavior are *symptoms* of illness—of deprivation of his social and egoistic needs.

The man whose lower-level needs are satisfied is not motivated to satisfy those needs any longer. For practical purposes they exist no longer. (Remember my point about your need for air.) Management often asks, "Why aren't people more productive? We pay good wages, provide good working conditions, have excellent fringe benefits and steady employment. Yet people do not seem to be willing to put forth more than minimum effort."

The fact that management has provided for these physiological and safety needs has shifted the motivational emphasis to the social and perhaps to the egoistic needs. Unless there are opportunities *at work* to satisfy these higher-level needs, people will be deprived; and their behavior will reflect this deprivation. Under such conditions, if management continues to focus its attention on physiological needs, its efforts are bound to be ineffective.

People *will* make insistent demands for more money under these conditions. It becomes more important than ever to buy the material goods and services which can provide limited satisfaction of the thwarted needs. Although money has only limited value in satisfying many higher-level needs, it can become the focus of interest if it is the *only* means available.

THE CARROT AND STICK APPROACH

The carrot and stick theory of motivation (like Newtonian physical theory) works reasonably well under certain circumstances. The *means* for satisfying man's physiological and (within limits) his safety needs can be provided or withheld by management. Employment itself is such a means, and so are wages, working conditions, and benefits. By these means the individual can be controlled so long as he is struggling for subsistence. Man lives for bread alone when there is no bread.

But the carrot and stick theory does not work at all once man has reached an adequate subsistence level and is motivated primarily by higher needs. Management cannot provide a man with self-respect, or with the respect of his fellows, or with the satisfaction of needs for self-fulfillment. It can create conditions such that he is encouraged and enabled to seek such satisfactions *for* himself, or it can thwart him by failing to create those conditions.

But this creation of conditions is not "control." It is not a good device for directing behavior. And so management finds itself in an odd position. The high standard of living created by our modern technological know-how provides quite adequately for the satisfaction of physiological and safety needs. The only significant exception is where management practices have not created confidence in a "fair break"—and thus where safety needs are thwarted. But by making possible the satisfaction of low-level needs, management has deprived itself of the ability to use as motivators the devices on which conventional theory has taught it to rely—rewards, promises, incentives, or threats and other coercive devices.

NEITHER HARD NOR SOFT

The philosophy of management by direction and control—*regardless of whether it is hard or soft*—is inadequate to motivate because the human needs on which this approach relies are today unimportant motivators of behavior. Direction and control are essentially useless in motivating people whose important needs are social and egoistic. Both the hard and the soft approach fail today because they are simply irrelevant to the situation.

People, deprived of opportunities to satisfy at work the needs which are now important to them, behave exactly as we might predict—with indolence, passivity, resistance to change, lack of responsibility, willingness to follow the demagogue, unreasonable demands for economic benefits. It would seem that we are caught in a web of our own weaving.

In summary, then, of these comments about motivation:

Management by direction and control—whether implemented with the hard, the soft, or the firm but fair approach—fails under today's conditions to provide effective motivation of human effort toward organizational objectives. It fails because direction and control are useless methods of motivating people whose physiological and safety needs are reasonably satisfied and whose social, egoistic, and self-fulfillment needs are predominant.

For these and many other reasons, we require a different theory of the task of managing people based on more adequate assumptions about human nature and human motivation. I am going to be so bold as to suggest the broad dimensions of such a theory. Call it "Theory Y," if you will.

1. Management is responsible for organizing the elements of productive enterprise—money, materials, equipment, people—in the interest of economic ends.
2. People are *not* by nature passive or resistant to organizational needs. They have become so as a result of experience in organizations.
3. The motivation, the potential for development, the capacity for assuming responsibility, the readiness to direct behavior toward organizational goals are all present in people. Management does not put them there. It is a responsibility of management to make it possible for people to recognize and develop these human characteristics for themselves.
4. The essential task of management is to arrange organizational conditions and methods of operation so that people can achieve their own goals *best* by directing *their own* efforts toward organizational objectives.

This is a process primarily of creating opportunities, releasing potential, removing obstacles, encouraging growth, providing guidance. It is what Peter Drucker has called "management by objectives" in contrast to "management by control."

And I hasten to add that it does *not* involve the abdication of management, the absence of leadership, the lowering of standards, or the other characteristics usually associated with the "soft" approach under Theory X. Much on the contrary. It is no more possible to create an organization today which will be a fully effective application of this theory than it was to build an atomic power plant in 1945. There are many fromidable obstacles to overcome.

SOME DIFFICULTIES

The conditions imposed by conventional organization theory and by the approach of scientific management for the past half century have tied men to limited jobs which do not utilize their capabilities, have discouraged the acceptance of responsibility, have encouraged passivity, have eliminated meaning from work. Man's habits, attitudes, expectations—his whole conception of membership in an industrial organization—have been conditioned by his experience under these circumstances. Change in the direction of Theory Y will be slow, and it will require extensive modification of the attitudes of management and workers alike.

People today are accustomed to being directed, manipulated, controlled in industrial organizations and to finding satisfaction for their social, egoistic, and self-fulfillment needs away from the job. This is true of much of management as well as of workers. Genuine "industrial citizenship"—to borrow again a term from Drucker—is a remote and unrealistic idea, the meaning of which has not even been considered by most members of industrial organizations.

Another way of saying this is that Theory X places exclusive reliance upon external control of human behavior, while Theory Y relies heavily on self-control and self-direction. It is worth noting that this difference is the difference between treating people as children and treating them as mature adults. After generations of the former, we cannot expect to shift to the latter overnight.

THE SUPERVISOR AS CHANGE AGENT: REPORTER

What precisely is the role of the supervisor in facilitating the introduction of change? With major innovations, he has little to do with the decision to make the change or with its timing and contents. In nine-tenths of the cases we are familiar with, these decisions are made by top management—the supervisor is cast in a passive role and has no more say than his own subordinates. Small wonder, then, that supervisors sometimes act as accomplices with their employees in resisting a change which, as they see it, threatens their psychic or material well-being.

One point is clear in the argument of whether top management should use participation, at any rate of the consultative kind, whenever it anticipates resistance to a major change. The balance sheet shows substantial debits as well as credits. But the argument operates in spades where the supervisors affected by the change are concerned. They are uniquely qualified to understand the mainsprings of resistance to the change and to make constructive suggestions for minimizing their force. By recognizing that first-line supervision has something to contribute, top management can substantially enhance the status of the line supervisors in their own eyes and those of their men—it can demonstrate to everyone that the line supervisor is not just the man in the middle, but a functioning member of management.

We have been talking about practices that are successful—but unfortunately exceptional. In most cases, the supervisor has the more modest and generally unappreciated role of helping to explain the change to those affected by it and of feeding back their reactions and criticisms to the appropriate management levels.

How skillful a job the supervisor does of explaining the change depends on many factors—his own skills as a communicator, his overall relations with his men, his attitude toward the company and his own superiors. But the most critical element is the assistance, or lack of it, provided by higher management. Has the supervisor been adequately briefed so that he understands the change and all its significant ramifications? Does he know the answers to most, if not all, of the questions his men are likely to ask? Most important, are his answers to their questions as accurate as the facts allow? In other words, has higher management leveled with the supervisor? If the answers to these questions are yes, the supervisor is likely to do at least an adequate job of explaining the change.

The hardest—and most important—part of his job is feedback. Again, the role of higher management is crucial. Key executives must encourage genuine feedback, entertaining grievances and criticisms as well as praise. They must be willing to modify the change wherever the criticisms warrant it. And lastly, they must encourage supervisors to fight for their men wherever they feel their criticisms are justified.

A classic industrial relations study at IBM reinforces this last point. Several years ago, the company introduced engineered work standards for most of its production employees. In some areas of the organization, the workers accepted the standards reasonably well, and in other parts they fought them tooth and nail. What was the reason for the contrasting, responses? It had nothing to do with how carefully the supervisor explained the standards or whether the employees understood them. The relevant factor was having a supervisor who would take the employees' case to higher management when they convinced him that the standard was wrong. Where the supervisor did not function as a representative of his men, they fought him every inch of the way.

Of course, the supervisors who represented their men in pointing out the errors made in implementing the standards program were only doing what every textbook on human relations and supervision says they should do. But look at what actually happened! IBM would rank high in any list of the best-managed companies in the United States. Its supervisory force is probably as carefully selected and as well paid as any comparable group in the country. Yet many IBM supervisors didn't fight for their men when they thought the employees were right—telling higher management that it was wrong apparently was too dangerous. We suspect that higher management's attitude toward criticism is healthier at IBM than in the average company. So the story dramatizes even more sharply the need for top management to consciously create an organizational climate in which negative feedback from any change is not merely tolerated but actively encouraged. Higher management needs to be told the truth, especially when it hurts.

At a deeper level of symbolic meaning, the supervisor is uniquely qualified to report this feedback. He has a greater sensitivity than anyone else in management to the sentiments in his unit that have an emotional significance far more important than their apparent real value. For example, the introduction of some complex new machine may seem to be the logical moment to compel the early retirement of a worker who has just been making the grade on the easier-to-operate equipment with which he is thoroughly familiar. It's possible that the employee himself may not resent the early retirement. But let's assume that the rest of the department will do his resenting for him. His production record isn't noteworthy, but as a man, he represents to his coworkers just about everything that is good about the organization. His forced retirement has ramifications that higher management doesn't suspect and to which the supervisor should draw its attention.

THE SUPERVISOR AS CHANGE AGENT: INITIATOR

We have stressed repeatedly the passive role of the supervisor in the initiation of any important change. However, in the implementation of some changes, the supervisor has a major responsibility for seeing that the technical side of the change works smoothly. This is in contrast to his responsibility for reporting back defects in the technique and strategy of the change to others who are responsible for modifying them.

What do we mean by technical errors versus errors of technique? In the IBM case, the engineered work standards although generally correct, contained some basic faults of design, attributed to the engineers in charge, who had to correct them. These were errors of technique. In contrast, think of what happens whenever a new and complex machine is introduced into the plant or office. Chaos—over the short run or the long. Given a machine that is capable of the job it is supposed to do and a work force capable of operating the equipment, the time is takes his work group to adjust is largely up to the supervisor. If he anticipates the kinds of mistakes his subordinates are likely to make and tells them in advance the most effective way of correcting them, the technical side of the adjustment process will run a fast course.

We know of a case of an inexperienced punch-card reader whose machine jammed frequently. Each time this happened, the unhappy girl went back to the beginning of the series and repeated the entire procedure, when all she needed to do was pull out the faulty card by hand, repunch it, and replace it. A sad chore, easily avoided: The supervisor need merely lay out a detailed recovery procedure for anticipated mistakes and make sure that every operator understood it. Of course no supervisor will anticipate all the possible errors and few employees will master all the techniques for correcting them— no matter. In the league of avoiding errors with new equipment, .600 is a fine batting average.

THE SUPERVISOR AS SOURCE OF RESISTANCE

What happens when the supervisors themselves are the source of resistance? The change will be much more difficult to install if the supervisors continue to oppose it tacitly—the ways of opposition are many, subtle, and frequently very difficult to prove. Besides, to compel supervisory compliance to a change is to threaten the whole structure of good higher management–supervisor relations.

How can top management overcome antagonism? The management boys obviously hold all the authority cards—they can order the supervisors to comply. But they may be reluctant to play their aces.

Most top managements, faced with stiff opposition from their supervisory force, find that it pays to take the long way around the problem—to employ discussion, persuasion, and participation. One classic case, reported by Marrow and French, concerned the resistance of the first-line supervisors in a pajama factory to hiring and training older workers. Research studies, conducted by a psychologist and fully supported by top management, had proved that the older workers on the payroll rated as well as, or better than, the rest of the work force by four critical criteria: man-hour production per worker per day, velocity of learning, attendance, and annual rate of turnover. A representative forelady conceded that her personal experience with the older workers in her group was favorable and agreed with the research findings, but she clung resolutely to the stereotype that older people learn more slowly, are absent more frequently, and quit after a short time. Facts succumbed to prejudice.

Higher management handled the problem by submitting the research findings to first-line supervisors in group discussions. Topics included the origin of the stereotype of older workers and the reasons for accepting it. Insights into the bias slowly developed, and after many sessions the group decided to recommend an experiment in training older workers. With the group's shift in attitude, the new policy finally became a reality.

SUMMARY

You have probably noticed the shift of focus in this chapter away from the supervisor and toward the actions of higher and even top-level management. The shift was a necessary one, dictated by the realities of the power situation. We continue, as we have throughout the book, to be primarily interested in the supervisor and his role in the organization. At the same time, in discussing the supervisor and his relation to any major change, we must recognize that in the process he is not the prime mover and shaper, but more frequently a pawn and a victim. It is decisions made several levels higher in the organization that weigh the heaviest in determining whether or not the change will be accepted and implemented successfully within the supervisor's own unit—including the decisions that will determine whether the supervisor himself spearheads the implementation or heads the resistance.

Not that the supervisor's role is a small one. That he understands the ramifications of the change in the little social system which he heads better than anyone else in management; that he is the management man best qualified to empathize with his work force, to measure the depth of their criticisms and determine what modifications will overcome their reservations; that he knows the importance of fighting for his men when he feels their criticisms are justified, is a partial measure of the supervisor's potential contribution to the change process. In short, he is a resource person with a vital contribution to make before, during, and after the change—if higher management only has the wits to use him properly.

SELECTED REFERENCES

Bennis, W., K. Benne, and R. Chin, *The Planning of Change,* Holt, New York, 1961, chap. 10.

Ford, R., *Motivation Through the Work Itself,* American Management Association, New York, 1969.

Grenier, L., "Patterns of Organizational Change," *Harvard Business Review,* vol. 45, no. 3, May-June 1967, p. 119.

Guest, R., *Organizational Change: The Effect of Successful Leadership,* Irwin, Homewood, Ill., 1962.

Judson, A., *A Manager's Guide to Making Changes,* Wiley, New York, 1966.

Ronken H., and P. Lawrence, *Administering Changes,* Harvard Graduate School of Business Administration, Boston, 1952.

Schon, D., *Technology and Change,* Delacorte, New York, 1967.

THE EDUCATION OF GREG HORNING: JUNE 22

Phil Martello had never told Greg exactly what he'd said to the boys at the union meeting. Actually Greg preferred not to know anyway. But whatever it was, it worked. There were no miracles, but there was less unfinished work, fewer shoddy pieces, and generally less of a mess each morning.

Maybe this was the reason why the crew finally had achieved the goal—110 percent of standard. In the past three weeks they had hit standard once and been 3 or 4 percent over on the other two weeks.

Phillips also hadn't forgotten his promise. He called Greg

to congratulate him and the company picked up the tab for the refreshments, including a big victory cake. Still Phillips, being Phillips, didn't put in an appearance at the party—too busy, he said.

Life always has its problems, though. Phillips told Greg that several customers had complained that some of the parts they got didn't meet quality specifications. Greg was sure that the reason was not because his crew was being careless or going too fast. They had installed the new mold that Creegmore had been testing back in April on all the machines, and Greg was positive that this was responsible for any substandard parts.

After all, it always took time to iron out the bugs in any new process. And that mold required special, careful handling; it was an intricate operation to get the hang of.

Greg had explained all this to Phillips and urged him to understand that it would take time to get everyone completely familiar with the new operation.

"Just wait and see," he'd stated. "In a few months we'll have any quality problems licked."

He hoped he was getting through to Phillips, but then with him you could never tell.

"What we need is an independent check in your department. Everybody is just too buddy-buddy with everyone else. I'll see whether industrial engineering can't come up with a real tough inspector."

Obviously Greg wasn't getting to Phillips. "Look, Steve, you're being unfair as hell. The reason production is up to where it is—and you're happy about it—is the fact that everyone is buddy-buddy with each other, as you put it. We're a team."

"Okay, Greg. You've done a good job. No one denies it. But I'm a production manager, not a cheerleader. And I say you need to tighten up inspections in your department."

"You're the boss, Steve," Greg said wearily, "and I guess you know what you're doing."

Still, it came as a shock to Greg a few days later when he received a memo from Frank Granto in industrial engineering, telling him that the new inspector, Sylvia Gould, would start in the molding department tomorrow and would report directly to Granto on Phillips' orders. She would concentrate on sorting and inspecting and wouldn't do any of the flashing and packing work done by the other women. Furthermore, she was to be paid 75 cents an hour more than Helen and 50 cents an hour more than Jeannette.

"What a bastard," Greg muttered to himself as he read the memo for the third time and let the words sink in. He hadn't realized until now what Phillips had meant by inspection—"a spy in the department, that's what she'll be."

His next impulse was to call Phillips. Greg even got as far as dialing the first two digits of his extension. "No—that won't do any good. I'm too riled up, and Phillips wouldn't listen anyway. My only chance of convincing him is to show that it hasn't worked out. I've got to put up with it for a while."

Greg's only consolation was that the crew resented the move as much as he did. Admittedly, he didn't show any enthusiasm when he announced that a new inspector was starting tomorrow.

Sylvia had arrived after lunch. A large young woman in her late twenties, she had walked slowly and solidly through the shop, resting narrowed looks here and there but speaking to no one.

"I'm Sylvia Gould, Mr. Horning. I believe Mr. Granto told you I'd be here this afternoon." She had stood, filling Greg's doorway, and had spoken without waiting for him to look up.

"Yes, Sylvia, he did," Greg had said, taking her in and doing his best to sound cordial. "Why don't you come in and sit down for a minute so we can get acquainted."

Sylvia stayed in the doorway. "If you don't mind, Mr. Horning, I'd rather get right to work. There's a lot to be done, I'm told."

"Well, of course, Sylvia. If you'd rather that's fine." There would be no gossiping problems with this dame, at any rate!

She had gone out to the shop with Greg following her. The crew responded to Greg's introductions with silence and cold stares. Sylvia had not seemed to notice. She was already examining the equipment and looking over pieces. Her eyes scanned the setup of the room.

Any minute, now, she'll be wanting to move the machines around so they'll be more convenient for her, Greg had thought. Well, I'll let the crew take care of her. They look like they can handle it.

But they hadn't been able to. They ignored her almost completely, but it had no effect. She seemed preoccupied with herself and totally uninterested in mixing. She brought her lunch and read detective stories while she ate. If she took a break at all, she went back to her reading.

Only when she felt compelled to give instructions or criticisms did she have anything to do with the others—and that was where the friction mounted.

She acted as if she were second only to Greg, saying things

like "Don't do that now, Helen. You have to sort those gears
before you start on that batch," or "Henry, those spools that
are coming off the runner now—they're too rough. I told
you—you have to fix your temperature dial a few degrees."
She made it quite clear that she was a supervisor giving
orders.

The reception her "orders" got was a different story: They
were completely ignored or shrugged off with a "You don't
know how we do things here. Ask Greg—he'll tell you."
Or, "If I don't do this batch right now, we'll be behind one
quota for today. Sorry about that."

Suddenly, late one afternoon Sylvia appeared at Greg's
door with a petulant look on her large face and interrupted
what he was doing with—"They plain won't listen to me,
Mr. Horning. I don't know what to do with them."

Greg was going to ask her to come in and sit down, but
she had entered and filled up the wooden armchair before
he had the chance.

"You can't blame them, Sylvia," he said quietly. "They're
used to taking orders from me and I don't give too many.
The crew knows what they're doing and they don't need
many orders."

"That's what you say, Mr. Horning," Sylvia lashed back.
"They make plenty of mistakes and Mr. Granto told me to
speak to them anytime I saw them do anything wrong."

"You're obviously talking to the wrong man," Greg
snapped. "If you're having trouble carrying out Mr. Granto's
orders, you'd better take it up with Mr. Granto."

"That's all you have to say?" asked Sylvia half in anger
and half in disbelief. She apparently thought the mention of
Granto's name would crumble Greg's defenses.

"That's all I have to say. Anything else I feel like saying
I couldn't say to a woman."

The trouble, of course, Greg mused to himself a few
minutes later, was that those were Phillips' orders, not Granto's.
Phillips was bound to hear that he wasn't cooperating with
Sylvia. And then the fat would be in the fire for sure.

QUESTIONS

1. Why do you think Phillips had the new inspector report to
Granto instead of Greg?

2. Is there anything Greg could have done to make Sylvia
acceptable to the group?

3. Should Greg have protested to Phillips as soon as he
heard about Sylvia?

4. What about Greg's handling of Sylvia's complaint? Would
you have handled her differently? Why?

12. The project manager:
*a new breed of supervisor**

Generally managers expect that most of their efforts will be concentrated on getting work done through their subordinates, so we have strongly emphasized leadership skills and the motivation of high performance. And we have pointed out that the supervisor has a parallel requirement for lateral coordination with other managers whose work and activities impinge on his assignments and jurisdiction.

But there are organizations in which nearly all the manager's time is spent with outsiders. He has almost no internal staff to do the work for which he is responsible. These are organizations that use a *project* form of structure. A project makes use of existing resources, most of which are located in existing divisions or departments and are *not* transferred to the control of the project manager. The purpose of this arrangement, which at first blush may seem a bit strange, is an obvious one. The organizations using it expect that their work will keep changing. Projects will come and go. Therefore, employees are given a permanent base with which to identify, regardless of the varying duration of the projects to which they are assigned.

These "home-base" work groups are typically put together on the basis of specialization. Specialists in manufacturing methods, financial matters, electronic circuits, drafting, and what have you—all have their own permanent departments, each of which will have its own supervision. But then projects with fixed lives will be organized, for example, to develop a new product, to design a new television set, to evaluate alternate computers the company might buy. Representatives from various relevant departments will be brought together, under a common project manager, to work through the project. These "specialists" will have two bosses—their project manager and their functional (or discipline, as it is sometimes called) boss.

Thus the project manager in the world of managerial jobs has the distinctive position of being largely dependent on outsiders to get his work done. To be sure, he is given some staff of his own to aid him in dealing with outsiders. For the most part, however, the real work of the project is performed by personnel who do not report to him but who work for line managers in various technical, functional, and

---

* This chapter is adapted from a larger study of management in the U.S. space program. The full study by Leonard Sayles and Margaret Chandler, *Managing Large Systems,* is to be published and copyrighted by Harper and Row Publishers, New York.

professional groups scattered throughout his parent institution
or who often are employed in contractors' companies. (The
traditional and project systems of work organization are
diagrammed in Figure 12-1.)

It would be a mistake to neglect the growing social
significance of project management. Whenever an organization, community, or agency seeks to get a new job done
without changing its basic structure or division of labor (that
is, without creating new jobs and lines of authority), it
typically establishes a project, task force, or working group
to complete this time-bounded activity. This is in sharp
contrast to traditional managerial thought. In scientific management, a job assignment implies the creation of specific
organizational slots under the direct control of a boss who
thus has authority and resources commensurate with the
responsibility given to him. The project and the project manager run in a very different direction: Clear responsibilities
are assigned to get some critical task accomplished, but
most of the resources are left where they are—in other people's departments.

The project manager thus has a very different supervisory
challenge: getting work done through outsiders. As we shall
see, this requires rather unique skills and a theory of management that differs from traditional supervision. The emphasis is on *monitoring* and *influencing decisions,* not order
giving and decision making in the usual meaning of those
terms. The project manager has overwhelmingly more responsibility than he has authority. The groups and employees
he will be dealing with not only work for other departments
and functions which have their primary loyalties, but they
have performance standards, built up over many years, that

Traditional Organization			Project Organization	
			Project Office	
Task A	Task B		Project A	Project B
Supervisor A	Supervisor B	Technical Line Department	Project Manager A	Project Manager B
∦∦∦∦	∦∦∦∦	X Supervisor X Workers	✓	
		Y Supervisor Y Workers		✓
A Workers	B Workers	Z Supervisor Z Workers	✓	✓

A uses X's workers and Z's workers.

B uses Y's workers and Z's workers.

*Figure 12-1 Comparison of traditional and project-
oriented organizations*

are consistent with these affiliations although perhaps inconsistent with the special needs of the limited-life project. The
project manager has the job of finding ways of correlating
the outsider's standards of performance and the needs of
the project in terms of cost, schedule, and performance
standards.

PROJECT INCEPTION

Most projects begin when upper management creates the
project office, assigns the project manager, and gives him a
budget which allows him to purchase "contributions" from
outside departments. Even with this budget, the project
manager may still have to woo and win reluctant line managers who will question whether they should assign their
better people or resources to the project, particularly if there
are other project managers shopping for these human and
technical resources and the line manager is skeptical about
the feasibility and prestige of this specific project. One such
manager explained:

I tried to keep most of our people off the X project even
though it was reasonably well funded. I knew it was the kind
of project that headquarters could cut off tomorrow and
then we would have all those disappointed engineers to
reassign who had just gotten all excited about the work
and then they have to do something else. This creates
serious morale problems and I try to get my people projects
that have a real chance of going down to the wire.

The critical skills for project inception can best be viewed
when upper management is either undecided or ambiguous
about a project or is allowing lower levels of management
to initiate some new projects. Under these circumstances,
the development and success of projects that will be funded
and that "will fly" depend upon the selling ability of the
would-be project managers. The men who are successful in
this entrepreneurial function—really in starting a new business, albeit with a short life expectancy—are those who can
generate enthusiasm and confidence in other managers who
can give the new project political and economic support.
Here is how one successful project manager described the
start-up function.

I had gotten the green light from my boss to try to get

support for a special computer project which would develop a technique for letting our large computer handle a
great deal of the test work we now do manually. First I
got every department head or his deputy to come to a
meeting. There my function was to get everyone to agree
first, that we had a problem with our current test procedures, and secondly on what kind of procedure would
cope with these problems. I then tried to generate enthusiasm for the solution: this computerization project.
This meant showing people that they would be in heaven
if we could pull it off and that everyone would benefit.
Of course, I wasn't above a little logrolling either, indicating
I would back them on some things they needed. I also
tried to play up the losses for those who stayed out. You
find after a while, when you keep talking something like
this up, the enthusiasm can become contagious, and
they'll convince one another.

Often the charismatic entrepreneurs who get new projects
off the ground resemble evangelists. They have so much
faith in their special project, its workability, and its long-run
value that they can convince doubting Thomases with all the
vigor of the good pitchmen of old. It is not unusual to
find that such zealots are hard on subordinates. They are
loath to delegate, keep making all the technical decisions
themselves, perhaps partially because, in the early stages, they
are the only ones who see the big picture, the grand design
or conception.

But such single-minded convictions—such strong desires
to clutch everything tightly to themselves—are inconsistent
with the needs of running an established and funded project.
It is the special managerial skill—the ability to push a project
through outside technical support and line departments—
that is our primary interest in this chapter. This skill and related ones come into play after the promoter or major organizational supporter has won the battle of getting the project
accepted. (At that point the originator may have trouble
adjusting as he sees his baby growing larger and being reared
by strange hands.)

KEEPING TIME BEHAVIORALLY

Although it is rarely stated this way, the program or project
manager is primarily dealing with rates or amounts (of time)
and organization process, not technical variables. He cannot
easily second-guess the technical prowess of his line-support

groups. Obviously, he and his staff often do or try to, but in the long run he is dependent upon both the good will and the technical judgment of the outside groups. This means, of course, that he must respect their professional expertise.

What he can and must do, however, is control the organizational participation—as distinct from the technical contribution—of the line or functional people. This means making sure that they cooperate in two very important ways:

1. They should make the right decisions at the right time. (For example, the line may want to study some problem extensively in order to arrive at an optimal solution, but the delay in making the decision may be much more costly than any increase in return generated by the improved decision. Of course, the opposite may be true. The program manager may want to encourage longer study of some issue that has profound "downstream" significance beyond the particular line manager's field of vision.)

2. They should tackle problems in the right sequence and the right time. (The line manager may be willing to tolerate, a certain problem buildup—e.g. in schedule delay or labor relations, that might be disastrous to the program. The program manager will pressure him to respond adequately to these "out-of-limit" situations and give them a priority based on program needs—even though such a step may be inconsistent with the management style or managerial appraisal of the line manager.)

It is this balancing act, resulting in technical decisions which reflect organizational considerations, that requires most of the program manager's time and influence. A nice example is furnished by one small aspect of a large area project.

On a construction job, fire-prevention equipment was being installed and the safety and equipment people were intending to use their usual criterion in design and installation. Traditionally, this was that every effort must be made to design a system which is *sure* to function in an emergency. From the project-management point of view, in this particular location, it was more important that the prime criterion for design and installation be that the system *not* function unless there is an emergency. (It may be noted that a subtle difference in philosophy has a major influence on such technical considerations as redundancy in circuits.)

The project manager acts in the role of a *marginalist*. He widens or narrows limits, speeds up or slows down actions, increases the emphasis on some activities and decreases it on others. He can't make very many of the decisions himself—both because of time and because he is not empowered to do so. That power resides in the line and functional groups, in most cases. Further, he wouldn't want to make the major decisions, since he usually can't know as much about the problem as someone closer to the work level. He chiefly wants to be sure that the decision is made at the proper time, within the proper framework of knowledge and concern, and by the proper people.

But the project manager must often seek to counter this inherent conservatism, particularly when one manager's "playing it safe" increases the risk for the total effort. A manager may wish to build only familiar hardware, use only well-known components or traditional standards, or "gold-plate" his contribution, any one of which approaches, in terms of time, dollars, or performance, may be destructive to the specific project at hand.

The project manager functions as a bandleader who pulls together his players, each a specialist with his score and his own internal rhythm. Under the leader's direction, they all respond to the same beat. To get people to adhere to his operational rhythm, the manager makes them see the consequences of their actions. In bringing the work of the various groups to his centralized beat, he may also seek to change their interplay. His project may require, for example, that group A now report to boss B instead of boss A, that group A be consulted earlier or more frequently, or that group A give its consent before x, y, and z are done. Such shifts in organizational relationships change the character of the response that any group will give to emerging problems and directions.

CONTRAST WITH TRADITIONAL MANAGEMENT

Professional employees and their managers are supposed to be left alone to sink or swim—as long as they appear to be motivated to meet their self-determined (in part) objectives. But the project manager must constantly try to penetrate the organizations upon whom he is dependent but whom he does not directly supervise. He must often get into the minutiae of decision processes to judge whether the desired system is being maintained (for example, whether adequate weight is being given to x factor, adequate consultation is taken with A group, the sign-offs are procured promptly from B group, or the appropriate appeal channels and conflict-resolution procedures are being used when stalemates appear). Time is of the essence and constant *monitoring* is the rule. The project manager must know *whom to contact, when,* and *how*.

If you watch one of these managers, you see him engaged in a ceaseless round of give and take. He appears to be trying, by the weight of various influence techniques, to counter the frictional forces and fatal drift in the human systems—forces that lead workers to use less than their full capabilities.

What we learn by watching project managers is that words don't mean what they seem to mean, that agreements can easily be misunderstood or ambiguous, that no agreement ever covers all the unanticipated contingencies, that temptations arise to lure committed people to take chances which they would not risk under less pressure or with less provocation—and many other factors that, if ignored, can sabotage the best-laid plans.

Bargaining

Project managers prefer to spend a great deal of time negotiating. In part this is due to the continuing appearance of unanticipated problems or opportunities. "What will it cost us to avoid this or take advantage of that?" the manager may ask, when dealing with a contractor. Part is due to inevitable differences in judgment. "I don't care what the tests show, I am sure we can get by with the extra five pounds, or at least that's what I am going to try to get approved." There are the individual differences in objectives. A subcontractor wants to use a manufacturing method in which he has an interest, but the prime contractor is fearful that this variation may upset an already tight schedule.

In addition, there are the foibles of organizational life. Estimates, specifications, and requests tend to have "fat" in them, or everyone believes so because he knows he is going to get less than he asked for.

Managers know there often are not precise, rational answers to most questions whatever their source, but that the answers are a product of flexible give and take.

WARREN G. BENNIS (1925–   )

Bennis is the swinger among our thinkers. His preoccupation is with the future—with a future that he sees as radically different from the past, and a future that he hurries to embrace.

But first, a few words about the past of Warren Bennis. He became interested in group dynamics as a student at Antioch when Douglas McGregor was president, received his Ph.D. in psychology from MIT, and has been student, colleague, disciple of McGregor—he co-edited his posthumous book, *The Professional Manager*—and has more claims than anyone to be regarded as his successor. In 1967 Bennis left the security of his MIT professorship to go where the action is and test out some of his theories of organizational change and growth: he became academic vice president of the State University of New York at Buffalo. Action he has seen aplenty and in public, at least, he has expressed no regrets over his decision.

His book, *The Temporary Society,* from which we made our selection, represents perhaps a midpoint in the development of Bennis' ideas toward his current position, which he calls "organic populism."

Just the sound of it has a radical ring. But what is organic populism? Or to ask a more precise question, what does organic populism seem to mean to Bennis? Organic populism is a vew of society in which two key words are *temporary* and *small:* Technology is forcing organizations of every kind and at every level to adapt at a progressively faster rate and in the long run only small organizations will demonstrate sufficient adaptability to survive. Bennis stakes his hopes for the future on the desirability and the necessity "for building a new generation of small institutions centered on the persons who develop them." The important work to be done in tomorrow's society will be more complex and technical than ever before; because of this complexity technically it can be accomplished successfully, if at all, by "task forces organized around problems to be solved by groups of relative strangers with diverse professional skills."

All of which brings us to the third key word in organic populism, *participation.* Participation in the decision-making process, which the new left sees as a natural right, Bennis views as a functional necessity. In a time of complexity and chronic change, society can't afford to lose the contribution of anyone with competence to the decision-making process. The very power of leaders in the future will arise from their ability to inspire the participation of others in decision making.

Radical Bennis's views certainly are. Correct? Obviously, only the future can answer the question. As a description of an evolving society, they impress these authors at least as a blend of shrewd observation with passionate wishful thinking. Take the matter of organic populism on the campus. An administrator committed to whittling down his own power is an interesting and sympathetic spectacle as Bennis is with his endorsement of student pressure for more participation.

The pressures for participation are real and doubtless must be accommodated. But where do we draw the line with student participation? Representation on joint faculty-student committees? The power to discipline their peers? A degree of control over the courses they take and the selection of the professors who teach them? Organic populism with its dual and conflicting bias towards competence and democracy offers few viable clues.

On the other hand, Dr. Bennis is still relatively youthful, energetic, and committed. There undoubtedly will be more books with more and possibly different answers. At present, we suggest the following books: With Edgar Schein, *Personal and Organizational Change* (John Wiley, New York, 1965); *Changing Organizations* (McGraw-Hill, New York, 1966); with Philip Slater, *The Temporary Society* (Harper and Row, New York, 1968).

Beyond Bureaucracy*

The increased level of education and mobility will change the values we place on work. People will be more intellectually committed to their jobs and will probably require more involvement, participation, and autonomy.

Also, people will be more "other-oriented," taking cues for their norms and values from their immediate environment rather than tradition.

* Printed by permission from Warren G. Bennis, and Philip E. Slater, *The Temporary Society*, Harper & Row, New York, 1968, pp. 72–75.

TASKS AND GOALS

The tasks of the organization will be more technical, complicated, and unprogrammed. They will rely on intellect instead of muscle. And they will be too complicated for one person to comprehend, to say nothing of control. Essentially, they will call for the collaboration of specialists in a project or a team form of organization.

There will be a complication of goals. Business will increasingly concern itself with its adaptive or innovative-creative capacity. In addition, supragoals will have to be articulated, goals that shape and provide the foundation for the goal structure. For example, one might be a system for detecting new and changing goals; another could be a system for deciding priorities among goals.

Finally, there will be more conflict and contradiction among diverse standards for organizational effectiveness. This is because professionals tend to identify more with the goals of their profession than with those of their immediate employer. University professors can be used as a case in point. Their inside work may be a conflict between teaching and research, while more of their income is derived from outside sources such as foundations and consultant work. They tend to be poor company men because they divide their loyalty between their professional values and organizational goals.

ORGANIZATION

The social structure of organizations of the future will have some unique characteristics. The key word will be "temporary." There will be adaptive, rapidly changing *temporary* systems. These will be task forces organized around problems to be solved by groups of relative strangers with diverse professional skills. The group will be arranged on an organic rather than mechanical model; it will evolve in response to a problem rather than to programmed role expectations. The executive thus becomes coordinator or "linking pin" between various task forces. He must be a man who can speak the polyglot jargon of research, with skills to relay information and to mediate between groups. People will be evaluated not according to rank but according to skill and professional training. Organizational charts will consist of project groups rather than stratified functional groups. (This trend is already visible in the aerospace and construction industries, as well as many professional and consulting firms.)

Adaptive, problem-solving, temporary systems of diverse specialists, linked together by coordinating and task-evaluating executive specialists in an organic flux—this is the organization form that will gradually replace bureaucracy as we know it. As no catchy phrase comes to mind, I call these new-style organizations "*adaptive* structures." Organizational arrangements of this sort may not only reduce the intergroup conflicts mentioned earlier; they may also induce honest-to-goodness creative collaboration.

MOTIVATION

Adaptive organizations should increase motivation and thereby effectiveness, because they create conditions under which the individual can gain increased satisfaction with the task itself. Thus, there should be a harmony between the educated individual's need for tasks that are meaning-ful, satisfying, and creative *and* an adaptive organizational structure.

Accompanying the increased integration between in-dividual and organizational goals, will be new modes of relating and changing commitments to work groups. Most of the research on the individual's relationship to his peer group at work indicates the significance of the work group on performance and morale. The work group creates and reinforces norms and standards, from the appropriate number of units produced to the appropriate amount of interaction and intimacy. The significance of the work group for the communication, control, and regulation of behavior cannot be overestimated. But in the new adaptive organizations I am talking about, work groups will be temporary systems, which means that people will have to learn to develop quick and intense relationships on the job and learn to bear the absence of more enduring work relationships. Thus we should expect to experience a con-centration of emotional energy in forming relationships quickly and intensely and then a dissolution and rapid relo-cation of personal attachments. . . . From an organizational point of view we can expect that more time and energy will have to be spent on continual rediscovery of the appropri-ate mix of people, competencies, and tasks within an am-biguous and unstructured existence.

In many ways, project managers are more like coaches than supervisors: They exhort, urge, cajole, browbeat, and pressure. By their very presence—their personal intervention and force of personality, their talking and pleading and demanding, they try to counteract the various frictions that would slow down or misdirect the activities of other groups, particularly the primary contractors and functional groups.

As in life itself, complex projects produce a variety of oppressive frustrations as well as destructive temptations. When parts shortages appear or facilities are not available or parallel activities (under others' control) are slowed down, everyone tends to relax, to wait, to take a somewhat easier way out. Like an ever present conscience, an effective project manager keeps urging the key people on whom the work depends to keep fighting a recalcitrant Mother Nature, to keep pushing against time, to pretend that everyone else will be on time, to seek equally satisfactory alternatives when the original plans are no longer feasible.

The pressuring includes keeping people from falling back to old, familiar routines and ways of doing business. The project often requires nonstandardized approaches that may be inconsistent with habitual patterns and methods for any particular organization or group. "We never do it this way" has to be a call to arms for the project manager. The tempo of work in a university laboratory and an industrial fabrication shop starts out miles apart. The project manager has the job of getting these incompatible habitual patterns into more congruent form. Sometimes, his problem is that the functional group wants to "gold-plate" something, to overprotect or overtest. Or the opposite may be the case: the group is taking shortcuts, conducting inadequate tests.

Confrontations and Challenges

One of the techniques most often used in deterring what we might call backsliding is deceptively simple and direct. The project manager confronts and challenges, raising questions like these:

What makes you think that those bearings are comparable to the ones we discussed last week?

What is your evidence that this redesign is likely to solve the problem? Prove it to me.

Have you checked all the sources of stray magnetism?

What have you done to correct the malfunctioning that
showed up on the special test we agreed upon?

How can you expect to catch up on the lost time when
you haven't authorized overtime and there is no additional
staffing?

The project staff is in the position of trying to get those with
whom it works to justify their present course of actions,
decisions, and choices. It is one thing to do something which
seems reasonable to yourself under the circumstances—it is
another to try to prove or rationalize your act to an inquir-
ing, reasonably well-informed, and potentially critical ob-
server-interested person.

The challenge is a process used by the project manager to
force people to face up to unpleasant realities. It is a
technique of giving both constant reminders and the stimulus
of a friendly critic who will demand answers to a somewhat
unpredictable set of potentially embarrassing questions. Telephone calls, visits, and regular meetings are used for the
purpose.

The confrontation process also visibly demonstrates and
reminds people that the project manager is vitally interested,
alert, and aware that everything is open to question. This is
consistent with the unusual potential for problems inherent in
complex endeavors where hundreds, if not thousands, of
variables interact and where problems are inevitable, although you can never be sure where and how they will
appear.

Intervention and Participation

Many of the behavior patterns we have been describing have
both before-the-fact and after-the-fact qualities. The project
manager is seeking to avoid problems or to solve problems.
And he also plays a more immediate, real-time role.

In working to maintain a forward momentum, the manager
attempts to avoid stalemates, polarization of issues, and
entrenchment of vested interests. Fluidity and movement, accommodation, solving problems rather than assessing blame—
all these are part of the distinctive point of view of program
management.

To demonstrate his concern as well as to get a feel for
what is happening and the many facets that cannot be
documented or transmitted in either verbal or written reports,

the project manager appears on the scene. During crucial tests, for example, many managers want to be present to observe as much as possible themselves.

The project manager also has the job of keeping things moving by maintaining a consensus, jelling decisions, and resolving holdups when those immediately involved are unwilling or unable to do so. In this regard, he will often be faced with conflicting technical judgments. It is difficult to decide who among a group of conscientious experts is correct. While a manager may feel obliged to suffer through this kind of choice, it is not realistic under most circumstances to try to prove who is right.

It's more important that a decision be reached so that forward momentum can be resumed. Insecure, risk-fearing managers fret and fume so long over such decisions that, regardless of who is right, it is too late to avoid schedule delays. First and foremost, then, the manager wants to force a choice when indecision may delay his work. His own dispassionate position, somewhat removed from the battle-front, may aid this resolution—as do his prestige and force of personality. Furthermore, his intervention is also a means of gaining familiarity, a feel for the real situation, and of keeping in touch with technical realities.

Indirection versus Orders

Thus, in contrast to direct supervision, there is comparatively little ordering in the relationship between the project manager and the outside groups and individuals he seeks to influence. There are many reasons for this, aside from the fact that they are not immediate subordinates.

For one thing, orders may raise legalistic questions like "Is this a change in our original commitment? Who is to pay for the change?" They also encourage a similar rigidity based on an opposite reaction: "No, we can't do it; this is our only choice under the present circumstances."

Further, the project manager often lacks the information needed to give a specific order. He is never as close to the situation as the individual immediately responsible, and must therefore trust the specialist. On the other hand, he may have broader knowledge than the technical expert has (for example, concerning other parts of the system or external pressures). By sharing this knowledge, the manager can often help the specialist do a better job.

CAPABILITY FOR QUICK RESPONSE

The heart of both intervention and decision making is quickness of response—the focusing of collective energies on the solution of a very critical problem. Given the many unanticipated barriers to working through original plans, the interdependencies (which multiply the impact of any holdup) and the ever-present schedule problems of fighting time, the manager must be capable of rapid adaptation to changed circumstances. Sometimes rules must be violated and established procedures ignored.

In fact, many effective managers insist that they can't wait for a problem to make itself known officially. Anticipating trouble requires very close contact—keeping in touch with the thinking and the planned next moves of the key participants. Daily or twice daily calls, weekly visits, and bimonthly meetings are therefore par for the course.

One penalty for slow response is that a good many situations allow for corrective action only during a brief "window," in space jargon. Quick action is the essence of the problem—to avoid a costly mistake, a lost customer or opportunity.

In these circumstances, the project manager and his associates talk to people face to face and on the telephone almost every minute, checking out the new requirements and exploring the feasibility of changed circuitry, access routes to enclosed equipment, test improvisations, and the rest. Decisions require enormous quantities of interaction!

Waiting

Perhaps the hardest thing the manager must often do is *nothing.* Seeing a potentially upsetting problem and not attempting to rearrange its components so that it is attacked differently or more massively takes great restraint.

An experienced, astute manager knows when to let the other person have the time to work through the difficulty and when it is necessary to intervene, urge reinforcements, insist on a different approach, and the like. Not only is moving in too early costly and disrupting—it also wastes the distinctive capacities of the contractor or support group handling the problem.

Staying out for an appropriate time also provides perspective which may be lost when one becomes personally involved in the emotional effort of struggling to solve recalcitrant problems. Surely many of the truly costly mistakes in any large program are the result of overlooking rather obvious trends.

In a sense, the project manager wants to play both sides of the street, to be an outsider as well as an insider, a dispassionate observer as well as an accepted member of the team.

Providing Assistance

The project manager is not just an impersonal goad, a timing mechanism, a conductor. He also has a set of comparatively direct contacts which can balance off his more stressful relationships, particularly from the point of view of those being pressured. Therefore he can aid them by providing priority access to scarce external resources (in effect, acting as an expediter), or at least to resources beyond the organizational reach of the line or functional manager. He can serve as an "honest broker," bringing together conflicting groups of factions.

USE OF MEETINGS

Some meetings are useful for the same reason that managers prefer to confront subordinates directly rather than by mail or telephone. Where groups are interdependent and risks are substantial, management hopes that face-to-face questioning will dispel doubts and answer nagging worries such as the question of whether the other fellow is working in a way that will wreak havoc on one's own budget, schedule, or performance.

Clearly, even among like-minded professionals who share a common language and respect for technical approaches, the data are not always self-evident. There will always be innumerable ambiguities and questions that cannot be answered definitively except in confrontations that impart trust and confidence. The in-person contact is also useful to encourage the conviction that highly responsible people have left no stone unturned in trying to come up with the best answers available.

Meetings also impart a sense of personal participation, of seeing and comprehending with your own senses without having to use intermediary people or paper or data. Moreover, meetings help to dispel the doubt that arises in any hierarchical system where artificial barriers separate people— that information or unpleasant facts are being kept from you.

Thus various techniques involving direct confrontation are useful in imparting reassurance and dispelling fears that a disagreeable surprise may come tomorrow although everything looks rosy today. In addition, there is the requirement to show through overt action that all groups are first-class citizens. Being personally involved and allowed to hear firsthand progress reports, status reviews, and debates concerning alternate approaches demonstrates that one is an accepted member of the team. On the opposite side, exclusion from these get-togethers communicates second-class membership: "They only call on us when there are troubles, when we've done something wrong, or when they're looking for a scapegoat."

Technical Coordination

Of course the most important and frequent use of meetings is to provide technical coordination, to interrelate the work of interdependent groups and individuals. Such meetings review progress and plans and try to evolve solutions to actual or foreseeable problems. Plans for future activities and problem solution, when handled successfully, take the following operational form:

What is needed, is wrong, or is foreseen. ("We are going to require additional backup teleprinting equipment.")
Why this is needed for technical or organizational purposes. ("If we should experience an equipment failure, it could abort the mission and we have had one or two problems from this already.")
Who is responsible for taking what actions, utilizing what decision-making criteria with *whom, when,* and *where.* (Through group discussion, an implementing procedure is worked out, and the persons responsible for specific actions are explicitly named.)
Validation is planned and arrangements are made for the organizational process by which the completion and effectiveness of the program can be validated and for the time and method for reporting this validation back to those who need to know. ("We'll put this down as an action item, to be reported back at our next meeting by Smith and Brown, who have agreed to meet within seventy-two hours to check out the new equipment.")

At these meetings, individuals find ways of expressing both

their concern and anxiety, and such open expressions fulfill a very important function. Thus, one hears comments like "I want to reemphasize our very real concern that the existing reinforcing may be inadequate," or "While I know you are doing all you can to speed things up, we want to underline how important an earlier delivery date would be to our schedule problems." Many times, the same underlying problem is dealt with by multiple questions that endeavor to ensure that things really are going well.

CONCLUSION

There is a maxim of scientific management: Authority ought to equal responsibility. To the manager, this means that he deserves to have under his direct control all the resources he is likely to need to fulfill the responsibilities he has been assigned. Any manager may become uncomfortable and just plain worried when he feels that he doesn't have enough authority to get his job done but must depend upon outsiders.

Yet, as we saw in Chapter 9, the modern organization creates a number of specialists whose activities and resources impinge on the manager. Sometimes these groups control scarce services (like repairs, typing, or computational facilities). Sometimes they control scarce "permissions" (like authorization for a raise for a key employee). But the result is the same: The manager doesn't control everything he needs to get his work done. He must depend upon outsiders.

In project management, we see the most extreme form or extension of this new development. Here authority isn't even close to responsibility since almost all the resources are located in other people's departments. The manager depends upon employees of other managers to do nearly all his work. To make matters worse, many of these employees are simultaneously working for other managers, and of course they are being supervised by another boss.

A project manager must therefore find a variety of new techniques, different from the order giving, communications, discipline, group relationships, and other skills we have described in previous chapters. These are the techniques of influencing and persuading others and effective use of meetings.

Further, these other employees have different standards as to what constitutes good work because of their profes-

sional training and identifications. They have different conceptions of cost and schedules, too.

Thus the project manager's function is not to impose his
own knowledge on theirs, but rather to establish clear-cut
limits on their discretion. He seeks to define the constraints
which will influence their decision making in the desirable
direction.

I keep telling them that we can't afford the best in this
project but time is of the essence. We just need a fan
that will work for a short period of time where there is
extreme heat. It only has to last forty-eight hours, not a
lifetime. They would love to design a really great new
fan, but they know now they can't.

After constraints are established, he works to keep the
project from stagnating or getting hung up on problems.
Every project, because by definition it represents a job that's
never been done before, is going to meet unanticipated
problems. Some can readily be solved. Others may take much
more time or money than anyone anticipated. It's up to the
project manager to find ways of spotting these holdups, to
help work out procedures which will quicken the development
of a solution, and to keep people from slowing down because they think the schedule will never be met anyway.

These are surely the most difficult and challenging kinds
of managerial assignments because the manager can't fall
back on power and authority. He uses a variety of fast-paced
techniques to confront, to persuade, to cajole, and to pressure
people to keep their eyes on the critical elements and to
ignore the noncritical elements. Thus he is a catalyst, a
goad, a kind of coxswain—or, as we have said, a bandleader—
who keeps the system moving.

SELECTED REFERENCES

Bester, A., *The Life and Death of a Satellite,* Little, Brown,
Boston, 1966.

Miles, M., "On Temporary Systems," in *Innovation in
Education,* M. Miles (ed.), Teachers College Press, New York,
1964.

Steiner, G., and W. Ryan, *Industrial Project Management,*
Macmillan, New York, 1968.

THE EDUCATION OF GREG HORNING: JUNE 30

Given the circumstances, production had not fallen off as much as Greg had expected—only 5 percent. The crew resented Sylvia, but they knew that he felt at least as bad about her as they did and they had faith that he would get rid of her in time.

Still, it did not surprise Greg when Phillips called him up to his office. His anger had built up to the point that he welcomed a confrontation. He had a lot to say to the production manager and he was going to say it—even if it meant his job.

The surprise came when Greg got upstairs.

"Greg—good to see you! Come on in! Sit down!" It was the most cordial greeting Greg could remember Phillips giving him.

He waited for Phillips to reprimand him for the production drop. He waited for questions about Sylvia Gould and he waited for his opportunity to sound off to Phillips and then get fired.

Instead, Phillips began telling him about plans for a new tape spool that the company was thinking of developing. It would take a new plastics mix and the formula would have to be worked out; the larger machines in Greg's shop would have to be retooled to include at least two new operations; a new packaging procedure would have to be worked out because the spools had to be individually wrapped.

It sounded pretty exciting, but he couldn't understand what a close-mouthed man like Phillips was going on like this to him for.

"It sounds exicting, Steve," he said, uncertainly, "but what's it got to do with me?"

"What do you mean, Greg? What do you think I'm telling you all this for? It's yours. I want you to take it over and run it for us."

"But what about my department?" Greg asked.

"Oh, don't worry about it, Greg. You've got things under control there, now it practically runs itself. Besides, you've got that Gould girl in there now. She's pretty competent, isn't she? Is she working out all right?" He did not give Greg time to answer before he went on. "I'm sure it'll all work out. You'll still be in charge of your department and keep your eye on things. But this will be your primary concern. You'll be the project manager. I'll get you a secretary, if you need one, and besides your own crew, you can have access to anyone in any department. We've got a big budget for this, so you don't have to worry about money. You can have a completely free hand. What do you say?"

The offer naturally appealed to Greg: It meant recognition, a big budget, a bigger, more challenging job. And last but maybe not least it meant an extra $1,500 a year right from the start.

"Fine, Greg. You've made the right decision, let me tell you. It'll be damned exciting. Go down to see Frank, now, and arrange for a secretary. We'll work out the space allocation next week. Here are some of the background reports. Read them over. Get filled in, then we'll talk some more. We'll be working on this together." Phillips thrust a pile of folders into Greg's arms and sent him on his way.

As he made his way back to the shop, Greg was not so sure he had made the right decision. First the prospect of working even more closely with this difficult man dampered his enthusiasm.

Then he thought about the project itself. He'd had a little contact with that sort of thing, working part-time, when he'd been in school. It was no bed of roses. You were outside every department—even your own—you had no authority to get things done, just wheedling and wheeling and dealing. It meant a hell of a lot of responsibility but damned little power. Everything depended on Phillips' willingness to go to bat for you. Then, if the project didn't work out, you were left holding the bag.

And what about the crew? They'd stayed loyal to him; in spite of the Sylvia, they'd pushed hard to keep production up. Greg was sure they didn't want to let him down. Now would they think he was letting them down?

"Oh, Greg. There you are. I've been looking for you." It was Creegmore coming over to get him as he returned to the shop. "Could you come over here a minute? I'd like to show you something."

"Sure, Henry. What is it?"

"Well, it's this operation we do on this spool. I was thinking, if we skipped this one step, see . . ."

"That's interesting, Henry," Greg said, leaning over his machine to look. "As a matter of fact, it might fit in with this new project we're going to be working on."

"What project's that, Greg?"

"Come into the office, Henry. I'll tell you about it. I think you'll be interested."

Yes, it was worth a try, Greg thought. If the project was as good as it sounded, it would be worth it. He'd learn a lot. And, if he could get the crew involved maybe it wouldn't be so hard after all to keep in close touch with them.

He'd do his best and ... well, he'd just have to wait and see.

QUESTIONS

1. Try to predict some of the problems that will arise in Greg's department when the maintenance people start doing some retooling at the same time his employees are expected to turn out normal production.

2. Describe how Greg can handle maintenance and his people to minimize the conflict over the timing of any new installations.

3. Assuming there is a conflict with shipping over Greg's people moving into their jurisdiction by doing wrapping, how should he handle this?

4. What skills as a project manager will Greg need that he hasn't used before?

DEFINING JOB CHARACTERISTICS

*While job analyses are conducted by personnel adminis-
tration specialists in larger organizations, every manager
ought to be able to define the requirements of each job
he supervises in order to facilitate training new employees, evaluating their performance, and providing
them with assistance.*

JOB TITLE

(Remember many titles are not descriptive of the real duties
required)

ORGANIZATIONAL LEVEL

(Who does employee report to and salary range)

PERFORMANCE REQUIREMENTS AND SKILL REQUIREMENTS

Task and equipment responsibilities

a. Work-load standards
b. Maintenance standards

Analytical skills and judgment required
Manual or physical skills required; dexterity, accuracy
How job is to be performed:

a. Criteria for satisfactory work—quality standards
b. Criteria for requesting assistance or for identifying
critical emergencies and whom to call for what
c. Working relationships required with other employees in the
work group or the flow of work
d. How much opportunity to vary pace

WORKING CONDITIONS

(Any unusual physical requirements, degree of arduousness,
environmental conditions such as physical exertion, unpleasant
humidity, or temperature)

PROMOTIONAL OPPORTUNITIES

(Job ladders or career lines available to those satisfactory in
performing this job)

QUALIFICATION PERIOD

(Length of probationary period and/or length of training or
apprenticeship period required to become fully qualified on
the job)

DEFINING EMPLOYEE CHARACTERISTICS

On the basis of the previous job analysis, the supervisor ought to seek to make explicit the selection criteria he would utilize when a job opening occurs. Keep in mind the temptation to add unnecessary or excessively high requirements which will tend to limit the number of available candidates.

EDUCATIONAL REQUIREMENTS

School level (e.g., high school diploma)
Special course requirements (e.g., algebra, manual drawing)

EXPERIENCE REQUIREMENTS

a. Jobs or tasks must have demonstrated competence in performing (e.g., at least eight months of experience as switchboard operator)
b. Familiarity and experience with equipment (e.g., use of addressograph machine)

SPECIAL PERSONALITY REQUIREMENTS

(e.g., job requires handling complaints from the general public and coping with stressful interpersonal situations)

SPECIAL PHYSICAL AND HEALTH REQUIREMENTS

EMPLOYEE EVALUATION FORM

A record such as this for each subordinate should facilitate such decisions as the following: Who should receive merit salary increases? is qualified for promotion? should be considered for discharge? needs more training or special attention? Also these semi-annual reviews should be compared with initial impression of new employee in order to evaluate the usefulness of selection criterion that are being utilized.

	Almost Always	2/3 of Time	Half of the time	1/3 of the time	Never or Rarely	Examples (with date) and Comments
Does the employee follow instructions?						
Are habits of regularity and punctuality shown?						
Is assigned work completed on schedule?						
Is quality maintained?						
Are relationships with other employees good including: a. those in work group						

EMPLOYEE EVALUATION FORM (continued)

	Almost Always	2/3 of Time	Half of the time	1/3 of the time	Never or Rarely	Examples (with date) and Comments
b. those in preceding stages of the work flow						
c. those in succeeding stages of the work flow						
Knows and follows accepted rules and procedures						
Distinguishes the relative priority of different tasks and handles them accordingly, doing the most important first						
Distinguishes between problems he or she can handle himself or herself and those which should be referred to me for assistance or decision						

Effective in detecting difficulties
which will cause production or
service problems and contributes
to their solution

Makes useful suggestions to improve
job or work environment

Takes on added or changed duties
willingly when situation requires
or when assigned work completed
or unavailable

Index